Y0-BRY-330

POLITICS AND INDUSTRIALIZATION

PRINCETON STUDIES IN AMERICAN POLITICS: HISTORICAL, INTERNATIONAL, AND COMPARATIVE PERSPECTIVES

SERIES EDITORS

IRA KATZNELSON, MARTIN SHEFTER, THEDA SKOCPOL

Labor Visions and State Power: The Origins of Business Unionism in the United States, by Victoria C. Hattam

PRINCETON STUDIES IN BUSINESS AND TECHNOLOGY

SERIES EDITOR

DAVID HOUNSHELL

Before the Computer: IBM, NCR, Burroughs, and Remington Rand and the Industry They Created, 1865-1956, by James W. Cortada

POLITICS AND INDUSTRIALIZATION

EARLY RAILROADS

IN THE UNITED STATES

AND PRUSSIA

Colleen A. Dunlavy

PRINCETON UNIVERSITY PRESS

Library of Congress Cataloging-in-Publication Data
Dunlavy, Colleen A., 1950–
Politics and industrialization : early railroads in the
United States and Prussia / Colleen A. Dunlavy.
    p.   cm. — (Princeton studies in American politics.
Historical, international, and comparative perspectives)
(Princeton studies in business and technology)
  Includes bibliographical references and index.
  ISBN 0-691-04769-3
  1. Railroads and state—United States—History—19th century.
2. Railroads and state—Germany—Prussia—History—
19th century. 3. Railroads—United States—History—19th century.
4. Railroads—Germany—Prussia—History—19th century.
I. Title. II. Series. III. Series: Princeton studies in
business and technology.
HE2757.D86   1993
385'.068—dc20   93-17455

This book has been composed in Trump

Princeton University Press books are printed on
acid-free paper, and meet the guidelines for
permanence and durability of the Committee
on Production Guidelines for Book Longevity
of the Council on Library Resources

Printed in the United States of America

10 9 8 7 6 5 4 3 2 1

IN MEMORY OF

Peggy Phillips _____

AND FOR MY FAMILIES

Contents

List of Figures and Tables _____

Figures

Tables

Preface

THIS BOOK explores the manifold ways in which two contrasting political structures—the antebellum American and the *Vormärz*[1] Prussian—shaped the contours of early railroad development. Implicit in the study is an effort to construe "politics" more broadly than usual. We normally think of politics in terms of ideas and actors, whether individuals (voters, politicians, judges, presidents) or institutions (political parties, legislatures, bureaucracies, and so on). This book forwards a sense of everyday politics that encompasses the larger *structure* of political institutions as well. Much of the book seeks to demonstrate why political structure matters for political and economic affairs alike and why, therefore, it should be part of our customary understanding of politics, past as well as present.

It would be too much to say that I set out with that goal firmly in mind. All that remains of my initial formulation is a portion of its empirical core, the comparison of early American and Prussian railroad development. Alternating bouts of research, reading, and rumination brought the initial puzzle into sharper focus. In the process, I became persuaded that the key to understanding systematic differences in the political and economic contours of early railroad development in these two industrializing nations lay in the two political structures themselves.

The historical understanding at which I arrived may be summed up as follows: The ambient political structure,[2] which defined the political context within which (capitalist) industrial change took place, had an enduring impact on that process. In ways that have been largely overlooked, it shaped the process of economic policy-making, the content of economic policy, the organizational form of economic institutions, the nature of the technological community in the newly industrializing nations of the nineteenth century, and, ultimately,

---

[1] *Vormärz* refers here to the period from the Congress of Vienna in 1815 to the revolution in March of 1848. On periodization, see Wolfgang Hardtwig, *Vormärz: Der monarchische Staat und das Bürgertum* (Munich: Deutscher Taschenbuch Verlag, 1985), pp. 7–8.

[2] On the ambience of technological change, see John M. Staudenmaier, S.J., *Technology's Storytellers: Reweaving the Human Fabric* (Cambridge: Society for the History of Technology and M.I.T. Press, 1985), esp. p. 6.

the very process of technological choice itself. In short, the ambient political structure left its indelible imprint on the polity (policy), on the economy (technology), and on the institutional interface between them (economic institutions). In time, however, the railroads—as the nation's "first big business," to borrow Alfred Chandler's phrase—set in motion a process of industrial change that worked its own changes on the ambient political structure. The basic lesson is simple: understanding the process of industrial change requires due attention to its political context, just as understanding the process of political change must take account of its industrial context. Understood in structural terms, the two are inextricably linked.

LIKE ALL such works, this one owes a great deal to many people. Richard M. Abrams at the University of California-Berkeley started it off by encouraging me long ago to shift my undergraduate major from physics to the history of technology. I remain deeply grateful. At the Massachusetts Institute of Technology, my graduate experience turned out to be all that one dreams of, due to the remarkable collection of faculty and students who enlivened the Program in Science, Technology, and Society, the Department of Political Science, and various niches at Harvard University. The reader will find in these pages clear traces of those with whom I worked most closely: Suzanne Berger, Alfred D. Chandler, Jr., Joshua Cohen, and Merritt Roe Smith. This book, like the dissertation from which it stems, seeks to integrate the diverse perspectives that they represent and, to the extent that it is successful, it casts their own work, I believe, in a new light. A number of others who populated the Cambridge community in the early 1980s also shaped my thinking: Lindy Biggs, Joel Genuth, Peter Hall, Victoria Hattam, George Hoberg, Gary Herrigel, Frank Laird, David F. Noble, Charles F. Sabel, Richard Sclove, and Langdon Winner. For the conceptualization of this project, the writings of Jürgen Kocka, Harry N. Scheiber, Theda Skocpol, Stephen Skowronek, and Richard Tilly meant much more than the footnotes alone convey. During my research in West Berlin and environs, Rainer Fremdling of the Free University (now at the University of Groningen, The Netherlands) consistently offered encouragement and sound advice, as did Elfriede Rehbein and her colleagues at the now-defunct *Hochschule für Verkehrswesen "Friedrich List"* in Dresden. At a critical moment,

Elmer Altvater's lectures at the Free University also reoriented my thinking in a fundamental way that I am at a loss to reconstruct. On the American side, Robert C. Post, Joan Mentzer, Carlene Stephens, and John H. White, Jr., aided and abetted my research in a variety of ways at the National Museum of American History (Smithsonian Institution), while my "fellow fellows"—especially Elizabeth Blackmar, Carolyn Cooper, Gail Cooper, Wayne Durrill, Grace Palladino, and honorary-fellow-for-life Pete Daniel—made it a real community, particularly on Tuesday evenings. The study of American history would be much the poorer if the Museum were ever to abandon its fine tradition of encouraging academics engaged in broad-based studies to mix it up with museum professionals. During the process of revision, I benefited at various points from the research assistance of Sean Adams, Susan Boettcher, Andrew Larsen, Elizabeth Miller, and David Varana; from the continued advice of individuals named above; and from another collection of generous people who read all or part of the book-in-the-making: Richard Bensel, Frank Dobbin, David Hounshell, Thomas P. Hughes, Richard R. John, Peter Katzenstein, Maury Klein, Stanley Kutler, Steven Lewis, Diane Lindstrom, Philip Scranton, Theda Skocpol, Cecil O. Smith, Jr., Ulrich Wengenroth, Glenn Yago, and Jonathan Zeitlin.

Along the way, archivists and librarians provided vital aid at a number of institutions: the *Zentrales Staatsarchiv, Historische Abteilung II* in Merseburg; the *Staatsarchive* in Dresden, Hamburg, and Magdeburg; the *Staatsbibliothek Preußischer Kulturbesitz Berlin*; the Library of Congress; the Baker Library, Harvard Business School; the library of the Association of American Railroads in Washington, D.C.; and the libraries of the University of Wisconsin-Madison. I am particularly indebted to Dr. Kohnke at the *Zentrales Staatsarchiv*, for making my stay in Merseburg as productive as it was; and to Dr. Hans-Günter Klein, curator of the *Mendelssohn-Archiv* in the *Musikabteilung* of the *Staatsbibliothek Berlin* for allowing me early access to the *Bankhaus Mendelssohn* papers.

For financial support during the research, writing, and revising, I thank the Council for European Studies (Columbia University); the German Academic Exchange Service; the Lincoln Educational Foundation; the Fulbright Commission; the Social Science Research Council; the International Research and Exchanges Board; the Smithsonian Institution; the American Council of Learned Societies (with funding from the National Endowment for the Humanities); and at the University of Wisconsin-Madison the Graduate School and the Cartographic Laboratory. Responsibility for the fruits of their aid is, of course, my own.

Portions of this book have appeared previously in *Wissenschaftliche Zeitschrift* (Dresden), Sonderheft 54: *Friedrich List—Leben und Werk* (1990): 51–60; *Business and Economic History*, 2d ser., 19 (1990): 133-42; *Studies in American Political Development* 5 (Spring 1991): 1–35; and *Structuring Politics: Historical Institutionalism in Comparative Analysis*, ed. Sven Steinmo, Kathleen Thelen, and Frank Longstreth (Cambridge: Cambridge University Press, 1992), pp. 114–54. I am grateful to be able to use the material in revised form here.

Finally, some special people deserve special mention: my parents, who teach by example; Victoria Hattam, for more than a decade of intellectual and personal give-and-take; Christiane Hartmann, for a modern-day kinship that transcends culture and distance; my colleagues in the Department of History at the University of Wisconsin-Madison, for their early confidence; Howard Dunlavy, Nancy Dunlavy, Thomas Dunlavy, and Helena Wright, for standing by when my fellowship luck ran out; and Barbara Davis and Patricia Weets, for all of that and much more over the last twenty-odd years. For Ronald M. Radano, who makes life interesting in so many ways (not least because he types his own manuscripts, seldom reads mine, and disagrees with almost all of it), no words are quite good enough.

Note on Weights, Measures, and Currency

FOR converting weights, measures, and currency, a number of foreign reports on American railroads provide valuable assistance. See especially Franz Anton Ritter von Gerstner, *Die innern Communicationen der Vereinigten Staaten von Nordamerica* (Vienna: L. Förster, 1842–43), 1:ii, 2:viii; and G. Tell-Poussin, *Öffentliche Bauwerke in den Vereinigten-Staaten von Amerika*, Part II: *Eisenbahnen*, trans. H. F. Lehritter (Regensburg: Friedrich Pustet, 1837), pp. 175n, 407. Following these sources,

  1 German mile (*deutsche Meile*) = 7.4 kilometers
  1 American (English) mile = 1.6 kilometers
  1 Prussian *Fuß* = 0.31 meters
  1 American (English) foot = 0.30 meters
  1 Prussian *Pfund* = 0.47 kilograms
  1 American (English) pound = 0.453 kilograms.

The Prussian currency, the *Thaler* (or *Taler*, as it is spelled today), I have converted at a rate of $.70. For contemporary reports on exchange rates, see the sources cited above and Kgl. Legations-Kasse, Berlin, September 17, 1840, Zentrales Staatsarchiv Merseburg, Historische Abteilung II, Rep. 2.4.1, Abt. II, no. 7694, vol. 1, p. 34r; [Ministry of Foreign Affairs] to Royal Prussian General Consul König in Alexandria [Egypt], February 25, 1861, in ibid., p. 108r. In using secondary-source data that have been converted to marks, I have reconverted at a rate of 3 marks per *Taler*.

POLITICS AND INDUSTRIALIZATION

1

Introduction

AN AMERICAN railroad man,[1] touring Prussian railroads in 1847, would have envied their uniformity, solidity, and harmony (as he would have put it). Prussian railroads had all adopted the English gauge (4'8-1/2"). They enjoyed the operating advantages of comparatively moderate grades, easy curves, and heavy iron rails. They were in the midst of forming a national association that would facilitate the movement of traffic over what would rapidly become a national "system" of railroads.[2] Two decades into the "railroad era," American railroads, in contrast, remained mired in diversity. The United States could at least claim more than four times the track mileage of Prussia, but in what would become the birthplace of managerial hierarchies and scientific management,[3] paradoxically, the railroads

[1] Although a few women (such as Rebecca Lukens of Lukens Iron in the United States) headed industrial enterprises in the 1830s and 1840s, no women were to be found among railroad promoters or managers in either country, to my knowledge. Scattered evidence for Prussia indicates that they were more common among railroad stockholders, although still not numerous. See, for example, "Verzeichniss der Actionaire zur beabsichtigten Verlängerung der Berlin-Potsdam Eisenbahn über Brandenburg nach Magdeburg und Hamburg," in Zentrales Staatsarchiv Merseburg (hereafter, ZStAM), Rep. 93E, no. 3305/1, vol. 2, pp. 214r–223r and Rep. 77, Tit. 258a, no. 30, vol. I, pp. 91r–99v; and "Liste der Actien-Zeichnungen zur Berlin-Stettiner Eisenbahn," in Staatsbibliothek Preußischer Kulturbesitz, Musikabteilung, Mendelssohn-Archiv (hereafter, MA Nachl. 5), VIII. (I have generally preserved the original spelling and punctuation of bibliographic information and quoted material.) On railroad men, see Thomas Cochran, *Railroad Leaders, 1845–1890: The Business Mind in Action* (New York: Russell & Russell, 1965); Kurt Wiedenfeld, "Deutsche Eisenbahn-Gestalter aus Staatsverwaltung und Wirtschaftsleben im 19. Jahrhundert (1815–1914)," *Archiv für Eisenbahnwesen* 63 (1940): 733–824; T. Pierenkemper, "Die Zusammensetzung des Führungspersonals und die Lösung unternehmerischer Probleme in frühen Eisenbahn-Gesellschaften," *Tradition* 21 (1976): 37–49.

[2] On large-scale technological systems, see Thomas P. Hughes, "The Order of the Technological World," *History of Technology* 5 (1980): 1–16; idem, "The Evolution of Large Technological Systems," in *The Social Construction of Technological Systems*, ed. Wiebe E. Bijker, Thomas P. Hughes, and Trevor Pinch (Cambridge: M.I.T. Press, 1987), pp. 51–82.

[3] See Alfred D. Chandler, Jr., *The Visible Hand: The Managerial Revolution in American Business* (Cambridge: Harvard University Press, Belknap Press, 1977); Glenn Porter, *The Rise of Big Business, 1860–1920*, 2d ed. (Arlington Heights, Ill.: Harlan Davidson, 1992). For comparative perspectives, see Alfred D. Chandler, Jr., and

lagged far behind in building a national system. Some lines had the English gauge, but many did not. Some had been built in a style that resembled the Prussian, but others coped with high grades, sharp curves, and light rails (some even with wooden rails capped by strips of iron, a hallmark of what railroad men around the world knew as the "American system" of railroad construction). American railroads, moreover, had just embarked on what would become a forty-year struggle to build a national railroad association of sufficient permanence to turn a fractured collection of railroads into a national system. To compound the paradox, Prussian railroad men had accomplished all this on their own, without the guiding hand of the state. Indeed, the Prussian central state had adopted a largely hands-off policy toward the railroads. The American state, in contrast, had taken a comparatively interventionist stance, actively promoting and regulating early railroads.

Understanding why early railroad development proceeded so differently in these two countries demands attention to a critical, but largely neglected, parameter of industrial change in our own time: the overall structure of political institutions. For the key to this paradox of the early nineteenth century, this book argues, lies neither in the realm of national culture nor in the actions of the state, but in the structuring presence of the two states themselves. Thus the story told here carries lessons for the world's political economies in the late twentieth century, as they cope with change and confront the need to rework institutions. "In the real world," as Ronald H. Coase observes, "to influence economic policy, we set up or abolish an agency, amend the law, change the personnel and so on: we work through institutions. The choice in economic policy is a choice of institutions."[4] In attending to institutions, however, we should not limit our horizons to isolated or mid-level institutions. To contemporary nations, early American and Prussian railroad development shows how the constitutional structure—the larger, overarching structure of national political institutions—plays a constitutive role in industrial change.

Herman Daems, eds., *Managerial Hierarchies: Comparative Perspectives on the Rise of the Modern Industrial Enterprise* (Cambridge: Harvard University Press, 1980); Alfred D. Chandler, *Scale and Scope: The Dynamics of Industrial Capitalism* (Cambridge: Harvard University Press, Belknap Press, 1990).

[4] Ronald H. Coase, "The New Institutional Economics," *Journal of Institutional and Theoretical Economics* 140 (1984): 230.

The New Institutionalisms

In the central place that it accords to national political structures, this book builds on the "new institutionalism" that has emerged both in business history and in the history of technology (I will argue) in recent years. But it expands the frame of reference within which historians of business and technology work by drawing on recent insights generated by "historical institutionalism" in the social sciences and showing how politics might be—and why it should be— more thoroughly integrated into their analyses. A brief review of institutionalism in these fields will indicate where the current shortcomings lie and how historical institutionalism enlarges the analytical frame of reference for understanding the relationship between politics and industrial change.[5]

In business (and economic) history, a "new institutionalism" with roots extending back to the 1930s has brought institutions—and therefore politics—front and center. The process began when historians shifted from neo-classical theory's traditional concern with production costs and relative factor prices to firm structure, corporate strategy, and transaction costs (that is, the costs of buying and selling, of organizing production, and so on). With this analytical turn, historians such as Alfred D. Chandler, Jr., and Douglass North came to regard institutions as central to economic performance.[6]

---

[5] The boundaries between business and technological history should not be sharply drawn, for they are highly artificial and, together with those demarcating labor history, have become quite porous in recent years. See especially William Lazonick, "Technological Change and the Control of Work: The Development of Capital-Labour Relations in US Mass Production Industries," in *Managerial Strategies and Industrial Relations: An Historical and Comparative Study*, ed. Craig R. Littler and Howard F. Gospel (London: Heineman, 1983), pp. 111–36; and Philip Scranton, *Proprietary Capitalism: The Textile Manufacture at Philadelphia, 1800–1885* (Cambridge: Cambridge University Press, 1983).

[6] See, most recently, Chandler, *Scale and Scope*; Douglass North, *Institutions, Institutional Change and Economic Performance* (Cambridge: Cambridge University Press, 1990); and, for historiographic insight, Thomas K. McCraw, "Introduction: The Intellectual Odyssey of Alfred D. Chandler, Jr.," in Alfred D. Chandler, *The Essential Alfred Chandler: Essays Toward a Historical Theory of Big Business*, ed. and intro. by Thomas K. McCraw (Boston: Harvard Business School, 1988), pp. 2, 13–15, 18–19. In economics, the classic works are Ronald H. Coase, "The Nature of the Firm," *Economica*, n.s., 4 (November 1937), which is reprinted in R. H. Coase, *The Firm, The Market, and the Law* (Chicago: University of Chicago Press, 1988), pp. 33–55; and Oliver Williamson, *The Economic Institutions of Capitalism: Firms, Markets, Relational Contracting* (New York: The Free Press, 1985). I would include in this literature "positive political economy," since it represents the fruits of this perspective applied to the

Although substantial differences distinguish various approaches within the new "economic institutionalism," they all, in effect, open up a way of putting politics back into history.[7] For institutions of any kind consist of rules, compliance procedures, and norms that order relations among individuals.[8] This means that institutions, by their very nature, spell out a distribution of power.[9] In this sense, politics is as inherent in the institutions that reduce economic uncertainty and facilitate economic exchange as it is in what we conventionally regard as political institutions. Institutionalist business history is thus well positioned to explore the relationship between politics and industrial change.

Historical analysis in this vein, moreover, has illuminated the workings of institutions at various levels of aggregation. Research at the level of the firm or industry still commands the field, but even in this domain comparative research has required historians to broaden their view. As Chandler's comparative study of the rise of managerial capitalism suggests, the behavior of individual firms cannot be fully understood without reference to political institutions, especially those that govern collusive behavior. This confirms what Douglass C. North and Barry R. Weingast argue: that economic development cannot be understood apart from its political context, that constitutions and states demand attention because they specify and enforce property rights. Taking a different tack, Steven Tolliday, Jonathan Zeitlin, and colleagues explore the institutional underpinnings of industrial relations, treating "firms and employers' associations, like trade unions and the state, . . . as complex institutions whose decisions are

---

political sphere. See James E. Alt and Kenneth A. Shepsle, eds., *Perspectives on Positive Political Economy* (Cambridge: Cambridge University Press, 1990).

[7] On efforts to put politics back into other fields, see William E. Leuchtenburg, "The Pertinence of Political History: Reflections on the Significance of the State in America," *Journal of American History* 73 (December 1986): 585–600; Robert W. Gordon, "Critical Legal Histories," in *Critical Legal Studies*, ed. Allan C. Hutchinson (Totowa, N.J.: Rowman & Littlefield, 1989), pp. 79–103; Eric Foner, ed., *The New American History* (Philadelphia: Temple University Press, 1990).

[8] For essentially similar definitions of institutions across disciplines, see Peter A. Hall, *Governing the Economy: The Politics of State Intervention in Britain and France* (New York: Oxford University Press, 1986), p. 19; Douglass C. North, *Structure and Change in Economic History* (New York: W. W. Norton, 1981), pp. 201–2; Rogers M. Smith, "Political Jurisprudence, The New Institutionalism, and the Future of Public-Law," *American Political Science Review* 82 (1988): 91; Williamson, *Economic Institutions*, p. 385.

[9] For theoretical insight, see Steven Lukes, *Power: A Radical View* (London and Basingstoke: The Macmillan Press, Ltd., 1974).

the product of the internal political processes as well as external pressures."[10] In shifting emphasis away from individual entrepreneurs or autonomous markets, institutionalists impart to business history a heightened sensitivity to political context—but only up to a point, as we will see.[11]

In the history of technology, an "institutionalist" school has not yet coalesced, but the materials are at hand. As historians of technology discovered, when they pushed back the boundaries of their field to make room for "contextual" and "externalist" perspectives, institutions pervade the history of technology.[12] This is evident both in the treatment of mass production, one of the field's mainstays, and in the newest work on the social construction of technology and on historical alternatives in technological development. As Merritt Roe Smith shows, the genesis of mass production technologies early in the nineteenth century was intimately bound up with a political institution (the military); the historical evolution of mass production, as recounted by David Hounshell, culminated in the creation of one of the premier institutions of the twentieth century, Fordism; and the military again played a central role, David F. Noble argues, in the development of numerically controlled machine tools in the twentieth century.[13] Thomas P. Hughes's influential work on "tech-

[10] Chandler, *Scale and Scope*; North, *Structure and Change*; Douglass C. North and Barry R. Weingast, "Constitutions and Commitment: The Evolution of Institutions Governing Public Choice in Seventeenth-Century England," *Journal of Economic History* 49 (December 1989): 803–32; Steven Tolliday and Jonathan Zeitlin, "Introduction: Employers and Industrial Relations between Theory and History," in *The Power to Manage? Employers and Industrial Relations in Comparative-Historical Perspective*, ed. idem (London: Routledge, 1991), p. 2.

[11] For a renewed defense of entrepreneurial history, however, see Harold C. Livesay, "Entrepreneurial Dominance in Businesses Large and Small, Past and Present," *Business History Review* 63 (1989): 1–21.

[12] On internalist-externalist debates in the history of technology, see David A. Hounshell, "Commentary: On the Discipline of the History of American Technology," *Journal of American History* 67 (March 1981): 854–65; Darwin Stapleton and David A. Hounshell, "The Discipline of the History of Technology: An Exchange," *Journal of American History* 68 (March 1982): 897–902; David A. Hounshell, ed., *The History of American Technology: Exhilaration or Discontent?* (Greenville, Del.: Hagley Papers, 1984); Staudenmaier, *Technology's Storytellers*; Stephen H. Cutcliffe and Robert C. Post, eds., *In Context: History and the History of Technology* (Bethlehem: Lehigh University Press; London: Associated University Presses, 1989); and John M. Staudenmaier, "Recent Trends in the History of Technology," *American Historical Review* 95 (1990): 715–25.

[13] Merritt Roe Smith, *Harpers Ferry and the New Technology: The Challenge of Change* (Ithaca: Cornell University Press, 1977); David Hounshell, *From the American System to Mass Production, 1800–1932: The Development of Manufacturing Technology in the United States* (Baltimore: Johns Hopkins University Press, 1984); David F.

nological systems," moreover, suggests a marked affinity with institutionalism. The rise of technological systems since the late nineteenth century has turned on the creation, expansion, and maintenance of a complex of institutions—economic, professional,
educational, political, and so on.[14] These changes in the realm of
technology, Melvin Dubofsky and William Lazonick argue, had pro-
found institutional implications for industrial relations as well.[15]

In the new literature on the social construction of technology
and on historical alternatives in technological development, institutions have also proven pivotal. In a pioneering work in this vein,
Ruth Schwartz Cowan points to the constitutive role of social and
economic institutions in determining the viability of alternative
household technologies.[16] Institutions are deeply embedded in a
paradigm-breaking essay by Charles Sabel and Jonathan Zeitlin,
which examines alternative ways in which relations among producers have been organized historically and thus highlights the institutions that underpinned mass production as well.[17] The social con-
structivist perspective advanced by Wiebe E. Bijker and Trevor J.
Pinch explicitly includes institutions among the "relevant social
groups" that, by definition, attach a particular meaning to a given
technology.[18] Meanwhile, Langdon Winner has revitalized the field's

---

Noble, *Forces of Production: A Social History of Industrial Automation* (New York:
Alfred A. Knopf, 1984). See also Merritt Roe Smith, ed., *Military Enterprise and Technological Change: Perspectives on the American Experience* (Cambridge: M.I.T. Press,
1985).

[14] Hughes, "The Order of the Technological World"; idem, *Networks of Power:
Electrification in Western Society, 1880–1930* (Baltimore: Johns Hopkins University
Press, 1983); idem, "Evolution of Large Technological Systems"; idem, *American
Genesis: A Century of Invention and Technological Enthusiasm* (New York: Penguin,
1989). See also David F. Noble, *America By Design: Science, Technology, and the
Rise of Corporate Capitalism* (Oxford: Oxford University Press, 1977); Walter A.
McDougall, . . . *the Heavens and the Earth: A Political History of the Space Age* (New
York: Basic Books, 1985).

[15] Melvin Dubofsky, "Technological Change and American Worker Movements,
1870–1970," in *Technology, The Economy, and Society: The American Experience,* ed.
Joel Colton and Stuart Bruchey (New York: Columbia University Press, 1987), pp. 162–
85; Lazonick, "Technological Change and the Control of Work."

[16] Ruth Schwartz Cowan, *More Work for Mother: The Ironies of Household Technology from the Open Hearth to the Microwave* (New York: Basic Books, 1983).

[17] Charles Sabel and Jonathan Zeitlin, "Historical Alternatives to Mass Production:
Politics, Markets and Technology in Nineteenth-Century Industrialization," *Past and
Present,* no. 108 (August 1985): 133–76. See also Scranton, *Proprietary Capitalism*;
idem, "Diversity in Diversity: Flexible Production and American Industrialization,
1880–1930," *Business History Review* 65 (1991): 27–90.

[18] Trevor J. Pinch and Wiebe E. Bijker, "The Social Construction of Facts and Arti-

traditional concern with the social impact of technology by exploring from a philosophical standpoint the impact of alternative technologies on the institutional configuration of society and polity.[19] Examples could easily be multiplied, for the institutional thread runs throughout the literature.

Yet, in the treatment of politics, a curious lopsidedness prevails in both business and technological history. Not only have historians in both fields directed attention to political institutions more haphazardly than to economic institutions, but even those who give the most sustained attention to politics work within limited horizons. To be sure, they conceive of political institutions as much more than mere actors, recognizing instead the manifold ways in which political institutions structure social action. Yet, almost without exception, historians overlook the way that the larger configuration of national political institutions structures social life in the business world and technological realm alike.

To clarify the nature of the problem, it helps to draw a broad distinction between the individual *elements* of a national economy or polity, on the one side, and the overall *structure* of the two spheres, on the other.[20] Studies of the multitude of discrete elements that compose economies or polities appear in abundance: they focus on capitalists or politicians; engineers or state officials; workers or voters; firms, technological systems, or political parties; markets or elections; unions, trade associations, or bureaucracies; and so on. Studies attentive to overall structure, in contrast, are concerned not with discrete elements but with the relationships among them and with the structures thus created. Applied to the economic sphere, this perspective yields studies sensitive to national industrial structure, labor-market structure, economic structure, and so on. Indeed, these are familiar terms because industrialization itself is normally construed as a process of structural change. But the perspective is rarely extended to the structure of the national polity itself.[21] By and large,

---

facts: Or How the Sociology of Science and the Sociology of Technology Might Benefit Each Other," in *Social Construction*, ed. Bijker, Hughes, and Pinch, p. 30.

[19] Langdon Winner, *The Whale and the Reactor: A Search for Limits in an Age of High Technology* (Chicago: University of Chicago Press, 1986).

[20] Reference to polity and economy as "two spheres," while useful for analytical purposes, should not be taken to imply autonomous realities.

[21] Harry N. Scheiber, "Federalism and the American Economic Order, 1789–1910," *Law & Society Review* 10 (Fall 1975): 57–118 constitutes a noteworthy exception,

the new institutionalism in business and technological history has neglected the role of national political structures in the process of industrial change.

What is missing can be seen by analogy in the new "historical institutionalism" that has coalesced in political science and sociology in recent years. Like its counterpart in economic thinking, this line of inquiry sees institutions and individuals as intimately intertwined: individuals pursue their goals, formulate policy, even create or alter institutions, all in the familiar, volitional sense; but, as they do so, their own strategic choices are shaped by the institutional context in which they operate.[22] In applying this insight to the political realm, however, historical institutionalists have taken it a step further, using it to explore the consequences not only of particular institutions but also of the structure of political institutions on a national scale. As Theda Skocpol writes:

> In this perspective, states matter not simply because of the goal-oriented activities of state officials. They matter because their organizational configurations, along with their overall patterns of activity, affect political culture, encourage some kinds of group formation and collective political actions (but not others), and make possible the raising of certain political issues (but not others).[23]

Political structures matter, in other words, because their presence defines the ambient political environment.

Although this perspective derives largely from the study of politics in the conventional sense, a handful of studies suggests that it is equally well suited to analysis in the economic sphere. In a study of

---

although Hughes, *Networks of Power*, and Chandler, *Scale and Scope*, may be read to imply the centrality of national political institutions.

[22] For reviews of the literature, see Smith, "Political Jurisprudence"; James G. March and Johan P. Olsen, *Rediscovering Institutions: The Organizational Basis of Politics* (New York: Free Press, 1989), pp. 1–19; Timothy Mitchell, "The Limits of the State: Beyond Statist Approaches and Their Critics," *American Political Science Review* 85 (March 1991): 77–96; Sven Steinmo and Kathleen Thelen, "Historical Institutionalism in Comparative Politics," in *Structuring Politics: Historical Institutionalism in Comparative Analysis*, ed. Sven Steinmo, Kathleen Thelen, and Frank Longstreth (New York: Cambridge University Press, 1992), pp. 1–32, from which I have borrowed the term.

[23] Theda Skocpol, "Bringing the State Back In: Strategies of Analysis in Current Research," in *Bringing the State Back In*, ed. Peter B. Evans, Dietrich Rueschemeyer, and Theda Skocpol (Cambridge: Cambridge University Press, 1985), p. 21.

working-class formation in the late nineteenth-century United States, for example, Victoria Hattam explores the complex interaction between labor ideology and the distinctive American political structure—the "state of courts and parties," as Stephen Skowronek dubbed it—in explaining why American labor never developed its own political party. Peter Hall's work on post–World War II economic policy in Britain and France demonstrates the impressive power of an analysis that is sensitive to the institutional organization of capital, labor, and the state; in effect, he views both economy and polity in structural terms.[24] In its attention to the silent presence of national political structures, in short, historical institutionalism pushes back the analytical horizon, offering historians of business and technology a new vantage point for understanding industrial change.

In that spirit, this book offers a comparative study that mines the experience of an earlier age for insight into the relationship between political structures and industrial change. The basic questions are deceptively simple: In what ways did the structure of political institutions shape patterns of industrial change? To what extent did the process of industrial change, in turn, alter domestic configurations of power? Comparing early railroad development in the United States and Prussia, the bulk of the study addresses the first question. It begins with the content and process of early railroad policy-making in the two countries, then compares the process of organizing railroad interests, and concludes by delving into the murky world of technological choice in the 1830s and 1840s. Political structure serves as the analytical fulcrum, in other words, while the analysis moves from the political to the economic sphere, focusing successively on state policies, economic institutions, and technological choice.[25] The final

[24] Victoria Hattam, "Economic Visions and Political Strategies: American Labor and the State, 1865–1896," *Studies in American Political Development* 4 (1990): 82–129; idem, *Labor Visions and State Power: The Origins of Business Unionism in the United States* (Princeton: Princeton University Press, 1992); Stephen Skowronek, *Building a New American State: The Expansion of National Administrative Capacities, 1877–1920* (Cambridge: Cambridge University Press, 1982); Peter A. Hall, "Patterns of Economic Policy: An Organizational Approach," in *The State in Capitalist Europe*, ed. S. Born, D. Held, and J. Krieger (London: Allen and Unwin, 1983), pp. 21–53; Hall, *Governing the Economy*. See also Amy Bridges, "Becoming American: The Working Classes in the United States before the Civil War," in *Working Class Formation: Nineteenth-Century Patterns in Western Europe and the United States*, ed. Ira Katznelson and Aristide R. Zolberg (Princeton: Princeton University Press, 1986), pp. 157–96.

[25] In the language more familiar to political scientists, political structure serves as

chapter then briefly addresses the second question, carrying the story forward to the 1850s and beyond, when the industrial changes set in motion by railroad development itself initiated a process of institutional change that ultimately transformed the American and Prussian political structures.

The Comparative Rationale

All historical knowledge, Marc Bloch once observed, necessarily relies on "the mark, perceptible to the senses, which some phenomenon, in itself inaccessible, has left behind."[26] But tracing the impact of something so intangible as political structures poses special problems of evidence, and it is partly for this reason that the study proceeds comparatively. Even if one could work with a manageable body of evidence, as is not the case with railroad history, tackling the subject in a single national context would magnify the difficulties of interpretation. As David Hackett Fischer observes, explicit comparison at least reduces the risk of committing the "fallacy of appositive proof," which occurs when one attempts "to establish a quality in A by contrast with a quality in B—and B is misrepresented or misunderstood."[27] This has been a long-standing problem in American and German historiography, for the concepts of American exceptionalism and the German *Sonderweg* both imply some standard from which they deviate. But that standard remains, at best, ill-defined and underspecified. This is what several British students of German history contended, sparking the first round in the *Historikerstreit* of the 1980s. Geoff Eley, David Blackbourn, and others charged that the central tenets of the German *Sonderweg*—the weakness of the German bourgeoisie, the failure of the revolution of 1848, and Germany's general misdevelopment—are grounded implicitly in comparisons with models of French, American, and, above all, British development that are either unsubstantiated or outdated.[28] During the same

---

the independent variable, while the components of industrial change—state economic policy, economic institutions, and technological choice—serve successively as dependent variables.

[26] Marc Bloch, *The Historian's Craft*, trans. Peter Putnam (New York: Vintage Books, 1953), p. 55.

[27] David Hackett Fischer, *Historians' Fallacies: Toward a Logic of Historical Thought* (New York: Harper & Row, 1970), p. 56.

[28] The path-breaking work was David Blackbourn and Geoff Eley, *Mythen deutscher*

years, moreover, the concept of exceptionalism lost its vigor in economic history, as comparative research undermined the notion of a
unitary process of industrialization modeled on the British experience.[29] Without a "model" pattern of political or economic development, all patterns become "exceptional." Although the notion of
German exceptionalism seems to have survived the challenge, American historians would do well to take note, given the paucity of comparative research on the American *Sonderweg*.

Another reason for casting this as a comparative study is difficult to
convey to those who have not had hands-on experience with comparative research. This is its almost magical ability to expose the otherwise invisible paradigms that become second-nature in the historiography of every nation. In the most general terms, the reigning
paradigm in American history reflexively privileges society over state;
in German history, the opposite occurs. Only when one tries out a
given paradigm in another context, and discovers that it alters the
historical landscape, does it become apparent how profoundly these
invisible paradigms structure understanding of our past, accentuat-
ing some facets while shielding others from view. The great value of
comparative research, as Carl Degler observes, resides in the way that
it "emphasize[s] aspects of our past that may have gone unnoticed
before, just as it . . . call[s] for explanations where none was thought
necessary before."[30] Comparing processes of industrial change in the
United States and Prussia enriches and deepens our historical understanding of both countries in provocative and unforeseen ways.

Finally, this study takes a comparative form because, as Erich An-

---

Geschichtsschreibung: Die gescheiterte bürgerliche Revolution von 1848, trans. Ulla
Haselstein (Frankfurt/Main: Verlag Ullstein, 1980). An English-language edition,
which includes a survey of the response to the German edition, was published as *The
Peculiarities of German History: Bourgeois Society and Politics in Nine-
teenth-Century Germany* (Oxford: Oxford University Press, 1984). Since then, this
Historikerstreit has been overtaken by another that centers more directly on the Nazi
period. For a thoughtful review of the former and an introduction to the latter, see
Charles Maier, *The Unmasterable Past: History, Holocaust, and German National
Identity* (Cambridge: Harvard University Press, 1988). For a recent contribution to the
original debate, see Bernd Weisbrod, "Der englische 'Sonderweg' in der neueren Geschichte," *Geschichte und Gesellschaft* 16 (1990): 233–52.

[29] Rondo Cameron, "A New View of European Industrialization," *Economic History
Review*, 2d ser., 38 (February 1985): 1–23; P. K. O'Brien, "Do We Have a Typology for
the Study of European Industrialization in the XIXth Century?" *Journal of European
Economic History* 15 (Fall 1986): 291–333.

[30] Carl N. Degler, "In Pursuit of an American History," *American Historical Review*
92 (February 1987): 7.

germann rightly observes, "it is fun!" In reality, some compulsion also enters in, for it becomes practically impossible to stop thinking comparatively, once one has learned the habit. But the sheer pleasure of confronting "the challenges of ambiguity," to borrow Angermann's phrase, makes it worth the risk, as he puts it, "of being torn to pieces by all kinds of specialists."[31]

Fortunately, comparative historians are neither as scarce nor as beleaguered as they once were.[32] For this, they have some distinguished colleagues to thank: Jürgen Kocka, one of the first to draw the United States and Germany into comparative perspective; Thomas P. Hughes, whose study of electrical power systems in the United States, Britain, and Germany introduced historians of technology to comparative history; Peter Kolchin, whose prize-winning study of American slavery and Russian serfdom did so much to validate the method; and Alfred D. Chandler, Jr., who juxtaposes the American experience with managerial capitalism to that of Britain and Germany.[33] These provide just a hint of the unprecedented vitality that comparative studies, especially of the United States and Prusso-Germany, enjoyed in the 1980s. Nearly a dozen such studies appeared during the decade, their topics ranging from landed elites, populism, and labor history to urban transportation and technical regulation to adolescence and kindergarten movements.[34]

[31] Erich Angermann, *Challenges of Ambiguity: Doing Comparative History*, German Historical Institute Annual Lecture Series No. 4 (New York: Berg, 1991), p. 6.

[32] Among more recent calls for a comparative approach to American history, see George M. Frederickson, "Giving a Comparative Dimension to American History: Problems and Opportunities," *Journal of Interdisciplinary History* 16 (Summer 1985): 107–10; Raymond Grew, "The Comparative Weakness of American History," ibid., pp. 87–101; Degler, "In Pursuit of an American History"; David A. Hounshell, "Rethinking the History of 'American Technology,'" in *In Context*, ed. Cutcliffe and Post, pp. 216–29.

[33] Jürgen Kocka, *White Collar Workers in America, 1890–1940: A Social-Political History in International Perspective*, trans. Maura Kealey, SAGE Studies in 20th Century History, vol. 10 (London and Beverly Hills: SAGE Publications, 1980); Hughes, *Networks of Power*; Peter Kolchin, *Unfree Labor: American Slavery and Russian Serfdom* (Cambridge: Harvard University Press, Belknap Press, 1987); Chandler, *Scale and Scope.*

[34] In order of appearance: Shearer Davis Bowman, "Antebellum Planters and *Vormärz* Junkers in Comparative Perspective," *American Historical Review* 85 (1980): 779–808; Glenn Yago, *The Decline of Transit: Urban Transportation in German and U.S. Cities, 1900–1970* (Cambridge: Cambridge University Press, 1984); Shearer Davis Bowman, "Planters and Junkers: A Comparative Study of Two Nineteenth-Century Elites and Their Regional Societies," (Ph.D. diss., University of California, Berkeley, 1986); Peter Lundgreen, "Measures for Objectivity in the Public Interest: The Role of Scientific Expertise in the Politics of Technical Regulation: Germany and the U.S.,

The present study contributes to this new and growing literature in a way that must be seen as suggestive rather than conclusive. Adopting a comparative methodology reduces the interpretive difficulties, as noted earlier; and organizing the exposition in a largely comparative fashion throughout the book reduces the "dirty work" of comparison that the reader has to do. But the two together magnify the historian's task (in ways for which the tenure track makes no allowance). Because of the many ramifications of railroad development itself, moreover, research on the subject in any country means dealing with an overwhelming wealth of sources. In an effort to keep it to manageable proportions, I oriented my research around the major railroad lines in both countries, but differences in the history of railroads in the two countries have produced discrepancies in the available sources. Both sides of the story rely on secondary sources where they are helpful, but the German side draws more on government archival materials, while the American is based to a larger degree on printed primary materials. In any event, this foray into comparative industrial history will have served its purpose if it convinces historians of both countries to think anew about the relationship between politics and industrialization. The remainder of this chapter explains

---

1865–1916," in idem, *Standardization, Testing, and Regulation: Studies in the History of the Science-based Regulatory State (Germany and the U.S.A., 19th and 20th Centuries)*, Forschungsschwerpunkt Wissenschaftsforschung (Bielefeld: B. Kleine, 1986); Irmgard Steinisch, *Arbeitszeitverkürzung und sozialer Wandel. Der Kampf um die Achtstundenschicht in der deutschen und amerikanischen Eisen-und Stahlindustrie 1880–1929* (Berlin and New York: Walter de Gruyter, 1986); Tom Taylor, "The Transition to Adulthood in Comparative Perspective: Professional Males in Germany and the United States at the Turn of the Century," *Journal of Social History* 21 (1987–88): 635–58; Ann Taylor Allen, " 'Let Us Live with Our Children': Kindergarten Movements in Germany and the United States, 1840–1914," *History of Education Quarterly* 28 (1988): 23–48; David Peal, "The Politics of Populism: Germany and the American South in the 1890s," *Comparative Studies in Society and History* 31 (April 1989): 340–62; Gary Marks, *Unions in Politics: Britain, Germany, and the United States in the Nineteenth and Early Twentieth Centuries* (Princeton: Princeton University Press, 1989); Shearer Davis Bowman, "Honor and Martialism in the U.S. South and Prussian East Elbia during the Mid-Nineteenth Century," in *What Made the South Different?* ed. Kees Gispen (Jackson: University Press of Mississippi, 1990), pp. 19–48; Thomas Welskopp, "Arbeit und Macht im Hüttenwerk. Arbeits- und industrielle Beziehungen in der deutschen und amerikanischen Eisen- und Stahlindustrie von den 1860er bis zu den 1930er Jahren," Ph.D. diss., Freie Universität Berlin, 1991. See also Erich Angermann and Marie-Luise Frings, eds., *Oceans Apart? Comparing Germany and the United States; Studies in Commemoration of the 150th Anniversary of the Birth of Carl Schurz* (Stuttgart: Klett-Cotta, 1981); Chandler and Daems, eds., *Managerial Hierarchies*; and Hans-Jürgen Puhle, "Comparative Approaches from Germany: The 'New Nation' in Advanced Industrial Capitalism, 1860–1940—Integration, Stabilization and Reform," *Reviews in American History* 14 (December 1986): 614–28.

why these two countries and this industry are appropriate choices for comparison and how the argument proceeds.

Parallel Patterns of Industrialization

Why compare the antebellum United States and *Vormärz* Prussia? Because the timing, pace, and nature of industrialization over the nineteenth century make the two countries ideal cases for comparison—or as close as one is likely to come in historical research. The earmarks of early industrialism had become visible in both countries by the 1830s, and structural change proceeded apace in subsequent decades. During the last half of the century, consequently, "the distribution of the labor force among the economic sectors was remarkably similar," according to Kocka, although the American labor force grew faster than the German. In both, moreover, the process of industrial change took a largely capitalist form, even though both had a fairly well developed public sector of the economy as the railroad era opened. In Prussia, the state, particularly through the Overseas Trading Corporation (*Seehandlung*) and the Mining Office (*Oberbergsamt*), owned a number of manufacturing and mining enterprises. In the United States, state enterprise came primarily in the form of state government participation in banking and transportation. Yet, in neither country did the public sector carry so much weight that the economy could not be called capitalist. By the end of the century, the United States and the German empire with its Prussian core had emerged as the leading challengers to British industrial power, and by then striking parallels were also evident in the organizational nature of American and German industrialism: where the United States saw the emergence of giant trusts, Germany, of course, had its giant cartels. To a greater degree than in any other country, moreover, American and German businesses built managerial hierarchies staffed by professional managers. "Competitive capitalism" in the United States and "cooperative capitalism" in Germany (as Chandler terms them) differed in degree, not in kind.[35] Both coun-

---

[35] Kocka, *White Collar Workers*, pp. 16–23; idem, "The Rise of the Modern Industrial Enterprise in Germany," in *Managerial Hierarchies*, ed. Chandler and Daems, pp. 99–105; Chandler, *Scale and Scope*, pp. 12, 393–95; Jürgen Kocka, "Germany: Cooperation and Competition," in "*Scale and Scope*: A Review Colloquium," *Business History Review* 64 (1990): 711–16. On state enterprise, see W. O. Henderson, *The State and the Industrial Revolution in Prussia, 1740–1870* (Liverpool: Liverpool Uni-

tries, in short, might usefully be viewed as moderately "backward" industrializers.[36]

This characterization is apt for another reason as well. *Vormärz* Prussia and the antebellum United States were once thought to map out opposite ends of a "strong-state, weak-state" spectrum, but several decades of research have rendered these images increasingly untenable (although the invisible paradigms make them difficult to dislodge). On the American side, revisions began in the 1940s when a group of scholars set out to reevaluate the state governments' role in antebellum American industrialization.[37] These studies—the first

---

versity Press, 1958), pp. 59–75, 119–47; Ulrich Peter Ritter, *Die Rolle des Staates in den Frühstadien der Industrialisierung: Die preußische Industrieförderung in der ersten Hälfte des 19. Jahrhunderts* (Berlin: Duncker and Humblot, 1961), pp. 76–92; Guy S. Callender, "The Early Transportation and Banking Enterprises of the States in Relation to the Growth of Corporations," *Quarterly Journal of Economics* 17 (November 1902): 111–62; George Rogers Taylor, *The Transportation Revolution, 1815–1860* (New York: Holt, Rinehart and Winston, 1951; reprint ed., New York: Harper & Row, Harper Torchbooks, 1968), pp. 352–83; Carter B. Goodrich, *Government Promotion of American Canals and Railroads, 1800–1890* (New York: Columbia University Press, 1960), pp. 51–165; and the sources cited in notes 37–42 below. The extent to which agriculture in the Prussian East and American South took a capitalist form is a matter of considerable controversy; for an introduction, see Helmut Bleiber, "Staat und bürgerliche Umwälzung in Deutschland: Zum Charakter besonders des preußischen Staates in der ersten Hälfte des 19. Jahrhunderts," in *Preußen in der deutschen Geschichte nach 1789*, ed. Gustav Seeber and Karl-Heinz Noack (Berlin: Akademie-Verlag, 1983), esp. pp. 102–6; Hartmut Harnisch, "Zum Stand der Diskussion um die Probleme des 'preußischen Weges' kapitalistischer Agrarentwicklung in der deutschen Geschichte," in ibid., pp. 116–44; Bowman, "Planters and Junkers," pp. 36–67; and for a broader take on the question, Steven Hahn, "Class and State in Postemancipation Societies: Southern Planters in Comparative Perspective," *American Historical Review* 95 (1990): 75–98.

[36] The classic statement is Alexander Gerschenkron, *Economic Backwardness in Historical Perspective: A Book of Essays* (Cambridge: Harvard University Press, Belknap Press, 1966).

[37] The pioneering studies were Oscar Handlin and Mary Flug Handlin, *Commonwealth: A Study of the Role of Government in the American Economy: Massachusetts, 1774–1861*, rev. ed. (Cambridge: Harvard University Press, Belknap Press, 1969; orig. pub. 1947); Louis Hartz, *Economic Policy and Democratic Thought: Pennsylvania, 1776–1860* (Cambridge: Harvard University Press, 1948; reprint ed., Chicago: Quadrangle Books, Quadrangle Paperbacks, 1968); Milton Sydney Heath, *Constructive Liberalism: The Role of the State in Economic Development in Georgia to 1860* (Cambridge: Harvard University Press, 1954); James Neal Primm, *Economic Policy in the Development of a Western State: Missouri, 1820–1860* (Cambridge: Harvard University Press, 1954). These grew out of a cooperative project of the Committee on Research in Economic History (under the sponsorship of the Social Science Research Council) and had their origins in the New Deal era. For details on the project, see Handlin and Handlin, *Commonwealth*, pp. viii–x and Appendix G. Related works include Harry H. Pierce, *Railroads of New York: A Study of Government Aid, 1826–1875* (Cambridge: Harvard University Press, 1953); Goodrich, *Government Promotion*; Harry N. Scheiber, *Ohio Canal Era: A Case Study of Government and the Econ-*

to take federalism seriously, one might say—effectively laid to rest the myth of laissez-faire during the antebellum period (or should have). Yet, the wealth of follow-up research that they should have generated never quite materialized. Since then, scholars of the antebellum political economy have examined the American state from another angle, shifting attention to the role of the state and federal courts in economic growth.[38] Others, meanwhile, began to look anew at the federal government's role before the Civil War and discerned interventionist tendencies in the federal legislature and executive as well.[39] The core of the old myth, to be sure, remains unchallenged:

omy, 1820–1861 (Athens: Ohio University Press, 1969). On the progress of the literature, see Robert A. Lively, "The American System: A Review Article," *Business History Review* 29 (March 1955): 81–96; Harry N. Scheiber, "Government and the Economy: Studies of the 'Commonwealth' Policy in Nineteenth-Century America," *Journal of Interdisciplinary History* 3 (Summer 1972): 135–51; Donald J. Pisani, "Promotion and Regulation: Constitutionalism and the American Economy," *Journal of American History* 74 (December 1987): 740–68. For a recent study that brings new questions to this line of inquiry, see L. Ray Gunn, *The Decline of Authority: Public Economic Policy and Political Development in New York State, 1800–1860* (Ithaca: Cornell University Press, 1988). We still know far too little about the details of antebellum public administration at the state level.

[38] Here scholars have followed the lead of James Willard Hurst, *Law and the Conditions of Freedom in the 19th-Century United States* (Madison: University of Wisconsin Press, 1956). Among subsequent works, see especially Lawrence M. Friedman, *A History of American Law* (New York: Simon & Schuster, Touchstone Books, 1973); and Morton J. Horwitz, *The Transformation of American Law, 1780–1860* (Cambridge: Harvard University Press, 1977). For a case study that reflects both traditions, see Stanley I. Kutler, *Privilege and Creative Destruction: The Charles River Bridge Case* (Philadelphia: J. B. Lippincott, 1971; New York: W. W. Norton, 1978). For an innovative structural perspective on the courts, see Hattam, "Economic Visions"; and idem, *Labor Visions*. For overviews of the literature, see Harry N. Scheiber, "Regulation, Property Rights, and Definition of 'The Market': Law and the American Economy," *Journal of Economic History* 41 (March 1981): 103–9; idem, "Public Economic Policy and the American Legal System: Historical Perspectives," *Wisconsin Law Review* (1980): 1159–89; Pisani, "Promotion and Regulation," pp. 740–68.

[39] John G. Burke, "Bursting Boilers and the Federal Power," *Technology and Culture* 7 (Winter 1966): 1–23; Smith, *Harpers Ferry*; Merritt Roe Smith, "Army Ordnance and the 'American System' of Manufacturing, 1815–1861," in *Military Enterprise*, ed. idem, pp. 39–86; Charles F. O'Connell, Jr., "The Corps of Engineers and the Rise of Modern Management, 1827–1856," in ibid., pp. 87–116; Keith W. Hoskin and Richard H. Macve, "The Genesis of Accountability: The West Point Connections," *Accounting, Organizations and Society* 13 (1988): 37–73; Frank Bourgin, *The Great Challenge: The Myth of Laissez-Faire in the Early Republic* (New York: George Braziller, 1989); Todd Shallat, "Building Waterways, 1802–1861: Science and the United States Army in Early Public Works," *Technology and Culture* 31 (January 1990): 18–50; Linda Ann Moore, "The Failure of Federal Social Programs in the Early 19th Century," paper presented to the Society for the History of the Early American Republic, Madison, Wis., July 26–28, 1991; Hugh R. Slotten, "Patronage, Politics, and Practice in Nineteenth-Century American Science: Alexander Dallas Bache and the U.S. Coast Survey," Ph.D. diss., University of Wisconsin-Madison, 1991. Although published re-

throughout the antebellum period, the federal executive remained comparatively weak, while the federal legislature inclined toward stalemate. Precisely because of its peculiar, fractured structure, moreover, the American state does not fit neatly with conventional understanding of an interventionist state. But the cumulative effect is clear: it has become impossible to speak of "laissez-faire" in the antebellum American context. Taking federalism into account, the antebellum American "state" was much more than "a mere shell."[40]

On the Prussian side, too, historians began to rethink the state's role in industrialization as mounting evidence undermined the conventional image. Initially, few historians questioned the extent of the state's involvement in economic activity during the first half of the nineteenth century; instead, they debated its consequences—beneficial or not, intended or not. On balance, the first round of revisions found *Vormärz* Prussian policies to have been rather contradictory in nature, some encouraging industrialization but others either hampering economic change or proving irrelevant.[41] Historian Clive Trebilcock has gone a step further, however, debunking what he labels "myths of the directed economy" in nineteenth-century Germany. By 1840, he argues, even the Prussian state had shifted away from the "regimented" forms of state involvement that had characterized the eighteenth century, turning instead to a collection of indirect policies that aimed to encourage industrialization mainly by offering advice and guidance. As he rightly notes, "these methods are not easily reconciled with traditional expectations as to the behaviour of 'authoritarian' German states."[42] In the 1980s other historians—Thomas Nipperdey, Wolfgang Hardtwig, W. R. Lee

---

cently, Bourgin's book, like the SSRC studies, had its origins in the New Deal; for details see the foreword by Arthur Schlesinger, Jr.

[40] Richard Franklin Bensel, *Yankee Leviathan: The Origins of Central State Authority in America, 1859–1877* (Cambridge: Cambridge University Press, 1990), p. ix. Bensel is referring, of course, to the federal government.

[41] See Karl W. Hardach, "Some Remarks on German Economic Historiography and its Understanding of the Industrial Revolution in Germany," *Journal of European Economic History* 1 (Spring 1972): 73–77; Jonathan Sperber, "State and Civil Society in Prussia: Thoughts on a New Edition of Reinhart Koselleck's *Preußen zwischen Reform und Revolution*," *Journal of Modern History* 57 (June 1985): 280–84. Eric Dorn Brose explores the origins of this contradictory quality in *The Politics of Technological Change in Prussia: Out of the Shadow of Antiquity, 1809–1848* (Princeton: Princeton University Press, 1993).

[42] Clive Trebilcock, *The Industrialization of the Continental Powers, 1780–1914* (New York and London: Longman, 1981), pp. 74–78 (quotation from p. 78).

among them—have come to this view as well.[43] "Despite much evidence for specific kinds of economic promotion," Hans Jaeger notes, "the significance of the state for the industrialization of the nineteenth century in Germany—especially with regard to Prussia—is very much contested."[44] Revisions from both sides, in short, have blurred traditional images of the two states: the antebellum United States had more of a state than previously thought, while Prussia apparently had less. In this sense, too, "*moderately* backward" seems an appropriate characterization.

Contrasting Political Structures

Yet, despite parallel patterns of capitalist industrialization, the American and Prussian political structures differed substantially in the first half of the nineteenth century. In this respect, they confirm Skocpol's warning not to conflate capitalism and democracy: "capitalism in general has no politics," she observes, "only (extremely flexible) outer limits for the kinds of support for property ownership and controls on the labor force that it can tolerate."[45] Both structures exhibited a significant degree of decentralization, but the critical difference lay in the degree to which governmental powers were separated, both vertically among levels and horizontally among branches of government. These formal differences defined two distinct types of structure, one federal-legislative and the other unitary-bureaucratic.

In the United States, decentralization operated within a federal structure that gave the American state governments a strong voice. The crucial distinction, as Carl J. Friedrich explains, was that the American state governments enjoyed the basic right of "amending of

---

[43] Thomas Nipperdey, *Deutsche Geschichte, 1800–1866: Bürgerwelt und starker Staat* (Munich: Verlag C. H. Beck, 1983), pp. 182–85; Hardtwig, *Vormärz*, pp. 93–95; W. R. Lee, "Economic Development and the State in Nineteenth-Century Germany," *Economic History Review*, 2d ser., 41 (1988): 346–67; idem, "The Paradigm of German Industrialisation: Some Recent Issues and Debates in the Modern Historiography of German Industrial Development," in *German Industry and German Industrialisation: Essays in German Economic and Business History in the Nineteenth and Twentieth Centuries*, ed. idem (London: Routledge, 1991), pp. 8, 12. See also Richard H. Tilly, *Vom Zollverein zum Industriestaat: Die wirtschaftlich-soziale Entwicklung Deutschlands 1834 bis 1914* (Munich: Deutscher Taschenbuch Verlag, 1990).

[44] Hans Jaeger, *Geschichte der Wirtschaftsordnung in Deutschland* (Frankfurt/Main: Suhrkamp Verlag, 1988), p. 81.

[45] Theda Skocpol, "Political Response to Capitalist Crisis: Neo-Marxist Theories of the State and the Case of the New Deal," *Politics and Society* 10 (1980): 200.

the constitutional charter itself."[46] In the antebellum years, more-over, they constituted the primary policy-making arena. As Harry N. Scheiber writes, "the states enjoyed virtually exclusive control over elections, civil rights, education, family and social relations, and criminal law," as well as extensive powers over labor relations, corpo-rations, commercial law, and the expropriation of private property under eminent-domain law.[47] The federal arrangement also gave the states the power to determine their own internal structure and to control the activities of lower levels of government. The structure of the state governments themselves depended on the arrangements spelled out in their constitutions, subject only to the stricture of the national constitution that they have "a Republican Form of Govern-ment."[48] Hence, most had bicameral legislatures and a single execu-tive, although the specific arrangements and relative strength of the branches varied from state to state.[49] And, regardless of their specific structure, the state governments generally determined what powers could be exercised by county and city governments. Thus, under "decentralized federalism," as Scheiber terms it, power in most pol-icy areas was concentrated at the middle level of the American politi-cal structure, rather than above or below that point.[50]

In Prussia, decentralization functioned within a unitary structure, the hallmark of which was enduring domestic conflict "between ministerial centralism and provincial regionalism."[51] This is worth emphasizing, for regionalism placed real limits on the power of the central state. Prussian regionalism reflected the country's persis-tently heterogeneous economic and social structure. Although per-

[46] Carl J. Friedrich, *Trends of Federalism in Theory and Practice* (New York: Freder-ick A. Praeger, 1968), pp. 5–6. Cf. Daniel J. Elazar, "Federalism," *International Encyclo-pedia of the Social Sciences*, vol. 5 (1968), pp. 355–57; idem, *Exploring Federalism* (Tuscaloosa: University of Alabama Press, 1987).

[47] Friedrich, *Trends of Federalism*, pp. 5–8, 17–18; Scheiber, "Federalism and the American Economic Order," pp. 83–84.

[48] U.S. *Constitution*, art. IV, sec. 4. The Constitution does not elaborate on the subject, and it has generally been accepted that the form of the state governments that existed when the Constitution was adopted implicitly defined "republican." *The Con-stitution of the United States of America (Annotated)*, Senate Doc. No. 232, 74th Congress, 2d sess., 1938, pp. 548–49.

[49] Richard B. Morris and Jeffrey B. Morris, eds., *Encyclopedia of American History*, 6th ed. (New York: Harper & Row, 1982), pp. 132–33 and 198.

[50] Scheiber, "Federalism and the American Economic Order," pp. 72–96.

[51] Rüdiger Schütz, "Preußen und seine Provinzen," in *Preußen-Ploetz: Eine histo-rische Bilanz in Daten und Deutungen*, ed. Manfred Schlenke (Würzburg: Verlag Ploetz Freiburg, 1983), p. 29.

haps not quite as diverse as the United States, Prussia was still a
nation marked, as Reinhart Koselleck writes, by "social, religious,
linguistic, and legal pluralism,"[52] and by pockets of local autonomy.
After the Congress of Vienna (1815), when Prussia acquired West-
phalia and the areas that would be consolidated into the province of
the Rhineland, the main lines of divergence ran along a gradient from
the agrarian East to the industrial South-Central and West.[53] In their
administrative, legal, and economic practices, the new western provinces reflected their geographical separation from the East, their
proximity to France and Belgium, and years of occupation by
Napoleon. In the face of provincial heterogeneity, the Prussian state
adopted an integration policy characterized by a willingness to compromise when it would not interfere unduly with the power of the
central state. As Thomas Nipperdey observes, "Prussia sought to
solve the problem of integration and regionalism not through federal-
ization but through decentralization."[54] The national legal code (Allgemeines Preußisches Landrecht) adopted in 1794, for example, did
not extend to each and every individual in the nation. In some cases it
did take precedence, but it generally remained subordinate to provincial law. In the Rhineland, moreover, French law superseded it altogether; in the premier example of "accommodation to provincial regionalism," as Rüdiger Schütz notes, the Rhineland retained its
distinctive legal and judicial system, based on the Code Napoléon,
when it became a Prussian province. Decentralization within the
unitary Prussian structure developed, not unlike American federalism, as a pragmatic concession to the reality of persistent
regionalism.[55]

[52] Reinhart Koselleck, "Staat und Gesellschaft in Preußen 1815–1848," in *Moderne
deutsche Sozialgeschichte*, ed. Hans-Ulrich Wehler, 5th ed. (Cologne: Verlag
Kiepenheuer & Witsch, 1976), p. 63. For a discussion of political structure and diversity
in the American case, see C. D. Tarlton, "Symmetry and Asymmetry as Elements of
Federalism: A Theoretical Speculation," *Journal of Politics* 27 (1965): 861–74.

[53] Knut Borchardt, *Perspectives on Modern German Economic History and Policy*,
trans. Peter Lambert (Cambridge: Cambridge University Press, 1991), pp. 30–47; Lee,
"Economic Development and the State." See also Frank B. Tipton, Jr., *Regional Variations in the Economic Development of Germany During the Nineteenth Century*
(Middletown, Conn.: Wesleyan University Press, 1976); Rainer Fremdling and Richard
H. Tilly, eds., *Industrialisierung und Raum: Studien zur regionalen Differenzierung
im Deutschland des 19. Jahrhunderts*, Historisch-Sozialwissenschaftliche Forschungen, vol. 7 (Stuttgart: Klett-Cotta, 1979).

[54] Nipperdey, *Deutsche Geschichte*, p. 332.

[55] Koselleck, "Staat und Gesellschaft," pp. 58, 63; Schütz, "Preußen und seine Provinzen," pp. 28–31; Nipperdey, *Deutsche Geschichte*, pp. 331–37. For a detailed study of

Nonetheless, Prussia's unitary structure meant that the uppermost level of government wielded much more power than the federal government in the United States.[56] A series of reforms after the Napoleonic Wars produced a degree of administrative uniformity throughout the country. At the top of the structure before 1848 stood the king, his personal authority limited mainly by the power of the bureaucracies, sometimes referred to as Prussia's "Quasi-Parliament." Where legislative matters were concerned, two bodies served the king directly in an advisory capacity. The Council of State (*Staatsrat*) included the royal princes, current and former ministers, senior members of the military and the bureaucracies, the provincial governors, and representatives of the churches and universities. The Council of Ministers (*Staatsministerium*) functioned as a collegial organization, whose members presided over the various, functionally organized ministries. On an informal basis, finally, a ring of personal advisors around the king could be as powerful as the Council of State or Council of Ministers. These institutions, formal and informal, together constituted the Prussian central state.

At the regional level, the political structure consisted of eight provinces (reduced from ten in 1824), divided into twenty-five districts (*Regierungsbezirke*) and further subdivided into several hundred counties (*Kreise*). At the head of the each province stood a senior president (*Oberpräsident*), who possessed only limited executive powers but nonetheless wielded considerable influence as mediator between the ministries and the provincial governments. Provincial assemblies (*Provinziallandtage*) were established in 1823/24 as a partial concession to demands for political liberalization, but these were headed by marshals, whom the king appointed personally. Here, the

---

Prussia's "integration policy" in the *Vormärz* period, see Rüdiger Schütz, *Preußen und die Rheinlande: Studien zur preußischen Integrationspolitik im Vormärz* (Wiesbaden: Franz Steiner Verlag, 1979).

[56] The description in this and the following paragraph draws on the diagram of the Prussian administrative structure after 1815 in Peter Ruf, "Ansätze zur Erneuerung: Die preußischen Reformen 1807–1815," in *Preußen-Ploetz*, ed. M. Schlenke, p. 175; Koselleck, "Staat und Gesellschaft," pp. 65–68; Schütz, *Preußen und die Rheinlande*, pp. 36–83, 242–45; Bleiber, "Staat und bürgerliche Umwälzung," pp. 99–100; Koselleck, "Altständische Rechte, außerständische Gesellschaft und Beamtenherrschaft im Vormärz," in *Preussen in der deutschen Geschichte*, ed. Dirk Blasius (Königstein/Ts.: Verlagsgruppe Athenäum-Hain-Scriptor-Hanstein, 1980), pp. 219–36; Nipperdey, *Deutsche Geschichte*, pp. 331–37. King Friedrich Wilhelm III reigned from 1797 until his death in 1840; he was succeeded by Friedrich Wilhelm IV, who died in 1861.

landed nobility retained the upper hand. Noble landowners held half
of the votes, urban landowners a third, and peasant landowners a
sixth, the nobility voting as individuals and the others holding votes
as a group (with a somewhat different arrangement in the Rhine provinces). These assemblies had responsibility for certain provincial
matters but otherwise their powers were largely advisory. Unlike the
American states, moreover, they enjoyed no constitutional right to
alter the structure of the state itself, not even after the revolution of
1848. At the next level down were the district governments, organized on a collegial basis but headed by strong district presidents
(*Regierungspräsidenten*). The district governments, however, were directly under the authority of the ministries (with the exception of the
Justice Ministry), rather than provincial officials, and they played an
important role in the formulation of legislation in the ministries. At
the next lower level of government was the county magistrate (*Land-
rat*), chosen by the central government from candidates nominated by
the district assemblies. The latter were firmly under the control of
the local nobility, who took care to see that the nominees for county
magistrate came from their own ranks.[57] Completing the structure,
finally, were the municipal governments, their powers exercised formally at the pleasure of the central state. In the administration of city
affairs, the landed nobility had less influence, but in the countryside
its power remained virtually unchecked.

Thus the Prussian structure exhibited a polarization of power between top and bottom, unlike the American structure with its mid-
level concentration of power. The fingers of ministerial power
reached down to the district level but not much further. The formal
power of the landed nobility, conversely, was concentrated at the
lower levels of the structure. It maintained its power at the national
level primarily through informal channels—personal connections to
the royal household or individuals appointed to the ministries. To the
extent that the interests of the ministries and the landed nobility
coincided, of course, the two together could form an interlocking
power structure, although they did not always do so.

---

[57] In 1812 the county magistrate was replaced by a county director named directly by
the central state rather than by the district assembly; due to opposition from the
nobility, however, the county-magistrate system was soon reinstated. Not until 1872
was the magistrate made a civil servant. Ruf, "Ansätze zur Erneuerung," p. 176.

At each level of government, moreover, the two structures differed in another crucial respect: the degree to which power was separated among branches of government. In the United States, a relatively well developed horizontal separation of powers served to limit executive power both at the national and at the state level. This naturally gave greater prominence to legislative bodies and carried with it a fairly high degree of formal popular representation at both the state-government and the national level.[58] In practice, therefore, Congress and the state legislatures tended to dominate the policy-making process at their respective levels of government, their power tempered mainly by the courts and in a few cases by strong executives at the state level.[59] In *Vormärz* Prussia, governmental powers were less distinctly separated. The executive (*Verwaltung*) and judiciary had been partially disengaged as part of the Stein-Hardenburg reforms early in the century, but the executive and legislative functions in Prussia remained formally combined. Since representative bodies played only an advisory role, the bureaucracies at the national and district level dominated the policy-making process.[60]

Viewed both vertically and horizontally, then, the American and Prussian political structures that early railroad promoters confronted looked quite different, despite a common tendency toward decentralization. The distinguishing mark of the Prussian unitary-bureaucratic state before 1848 was its twofold concentration of policy-making power at the national level in the executive branch. In the United States, federalism and (horizontal) separation of powers combined to produce a highly fragmented political structure, one marked by a

[58] By 1830 only five state governments still retained property qualifications on suffrage while another eight required voters to be taxpayers. In addition, most had moved to popular election of governors and presidential electors. A glaring exception to the shift toward manhood (not to mention universal) suffrage remained in place, of course, as long as slaves and (in some states) free blacks had no voting rights. Morris and Morris, eds., *Encyclopedia*, p. 198; Kirk H. Porter, *A History of Suffrage* (Chicago: University of Chicago, 1918), pp. 110, 148.

[59] See note 49. By the 1830s New York state under the Albany Regency had developed one of the strongest executives, its powers particularly noticeable in the areas of banking, education, and internal improvements. "For some time there has appeared in the administration of the State of New York," Michel Chevalier noted with approbation in 1835, "a character of grandeur, unity, and centralisation, that has procured it the title of the *Empire-State*." Michael Chevalier, *Society, Manners and Politics in the United States* (New York: Burt Franklin, 1969; orig. pub. Boston, 1839), pp. 370–77 (quotation from p. 371; original italics).

[60] See note 56.

twofold dispersion of power that gave the state legislatures a prominent place in policy-making.

The structure of the antebellum American state poses special problems, as historians well know, for federalism produced a policy "mosaic" (in Scheiber's words) to which each state contributed "its own coloration and design."[61] This makes generalization difficult, though nonetheless necessary. The large differences among the states notwithstanding, it is essential to adopt a more comprehensive vision—to view events from the perspective of "the American state" writ large—in order to perceive the full dimensions of the antebellum American state. As Oscar and Mary Handlin observed nearly fifty years ago:

> In America, the peculiar complexity of federalism has often, in the last half-century, misled those who have touched upon the subjects of government and business enterprise. . . . Too often the absence of activity by the federal government has been taken for the absence of all activity, the denial of its right to act, the denial of the right of any government to act.

In a decentralized federal system, this is the predictable result, when the states are not taken into account. Understanding the antebellum American state demands close attention to the activities of the states, because, as the Handlins explain, "the affairs of the states were not only of greater public concern than those of the nation but they also had a more pervasive and more significant influence."[62] But policy variations among the states, while worth exploring in their own right, are not of intrinsic interest for this study. They matter no more or less than differences in the Prussian central state's treatment of its provinces, for assessments of state intervention do not depend on the geographical uniformity of policy.

If these various methods of curbing autocratic or oligarchic power—horizontal and vertical separation of powers, greater formal representation—may be taken as essential characteristics of a "liberal" political structure in the classical sense, then it seems reasonable to characterize the American structure as more liberal and the Prussian as less. Notwithstanding the limitations on formal representation in the United States and the existence of informal channels

---

[61] Scheiber, "Federalism and the American Economic Order," p. 97.
[62] Handlin and Handlin, *Commonwealth*, p. xvi.

of representation in Prussia, political liberalism prevailed to a greater extent in the antebellum United States than it did in Prussia.[63]

Because of these differences in structure, railroad policy in this period emanated from different levels and branches of government in the two countries. In the antebellum United States, the state legislatures decided, for example, whether to incorporate companies or to grant rights of eminent domain. In *Vormärz* Prussia, the central bureaucracies did so. Although most of the ministries (not to mention state financial institutions, the Post Office, and the provincial and local governments) had a strong interest in railroad policy, the Finance Ministry in Berlin had immediate responsibility for the issuing of charters, and early railroad men dealt most often with its officials. Comparing events and tendencies in these two countries thus should provide valuable clues to the impact of different political structures on the process of industrial change.[64]

Early Railroad Development

Early railroad development offers a remarkably rich basis for comparison. In the United States and Prusso-Germany alike, it served as an opening wedge in the process of industrial change that transformed the two nations into leading economic powers by the end of the century. Even though the magnitude of railroad construction in the United States quickly dwarfed that in any other country, as Jürgen Kocka observes, a fundamental similarity marked the timing, pace, and nature of railroad development in the two countries.[65] In both

---

[63] Cf. David G. Smith, "Liberalism," *International Encyclopedia of the Social Sciences*, vol. 9 (1968), p. 278. Friedrich treats the question whether a federal or a unitary structure is "more appropriate" in a given situation as a matter of "practical politics" (*Trends of Federalism*, p. 6), but, as Daniel J. Elazar notes, federalism "as a political device" is usually valued as "a means of safeguarding individual and local liberties" through the dispersion of power ("Federalism," p. 354).

[64] Marc Bloch, "Toward a Comparative History of European Societies," in *Enterprise and Secular Change: Readings in Economic History*, ed. Frederick C. Lane and Jelle C. Riermersma (Homewood, Ill.: Richard D. Irwin, Inc., 1953), pp. 494–521; William H. Sewell, "Marc Bloch and the Logic of Comparative History," *History and Theory* 6 (1967): 208–18; Theda Skocpol and Margaret Somers, "The Uses of Comparative History in Macrosocial Inquiry," *Comparative Studies in Society and History* 22 (April 1980): 174–97.

[65] Jürgen Kocka, "Eisenbahnverwaltung in der industriellen Revolution: Deutsch-Amerikanische Vergleiche," in *Historia Socialis et Oeconomica: Festschrift für Wolfgang Zorn zum 65. Geburtstag*, ed. Hermann Kellenbenz and Hans Pohl (Stuttgart: Franz Steiner Verlag Wiesbaden GmbH, 1987), pp. 261–62.

countries, plans for the first railroads surfaced in the 1820s. In the United States, the first railroads, powered by horses, were the Granite Railroad in Quincy, Massachusetts, and the Mauch Chunk Railroad, a mining railroad in Pennsylvania, completed in 1826 and 1827, respectively. The first Prussian railroads, also horse-powered mining railroads, were built in 1828 and 1829.[66] Then in the 1830s railroad construction began in earnest, especially in the United States. As will become apparent in the following chapters, the rapidity of construction in the United States reflected the dynamics of legislative policy-making, coupled with the political exigencies of federalism, both of which made it much easier for American railroad promoters to obtain charters. By 1840 (table 1-1) construction had been completed on some 4,500 kilometers of track in the United States; in Prussia, only 185 kilometers had been completed. (The German states together claimed about 500 kilometers of track at that time.)[67]

The pace of construction in Prussia picked up in the 1840s, however, and in both countries national rail networks took shape in the late 1840s and 1850s. By the mid-1840s, several regional concentrations of railroads had emerged in Prussia. The most important of these centered on Berlin, from which railroads radiated in every direction (except to the northwest). Cologne formed a second nexus in the western provinces, while regional centers had also grown up in other German states.[68] Construction proceeded unevenly, depending on

[66] For an overview of Prussian railroad development, see Wolfgang Klee, *Preußische Eisenbahngeschichte* (Stuttgart: Verlag W. Kohlhammer, 1982); and Rainer Fremdling, *Eisenbahnen und deutsches Wirtschaftswachstum, 1840–1879: Ein Beitrag zur Entwicklungstheorie und zur Theorie der Infrastruktur*, 2d ed. enl., Untersuchungen zur Wirtschafts-, Sozial- und Technikgeschichte, vol. 2. (Dortmund: Gesellschaft für Westfälische Wirtschaftsgeschichte e.V., 1985). On antebellum American railroad development, see Robert William Fogel, *Railroads and American Economic Growth: Essays in Econometric History* (Baltimore: Johns Hopkins University Press, 1964); Albert Fishlow, *American Railroads and the Transformation of the Ante-Bellum Economy* (Cambridge: Harvard University Press, 1965); *History of Transportation in the United States before 1860*, prepared under the direction of Balthasar H. Meyer by Caroline E. MacGill and a staff of collaborators (Washington, D.C.: Carnegie Institution, 1917), hereafter cited as Meyer, *History of Transportation*; and Taylor, *Transportation Revolution*, pp. 74–103.

[67] For summary details on 178 American railroads completed or in planning by 1840, see Franz Anton Ritter von Gerstner, *Die innern Communicationen der Vereinigten Staaten von Nordamerika*, 2 vols. (Vienna: L. Förster, 1842–43), 2:334–37, who counts 4,600 kilometers. Early railroad mileage statistics, especially for the United States, must be viewed as rough estimates. For discussion, see Fogel, *Railroads*, pp. 257–60.

[68] *Festschrift über die Thätigkeit des Vereins Deutscher Eisenbahn-Verwaltungen in den ersten 50 Jahren seines Bestehens, 1846–1896* (Berlin: Nauck'schen Buch-

TABLE 1-1
Comparative Railroad Development
United States and Prussia, 1839/40–1860

	United States	Prussia
Population (millions)		
1820	9.6	11.3
1830	12.9	13.0
1839	16.7	
1840	17.1	14.9
1850	23.2	16.6
1860	31.5	18.3
Total Railroad Mileage (km)		
1840	4,500	185
1850	14,400	2,970
1860	49,000	5,760
Mileage per 10,000 Inhabitants (km)		
1840	2.6	0.1
1850	6.2	1.8
1860	15.6	3.1
Total Railroad Investment ($ million)		
1839/40[a]	$96	$5
1850	$301	$107
1860	$1,151	$268
Investment per Capita		
1839/40[a]	$5.75	$0.34
1850	$12.97	$6.45
1860	$36.54	$14.64

SOURCES: For Prussian population, Wolfgang Köllman, ed., *Quellen zur Bevöl-kerungs-, Sozial- und Wirtschaftsstatistik Deutschlands 1815–1875*, vol. 1: *Quellen zur Bevölkerungsstatistik Deutschlands 1815–1875*, prepared by Antje Kraus (Boppard am Rhein: Harald Boldt Verlag, 1980), p. 226. For American population and rail mileage, U.S. Bureau of the Census, *Historical Statistics of the United States, 1789–1945* (Washington, D.C.: Government Printing Office, 1949), Series A2, K1. For American investment, Fishlow, *American Railroads*, p. 358. For Prussian mileage and investment (*Kapitalstock zu Anschaffungspreisen [verwendetes Anlagekapital]*), Fremdling, *Eisenbahnen*, pp. 28, 48.

[a] U.S. in 1839; Prussia in 1840.

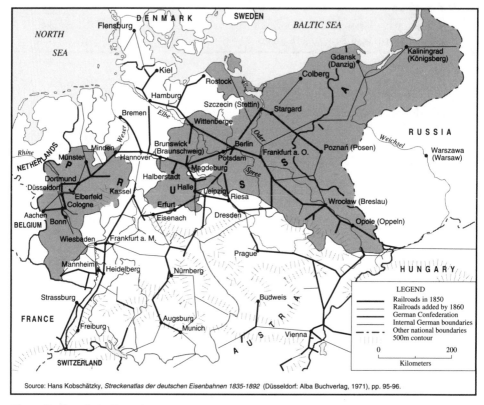

Source: Hans Kobschätzky, *Streckenatlas der deutschen Eisenbahnen 1835-1892* (Düsseldorf: Alba Buchverlag, 1971), pp. 95-96.

Fig. 1. Railroads in Prussia

general economic and political conditions, but by the end of the decade (see fig. 1), two great east-west thoroughfares had been constructed, one running from Berlin through Hannover to Düsseldorf on the Rhine and another connecting Berlin (by a rather circuitous route) through Halle with Frankfurt/Main. Other long-distance lines radiated from Berlin northwest to Hamburg and southeast to Breslau and beyond. Additional construction during the 1850s had fleshed out the network considerably by 1860.

druckerei, 1896), p. 410. Hereafter, this source is cited as *Festschrift*. See also Hans Kobschätzky, *Streckenatlas der deutschen Eisenbahnen, 1835–1892* (Düsseldorf: Alba Buchverlag, 1971), pp. 94–95.

During the same years, the American system also began to fill in (fig. 2). After the economic hard times of the late 1830s and the early 1840s, the pace of railroad construction picked up, first, in New England, where the density of track was already the greatest, and by the late 1840s in the rest of the country. Subsequently, the capstone of the antebellum American system was put in place when the four great east-west trunk-line railroads (the New York and Erie, New York Central, Baltimore and Ohio, and Pennsylvania railroads) were completed in rapid succession between 1851 and 1854. Meanwhile, construction of new railroads in the Old Northwest extended the trunklines' reach further westward and set the United States off on a railroad-building boom without parallel.[69]

By mid-century, then, the United States boasted roughly 14,000 kilometers of track (table 1-1), while the Prussian system had grown to nearly 3,000. (The German states, which led the Continental countries in railroad construction, claimed close to 6,000 kilometers.)[70] In per capita terms, this represented more than three times as much mileage in the United States as in Prussia. Then came a great spurt of construction in the United States in the 1850s, which widened the gap between the two countries. By 1860, the American network had grown to more than eight times the size of the Prussian system. In per capita terms, this represented five times more railroad mileage in the United States than in Prussia.

The bulk of this study focuses on the 1830s and 1840s, mainly because these were the years in which the contours of the industry took shape in both countries. Thus they were the years in which the two contrasting political structures exercised a formative influence on railroad development. In subsequent decades, moreover, the history of railroads in these two countries diverged in ways that would vitiate the comparative rationale that undergirds this study, if it were extended to those years. When American railroad construction penetrated the West in the 1850s and especially from the late 1860s on, not only the scale but also the nature of railroad development changed. As lines were constructed through sparsely populated areas in which

---

[69] On the post-1850 railroad business, see Chandler, *Visible Hand*, pp. 83–121.

[70] By 1850 France had built slightly less track than Prussia, Belgium had constructed less than 1,000 kilometers, and Britain claimed 10,000 kilometers. Fremdling, *Eisenbahnen*, p. 48; B. R. Mitchell, *European Historical Statistics, 1750–1970*, abridged ed. (New York: Columbia University Press, Macmillan Press, 1978), pp. 315–16.

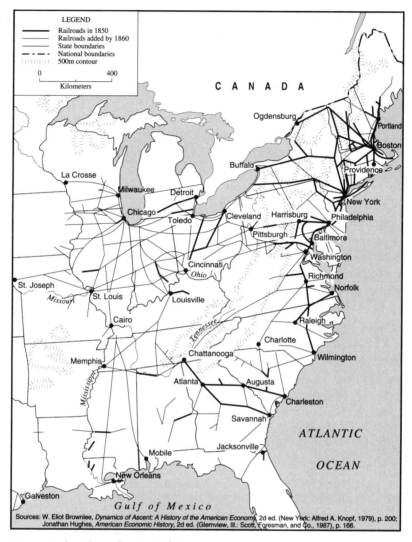

Fig. 2. Railroads in the United States

the federal government still owned much of the land, American railroad development became increasingly "developmental" in nature. That is, railroads no longer generated profits directly from the thriving local economies through which they passed; instead they themselves shaped the lines of subsequent settlement and stimulated eco-

nomic development. Railroad construction in the more sparsely settled regions of eastern Prussia in the 1860s and 1870s did not have
comparable ramifications. The American federal and local governments, moreover, began to pick up the burden of promotion from
financially strapped states, some of whose constitutions now prevented them from providing further aid. During the 1880s, finally, as a
modicum of federal regulation was instituted in the United States,
Prussia (by then a part of the German empire) nationalized its major
lines.[71] As the industry matured in both countries, in short, the divergence between the two widened along several dimensions.

In the earlier period, however, railroad development had a more
comparable significance in the two countries, despite discrepancies
in the scale of construction. Indeed, it meant more to their industrial
development than it did for any of their contemporaries. "In both
countries," Kocka observes, "the initial construction phase (1840s to
1870s) coincided approximately with the breakthrough phase of industrialization, which was, accordingly, marked strongly by railroad
construction."[72] The railroads contributed to that transformation by
introducing the twin phenomena that would define a new industrial
order: large geographic scale and capital intensity. The railroads
brought a vast extension of the geographic scale of enterprise, for they
were the first businesses whose transactions and property holdings
alike extended over large distances. In tandem with capital intensity,
moreover, large geographic scale prompted the railroad men to pioneer management techniques new to the private sector.[73] But the
second phenomenon, capital intensity, had much wider ramifications, for it also prompted new methods of mobilizing capital, acted
as a stimulus to industrial activity in other sectors, and radically
changed competitive behavior.

[71] Goodrich, *Government Promotion*, pp. 169–204, 265–97; and idem, "Internal
Improvements Reconsidered," *Journal of Economic History* 30 (June 1970): 289–311,
esp. pp. 305–6. The developmental aspects in the United States may be seen most
clearly in construction of the transcontinental railroads. See Robert William Fogel,
The Union Pacific Railroad: A Case in Premature Enterprise (Baltimore: Johns Hopkins University Press, 1960). For an overview of Prussian (and German) railroads from
the 1860s through nationalization, see Klee, *Preußische Eisenbahngeschichte*, pp.
132–78. Amy Elaine Sanders has a dissertation in progress at Columbia University on
the nationalization of Prussian railroads.

[72] Kocka, "Eisenbahnverwaltung," p. 262. See also Richard Tilly, "The 'Take-Off' in
Germany," in *Oceans Apart?*, ed. Angermann and Frings, p. 48.

[73] Chandler, *Visible Hand*, pp. 94–120; O'Connell, "Corps of Engineers"; Kocka,
"Eisenbahnverwaltung," pp. 263–64.

Capital intensity manifested itself in several ways. First, and most obvious to contemporary observers, it meant that single enterprises and the industry as a whole commanded unprecedented amounts of capital. As Rainer Fremdling comments, "between 1840 and 1880 no other modern sector in Germany accumulated capital on [the] scale [of the railroads]."[74] In the United States, where railroad development proceeded so much more rapidly from the outset, railroads absorbed an even larger proportion of domestic capital. By 1850 (see table 1-1) something on the order of $300 million had been invested in American railroads and more than $100 million in Prussian lines; in per capita terms, Americans had invested roughly twice as much as Prussians had. In the United States, total railroad investment in 1850 reached a level equal to nearly 7 percent of the nation's domestic capital stock (table 1-2); in Prussia, it constituted about 3 percent. Ten years later, investment reached more than $1 billion and $268 million, respectively. In per capita terms, this meant two and a half times as much investment in the United States as in Prussia; total railroad investment now equalled nearly 13 percent of domestic capital stock in the United States and more than 5 percent in Prussia.

Because most railroads in both countries were privately owned and operated and because they demanded such large sums of capital, they made important contributions to the development of modern business methods. Even though American lines tended to rely more heavily on state aid (as chapter 2 argues), railroads in both countries were the first enterprises to make widespread use of the joint-stock form of corporate organization, and they were also the first to introduce broad segments of the public to the stock market. Through the 1840s, railroad investment in both countries came largely from private, domestic sources of capital. Foreign capital took on some importance in the United States during the 1830s, but only after 1850, as Carter B. Goodrich observes, were American railroads "able to raise substantial sums in the European market," and the bulk of foreign investment came after the Civil War. To raise large sums of capital, which reached millions of dollars per enterprise, railroad promoters in both countries turned mainly to private bankers (in Prussia) or merchant-capitalists (in the United States), who were often to be

[74]Rainer Fremdling, "Railroads and German Economic Growth: A Leading Sector Analysis with a Comparison to the United States and Great Britain," *Journal of Economic History* 37 (September 1977): 586.

TABLE I-2

Total Railroad Investment as a Percentage of
Domestic Capital Stock (Current Market Prices)

Year	U.S.	Prussia
1850	6.8%	3.0%
1860	12.7%	5.4%

SOURCES: Table 1-1; Robert E. Gallman, "The United
States Capital Stock in the Nineteenth Century," in
Long-Term Factors in American Economic Growth, ed.
Stanley L. Engerman and Robert E. Gallman (Chicago:
University of Chicago Press, 1986), p. 204, variant B; Wal-
ther G. Hoffman, *Das Wachstum der deutschen Wirt-
schaft seit der Mitte des 19. Jahrhunderts* (Berlin:
Springer-Verlag, 1965), p. 255. German capital stock
(*Kapital-stock zu laufenden Preisen*) adjusted to the
Prussian population on the basis of Köllmann, ed. *Quel-
len,* pp. 226, 338. Most of the components of Gallman's
data are in market prices or in net reproduction costs.

found among the ranks of their own stockholders. The companies
relied on these private capitalists to help them in placing railroad
stocks and bonds, which in both countries were the first industrial
securities to be offered publicly in large volume. Indeed, they were
virtually the only ones until the last decades of the nineteenth century: in Germany, other industrial securities did not appear on stock
exchanges in any number until the 1870s; in the United States, it was
only in the 1890s that manufacturers turned to the stock exchange for
outside funds.[75] This is one reason why Chandler terms the railroads

[75] Kurt Bösselmann, *Die Entwicklung des deutschen Aktienwesens im 19. Jahrhundert: Ein Beitrag zur Frage der Finanzierung gemeinwirtschaftlicher Unternehmungen und zu den Reformen des Aktienrechts* (Berlin: Walter de Gruyter, 1939),
pp. 30, 48–49, 102; Karl Obermann, "Zur Beschaffung des Eisenbahn-Kapitals in
Deutschland in den Jahren 1835–1855," *Revue Internationale d'Histoire de la Banque*
5 (1972): 315–52; Richard H. Tilly, "Zur Entwicklung des Kapitalmarktes und Industrialisierung im 19. Jahrhundert unter besonderer Berücksichtigung Deutschlands,"
Vierteljahrschrift für Sozial-und Wirtschaftsgeschichte 60 (1973): 154–58; Leland H.
Jenks, "Railroads as an Economic Force in American Development," *Journal of Economic History* 4 (1944): 7–10; Chandler, *Visible Hand,* pp. 90–93. For insight into the
railroad activities of private bankers in Prussia, see the Bankhaus Mendelssohn & Co.
collection, MA Nachl. 5. For background on Mendelssohn and this collection, see
Wilhelm Treue, "Das Bankhaus Mendelssohn als Beispiel einer Privatbank im 19. und
20. Jahrhundert," *Mendelssohn Studien* 1 (1972): 29–80; and Hans-Günter Klein, "Das
'Bankarchiv' der Mendelssohns," Staatsbibliothek Preussischer Kulturbesitz, *Mitteilungen* 16 (1984): 94–105.

the "first big business" in the United States, a designation that applies equally well in Prusso-Germany.[76]

In both countries, the railroads also generated considerable demand for industrial products and thereby stimulated activity elsewhere in the economy. To see their importance in this respect, we need not wade into controversies about the railroads' "social savings."[77] The point here is merely to convey a sense of the railroads' economic weight in these two countries during the middle decades of the nineteenth century. Relying on the data of Robert W. Fogel and Albert Fishlow for the American side, Rainer Fremdling has compared the railroads' demand for iron products in the United States and Germany. Throughout the period 1840–1860, railroad-derived demand accounted for a substantial percentage of total domestic production and consumption of pig iron in both countries, although a larger percentage in the German states than in the United States. By the end of the period, American railroad demand approached 20 percent of domestic consumption and production—not insignificant, in itself. In Germany, however, railroad demand remained above 20 percent of both consumption and production after 1845, and by the late 1850s railroad demand approached 30 percent of production. In this regard, Fremdling concludes, railroad construction meant more for German iron producers and processors than it did for their American counterparts.[78]

Important differences also obtained in the timing of the process of import substitution in the two countries. Railroads in both initially relied almost entirely on Britain for locomotives and rails, and in both they moved quickly to substitute domestically produced locomotives for imports. But the German states moved more quickly through two subsequent stages in the process of import substitution: first, using imported coke pig iron to roll their own rails in the 1840s, and then substituting domestically produced coke pig iron for imports in the 1850s. The United States, in contrast, developed some

[76] Alfred D. Chandler, Jr., comp. and ed., *The Railroads: The Nation's First Big Business, Sources and Readings* (New York: Harcourt, Brace & World, Inc., 1965).
[77] To survey the American debate, see Fogel, *Railroads;* Fishlow, *American Railroads;* Patrick O'Brien, *The New Economic History of Railways* (London: Croom Helm, 1977); Robert W. Fogel, "Notes on the Social Saving Controversy," *Journal of Economic History* 39 (March 1979): 1–54. For Germany, see Fremdling, *Eisenbahnen.* For a wider European perspective, see Patrick O'Brien, ed., *Railways and the Economic Development of Western Europe, 1830–1914* (New York: St. Martin's Press, 1983).
[78] Fremdling, "Railroads and German Economic Growth," p. 593.

domestic rolling capacity in the late 1840s, but domestically produced rails did not provide serious competition to British imports
until the late 1850s.[79] These divergent patterns, Fremdling argues,
reflected differences in political context, for the tariff structure of the
German *Zollverein* allowed duty-free imports of pig iron but placed
heavy duties on finished iron until 1844. With a change of policy that
year, the tariff structure protected both domestic coke (but not char-
coal) pig iron producers and bar iron producers. This quickened the
process of import substitution in two stages, as noted above. In the
United States, in contrast, the tariff structure favored imports of finished rails over pig iron, except for a brief interlude from 1843 to 1846.
This meant, in effect, that the United States exported the industry's
backward linkages in the production of rails to a greater extent. As
Fremdling observes:

> This tariff structure not only retarded the development of a modern
> iron processing industry based on imported pig iron, but also
> helped maintain the old-fashioned and costly charcoal furnaces.
> On this hypothesis the relatively small impact that American rail-
> road construction had on pig iron production until the mid-1850s
> may be understood.

In the end, as Fremdling emphasizes, "*both* countries exported significant income and employment effects, chiefly to Great Britain," although the United States did so longer.[80]

In a third way, finally, capital intensity set railroad development
apart from anything that had gone before. In this instance, capital
intensity expressed itself in the ratio of fixed (or constant) to variable
(or operating) costs. Fixed costs did not change significantly with an
increase or decrease in the volume of traffic or the distance traveled;
these included such items as administrative expenses, depreciation
on buildings and equipment, insurance, taxes, interest (as opposed to
dividends), and routine maintenance. Variable costs, as the term suggests, consisted of costs that varied with the volume of production—

[79] Ibid., pp. 587–92; Fishlow, *American Railroads*, pp. 132–40.
[80] Fremdling, "Railroads and German Economic Growth," pp. 595, 598–601 (original emphasis). Taking account of exports to countries such as the United States and
Germany, moreover, alters the weight of railroad construction in the development of
the British iron industry as well. Fremdling estimates roughly that worldwide railroad
demand accounted for 26 percent of British pig iron production in 1844–51 and 18
percent in 1852–59.

on the railroads, the volume of traffic. These included wages and the other expenses of loading, unloading, and running trains, as well as certain maintenance expenses that varied with the intensity of train operation. In the railroad business, fixed costs accounted for a higher proportion of total unit costs than in any industry at the time.[81] In a fascinating analysis of railroad problems in the late nineteenth century, Gerald Berk rightly emphasizes that overcapitalization and the resulting high levels of fixed costs must be understood as a political construction, the result of "capital-market organization, investor entitlements, and national policy."[82] But, as he also acknowledges, relatively high fixed costs were a reality in the business from the outset.

By the late 1830s, railroad men in both countries understood the practical significance of high fixed costs. "This elementary fact of economic life," George H. Miller notes in his excellent study of American railroad regulation, "was responsible for most of the early assumptions behind rate-making policies."[83] As the Prussian railroad promoter David Hansemann observed in 1837, it was essential to differentiate "between those costs that originate directly from the transport [of goods and passengers] and those costs that, quite apart from the volume of transportation, are entirely unavoidable." Because some costs were more or less fixed—he cited interest charges and a portion of maintenance costs—unit costs fall "with an increase in traffic," he noted.[84] A committee of directors of the Boston and Worcester Railroad reasoned along similar lines in 1840, in estimating what would have happened to costs in 1838, had the volume of freight doubled.[85] The company's directors also reported that they

---

[81] Chandler, comp. and ed., *Railroads*, pp. 159–60; idem, *Visible Hand*, pp. 116–19. For a general discussion, see Porter, *Rise of Big Business*, pp. 10–11.

[82] Gerald Berk, "Constituting Corporations and Markets: Railroads in Gilded Age Politics," *Studies in American Political Development* 4 (1990): 137.

[83] George H. Miller, *Railroads and the Granger Laws* (Madison: University of Wisconsin Press, 1971), p. 17.

[84] David Hansemann, *Die Eisenbahnen und deren Aktionäre in ihrem Verhältniß zum Staat* (Leipzig: Renger'sche Verlagsbuchhandlung, 1837), pp. 14, 18. Hansemann distinguished four types of expenses—transportation costs, road maintenance costs, general administrative costs, and interest—and acknowledged the difficulty of apportioning them between the two categories. Ibid., p. 6.

[85] *Report of a Committee of Directors of the Boston and Worcester Rail-road Corporation. On the proposition of the Directors of the Western Rail-road, to reduce the rates of fare and freight on the two Rail-roads* (Boston: Samuel N. Dickinson, 1840), pp.

were charging higher rates per mile for shorter trips, in part because the interior segments did not face water competition but also "on the ground, that freight when once loaded in the cars, . . . might be carried to the termination of the line at as little cost at least, as it can be delivered at any of the intervening stations."[86]

Because the railroads labored under relatively high fixed costs, their cost efficiency depended critically on the volume of traffic—what Chandler terms "throughput"—and the distance that it traveled, and this, in turn, generated multiple incentives for rate discrimination. As Miller summarizes:

> Since the total cost of operation did not increase in proportion to the amount of traffic, a large volume of business was thought to be desirable, permitting overhead expenses to be distributed over a maximum number of units. This in turn seemed to justify low inducement rates. It was also evident that costs did not increase in proportion to the distance traveled because switching and terminal expenses were the same for short as for long hauls. It seemed practical therefore to seek long-haul traffic at lower rates per mile than were asked for short hauls.

Assymetries in track grades and in the flow of traffic back and forth provided additional grounds for discrimination. "Almost from the

---

23n, 31. They divided expenses into the following categories: general (including road repairs), locomotive, freight, and passenger, each of the latter three including wages, repairs, and depreciation. Ibid., p. 30. Since 1837, they reported, they had been charging "depreciation," that is, "an equivalent for the estimated amount of wear and decay beyond what was made good by the repairs," to current expenses. *Report of the Directors of the Boston & Worcester Rail Road, to the Stockholders, at Their Ninth Annual Meeting, June 1, 1840* (Boston: Samuel N. Dickinson, 1840), p. 19.

86 *Report of the Directors of the Boston & Worcester Rail Road . . . at Their Ninth Annual Meeting*, pp. 7–8. Fourteen years later, however, the company was having trouble maintaining higher rates on local traffic: "It has been found that high rates for short distances cannot be maintained against wagons, as much of the cost of handling and truckage at each end of the transit is saved to the latter." *Twenty-Fifth Annual Report of the Directors of the Boston and Worcester Railroad Corporation, for the Year Ending November 30, 1854* (Boston: David Clapp, 1855), p. 15. The following year they complained that, because of the novelty of the business, the industry had from the outset underestimated the cost of running a railroad: "an undue appreciation was made of the wear and depreciation of all its parts. . . . it must not be forgotten that railways are, at best, expensive establishments." *Twenty-Sixth Annual Report of the Directors of the Boston and Worcester Railroad Corporation, for the Year Ending November 30, 1854* (Boston: David Clapp, 1856), pp. 17–18.

outset," Miller observes, such cost considerations "produced wide departures from a rate structure based simply on distance."[87]

More broadly, the railroads' experience with high fixed costs introduced the distinctively modern business practices and regulatory problems associated with industrial capitalism. The new conditions of operation transformed the incentives acting on businessmen (and the occasional businesswoman), radically altering competitive behavior. In hard times, businesses that did not labor under high fixed costs could curtail production in the time-honored fashion, thereby reducing the bulk of their expenses proportionately. But capital-intensive businesses no longer had this option, for reducing production levels, while fixed costs remained nearly constant, merely increased their unit costs. Under the new incentives, therefore, they maintained or even increased production levels when demand slackened, so that they could at least spread their fixed costs over a larger volume of output. This reduced their unit costs and thus enabled them to cut prices.[88]

This peculiar new competitive behavior had a widening circle of consequences, many of which first appeared in the railroad industry and then emerged in full force in the mass-production industries of the late nineteenth century. It made cooperation among firms to control output or prices both more important (because competition was more "virulent," as Naomi Lamoreaux puts it) and more difficult from an economic standpoint (because decreasing production entailed greater costs for the capital-intensive producer). Other things being equal, the new conditions of competition compounded the obstacles to collective action among firms. They also altered the balance of power between labor and management, Dubofsky argues, making capital-intensive companies *more* vulnerable to labor unrest

---

[87] Miller, *Railroads and the Granger Laws*, p. 17. Competition with parallel lines or alternative modes of transportation and value-based pricing also encouraged rate discrimination. On rate-making, see also Chandler, comp. and ed., *Railroads*, pp. 159–60; Rainer Fremdling and Günter Knieps, "Competition, Regulation and Nationalization: The Prussian Railroad System in the 19th Century," Institute of Economic Research, Faculty of Economics, University of Groningen, Research Memorandum No. 397, November 1990. On the concept of throughput, see Chandler, *Visible Hand*, p. 241, and idem, *Scale and Scope*, p. 24.

[88] Naomi Lamoreaux, *The Great Merger Movement in American Business, 1895–1904* (Cambridge: Cambridge University Press, 1985), pp. 14–86. "The industries most likely to erupt in price wars," she argues (p. 86), "were those in which fi[x]ed costs were high and in which expansion had been rapid and recent." See also Porter, *Rise of Big Business*, pp. 10–12.

and work stoppages. The combined effect, as William Lazonick emphasizes, was to put a premium on the ability to secure the raw materials, labor, and markets that were essential to maintaining a high volume of production and low unit costs. In the absence of perfect markets, this, in turn, encouraged backward and forward integration as well as the new techniques associated with modern labor relations, scientific management, welfare capitalism, and mass consumerism (all of which further increased fixed costs).[89] In the railroad business, moreover, the rate discrimination that high fixed costs encouraged profoundly undermined traditional American methods of government regulation that were geared to maximum prices.[90]

In short, the railroads introduced many, if not all, of the distinctive phenomena that marked industrial capitalism, as Chandler suggested some thirty years ago when he dubbed them "the first big business." They served as a bridge between the first and second phases of the industrial revolution in these two countries, constituting a vital element of the first but also ushering in the second, with all the novelty that attended large-scale, capital-intensive enterprise. Studying early railroad history, therefore, takes us into the first stages of a process of industrial change without parallel until our own time.[91] As the following chapters argue, however, this early encounter with industrial capitalism proceeded differently in the two countries, because of their contrasting political structures.

The Argument

This book offers neither a comprehensive history of American and Prussian railroads nor a general political history of the two nations. Instead, it explores certain ways in which political history and early railroad history intermeshed during the antebellum and *Vormärz*

[89] Dubofsky, "Technological Change"; Lamoreaux, *Great Merger Movement*, p. 45; Lazonick, "Technological Change." For an overview, see Porter, *Rise of Big Business*, pp. 1–28, and on the railroads, ibid., pp. 32–41. On railroad labor, see also Chandler, comp. and ed., *Railroads*, pt. 4; Walter Licht, *Working for the Railroad: The Organization of Work in the Nineteenth Century* (Princeton: Princeton University Press, 1983); Shelton Stromquist, *A Generation of Boomers: The Pattern of Railroad Labor Conflict in Nineteenth-Century America* (Urbana: University of Illinois Press, 1987).

[90] See Miller, *Railroads and the Granger Laws*; and chap. 6 of this book.

[91] Michael J. Piore and Charles F. Sabel, *The Second Industrial Divide: Possibilities for Prosperity* (New York: Basic Books, 1984).

years, thus affirming that industrial change is a complex process, at once political and economic in nature. It takes as its starting point the two political structures as they stood on the eve of the railroad era. The bulk of the study (chapters 2–5) explores their impact on various aspects of early railroad development during the formative decades of the 1830s and 1840s. In these chapters, political structure serves mainly as the independent variable, although the causal connections become increasingly complicated as the chapters progress from state policy through railroad associations to technological styles.

This exploration should not be read as an attempt to derive a rigorous "law" of political structure. That would surely be a fruitless exercise, for history may be structured but it is not so tightly constrained. Rather, it should be understood as an effort to understand the incentives and tendencies that different political structures created and how they shaped social action.

Briefly, chapters 2 and 3 describe and then suggest how to interpret the tenor of early American and Prussian railroad policies. Chapter 2 outlines systematic policy differences and concludes that the American state (that is, the state governments and to a lesser extent the federal government) intervened more extensively and more effectively during the 1830s and 1840s than the *Vormärz* Prussian state did. When functional equivalents—the Prussian central state and the American state governments—are set side by side, in other words, the "American state" receives higher marks on the interventionist scale during the 1830s and 1840s. Chapter 3 considers alternative ways of interpreting these divergent patterns and argues that they reflected neither prevailing interests nor ideas, but the distinctive patterns of policy-making that the two political structures engendered in a capitalist context. The American political structure encouraged more interventionist policies by allowing more effective expression of interests both supporting and opposing railroad construction. In Prussia, state officials at the apex of the unitary structure favored railroad development by the late 1830s, but they could not marshal the capital for state railroads without also ceding to demands for political liberalization. When push came to shove, they chose to rely on private capital to build the railroads, a decision that forced them to moderate regulatory demands so that the private companies would attract sufficient capital.

Chapter 4 suggests that the two political structures shaped relations among the railroads in equally distinctive ways. The Prussian
lines succeeded in forming a permanent national (indeed, inter-
German) association in the late 1840s, because they faced a unitary
state that had begun to take a more interventionist stance. American
lines tried valiantly to form similar associations. But the fragmented
American political structure compounded the obstacles to collective
action, and they uniformly failed to do so during the antebellum
period. The location of the policy-making process within each state
structure thus exercised a decisive impact on efforts to organize railroad interests.

Chapter 5 shows how attention to institutions also yields a new
perspective on the question of technological style. Prussian railroads
cost (per kilometer) roughly half again as much as American railroads, a difference that is best understood as the product of the complex interaction of state and capital. Railroad builders in both countries, as avid participants in a vibrant international colloquy on the
new technology, worked with a common pool of knowledge, and they
shared a common frame of reference, defined by the British paradigm
of railroad construction (sturdy construction, low grades, minimal
curves) and its polar opposite, the "American system." Out of these
commonalities the contrasting Prussian and American political
structures shaped distinctive national styles of technology in two
ways: indirectly, through their impact on state railroad policy, which
exacerbated a relative scarcity of capital in the United States but not
in Prussia; and, more immediately, by structuring the engineering
community itself, producing a more homogeneous engineering viewpoint in Prussia but encouraging a durable diversity of views in the
United States. As Prussian engineers moved toward a consensus in
the early 1840s that railroads should be constructed in a sturdier
fashion than the "American system" called for, but not as luxuriously as the British paradigm dictated, American engineers remained divided. This heterogeneity of views, combined with the relative scarcity of capital, produced a greater diversity of styles and
therefore lowered *average* construction costs in the United States.

Thus, from state policies through interest associations to the technology itself, these two contrasting political structures pushed early
railroad development in divergent directions. In all three domains,

the fragmented American structure impeded, and the centralized Prussian structure facilitated, the emergence of this large-scale technological system.

But these two political structures, taken as givens in chapters 2 through 5, were by no means impervious to change. Bringing the causal arrow full circle, the Epilogue surveys the complex transformation of both political structures that this peculiar new technology precipitated in the late 1840s and 1850s. In Prussia, the unprecedented amounts of capital that railroad construction demanded— *pace* Gerschenkron—ultimately forced a modicum of political liberalization. In the United States, the combination of high fixed costs and geographic sprawl undermined the states' traditional regulatory authority. These institutional changes, in turn, altered the interventionist thrust of railroad policy in the two countries. In newly liberalized Prussia, railroad policy took an "American turn" as state officials gained the political legitimacy to promote *and* regulate the railroads with greater energy. In the United States, the growth of interstate railroads laid bare the structural constraints on the American state legislatures' power, and the parameters that guided railroad policy-making were suddenly thrown open to redefinition. As railroad men used the weapons inherent in the American political structure to wage running battles with the state legislatures, the interventionist thrust of American railroad policy became increasingly attenuated. Only when their defensive maneuvers catapulted the issue to the national level was the American state's regulatory power partially reconstituted in the 1880s. And only then, when regulatory authority was clearly lodged at the national level, did the obstacles to collective action inherent in federalism abruptly recede. American railroads quickly responded to the new constellation of incentives and, like their Prussian counterparts forty years earlier, organized a permanent national association.

Shifting analytical gears in this way underscores the corollary importance of attending to industrial context in understanding political change, thus reinforcing the larger point: that a keener sensitivity to the intangible, yet very real presence of political structures enriches understanding of the complex interplay between industrial and political change.

2

American Intervention and Prussian Abstention

IMPLICIT IN the invisible paradigms that govern American and Prusso-German history seems to be a sense that economic policy follows from political structure: that is, states with strong administrative capacities—above all, well-developed, national bureaucracies—tend to intervene; those without such capacities do not. From this, the assumption easily follows that a country with a more liberal political system, such as the United States, must surely have adopted more liberal economic policies and, conversely, that one with a less liberal political structure, such as Prussia, must have adopted correspondingly less liberal economic policies.[1] This conception of state intervention, murky yet resilient, retains a powerful presence in both countries, predisposing historians to downplay the significance of state activity in the United States and to accentuate it in Prussia.

But research on both sides, as noted in chapter 1, has blurred traditional images of the two states. Something distinguished the American from the Prusso-German pattern of industrialization, but it was not the absence of a tradition of state intervention in the United States, nor was it the degree of interventionism practiced in Prussia. Bringing the two patterns of industrial policy back into focus requires comparative research, for the revisionist literature does not go far enough. It does not explain *why* industrial policy took the course that it did in each country. Why would a comparatively representative government have proven more interventionist in its policy-making? And why would a relatively authoritarian state have largely abstained from direct intervention? Until this puzzle is solved, the power of the invisible paradigms is not likely to attenuate.

This chapter takes the first step toward a solution to the puzzle by highlighting systematically some significant differences in early American and Prussian railroad policy. Viewed comparatively, the evidence confirms the emerging consensus on both sides of the com-

---

[1] See Trebilcock, *Industrialization*, p. 75, the thrust of whose comments applies equally well to American historiography.

parison: the American state legislatures actually tended to favor less liberal (or more interventionist) policies through the mid-1840s than the Prussian central state did. Why that should have been so is the question taken up in chapter 3.

Since the argument in these two chapters turns on a second kind of liberalism, a few words of definition may be in order. The subject of inquiry here is *economic* liberalism, a concept related to, yet distinct from, political liberalism. The central concern is not the structure of political institutions but rather the nature of the economic policies that those institutions produced. At issue, accordingly, is not the degree of individual autonomy in political affairs afforded by the structure of political institutions, but the degree of individual autonomy in economic matters admitted by the general pattern of economic policy—here, railroad policy.

Without being too precise about it, one may simply define economic liberalism by gesturing toward the school of thought popularly associated with Adam Smith.[2] To assess state policies in comparative terms, a first approximation will do: economic liberalism prevails more where the state does less, providing a suitable context for market operations but otherwise abstaining from action; conversely, it obtains less where the state does more. Put differently, the more that state economic policies shift the balance of decision-making power in favor of the state, the more "interventionist" and therefore less liberal they are.[3] This pragmatic, "no politics" definition assumes only that the economy in question is in some measure capitalist (since only when private economic actors have some sphere of action does the degree of state intervention become an issue at all). Under that minimal assumption, the state by definition does not monopolize

[2] For an influential neoclassical formulation of economic liberalism, see Milton Friedman, with the assistance of Rose D. Friedman, *Capitalism and Freedom* (Chicago: University of Chicago Press, 1962), pp. 22–36. Adam Smith himself envisioned a larger role for the state than is commonly recognized; see *An Inquiry into the Nature and Causes of the Wealth of Nations*, ed. Edwin Cannan (Chicago: University of Chicago Press, 1976), book 5. For historical and theoretical insight, see Phyllis Deane, *The Evolution of Economic Ideas* (Cambridge: Cambridge University Press, 1978); John A. Hall, *Liberalism: Politics, Ideology and the Market* (Chapel Hill: University of North Carolina Press, 1987); Samuel Brittan, *A Restatement of Economic Liberalism* (Atlantic Highlands, N.J.: Humanities Press International, 1988).

[3] On the various functions that the state may carry out, see Wolfram Fischer, "Government Activity and Industrialization in Germany (1815–70)," in *The Economics of Take-Off into Sustained Growth*, ed. W. W. Rostow (London: Macmillan & Co.; New York: St. Martin's Press, 1963), p. 84. The term "intervention" carries a sense of intrinsically autonomous political and economic spheres that runs counter to the broader argument in this book. In the interests of accessibility, however, I have retained it.

resources; private economic actors, therefore, have at least some means of wielding power vis-à-vis the state. This conception of economic liberalism thus serves to assess state policies not only in a capitalist democracy like the United States but also in a capitalist monarchy such as Prussia.

In practice, of course, railroad policy from the start was an extraordinarily complex affair. Quite apart from the policy "mosaic" that federalism created, relations between the railroads and the state comprehended a diverse array of topics. To keep the task to manageable proportions, therefore, this chapter is organized around a selection of issues that were central to railroad development in both countries in the 1830s and 1840s. The first section explores state efforts to promote railroad development: state enterprise, investment in private railroads, and the loan of state engineers; while the second addresses two ways in which the states sought to regulate private railroads: by imposing taxes on railroad traffic or revenue, and by controlling rates.

By no means should this survey be viewed as exhaustive. The data for the United States are, as always, less precise than one would like— a historical legacy of the American political structure itself, which makes generalization more difficult. Summarizing trends is also complicated because the first signs appeared in the early 1840s of a transformation in state policies that, as chapter 6 shows, took on greater salience in both countries in the 1850s. A comprehensive survey, moreover, would attend to other policy issues that could function either as promotion or regulation, depending on their thrust— for example, interpretation of liability laws,[4] procedures for exercising rights of eminent domain,[5] the military's influence on the loca-

---

[4] Liability laws, a topic that surfaces in chap. 4, seem to have been interpreted to favor American railroads, although the railroads were not happy with them in every state. In Prussia, the liability provisions of the 1838 railroad law served, on paper, as a form of regulation, and Prussian railroads clearly wanted them removed from the books. But it is not clear that the Prussian courts actually interpreted them stringently. "Experience certainly warrants the hope," railroad promoter and Rhenish liberal David Hansemann wrote, "that the judges, in this case as in the past, will seek by application to moderate a law that, by violating general legal rules, offends natural justice, to the detriment of enterprises whose existence and prosperity have the greatest utility for the state." But he still wanted to see the provision removed from the law. David Hansemann, *Kritik des Preußischen Eisenbahn-Gesetzes vom 3. November 1838* (Aachen und Leipzig: J. A. Mayer, 1841), p. 70. On the American side, see Leonard W. Levy, *The Laws of the Commonwealth and Chief Justice Shaw: The Evolution of American Law, 1830–1860* (New York: Harper & Row, Harper Torchbooks, 1957), pp. 140–82.

[5] Eminent-domain proceedings took on the flavor of promotion in the United States. In disputes with landowners, the doctrine of "offsetting benefits" lowered the cost of

tion of lines,[6] and relations with the Post Office,[7] to name a few. Although space does not permit treatment of these and other interesting questions, the issues reviewed in the following sections convey a good sense of the broad divergence in early American and Prussian railroad policies.

State Promotion of Early Railroads

When enthusiasm for railroad construction surged in the late 1820s and early 1830s, the western industrializing nations responded in diverse ways. At one extreme, states such as Belgium and Baden built and operated railroads themselves; at the other extreme, the

---

land for the railroads by requiring authorities to calculate the value of the land taken for railroad purposes and then *deduct* the increase in the value of the remaining land that would result from construction of the railroad. Levy, *Laws of the Commonwealth*, pp. 130–32; Scheiber, *Ohio Canal Era*, pp. 277–78; idem, "Federalism and the American Economic Order," p. 95. In Prussia railroad men thought that their rights of eminent domain were too narrowly construed. As was often the case, however, the law said one thing and the king another: although the railroads officially did not enjoy the same rights under the rules prevailing in 1837 as applied in the construction of highways, the king announced that he would grant such rights on an individual basis. *Allgemeine Zeitung* (Augsburg), Beilage zur Nr. 298, October 24, 1837, p. 2383. Still, in the western provinces of Prussia, David Hansemann reported, authorities calculated the enhanced value of the land due to railroad construction and then required the companies to pay the higher value. Hansemann, *Kritik des Preußischen Eisenbahn-Gesetzes*, pp. 40–41. This practice had changed by the 1850s. See August Bessel and Eduard Kühlwetter, *Das Preussische Eisenbahnrecht*, part 1 (Cologne: Verlag von Franz Carl Eisen, 1855), pp. 94–95, 107–8; Julius Herrmann Beschorner, *Das deutsche Eisenbahnrecht mit besonderer Berücksichtigung des Actien- und Expropriationsrechtes* (Erlangen: Verlag von Ferdinand Enke, 1858), pp. 98–99.

[6] This is a good candidate for comparison, given the American army engineers' role in the location and construction of early railroads. The question is tricky, however, because the demands of war and commerce often favored the same line of communication. Yet, on the few occasions when commercial and military considerations did conflict in *Vormärz* Prussia, events made clear that, despite strong divisions among the ministers, priority went to the commercially viable location. In the United States, the evidence is much more ambiguous. See Dunlavy, "Politics and Industrialization," pp. 132–52. On the military attractions of railroad construction in both countries, see chap. 3 of this book. On similar debates in a different national context, see Richard Mowbray Haywood, "The 'Ruler Legend': Tsar Nicholas I and the Route of the St. Petersburg–Moscow Railway, 1842–1843," *Slavic Review* 37 (1978): 640–50.

[7] This chapter and chaps. 3 and 4 touch on the subject. For an introduction to its complexities, see *History of the Railway Mail Service; A Chapter in the History of Postal Affairs in the United States* (Washington: Government Printing Office, 1885); Sautter, "General Postmeister von Nagler und seine Stellung zu den Eisenbahnen," *Archiv für Post und Telegraphie* 7 (1916): 223–38; Helmut Paul, "Die preußische Eisenbahnpolitik von 1835–1838: Ein Beitrag zur Geschichte der Restauration und Reaktion in Preußen," *Archiv für Eisenbahnwesen*," 50 (1938): 250–303; Klee, *Preussische Eisenbahngeschichte*, pp. 97–105.

British parliament offered little or no assistance to private railroad construction—indeed, it created obstacles in the cumbersome and expensive process that was required to obtain a corporate charter. On an intermediate terrain lay France, the United States, and Prussia. After considerable discussion and controversy, the French parliament marked out the middle of the state-private spectrum, opting in mid-1842 for a system of mixed enterprise in which its famed state engineers surveyed and constructed the state-owned roadbeds, while private companies contracted to equip and operate the lines.[8] American and Prussian policies lay between this midpoint and the British private-enterprise end of the spectrum, for *most* railroad mileage in both countries was privately owned and operated through mid-century and remained so until the last quarter of the nineteenth century. Yet American policies more closely approximated the quasi-statist French model, while Prussian policies before 1848 lay closer to the British private-enterprise model.

State Enterprise

The differences in American and Prussian policy emerged most clearly in the realm of state enterprise, which initially proceeded on a much grander scale in the United States than it did in Prussia. Although enthusiasm for railroad projects intensified about the same time in the two countries, Prussia, unlike the United States, had no state-owned railroads in operation through the 1840s. Private enterprise built all of the Prussian railroads that opened before the revolution of 1848. Later, to be sure, state construction proceeded rapidly. By 1850, sections of three state railroads (the Westphalen, Saarbrücken, and Eastern railroads) had been completed, the first

---

[8] A. Linters, ed., *Spoorwegen in België/Chemins de Fer en Belgique/Railways in Belgium* (Gent: GOFF pvba, 1985); Wolfgang v. Hippel, Joachim Stephan, Peter Gleber, and Hans-Jürgen Enzwieler, *Eisenbahn-Fieber: Badens Aufbruch ins Eisenbahnzeitalter*, Landesmuseum für Technik und Arbeit in Mannheim (Ubstadt-Weiher: Verlag Regionalkultur, 1990); Henry Parris, *Government and the Railways in Nineteenth-Century Britain* (London: Routledge & Kegan Paul; Toronto: University of Toronto Press, 1965), pp. 1–27; M. C. Reed, *Investment in Railways in Britain, 1820–1844* (London: Oxford University Press, 1974), pp. 76–98; Richard von Kaufmann, *Die Eisenbahnpolitik Frankreichs*, vol. 1, *Allgemeiner, Geschichtlicher Teil* (Stuttgart: J. G. Cotta'schen Buchhandlung, 1896), pp. 1–89; Kimon A. Doukas, *The French Railroads and the State* (New York: Columbia University Press, 1945), pp. 21–23; Cecil O. Smith, "The Longest Run: Public Engineers and Planning in France," *American Historical Review* 95 (June 1990): 665–80. See also O'Brien, ed., *Railways*.

state line opening in its entirety in 1852. During the remainder of the decade, state railroad construction accelerated as state officials not only declined to charter new private lines but also took over the management of some of the major private railroads.[9] By 1860, consequently, the Prussian state owned roughly a quarter of Prussian track, while somewhat less than a quarter was privately owned and state-operated; private capital owned and operated the remaining 50 percent or so. These proportions held roughly steady until 1879, when the Prussian government began a concerted campaign to buy up the major railroads.[10] Then the kind of statist policy so often associated with Prussia finally emerged in full force. But during the period under consideration here, the years before the revolution of 1848, all of the Prussian railroads brought into operation were in private hands.

In the United States, in contrast, relations between the state and private interests in the railroad industry initially took on a more statist complexion, as Carter B. Goodrich's masterful survey of government promotion amply demonstrates.[11] A number of state governments entered the field of state enterprise boldly in the 1830s, building and operating railroads themselves. The fruits of their efforts included Georgia's Western and Atlantic Railroad as well as the Michigan Central and Michigan Southern railroads. Indiana and Illinois also engaged in state enterprise, while Pennsylvania constructed two lines to link canals in its Main Line system of public works.[12] By the early 1840s, economic depression and fiscal troubles had stimulated what Goodrich terms a popular "revulsion" against state enterprise, and some state governments consequently privatized their railroads. But, even then, not all governments divested immediately. Pennsylvania retained ownership of the Philadelphia and Columbia Railroad until 1857, while Georgia's Western and Atlantic Railroad remained a state-owned railroad throughout the nineteenth century.

---

[9] Henderson, *The State and the Industrial Revolution*, p. 172; Klee, *Preußische Eisenbahngeschichte*, pp. 114–26. For a railroad-by-railroad summary of changes in management or ownership, see Kobschätzky, *Streckenatlas*. On the post-1848 period, see chap. 6 and James M. Brophy, "Capitulation or Negotiated Settlement? Entrepreneurs and the Prussian State, 1848–1866," Ph.D. diss., Indiana University, Bloomington, 1991.

[10] Klee, *Preußische Eisenbahngeschichte*, pp. 157–78, 224.

[11] Goodrich, *Government Promotion*, pp. 51–165.

[12] In addition to Goodrich, *Government Promotion*, see Ulrich B. Phillips, "An American State-Owned Railroad: The Western and Atlantic," *Yale Review* 15 (November 1906): 259–82; Robert J. Parks, *Democracy's Railroads: Public Enterprise in Jacksonian Michigan* (Port Washington, N.Y., and London: Kennikat Press, Inc., 1972).

Virginia and Tennessee, meanwhile, moved against the trend, first assuming the role of railroad entrepreneur in the 1850s.[13] The depression of the late 1830s and early 1840s dealt a blow to the American tradition of state enterprise but did not obliterate it altogether.

State Investment in Private Railroads

The pattern of state investment in private railroads followed similar contours, for the American state governments—and, with their approval, the municipalities—proved far more generous in providing financial aid for private railroads than the Prussian state initially did. In individual cases, their investment in railroads matched or exceeded the contributions of private capital, producing a wealth of privately managed "mixed enterprises" in the transportation sector. To cite an extreme case, Maryland's investment in the Baltimore and Susquehanna Railroad represented 63 percent of its total capital by 1839, while the city of Baltimore had contributed more than 28 percent; hence, private capital accounted for less than 9 percent. Beginning in the 1830s, the state of Virginia extended to railroads its policy of subscribing 40 percent of the shares of worthy internal-improvements projects as soon as the public had taken 60 percent; by the late 1840s, it was, in practice, buying 60 percent of their shares itself. The Tennessee legislature passed legislation in 1838 authorizing the state to subscribe one-half of the shares of all railroads (and turnpikes), up to a total of $3.7 million. The state of Massachusetts provided 70 percent of the capital that had been invested in the Western Railroad by its completion in 1841. By the late 1850s, the state of Maryland, together with the cities of Baltimore and Wheeling (Virginia), had contributed nearly half of the Baltimore and Ohio Railroad's share capital and more than half of its loan capital. And so on.[14]

In aggregate terms, the investment of state and substate governments in American railroads—state and private—reached impressive levels during the antebellum period. Indeed, "among the earliest railroads," as Goodrich observes, "the only completely private undertak-

[13] In addition to Goodrich, *Government Promotion*, see idem, "The Revulsion Against Internal Improvements," *Journal of Economic History* 10 (November 1950): 145–69.
[14] Best on details is Goodrich, *Government Promotion*, pp. 51–165. For contemporary, state-by-state observations, see von Gerstner, *Die innern Communicationen*.

ings were a few short lines in settled areas of the East."[15] By the late 1830s, the state governments alone had contributed nearly 45 percent of the capital invested in American railroads.[16] (This came in the form of loans and stock purchases; interest guarantees do not seem to have been entertained until the postbellum years.) In the early 1840s, the revulsion against state enterprise slowed the pace of state investment in private railroads, and prohibitions on such aid were written into the new constitutions of a number of states. But, as Goodrich notes, "the shift in policy was by no means final." Except in the Old Northwest, state aid soon flowed again and, where it did taper off, local governments (with the permission of the legislatures) tended to take up the slack.[17] Altogether, investment by state and local governments still accounted for an estimated 25 to 30 percent of the more than $1 billion invested in railroads before the Civil War.[18] To a Prussian railroad promoter, the Berlin banker Joseph Mendelssohn, the state governments' contributions seemed self-evident; American railroads had been built by the state governments, he declared in 1844, unlike German railroads, which had been and would be built "through thick and thin" by private capital with little state assistance.[19]

In fact, the Prussian state invested very little capital in private railroads during the first phase of Prussian railroad development, which ran from the 1820s to 1842. Only on two occasions during those years did the state step in when railroad promoters encountered financial difficulties. Through the *Seehandlung* or Overseas Trading

---

[15] Carter B. Goodrich, "State In, State Out—A Pattern of Development Policy," *Journal of Economic Issues* 2 (1968): 366–67.

[16] As early as 1838, the state governments alone had incurred debts totalling $42.9 million for railroad development. Taylor, *Transportation Revolution*, pp. 92, 374; Dorothy R. Adler, *British Investment in American Railways, 1834–1898*, ed. Muriel E. Hidy (Charlottesville: University Press of Virginia for the Eleutherian Mills-Hagley Foundation, 1970), p. 10. If one takes Fishlow's estimated investment of $96 million in 1839 (see table 1-1) as the maximum a year earlier, then the state governments had contributed a minimum of 44.6 percent by then.

[17] Goodrich, "The Revulsion Against Internal Improvements," pp. 148–51 (quotation from p. 148); "Report of the Superintendent of the Census, December 1, 1852," in Sen. Exec. Doc., 32d Cong., 2d sess., 1852–53, vol. 2, no. 1, p. 564.

[18] This excludes federal land grants. After the initial burst of railroad investment, the share contributed by state and substate governments fell to about 10 percent during the 1860s (again excluding massive federal land grants); then between 1873 and 1890 it declined further to a mere 1 percent. Goodrich, "State In, State Out," pp. 366–67; idem, *Government Promotion*, pp. 270–71.

[19] Joseph Mendelssohn to [August] Leo in Paris, June 29, 1844, in MA Nachl. 5, IX.

Corporation, the state invested about $1 million (about 1.5 million *Taler*) in the Berlin-Saxon (later, the Berlin-Anhalt) Railroad in 1839.[20] The Finance Ministry also invested 500,000 *Taler* in Berlin-Stettin Railroad bonds some time between mid-1842 and mid-1843, buying them at par when they were selling below par on the stock exchange and agreeing to forego 0.5 percent interest for six years.[21] The Berlin-Stettin, like many American railroads, also received aid from the local government in early 1840, but this aid, in the form of an interest guarantee from the Old Pomeranian Communal Assembly, constituted an exception to the rule. On a strict reading of the ordinances governing the assemblies' organization, they did not have the power to undertake such activities. But the ministers urged (and the king granted) an exception, in order both to encourage construction of the line and to placate local interests, who felt that state policy had systematically slighted their region since the Napoleonic Wars.[22] Leaving aside the interest guarantee, however, direct state assistance to 1842 totalled a mere $1.4 million (2 million *Taler*) or less than 7 percent of the $21 million in railroad capital that had been chartered by then. Beyond that, the railroads received no systematic infusion of capital from the state before 1842. Prussian railroad construction, as W. O. Henderson notes, was simply "left to private enterprise."[23]

[20] "Die Berlin-Sächsische Eisenbahn," *Allgemeine Zeitung* (Augsburg), Beilage, no. 88, March 29, 1839, p. 679; K. Schreiber, *Die Preussischen Eisenbahnen und ihr Verhältniss zum Staat, 1834–1874* (Berlin: Ernst & Korn, 1874), p. 8. The former reports the Seehandlung's subscription to Berlin-Anhalt stock at 1.4 million *Taler*; the latter cites shares of 1 million *Taler* and a loan of 500,000 *Taler*. See also Fremdling, *Eisenbahnen*, p. 125n. On the *Seehandlung*, see Henderson, *The State and the Industrial Revolution*, pp. 119–47.

[21] Schreiber, *Die Preussischen Eisenbahnen*, pp. 8–9, dates this before the change in state policy in the fall of 1842, but it was not reported in the company's annual reports until mid-1843. See *Dritter Jahresbericht des Directorium der Berlin-Stettiner Eisenbahn-Gesellschaft über den Fortgang des Unternehmens im Jahre vom May 1842 bis 1843, zum Vortrag in der General-Versammlung der Aktionaire am 26. May 1843*, p. 26.

[22] See the documents in ZStAM, Rep. 90a, K.III.3, no. 9, vol. 1, pp. 11–20r. The Massachusetts General Court, in contrast, "interposed a firm veto" when the Boston City Council asked permission to subscribe to the Boston and Worcester Railroad's stock, but this seems to have been as exceptional in the American context as the ministers' permission was in the Prussian context. Edward Chase Kirkland, *Men, Cities, and Transportation: A Study in New England History, 1820–1900*, 2 vols. (Cambridge: Harvard University Press, 1948; reprint ed., New York: Russell & Russell, 1968), 1:114. For information on the way such matters were handled in Pennsylvania, see Hartz, *Economic Policy and Democratic Thought*, pp. 86–88.

[23] W. O. Henderson, *The Rise of German Industrial Power, 1834–1914* (Berkeley and Los Angeles: University of California Press, 1975), p. 48. According to Fremdling, *Eisenbahnen*, p. 127, chartered capital to the end of 1842 totalled 90.2 million marks.

In the early 1840s, however, just as the "revulsion" against American state enterprise set in, new circumstances forced Prussian officials to reevaluate their policy stance. By then, they had begun to take a positive view of the new transportation technology, encouraged both by a new (and younger) king, Friedrich Wilhelm IV, and by improvements in the technology itself. In 1841, moreover, some of the provincial assemblies had proposed that the crown use an anticipated budget surplus to promote railroad construction. But the timing of the change was perhaps most closely linked to events outside of Prussia. The king and his ministers surely knew that the French legislature had finally adopted a compromise plan to promote railroad development in June of 1842 (partly in fear of German railroad construction). Ten days after the French legislation passed, the king notified the provincial assemblies to form standing committees, and in August he gave notice that the standing committees would meet in October to consider, among other issues, a railroad aid package.[24]

Once he obtained the provincial delegates' stamp of approval, Friedrich Wilhelm IV authorized an aid package in late 1842 to assist the railroads that the standing committee agreed had national importance.[25] This package included a continuing expenditure of up to $1.4 million (2 million *Taler*) annually, to be used to guarantee interest on the shares of those railroads. These funds, he thought, could be siphoned from the general budget (*Staatshaushalt*) by reducing administrative expenses elsewhere; if not, the provincial delegates had agreed, the salt tax would be raised to provide the necessary revenue.[26] In exchange, railroads receiving an interest guarantee were

---

For details on early policy, see Paul, "Die preußische Eisenbahnpolitik," pp. 250–303; and Klee, *Preußische Eisenbahngeschichte*, pp. 97–105.

[24] "Die Verhandlungen der vereinigten ständischen Ausschüsse über die Eisenbahnfrage in Preussen im Jahre 1842," *Archiv für Eisenbahnwesen* (1881): 4; and on the new French policy the relevant sources in note 8.

[25] These were lines from Cologne to Minden (on the Hannover border); from Halle through Kassel to the middle Rhine; from Berlin to Königsberg and Danzig and possibly to the Russian border; extensions of the Upper Silesian Railroad from Breslau to Frankfurt a.O. and from Oppeln to the Austrian border; and from Posen to lines in the Prussian provinces to the north and in Silesia to the southwest. On the proceedings and discussions at these meetings, see "Die Verhandlungen"; and Friedrich Wilhelm Freiherr von Reden, *Die Eisenbahnen Deutschlands*, 1. Abt., 2. Abschnitt: *Statistischgeschichtliche Darstellung ihrer Entstehung, ihres Verhältnisses zu der Staatsgewalt, so wie ihrer Verwaltungs- und Betriebs-Einrichtungen* (Berlin: Ernst Siegfried Mittler, 1844), pp. 308–14.

[26] Extract, Friedrich Wilhelm to the Staatsministerium, November 22, 1842, in

required to pay the state a so-called superdividend (one-third of all profits above 5 percent), while the state reserved to itself rather extensive rights regarding the management of those lines.[27] The king also authorized Finance Minister Ernst von Bodelschwingh, the official then in charge of railroad policy, to spend up to $350,000 (500,000 *Taler*) for railroad surveys, these monies also to come from the general budget.[28] In the spring of 1843, finally, the king created a so-called Railroad Fund, initially capitalized at $4.2 million (6 million *Taler*) and subsequently augmented by specially earmarked government revenues. State officials used this fund to purchase stock in the railroads that received interest guarantees and then used the annual income on those shares to guarantee interest on additional railroad shares. In practice, when the state offered aid, it did so by purchasing one-seventh of a railroad's shares and guaranteeing 3.5 percent interest on the remaining, publicly held shares.[29]

But, even though the new policy looked ambitious on paper, state investment remained, in Rainer Fremdling's words, "quite modest." The share of total chartered capital on which it guaranteed interest slipped from a peak of 39 percent in 1843, just after the new policy

ZStAM, Rep. 93E, no. 546, vol. 1, pp. 2r–3v; Henderson, *The State and the Industrial Revolution*, pp. 165–66.

[27] Henderson, *The State and the Industrial Revolution*, pp. 163, 166. The state generally received special voting powers in the stockholders' meetings and reserved the following rights: approval over the amounts set aside annually in the reserve fund; approval over the hiring of upper-level employees; and the power to name the president and vice-president of the administrative council (*Verwaltungsrath*), an independent auditor, and one member of the board of directors (*Direction*) who did not need to be a stockholder. See F. Rapmund, *Die finanzielle Betheiligung des Preußischen Staats bei den Preußischen Privateisenbahnen* (Berlin: Verlag der Königlichen Geheimen Ober-Hofbuchdruckerei [R. v. Decker], 1869), pp. 3–4, 16–17; von Reden, *Die Eisenbahnen Deutschlands*, 1. Abt., 2. Abschnitt, pp. 316-18.

[28] Friedrich Wilhelm to Minister von Bodelschwingh, December 31, 1842, in ZStAM, Rep. 93E, no. 546, vol. 1, pp. 23r–v.

[29] Friedrich Wilhelm to Minister von Bodelschwingh, April 28, 1843, in ZStAM, Rep. 93E, no. 546, vol. 1, p. 31r; Josef Enkling, *Die Stellung des Staates zu den Privateisenbahnen in der Anfangszeit des preußischen Eisenbahnwesens (1830–1848)* (Kettwig: F. Flothmann, 1935), pp. 66–69; Henderson, *The State and the Industrial Revolution*, p. 166; Klee, *Preußische Eisenbahngeschichte*, pp. 108, 215n6. For a contemporary analysis of Prussian railroads' problems attracting capital and the importance of state assistance, see David Hansemann, *Über die Ausführung des Preußischen Eisenbahn-Systems* (Berlin: Alexander Duncker, 1843), pp. 41–71. The new policies generally followed principles sketched out by Christian von Rother, head of the *Seehandlung*. See Rother, "Bemerkungen zur Förderung des Eisenbahnbaues unter den in Preußen gegebenen Verhältnißen," February 21, 1843, in ZStAM, Rep. 93E, no. 546, vol. 1, pp. 43r–48r; and Henderson, *The State and the Industrial Revolution*, pp. 165–66.

took effect, to 19 percent in 1848. Meanwhile, its nominal stock holdings, relative to the total chartered capital, had peaked at 7 percent in 1844 and declined to little more than 4 percent in 1848. The new policy no doubt provided crucial encouragement to private railroad development.[30] In aggregate terms, however, state enterprise featured more prominently in American than in Prussian railroad development until the late 1840s. Prussia's parsimonious railroad policy, as Richard Tilly notes, "contrasts sharply with the substantial program of 'internal improvements' carried out in the United States after 1815."[31]

Lending State Engineers

Both states also promoted railroad development in another way: by lending state engineers to aid in surveying and often in constructing and operating early railroads. Unlike state investment, which came from the states and localities in the United States, this kind of aid came from the central state in both countries. The American federal government lent early railroad companies the services of its military engineers, while the Prussian state lent its state civil engineers. On the whole, however, the American state responded with greater alacrity than the Prussian state did.

That the federal government, rather than the states, provided this kind of aid reflected the state of American engineering in the early nineteenth century. The railroad constituted the "high technology" of its day, and among the industrializing nations of the nineteenth century, as Peter Lundgreen observes, "the earliest source of [technical] experts was the military." In the late 1820s, only three American institutions offered formal training in engineering: Rensselaer Polytechnic Institute; Alden Partridge's academy in Norwich, Vermont;

---

[30] Fremdling, *Eisenbahnen*, p. 126. His data do not include the one (possibly two) grants of aid before 1842, the details of which, as noted, remain murky. On the status of the Railroad Fund, see the 1846 report of the *General-Staats-Kasse* (General State Treasury) in ZStAM, Rep. 93E, no. 546, vol. 1, pp. 122r–231r; and "General-Dispositions-Plan für die Verwendung des Eisenbahn-Fonds in den Jahren 1847 bis einschließlich 1856" in ibid., 142r–143v. For details on the state's participation in individual railroad lines to 1869, see Rapmund, *Die finanzielle Betheiligung.* Bösselmann, *Entwicklung*, pp. 201–2, provides useful summaries of railroad stocks and bonds issued up to 1850.

[31] Richard Tilly, "The Political Economy of Public Finance and the Industrialization of Prussia, 1815–1866," *Journal of Economic History* 26 (December 1966): 485.

and the military academy at West Point. Of the three, West Point was by far the most important, producing roughly ten times as many engineers as the other two institutions. As a result, the War Department commanded a near-monopoly over the supply of engineers with "schooling." Moreover, the federal government, unlike its Continental counterparts, had no separate civil engineering corps. Constitutional conflict generally constrained expansion of the federal government's activities in the antebellum period, and the opposition of military officials helped to defeat occasional initiatives to create a civil engineering corps. In a de facto compromise, West Point cadets studied civil as well as military engineering. Consequently, the United States, as Lundgreen observes, "relied longer than any other comparable country on military engineers as experts for civilian purposes." Since national defense was one of the few policy areas that the Constitution clearly delegated to the federal government, it had both the technical and the political capability, as the French visitor Michel Chevalier put it, "[t]o supply the want of men of science, demanded by the spirit of enterprise."[32]

The War Department began sending engineers to work on railroad surveys in the late 1820s, as Forest G. Hill has shown, under the authority of the General Survey Act of 1824. This legislation, a compromise enacted after President James Monroe vetoed the Cumberland Road bill in 1822, did not allow the federal government to carry out internal-improvements projects itself, as some preferred, but it did empower the president to deploy War Department engineers to aid transportation projects that he deemed of national importance. In effect, as Hill notes, the act "formalized and systematized practices which had already evolved and gained general acceptance." When the railroad emerged as a potentially viable alternative to roads and canals, President John Quincy Adams extended use of the Survey Act to railroads as well.[33]

[32] Daniel Hovey Calhoun, The American Civil Engineer: Origins and Conflict (Cambridge, Mass.: Technology Press, 1960), pp. 37–46; Forest G. Hill, Roads, Rails, and Waterways: The Army Engineers and Early Transportation (Norman: University of Oklahoma Press, 1957), pp. 62–64; Lundgreen, "Measures for Objectivity," p. 14; Chevalier, Society, Manners and Politics, p. 274. On West Point, see Peter M. Molloy, "Technical Education and the Young Republic: West Point as America's École Polytechnique, 1802–1833," Ph.D. diss., Brown University, 1975; James L. Morrison, Jr., "The Best School in the World": West Point, the Pre-Civil War Years, 1833–1866 (Kent: Kent State University Press, 1986).

[33] Hill, Roads, Rails, and Waterways, pp. 37–56, 72 (quotation from p. 44). On these

The army engineers' experience on the first railroad to receive federal aid suggests the magnitude of the work that the engineers carried
out. Having requested aid from the War Department, the Baltimore
and Ohio Railroad received three brigades of engineers in 1827.
Headed by Dr. William Howard, Col. Stephen H. Long, and Capt.
(later, Maj.) William Gibbs McNeill, each brigade included three assistant engineers. Long and McNeill worked on the Baltimore and
Ohio surveys for three years; after two years of work, Dr. Howard and
his team were sent down to survey the South Carolina Railroad.
Better-known among the assistant engineers was Lt. George W. Whistler, who fathered the famous painter, went on to work on other
American railroads, and supervised construction of the St. Petersburg
and Moscow Railroad in the 1840s. During each of the three years, the
company employed ten to twelve army engineers; over the three
years, some fourteen government engineers worked on the railroad,
and all of them went on to work on other railroads as well. Initially,
the government absorbed all expenses, but within two years the War
Department began to feel the strain and from then on the government
paid only the engineers' salaries; the companies picked up the expenses of the surveys themselves. The engineers' work did not stop
with the surveys, however, for they also helped in organizing construction, taking bids from contractors, supervising the laying of
track, adapting the military's bureaucratic methods to railroad management, and so on. Once construction began, moreover, the company sent three engineers—Major McNeill and Lieutenant Whistler,
both West Point–trained, and Jonathan Knight, who had been hired
from the National Road—to England to gather the most up-to-date
information.[34]

McNeill, Long, and their colleagues represented the beginnings of a
flood of government engineers who provided vital engineering skills
to the early railroads, initially while on active duty or on leave but
increasingly after resigning from the military. The first engineers

and other activities of the army engineers during the antebellum period, see also
Calhoun, *American Civil Engineer*, pp. 37–47; Smith, *Harpers Ferry*; Smith, "Army
Ordnance and the 'American System' of Manufacturing"; O'Connell, "The Corps of
Engineers and the Rise of Modern Management"; Shallat, "Building Waterways."

[34] Hill, *Roads, Rails, and Waterways*, pp. 101–6. On Howard's subsequent work, see
Dr. William Howard, *Report on the Charleston and Hamburg Rail-Road* (Charleston,
1829). On the army engineers' contributions to modern management methods while
working on the Baltimore and Ohio Railroad, see O'Connell, "The Corps of Engineers
and the Rise of Modern Management."

carried out surveys and related work while on active duty, their expenses, as noted, paid by the companies from 1828 on. By then, however, the War Department was occasionally granting furloughs to allow the engineers to carry out surveys for lines that it viewed as important. When the War Department tightened its regulations concerning outside work in late 1831, engineers began to resign from the military in large numbers in order to remain with the railroads, a trend that accelerated in the mid-1830s.[35]

Altogether, at least 122 graduates of West Point, both active-duty and resigned, worked on American railroads in the antebellum years, their participation coming in two waves. The first, which the Baltimore and Ohio surveys set in motion, peaked in 1837. During that year at least 54 West Point graduates were occupied in railroad work, the large majority of them having resigned from the military. Their numbers declined in the late 1830s and early 1840s, not only because economic conditions temporarily dampened the pace of construction but also because of changes in government policy. As early as 1831 the War Department had backed away from its policy of lending or furloughing army officers to internal improvements projects because of the strains that it placed on departmental work, but it continued to lend topographical engineers on an exceptional basis. In the mid-1830s, however, the strain on the Department's engineering resources reached sufficiently alarming proportions that successive secretaries of war began to oppose the policy of loaning army engineers to private companies. In 1838, congressional legislation mandating a reorganization of the War Department finally prohibited army engineers from working on internal improvements or for private companies. This effectively repealed the General Survey Act. But a second wave began in the late 1840s and crested in 1854, when at least 52 graduates of the academy worked on railroad projects, the active-duty engineers now occupied with surveys for transcontinental railroads. Assuming that the West Pointers on average spent only half of each year with the railroads, then they devoted an estimated five hundred cumulative man-years to antebellum railroad construction. This estimate errs on the conservative side, it must be emphasized, for not all army engineers had graduated from West Point.[36]

[35] Hill, *Roads, Rails, and Waterways,* p. 111.
[36] These observations are based on data for 137 individuals, gleaned largely from George W. Cullum, *Biographical Register of the Officers and Graduates of the U.S.*

The full value of this assistance defies appraisal. According to one estimate, the direct cost of railroad surveys under the General Survey Act amounted to only $75,000. But in Hill's judgment this "estimate is probably much too low." At least half of the $424,000 spent under the Survey Act, as he points out, went to railroad surveys. The work of furloughed and resigned army engineers, moreover, must be viewed as a form of state aid, for the government had absorbed the cost of training many of them. Combined with investment by state and municipal government, engineering aid from the federal government made some nominally private railroads in reality a joint venture of the several levels of government. The Baltimore and Susquehanna Railroad serves as the best example: not only had it derived more than 90 percent of its capital in 1839 from the state of Maryland and the city of Baltimore, but it also employed nine West Point graduates between 1828 and 1839, including three who served successively as its chief engineer from 1828 to 1838. Two of the latter were retired or resigned, but one—the ubiquitous Major McNeill—did so while on active duty from 1830 to 1836. If the indirect costs of engineering aid were included, Hill concludes, "the figure of $75,000 would be insignificant in comparison."[37]

If the number of army engineers involved in railroad work appears impressive, the practice of working on several railroads at once multiplied their influence. "The most eminent engineers have always several works under their direction at once," Michel Chevalier reported in 1835; "it is understood, of course, that they are aided by skilful and intelligent assistants who do most of the work."[38] The busiest of the "eminent" engineers was probably the topographical engineer Major McNeill, who graduated from West Point in 1817. After the army engineers left the Baltimore and Ohio Railroad in 1830, McNeill

---

Military Academy, 2 vols. (Boston: Houghton, Mifflin and Company, Riverside Press, 1891), entries for graduates from 1802 through 1850 (nos. 1–1493). Excluded from consideration here are thirteen graduates who worked for railroads only during or after the Civil War, one who worked only as a railroad contractor, and one whose dates of service are uncertain. The details are summarized in Dunlavy, "Politics and Industrialization," appendix. The depression's effects on the engineering community are discussed in Calhoun, *American Civil Engineer,* pp. 141–81. For restrictions on the engineers' railroad work, see Hill, *Roads, Rails, and Waterways,* pp. 78–95, 112–16, 120–30.

[37] Hill, *Roads, Rails & Waterways,* p. 132n; Dunlavy, "Politics and Industrialization," appendix.

[38] Chevalier, *Society, Manners and Politics,* p. 273.

went on to conduct another dozen surveys while on active duty (table 2-1). Although the War Department prohibited non-Department work by its line officers from 1831 on, it made an exception "only with McNeill," his superior officer explained, "whose connexion with several private companies has been long and with the express sanction of the War Department." In the banner year 1835, McNeill served as chief engineer of six different railroads along the Eastern seaboard.[39]

No other army engineer quite matched McNeill's distinguished record, but others came close. Col. Stephen Long, for example, worked on ten railroads between 1827 and 1847, in the interim also serving as state engineer of Georgia in 1837, while on leave from the military. In Hill's judgment, Long, McNeill, and Whistler (of Russian railroad fame) enjoyed "the most famous railroad careers." Although many of the army engineers worked in the industry only a few years or with lengthy interruptions, lesser-known engineers also compiled impressive records. William H. Swift worked for railroads nearly continuously from 1828 to the 1870s, holding the office of president on three railroads toward the end of his career. Joshua Barney, a veteran of the Baltimore and Ohio surveys, had worked on another ten railroads in New England and the Midwest by 1854. His colleague on the Baltimore and Ohio surveys, William Cook, chose greater stability, serving simultaneously as chief engineer of the Camden and Amboy and Philadelphia and Trenton railroads from the 1830s until his death in 1865. Others who got their practical training on the Baltimore and Ohio surveys included Walter Gwynn, who worked on a dozen more railroads, mainly in the South, between 1832 and 1861; and Isaac R. Trimble, a veteran of six railroads. Among later graduates, Herman Haupt (class of 1835) enjoyed perhaps the longest and most active career. Having resigned from the service shortly after graduation, he worked on six railroads and taught engineering and mathematics at Pennsylvania College, before spending eight years with the Pennsylvania Railroad in the late 1840s and 1850s. He remained a railroad man for the rest of his long and distinguished career, holding the

---

[39] McNeill ended his career outside the railroad industry, serving first as president of the Chesapeake and Ohio Canal Company in 1842–43 and then as chief engineer of the dry docks at Brooklyn Navy Yard in 1844–45. Between those two positions, he commanded the Rhode Island militia during the Dorr Rebellion. Hill, *Roads, Rails, and Waterways*, pp. 113–16 (quotation from p. 115); Cullum, *Biographical Register*, 1: 164–65.

TABLE 2-1
Railroad Work of Maj. William Gibbs McNeill, 1827–40

1823	Promoted to brevet captain in general staff, assistant topographical engineer
1827–30	*Baltimore & Ohio Railroad:* surveys; member of the company's board of civil engineers
1830–36	*Baltimore & Susquehanna Railroad:* survey, 1830; chief engineer, 1830–36
1830–53	Consulting engineer of various railroads and other public works in U.S. and Cuba
1831	*Baltimore-Washington railroad:* survey for the Maryland General Assembly, House of Delegates, Committee on Internal Improvements
1831–34	*Paterson and Hudson River Railroad:* survey, 1831; chief engineer, 1831–34
1832–35	*Boston and Providence Railroad:* survey, 1832–33; chief engineer, 1832–35
1832–37	*Providence and Stonington Railroad:* survey, 1832–33; chief engineer, 1832–37
1834	Promoted to brevet major in general staff, topographical engineer
1834	Surveys of railroads in Florida and Alabama
1835	*Taunton and New Bedford Railroad:* surveys and chief engineer
1835	*Fayetteville and Yadkin Railroad:* surveys and chief engineer
1835–36	*Long Island Railroad:* surveys and chief engineer
1836–40	*Western Railroad:* surveys, 1836–37; chief engineer, 1836–40
1837	Resigned from the topographical engineers
1837–40	*Louisville, Cincinnati, and Charleston Railroad:* chief engineer

SOURCES: Cullum, *Biographical Register*, 1:161–66; "Report of the Committee on Internal Improvement, Delivered by Archibald Lee, Esq. Chairman," Committee on Internal Improvement, Maryland General Assembly, House of Delegates, December session, 1830–31 (Annapolis, 1831), p. 3.

position of Chief of Construction and Transportation with the U.S. Military Railroads during the Civil War and ending as president of the Dakota and Great Southern Railway in the mid-1880s.[40]

The significance of the army engineers' railroad work, despite Hill's valuable research, has never been fully appreciated—further evidence of the power of the invisible paradigms perhaps. "Up to 1855," one writer concluded, with only a touch of hyperbole, "there was scarcely a railroad in this country that had not been projected, built and in most cases managed by officers of the Corps."[41] As a result of the army engineers' work on internal improvements projects, a biographer of Major McNeill maintained in 1859, "Engineering knowledge was thus scattered abroad among the youth of our country— producing among them emulation and success in many a public work, that else had remained in embryo."[42] In any other country, the army engineers' impressive contributions to early railroad development would suggest a statist pattern of industrialization.[43]

In Prussia, central state officials also provided engineering assistance, sending state civil, rather than military, engineers to help the railroads. Although a handful of military men worked for the railroads in technical positions, the companies drew technical aid from the state corps of civil engineers, especially those who had specialized training in hydraulic engineering and road construction. Thus when King Friedrich Wilhelm III approved guidelines for granting furloughs to do railroad work in 1838, they applied to *Baubeamte* or construction officials, rather than to military engineers.[44] "In comparative perspective," Lundgreen observes,

> an explanation is at hand. Highly bureaucratized countries like Prussia/Germany commanded not only a complex civil service for general administration, but also for "technical administration.". . . [B]uilding officials, i.e. civil engineers employed in the

---

[40] See Dunlavy, "Politics and Industrialization," appendix; the relevant entries in Cullum, *Biographical Register*; and Hill, *Roads, Rails, and Waterways*, pp. 107–8, 111, 113, 122, 125, 127–32, 146n.

[41] Henry C. Jewett, "History of the Corps of Engineers to 1915," *The Military Engineer* 38 (1946): 344, quoted in Hill, *Roads, Rails, and Waterways*, p. 146n.

[42] *American Railway Review*, vol. 1, no. 2 (July 21, 1859), p. 12.

[43] Chap. 5 explores other dimensions of their railroad work.

[44] Von Alvensleben to [Friedrich Wilhelm III], December 29, 1837, and [Friedrich Wilhelm III] to von Alvensleben, January 19, 1838, in ZStAM, Rep. 2.2.1, no. 29524, pp. 1r–4r.

public sector constituted the most important body of expertise within the Prussian government.[45]

Although no study comparable to Hill's has been done of the Prussian state civil engineers' railroad work, the available evidence provides a basis for tentative generalization.

Information on two groups of railroad men confirms that state officials predominated and that the majority of them were civil engineers. The two, overlapping groups embraced those who had supervised construction of the major lines and those who held technical positions (chief engineer, technical director, special director, or director with technical specialty) on Prussian railroads in 1847. Of the 49 men in these two groups, more than 60 percent (31) were state officials of one kind or another. By comparison, state officials constituted a smaller proportion (40%) of all directors—inside and outside, technical and nontechnical—in 1847. Of the 31 state officials, in turn, more than 60 percent (20) were state civil engineers, nearly all of them specialists in hydraulic engineering (*Wasserbau*) or road construction (*Wegebau*). Another five among the state officials were military men, two of whom appear to have been military engineers.[46]

[45] Lundgreen, "Measures for Objectivity," pp. 14–15 (emphasis omitted).

[46] This information is by no means complete. It was gleaned from company-by-company listings in Julius Michaelis, *Deutschlands Eisenbahnen: Ein Handbuch für Geschäftsleute, Privatpersonen, Capitalisten und Speculanten* (Leipzig: C. F. Amelang's Verlag, 1854), which lists constructing engineers for some but not all railroads; and from Friedrich Wilhelm von Reden, *Eisenbahn-Jahrbuch für Bahn-Beamte und Staats-Behörden* 2 (1847), which lists current personnel. Supplementary information comes from "Subscriptions-Verzeichniß," *Journal für die Baukunst* 1 (1829): iii-xxii; "Nachtrag zum Subscriptions-Verzeichniß," ibid., 2 (1830); *Bericht des Comite für die Eisenbahn von Köln nach der belgischen Gränze, erstattet am 25. August 1835 und gedruckt auf Beschluß der Rheinischen Eisenbahn-Gesellschaft, zur Vertheilung an die Mitglieder desselben* (Cologne, [1835]), p. 2; *Handbuch über den königlich preussischen Hof und Staat für das Jahr 1839* (Berlin, [1839]); *Dritter Jahresbericht des Directorium der Berlin-Stettiner Eisenbahn-Gesellschaft*, pp. 24–25; von der Leyen, "Die Entstehung der Magdeburg-Leipziger Eisenbahn," *Archiv für Eisenbahnwesen* 5 (1880): 256, 267; *Zur Feier des Fünfundzwanzigsten Jahrestages der Eröffnung des Betriebes auf der Oberschlesischen Eisenbahn, den 22. Mai 1867* (Breslau: Wilh. Gottl. Korn, 1867), pp. 11–12, 25–26, 31, 38. The statement regarding all directors is based on an analysis of the occupations given for 386 of 444 board members in von Reden, *Eisenbahn-Jahrbuch*. Another scholar found roughly comparable proportions on the boards of the Rhenish Railroad between 1835 and 1879. Pierenkemper, "Die Zusammensetzung des Führungspersonals," p. 42. The military men had probably not been dispatched by the state. The only instance in which military engineers had been used, to my knowledge, came after the change of state policy in late 1842, when the king assigned military engineers to do preliminary surveys for what would become the state-owned Eastern Railroad to Königsberg. Friedrich Wilhelm to Minister von Bodelschwingh, December 31, 1842, in ZStAM, Rep. 93E, no. 546, vol. 1, pp. 231-v.

But none of the Prussian state engineers was as peripatetic as the most active of the American army engineers. The closest competitor in this regard may have been *Baurath* (roughly, Construction Councilor) Hess of Magdeburg, who served as chief engineer for construction of the Magdeburg-Wittenberge Railroad, chartered in 1845, and sat on the boards of the Berlin-Potsdam-Magdeburg and Magdeburg-Leipzig railroads two years later. In the common pattern, a state engineer took leave from state service, supervised construction of a railroad, stayed on as chief engineer or a member of the board of directors, and in the meantime perhaps constructed connecting lines as well. *Regierungs-Baurath* (District Construction Councilor) Hans Viktor von Unruh, for example, carried out surveys for a railroad from Potsdam to Magdeburg and then took leave from his state duties in 1844 to build the line. In late 1845, at the urging of the directors of the Magdeburg-Wittenberge Railroad, he received an extension of his leave in order to take charge of construction of the great bridge over the Elbe River. The following year he took charge of construction of that railroad as well, apparently replacing Hess. While on leave he was elected to two terms on the railroad's supervisory board.[47]

One of the better-known state civil engineers, *Ober-Wege-Bau-Inspektor* (Senior Road Construction Inspector) Georg Neuhaus initially took a similar path, then moved to the private sector. The promoters of the Berlin-Stettin Railroad borrowed his services from the state in 1836 and immediately sent him off at their expense to tour railroads in other German cities and in Belgium. Between then and 1840, while the venture remained uncertain, he also carried out surveys and prepared cost estimates for the company. In 1840 he requested a two- to three-year leave of absence to take charge of construction. But because state officials considered his position too important to fill with a substitute for so long, he left state service with the understanding that he could reclaim his position and salary

[47] See the correspondence in ZStAM, Rep. 2.2.1, no. 29524, pp. 14r–15r, 16r, 35r–37v, 38r–v; and Heinrich von Poschinger, ed., *Erinnerungen aus dem Leben von Hans Viktor von Unruh* (Stuttgart: Deutsche Verlags-Anstalt, 1895), pp. 69–71. After the revolution, Unruh's liberal activities attracted the attention of August von der Heydt, Minister of Trade, Commerce, and Public Works, when he set out to purge the railroads of democratic sympathizers. As a result of the minister's machinations, Unruh left the railroad and state service in the early 1850s and took charge of construction of a gas-lighting system in Magdeburg. Correspondence in ZStAM, Rep. 2.2.1, no. 29524, pp. 39r, 40r; Poschinger, ed., *Erinerungen*, pp. 135–36, 170–75. For further details on von der Heydt's initiatives in the 1850s, see chap. 6.

level when he returned and that his work with the railroad would count toward his pension time. In overlapping stints between 1840 and 1848, he supervised construction of the Berlin-Stettin, Stettin-Stargard, and Berlin-Hamburg lines. In 1848, he finally left state service altogether to become *Betriebs-Direktor* or general superintendent of the Berlin-Hamburg Railroad. In 1850 he also accepted the position of chairman of the inside board of directors (*Direktion*). Neuhaus held both positions until his death in 1876. "Seldom has a large railroad company been so centralized and so thoroughly controlled by a single person," observed an obituary writer.[48]

Other state civil engineers worked intermittently on railroad projects and then specialized in the subject as state officials. Construction Inspector (*Bauinspektor*) Ludwig Henz first acquired a hands-on knowledge of railroad surveying in 1835, when he carried out surveys in the western provinces while in state service. The same year, the promoters of the Magdeburg-Leipzig Railroad made him an honorary member of their committee in recognition of his contributions to railroad development. In the early 1840s, state officials again sent him off to do a railroad survey, this time for the Thüringian Railroad, which would run west from Halle to the Hessen border. Henz took charge of the surveys, which consumed a year of work; his deputy engineer, Mons, later became chief engineer and general superintendent of the railroad. By 1847 Henz had been promoted to construction councilor in the Finance Ministry and was also serving as technical director of the Lower Silesian-Mark Railroad, which ran from Berlin southeast to Breslau.[49]

[48] Correspondence between *Oberbürgermeister* Masche in Stettin and Joseph Mendelssohn in Berlin, March 22, March 25, April 1, May 2, May 9, 1836, and Neuhaus' initial estimate of costs for the Berlin-Stettin Railroad in MA Nachl. 5, VIII; correspondence in ZStAM, Rep. 2.2.1, no. 29524, pp. 5r–8r; *Deutsche Bauzeitung*, August 18, 1877, p. 328, and August 25, 1877, p. 338.

[49] Ludwig Henz, *Denkschrift zur Begründung des Projektes der Erbauung einer Eisenbahn zwischen Köln und Eupen* (1835), which was cited as an authoritative source in Hansemann, *Die Eisenbahnen und deren Aktionäre*, pp. 4n–5n; *Bericht des Comite für die Eisenbahn von Köln nach der belgischen Gränze*, p. 2; von der Leyen, "Entstehung der Magdeburg-Leipzig Eisenbahn," pp. 253–54; Louis Röll, *Die Entstehungsgeschichte der Thüringischen Eisenbahn* (1910), pp. 18–19, 22; von Reden, *Eisenbahn-Jahrbuch*, p. xxv. Ludwig Henz may be the *Wasserbaumeister* L. Henz who was involved in other early work on railroads in the western provinces. See Walter Steitz, *Die Entstehung der Köln-Mindener Eisenbahngesellschaft: Ein Beitrag zur Frühgeschichte der deutschen Eisenbahnen und des preussischen Aktienwesens*, Schriften zur Rheinisch-Westfälischen Wirtschaftsgeschichte, vol. 27 (Cologne: Rheinisch-Westfälischen Wirtschaftsarchiv zu Köln, 1974), pp. 137, 158, 164–67, 194.

Another state engineer, Construction Councilor Friedrich Mellin, carved out a career in railroad work that took him from the provinces into the Finance Ministry as a railroad specialist in the early 1840s. A native of Magdeburg, Mellin became involved with plans to build the Magdeburg-Leipzig Railroad, the first long-distance Prussian line, while working for the district government in Magdeburg. In the late 1830s and early 1840s, he served as the company's technical director, in charge first of construction and then of operation. During the same years, he also supervised construction of the Magdeburg-Halberstadt Railroad. Then in mid-1843, after state policy had taken a more activist turn, Finance Minister Ernst von Bodelschwingh sought to recruit Mellin and his special expertise for the ministry. To do so, however, he had to offer an unusually high salary. "Mellin, with his established qualifications," observed von Bodelschwingh, "would easily be able to find a much more advantageous position and would be taken on immediately as a chief construction engineer by any railroad corporation."[50] Mellin accepted the minister's offer and then, in order to hold him in the face of extraordinary competition from the private railroads, von Bodelschwingh and his successor, Finance Minister Eduard Heinrich Flottwell, rapidly secured a bonus, permanent status, and special pay for him. "With the progressive development of the railroad system," Flottwell explained, "a senior engineer (*oberer Techniker*) for railroad affairs has consequently become absolutely essential to the Finance Ministry." But retaining such a valuable man required special compensation "in view of the extraordinary conditions that prevail where the railroad engineer is concerned."[51] By 1849 Mellin had been promoted to privy senior finance councilor (*Geh. Ober-Finanz-Rath*) in the new Ministry of Trade, Commerce, and Public Works and headed the department responsible for railroad affairs.[52]

[50] Von Bodelschwingh to [Friedrich Wilhelm IV], June 20, 1843, and [Friedrich Wilhelm IV] to von Bodelschwingh, July 31, 1843, in ZStAM, Rep. 2.2.1, no. 29418, pp. 7r–14v; *Allgemeine Deutsche Biographie* 21 (1885): 299–300.

[51] Von Bodelschwingh to [Friedrich Wilhelm IV], May 13, 1844; [Friedrich Wilhelm IV] to von Bodelschwingh, May 24, 1844; Flottwell to [Friedrich Wilhelm IV], June 3, 1844; [Friedrich Wilhelm IV] to Flottwell, June 21, 1844, in ZStAM, Rep. 2.2.1, no. 29418, pp. 15r–19v.

[52] Minister von der Heydt to Räthen und Hülfsarbeitern bei [Department] II, February 24, 1849, in ZStAM, Rep. 93E, no. 1, pp. 7r–8r; Minister von der Heydt to [Friedrich Wilhelm IV], January 20, 1850, in ibid., pp. 11r–12v; Friedrich Wilhelm IV to Minister für Handel, Gewerbe, und öffentliche Arbeiten, January 22, 1850, in ibid., p. 13r.

By the mid-1840s, however, state officials had begun to rethink the furlough policy, as American officials did in the mid-1830s. Prospects for state construction officials (*Baubeamte*) were not particularly good, Finance Minister Flottwell noted in late 1844. They had to undergo five years of preparation and study, before taking the architecture examination; then came some ten years as *Bau-Kondukteure*, a probationary period when they had to find employment themselves. Only after that did they have a chance at a state position—where they confronted only low pay and an inordinate workload. At the same time, the railroads' demand for engineers remained strong, not only in Prussia but also in foreign countries. Some Prussian engineers, he warned, had even gone to work on state railroads in other countries.[53]

In early 1845, therefore, the king approved a change of policy. Like the American Congress eight years earlier, he sought not to make state service more attractive but to restrict the conditions under which state engineers could take positions with railroads. Now they would have to leave state service entirely, with no assurance that they could return at their pleasure. Moreover, when *Bau-Kondukteure* worked first for the railroads and then entered state service, no more than three years of their employment with a railroad company would be credited toward seniority and pension time with the state.[54] Despite occasional interministerial lobbying on behalf of individual engineers, Finance Minister Flottwell generally held fast to the new policy.[55]

State engineers made important contributions to private railroad construction in both countries, and their work placed a sufficient strain on the states' engineering resources that American and then Prussian officials took steps to curb it after a few years. On balance, however, the American federal government's largess meant more, because it did so much more with far fewer resources. Its most active

[53] Flottwell to [Friedrich Wilhelm IV], October 27, 1844, in ZStAM, Rep. 2.2.1, no. 29524, pp. 18r–20r. State engineer von Unruh complained both about low pay and about the administrative work required of state engineers; railroad construction offered not only better pay, he noted, but also more challenging and interesting work. See Poschinger, ed., *Erinnerungen*, pp. 40–45, 68.

[54] Flottwell to [Friedrich Wilhelm IV], October 27, 1844, and [Friedrich Wilhelm IV] to Flottwell, March 7, 1845, in ZStAM, Rep. 2.2.1, no. 29524, pp. 18r–21r.

[55] See the correspondence regarding *Regierungs- und Baurath* Hartwich, *Bau-Inspektor* Pickel, and *Regierungs-Baurath* von Unruh in ZStAM, Rep. 2.2.1, no. 29524, pp. 22r–38v.

officers, as we have seen, worked for several railroads at once and for a dozen or so over their career. The Prussian engineers' railroad work tended to be more limited in scope. In the best of times in the 1830s, moreover, the U.S. War Department had no more than fifty-five engineers at its disposal each year.[56] In contrast, the Prussian district governments, from which the state civil engineers were dispatched, commanded a larger pool of candidates. In 1839, for example, they employed some two hundred engineers with the training and experience demanded for railroad construction.[57]

Thus in providing not only investment capital but human capital, state efforts to promote railroad development figured more prominently in the United States than in Prussia through the 1840s. With its greater commitment to promotion, American policy plainly earned higher marks for "interventionism" than Prussian policy did through the mid-1840s. But promotion represented only one side of state intervention. As the next section implies, the state that promoted also regulated, and the one that pursued promotion with less energy encountered greater difficulties in regulating.

Regulating Early Railroads

For evaluating efforts to regulate private railroads,[58] conventional images of the two states provide equally little guidance. It would be wrong, for example, to suppose that the *Vormärz* Prussian state not only did little to aid railroad construction but also subjected the joint-stock companies to stringent regulatory controls; likewise, one would err in assuming that the antebellum American states promoted railroad construction with great enthusiasm and then left the private corporations to their own devices. Quite to the contrary, state regulation of private railroads in the two countries followed much the same pattern as state enterprise during the 1830s and 1840s: the

[56] According to Hill, *Roads, Rails, and Waterways*, p. 78, this included ten topographical engineers, ten to fifteen civil engineers, and twenty to thirty line officers.

[57] Estimated from the personnel listed as road (*Wegebau*), highway (*Chausseebau*), and waterway (*Wasserbau*) specialists in *Handbuch über den königlich preussischen Hof und Staat für das Jahr 1839*. This does not include other kinds of hydraulic engineers. Including all kinds of *Baubeamte* or construction officials, moreover, would increase the number substantially.

[58] The term private railroads encompasses both exclusively privately owned and operated lines and those that had attracted some state investment.

American states—and, to a lesser extent, the federal government—
tended to regulate private railroads more extensively than the Prussian central state did before 1848.

Commonalities

In some respects, it should be noted, the two followed similar policies in chartering the joint-stock corporations that built early railroads. The antebellum American legislatures incorporated railroad companies by means of special legislation, and by the 1840s these special acts frequently subordinated the company in question to generic railroad laws. Unlike general incorporation laws, which appeared later and allowed companies to incorporate through an administrative procedure, these generic laws merely allowed a streamlining of legislative charters. Whenever a new railroad was incorporated, as a Virginia act of 1837 explained, the generic provisions "shall be deemed and taken to be a part of the said charter or act of incorporation, to the same effect as if the same were expressly re-enacted in reference to any such charter or act, except so far as such charter or act may otherwise expressly provide."[59] The first general incorporation law for railroads was passed in New York in 1848 (replaced by new legislation in 1850), but, even when these became common, railroad promoters tended to opt for special charters, if allowed to do so, for general incorporation did not necessarily grant all the rights that the companies wanted. The New York law of 1848, for example, did not grant the right of eminent domain; for this, the companies had to apply separately to the legislature (from 1850, to the state Supreme Court).[60]

The *Vormärz* Prussian ministries also incorporated private railroads by issuing special charters and, like the American legislatures, they soon issued a generic railroad law (although general incorporation was not available until 1870). The generic law—in this case, national in scope—initially appeared in 1836 as a set of provisional

[59] Balthasar Henry Meyer, *Railway Legislation in the United States* (New York: MacMillan Company, 1903), pp. 81–82, 88–94; "An Act, Prescribing certain general regulations for the incorporation of railroad companies," in *Charter of the Richmond and Ohio Railroad Company* (n.p., [1847]), pp. 12–23.

[60] *Laws of New York* (1848), chap. 140; William S. Bishop, comp., *The General Rail Road Law of the State of New York. With Notes and References* (Rochester: D. Hoyt, 1853). On antebellum New York policy, see Gunn, *The Decline of Authority*, pp. 222–45.

guidelines for railroad incorporation, the *Allgemeine Bedingungen* or, roughly, General Stipulations. These generated considerable controversy and ministerial debate, so much so that charters issued while they were in effect included numerous exceptions. A commission of state officials from the various ministries then drafted a national law—without including any of the railroad men in their consultations. After further discussions in the Council of Ministers and Council of State and subsequent revision, the law took effect in November of 1838. Despite the revisions, it too raised a storm of protest, for railroad promoters, in David Hansemann's oft-quoted words, thought it "gave the government the means to destroy a railroad corporation." Coming at a time when state officials had begun to look quite favorably on railroad construction, its apparent stringency, as Wolfgang Klee notes, remains a "riddle." Hansemann himself probably explained it best: he interpreted it as an expedient measure aimed primarily at resolving policy disagreements among high state officials, thereby providing a starting point, however limited, from which railroad construction could at least move forward. In any event, the ministries continued to review and approve applications for individual charters; and, like many issued by the American states, these included a stipulation that the company abide by the provisions of the generic law.[61]

Aside from differences in process, however, early American and Prussian charters generally contained a number of common provisions (although with considerable variation by state in the United

[61] Hansemann, *Kritik des Preußischen Eisenbahn-Gesetzes* pp. 21–23 (quotation from p. 22); Klee, *Preußische Eisenbahngeschichte*, pp. 101–5 (quotation from p. 103); Paul, "Die Preußische Eisenbahnpolitik," pp. 250–303. The Berlin banker Joseph Mendelssohn also perceived considerable confusion among state officials in the mid-1830s. See Joseph Mendelssohn to *Oberbürgermeister* Masche, April 4, 1836, in MA Nachl. 5, VIII. A copy of the *Allgemeine Bedingungen* may be found in Staatsarchiv Magdeburg (hereafter, StA Magdeburg), Rep. C20Iª, no. 1626, vol. 1, pp. 116r–231; they are also reprinted in Steitz, *Entstehung*, pp. 288–89. On exceptions to the new rules, see "Eisenbahn zwischen Düsseldorf und Elberfeld," *Allgemeine Zeitung* (Augsburg), Außerordentliche Beilage, no. 235/6, May 20, 1837, pp. 938–39; Paul, "Die preußische Eisenbahnpolitik," p. 271. The railroad law, "Gesetz über die Eisenbahn-Unternehmungen, vom 3. November 1838," appeared in *Gesetz-Sammlung für die Königlichen Preußischen Staaten*, no. 35; was published in *Allgemeine Zeitung* (Augsburg), Außerordentliche Beilage, no. 638–39, December 2, 1838, pp. 2550–52, and no. 640–41, December 3, 1838, pp. 2559–61; and is reprinted in Steitz, *Entstehung*, pp. 309–20, and in Klee, *Preußische Eisenbahngeschichte*, appendix. In 1843 new railroad corporations also became subject to generic legislation governing joint-stock corporations. Bösselmann, *Entwicklung*, pp. 71–72.

States). Railroad corporations almost always received rights of eminent domain and were usually granted monopoly privileges for a specified number of years. The Prussian law of 1838 (§38) exempted the railroads from some taxes, and many American legislatures granted similar exemptions. The Prussian ministries and many American state legislatures also reserved the right to regulate rates or dividends, to purchase the railroads after a specified period of time (usually twenty to thirty years), and to alter the provisions of railroad charters at will.[62] The latter became necessary in the United States after the 1819 Supreme Court decision in the Dartmouth College case put state legislatures on notice that corporate charters should include explicit provisions regarding the state's rights.[63] In Prussia, however, the 1838 railroad law (§49) required the state to compensate the railroads for income lost or expenses incurred as a result of new regulations, provided that they pertained to matters not covered in the 1838 law.

Both states sought, moreover, to regulate the new transportation technology in the "public interest." Prevailing practice in both countries treated the railroads as quasi-public enterprises, even when their capital lay entirely in private hands. This reflected the twin facts that

[62] Railroad charters may be found in the published legislation of the American states; in Prussia they appeared in the *Amtsblatt* of the provincial governments to 1838 and thereafter in the national *Gesetzsammlung*. Numerous charters have also been reprinted in various forms. See, for example, W. P. Gregg and Benjamin Pond, comps., *The Railroad Laws and Charters of the United States*, 2 vols. (Boston: Charles C. Little and James Brown, 1851), which covers New England only; *Laws and Ordinances Relating to the Baltimore and Ohio Rail Road Company* (Baltimore: Jas. Lucas and E. K. Deaver, 1834); *An Act to Incorporate the Wilmington and Raleigh R. R. Co. Passed at the Session of 1833 of the Legislature of North Carolina: With an Act to Amend the Same Passed at the Session of 1835* (Raleigh: T. Loring, n.d.), *By-Laws of the Board of Directors, [Adopted April and May, 1847.] Together with the Charter of the Pennsylvania Railroad Company, Its Supplement, and Other Laws . . .* (Philadelphia: United States Book and Job Printing Office, 1847); *The Charter and Other Acts of the Legislature, in Relation to the South-Carolina Rail Road Company* (Charleston: Steam Power-Press of Walker and James, 1851); the charter of the Rhine Railroad, reprinted in Klee, *Preußische Eisenbahngeschichte*, appendix, and in Hansemann, *Die Eisenbahnen und deren Aktionäre*, pp. 155–63; the charter of the Cologne-Minden Railroad, reprinted in Steitz, *Entstehung*, pp. 342–55. On charter provisions, see Meyer, *Railway Legislation*, pp. 53–79, 88–96; Kirkland, *Men, Cities, and Transportation*, I: 267–84; Bösselmann, *Entwicklung*, pp. 106–11, 114–15.

[63] Meyer, *History of Transportation*, p. 558. On related developments, see Kutler, *Privilege and Creative Destruction*; and for contemporary perspectives, [David Henshaw], *Remarks Upon the Rights and Powers of Corporations, and of the Rights, Powers, and Duties of the Legislature Toward Them . . . By a Citizen of Boston* (Boston: Beals and Greene, 1837); and *On the Rights and Powers of Corporations. A Notice of the Pamphlet by a Citizen of Boston. By His Fellow Citizen* (Boston, 1837).

the railroads were organized as corporate enterprises and that they served as "common carriers," offering transportation services to the public. In both countries, a grant of incorporation implied that the company had passed a test of public usefulness, while their status as common carriers gave them a distinctive legal position. As Lemuel Shaw, Chief Justice of the Supreme Judicial Court of Massachusetts, remarked in 1836, because a railroad was privately owned and operated, it was "not the less a public work; . . . the public accommodation is the ultimate object."[64]

Besides regulating through the chartering process, state officials frequently appointed railroad commissioners, although it remains unclear whose interests they represented in practice. In Prussia the *Allgemeine Bedingungen* of 1836 and then the railroad law of 1838 (§46) required a commissioner to be assigned to each railroad company. But the law merely indicated that the commissioners, who had the right to call and attend meetings of the railroad's board of directors, should serve as a channel of communication between the companies and the state.[65] Hansemann of the Rhenish Railroad maintained already in 1837 that the commissioner system had doubtful utility: either the commissioners caused problems by being too rigidly bureaucratic or, what could happen just as easily, he warned, they "became friendlier with the board of directors than was compatible with effective supervision."[66] Four years later, he affirmed these reservations: experience showed how difficult it was to find commissioners who combined a practical understanding of the technology with the tact to look after both the state's and the company's interest without weakening the company through excessive interference. Thus far, he maintained, railroad commissioners had variously "aided and injured the railroads": aided, when they intervened with state officials on behalf of the railroads; injured, when they sought to function as "quasi-directors."[67]

In the United States, the practice of appointing commissioners, like so much else, varied considerably among the states. Commissioners were appointed for a variety of specific purposes. Railroad

---

[64] Levy, *The Law of the Commonwealth and Chief Justice Shaw*, pp. 118–39 (quotation from p. 121); Bessel and Kühlwetter, *Das Preussische Eisenbahnrecht*, esp. 1:9–12.
[65] "Gesetz über die Eisenbahn-Unternehmungen."
[66] Hansemann, *Die Eisenbahnen und deren Aktionäre*, pp. 102–3.
[67] Hansemann, *Kritik des Preußischen Eisenbahn-Gesetzes*, pp. 113, 113n–14n.

legislation in New England, for example, usually required commissioners to oversee the activities of interstate lines or the construction of bridges; these were appointed by the state governments, and the railroads bore the cost of their services. Commissioners also supervised eminent-domain proceedings. But railroad commissioners were sometimes given a wider scope of action. Rhode Island legislation in 1839 established a railroad commission whose three members oversaw the activities of railroads chartered in the state; the commission was reauthorized in 1844. Connecticut legislation passed in 1849 and revised in 1850 went a step further than the Prussian system, for it called for the appointment of three commissioners for every railroad and specially charged them to tend to public safety; after a railroad disaster three years later, the state also created a three-man railroad commission.[68] In other states, meanwhile, railroads were subjected to more or less supervision by boards of public works or internal improvement. Virginia's Board of Public Works exercised considerable power, although similar institutions in the Carolinas and Georgia were weaker or shorter-lived.[69]

More common in the United States was the practice of appointing directors to represent a state's or city's interests as a stockholder. Since so many of the early lines had attracted at least some public investment, many of them had state or city directors as well. When the state of North Carolina subscribed two-fifths of the Fayetteville and Western's stock in 1836, it appointed two-fifths of the company's directors; the same terms applied to two other railroads that year.[70] The Baltimore and Susquehanna Railroad, which, as noted earlier, had attracted massive state and city investment and employed a large number of army engineers, had five directors representing the state of Maryland and city of Baltimore by 1839; ten years later the state and city directors outnumbered those representing the private stockholders by more than three to one.[71] The same state and city also had

[68] Gregg and Pond, comps., *Railroad Laws*, e.g., 2:53, 343, 398, 428, 843–44, 849–50, 872, 1159, 1163–64; Kirkland, *Men, Cities, and Transportation*, II:233–37.

[69] Goodrich, *Government Promotion*, pp. 91–98, 103, 108–9, 115–16.

[70] Charles Clinton Weaver, *Internal Improvements in North Carolina Previous to 1860*, Johns Hopkins University Studies in Historical and Political Science, ser. 21, March–April 1903 (reprint ed., Spartanburg, S.C.: The Reprint Company, 1971), pp. 81, 83.

[71] *Report of a Committee of the Stockholders of the Baltimore and Susquehannah Rail Road Company: Appointed May 9, 1839* (n.p., n.d.), pp. 9–10, 17–20; *Twelfth Annual Report of the President and Directors of the Stockholders of the Baltimore and*

strong representation on the board of the Baltimore and Ohio Railroad in the early 1850s, when only twelve of thirty directors represented private stockholders.[72] The board of the Pennsylvania Railroad, a latecomer among major lines, included directors representing Philadelphia and other municipalities.[73] Further north, the Massachusetts legislature reserved three of nine board positions for state directors, when it incorporated the Western Railroad in 1836 and subscribed $1 million of the company's stock. When the legislature granted further aid in 1839, it raised the state's representation to four of nine directors.[74]

Whose interests the public directors represented is difficult to judge and no doubt varied. State directors played a "relatively passive role," Goodrich argues, in part because of the prevailing philosophy that private interests should hold the preponderance of power, even when the state provided much of the capital. In those cases—for example, in Virginia—state directors constituted a minority on the boards of directors, regardless what proportion of the capital the state supplied. As Goodrich explains, "Public and individual investors were thought of as sharing the overriding interest in the completion of a proposed improvement, and it was often believed that this common purpose would be better served under private leadership."[75]

But once operation got underway, interests could and did diverge, and some railroads clearly thought it mattered whether public directors sat on the board. The state directors on the board of the Western Railroad, according to Stephen Salsbury, "became committed to policies designed to protect the Commonwealth's financial interests," which clashed with those pursued by the private directors.[76] A committee of stockholders of the Baltimore and Susquehanna Railroad

---

Susquehanna Rail Road Company. October, 1839 (Baltimore: Joseph Robinson, 1840), pp. 1–2; *Twenty-Second Annual Report of the President and Directors of the Baltimore & Susquehanna Rail-Road Company* (Baltimore: James Lucas, 1849), p. 2.

[72] [William Prescott Smith], *A History and Description of the Baltimore and Ohio Rail Road* (Baltimore: John Murphy & Co., 1853), p. 83.

[73] George H. Burgess and Miles C. Kennedy, *Centennial History of the Pennsylvania Railroad Company, 1846–1946* (Philadelphia: The Pennsylvania Railroad Company, 1949), p. 785.

[74] George Bliss, *Historical Memoir of the Western Railroad* (Springfield, Mass.: Samuel Bowles & Co., Printers, 1863), p. 33; Stephen Salsbury, *The State, the Investor, and the Railroad: The Boston & Albany, 1825–1867* (Cambridge: Harvard University Press, 1967), pp. 143, 150.

[75] Goodrich, *Government Promotion*, pp. 289–91 (quotation from p. 290).

[76] Salsbury, *The State, the Investor, and the Railroad*, p. 298.

objected strongly in 1839 (though without effect) when public directors became a majority on the board. Recalling "the fable of the Dwarf and the Giant," they warned:

> The interests of the State are to be promoted by the increased commerce of her citizens and their augmented taxable property. It is clear that the lower the tolls can be made the greater will be the attraction to trade. The argument then is, that because it is the interest of the State to diminish the tolls as much as possible, therefore the Stockholders, whose interest it is that they should not be diminished, ought to entrust the management to the State. The correctness of the logic is not perceived.[77]

In the mid-1850s, the private directors on the Baltimore and Ohio's board actually tried, as individuals, to buy out the city's interest. As the city's directors reported to the City Council in 1855, "[t]he Directors of the [company], on the part of the private stockholders, desire you to retire from a participation in the direction and management of its affairs." The city directors recommended against sale of the stock, and in 1860 the private stockholders tried a different tactic, seeking legislation that would give them a majority on the board.[78] On balance, Hansemann's assessment probably held for the antebellum states as well: sometimes state (or city) directors allied themselves with the private stockholders, and other times they did not.

Yet, despite these very broad similarities, two characteristics distinguished American from Prussian regulation before 1848: in other ways, American policies gave the state a stronger voice in matters that intimately affected the management of private railroads; and, even when policies appeared very similar on paper, American regulatory efforts tended to be more effective in practice. "[T]he state interferes much more largely" with railroad corporations in the United States than in England, Dionysius Lardner observed in 1850; he could have said the same in comparing the United States with Prussia.[79]

---

[77] *Report of a Committee of the Stockholders*, pp. 10, 19–20.

[78] *Report of the Directors Representing the City in the Baltimore & Ohio Rail Road Company, to the Mayor and City Council of Baltimore* (Baltimore: James Lucas & Son, 1855), pp. 4–5; *Objections to Yielding to Northerners the Control of the Baltimore and Ohio Rail Road, on Which Depends the Development of the Farms, Mines, Manufactures and Trade of the State of Maryland, by a Marylander* (Baltimore, 1860).

[79] Dionysius Lardner, *Railway Economy: A Treatise on the New Art of Transport, Its Management, Prospects, and Relations, Commercial, Financial, and Social* (London: Taylor, Walton, and Maberly, 1850), p. 411.

This is the pattern that emerges from a review of American and Prussian efforts to impose taxes on the railroads (either to protect state investment in other forms of transportation or to generate new revenue) and their experience in regulating railroad rates.

Taxes on Railroad Traffic and Revenue

While the American states often exempted railroad property from state property taxes, this did not mean that the railroads escaped taxation altogether. Some states taxed the companies' stock instead of their property; or city and county governments imposed their own taxes on the railroads; or the state legislatures taxed railroad traffic or revenues. In pursuing this latter strategy, some of the American state legislatures not only chose more interventionist policies than the Prussian central state did in the 1830s and 1840s; they also proved more successful in their efforts.

In some of the American states, taxes on railroad traffic became, in effect, a way to ameliorate the disruptions brought on by technological change. After the War of 1812, massive amounts of state investment had gone into canal construction.[80] When the first railroad projects got underway in the late 1820s, the common assumption was that the new transportation technology would attract mainly passenger traffic, and, indeed, the railroads captured passenger traffic rather easily (though not without opposition). But a lengthier contest ensued over freight traffic. Throughout the antebellum years, rail transport remained relatively expensive and therefore unattractive to shippers of high-bulk, low-value goods, such as grain. However, it offered a more attractive alternative to shippers of higher-value, less-bulky goods. Railroad construction, therefore, quickly threatened a multiplicity of interests: not only the private canals, with which they competed for freight and passenger traffic, but also the holders of the state bonds that had financed state canal construction; the taxpayers who would bear the burden, if state canals ran a deficit; the boatmen who moved freight on the canals; and so on. In response to popular pressure, the state legislatures brought their powers to bear in an effort to take the rough edges off the process of technological change.

---

[80] For overviews, see Taylor, *Transportation Revolution*, pp. 32–55; Goodrich, *Government Promotion*, pp. 51–165.

They did so—those that had invested heavily in canals—by using taxes to raise the cost of freight transportation on railroads that competed directly with state canals.

The New York state legislature proved particularly energetic in this regard. At stake by the early 1830s were large sums of state investment in its canal system, including some $7 million in the Erie Canal alone. The 363-mile canal had proved profitable even before it opened in its entirety, and "beginning in 1835," as Goodrich explains, "the legislature made a substantial levy on the canal tolls for the general purposes of the state."[81] To protect the canals, therefore, the legislature inserted provisions in the charters of some of the short lines connecting Albany and Buffalo that effectively prohibited through traffic for nearly two decades. The lynchpin of the policy was put in place in 1833, when the legislature granted a charter to the Utica and Schenectady Railroad, which paralleled a midsection of the Erie Canal. Its charter allowed it to carry passengers and their baggage, but no freight. Over the next eighteen years, the legislature altered this restriction to allow the line to carry freight, but it required this and other lines along the canal to pay tolls to the canal fund as if their freight had gone by canal. Initially, these railroads had to pay canal tolls only in the winter months, when the canal was not navigable, but by the mid-1840s the requirement had been extended to the entire year. When the legislature passed its general railroad incorporation law in 1848, moreover, it generalized these restrictions, inserting a blanket provision requiring all lines that ran within thirty miles of and parallel to a state canal to pay canal tolls, if the legislature deemed that they were diverting business from the state canals. This policy it reaffirmed in the new general incorporation law passed two years later. Not until 1851 did the legislature abolish all such restrictions.[82]

---

[81] Goodrich, *Government Promotion*, pp. 54–55.

[82] Frank Walker Stevens, *The Beginnings of the New York Central Railroad: A History* (New York: G. P. Putnam's Sons, 1926), pp. 266–73; Meyer, *History of Transportation*, pp. 316–17, 354–55; Thurman W. Van Metre, *Early Opposition to the Steam Railroad* (n.p., n.d), pp. 52–57; Taylor, *Transportation Revolution*, p. 85; *Laws of New York* (1848), chap. 140, §25, and (1850), chap. 140, §29; Bishop, *General Railroad Law*, pp. 63–64. Two years after the restrictions were lifted, the lines paralleling the Erie were consolidated into the New York Central Railroad, which quickly became one of the nation's handful of trunk-line railroads. On subsequent developments, see David Maldwyn Ellis, "Rivalry between the New York Central and the Erie Canal," *New York History* 29 (1948): 268–300.

Even then, the idea of reimposing canal tolls on the railroads persisted. Competition not only between the canal and the railroads but now also among the trunk-line railroads brought a decline in railroad rates. Just as the state undertook expensive improvements to the Erie Canal, competition reduced its traffic and revenues.[83] Consequently, the idea of reviving the protective tolls found a powerful supporter in Governor Myron H. Clark, who endorsed the policy in a special message to the legislature in 1855:

> There is no interest of the State of greater importance, or which has a more extended influence upon its growth and prosperity than its works of internal improvement. They are enduring and valuable monuments of the wisdom and foresight of those who projected them and have, to an incalculable degree, developed the resources, increased the wealth, and contributed to the general prosperity of the commonwealth. It is the duty of the legislature, therefore, to guard jealously their interests and to secure to them that degree of protection which their importance and the vested right of the State alike demand.[84]

Although the "tolling movement" ultimately did not make much headway, this was not for lack of effort. For several more years, "canal conventions" around the state agitated to reimpose canal tolls on railroad freight traffic. In 1860 the New York Assembly passed a bill to that effect, but it did not survive the Senate. Later the same year, the state's attorney general sought without success to have the 1851 legislation that had removed the tolls declared unconstitutional. Only after the Civil War did this particular solution to the problem of railroad competition finally lose its force.[85]

The Pennsylvania legislature showed comparable energy in its efforts to protect its Main Line system of internal improvements,

---

[83] Van Metre, *Early Opposition*, pp. 55–57; Taylor, *Transportation Revolution*, p. 137.

[84] New York State Assembly, Doc. no. 97, 78th sess., 1855, quoted in Van Metre, *Early Opposition*, pp. 56–57.

[85] New York (pseud.), *Legislative Restrictions on the Carrying Trade of the Railways of the State of New York: Viewed in Connection with Outside Competition* (New York, 1860), pp. 3, 27–28; Frederick Merk, "Eastern Antecedents of the Grangers," *Agricultural History* 23 (January 1949): 1, 7; Stevens, *Beginnings*, pp. 273–74; Charles P. Kirkland, *An Inquiry into the Merits of the Suit Brought by the Attorney-General of the State of New York* ... (New York: Wm. C. Bryant, 1860). As Stevens remarks (p. 274), "An account of the struggles on this toll question ... would be one of the most interesting chapters in the history of the regulation of railroads."

which consisted mainly of canals. Completed in 1834, the Main Line canal spanned more than six hundred kilometers and had cost some $10 million. "[N]o nation, ancient or modern, has ever expended so much money, on such vast useful improvements *in the same space of time*," Mathew Carey proclaimed in 1831. To protect this impressive investment, Governor Joseph Ritner vetoed two "general improvement" bills in the late 1830s, because they would have aided railroad projects that ran parallel to the state works. It was a "ruinous policy," he declared. "If this course be pursued and particularly if the companies be also aided by the State in thus setting the State works idle, the latter had better at once be abandoned."[86] In 1846, the legislature did indeed charter a line—the Pennsylvania Railroad—which ran parallel to the state works across the length of the state. But, to protect the state works, it required the railroad (and its leasee, the Harrisburg and Lancaster Railroad) to pay a tax of five mills per ton-mile for freight carried more than twenty miles between March and December. The legislature reduced the tax to three mills in 1848 but made it effective throughout the year, reserving the right to raise it again if the reduction diminished state revenues. This tax remained in place through the 1850s. At the end of the decade, Governor James Pollock declared that it could "only be justified as a revenue measure," since the state works that it had been designed to defend had been sold to the railroad. Yet the tax was not eliminated completely until 1861.[87]

If protection proved successful, it could help to fill the state coffers, and some states pursued this end directly, levying taxes on railroads in an effort to generate new sources of state revenue. At least two states, for example, imposed "transit taxes" on certain early railroads

[86] Taylor, *Transportation Revolution*, pp. 43–45 (Carey quotation from p. 44); Joseph Ritner, "Annual Message to the Assembly, 1837," in *Pennsylvania Archives*, 4th ser., vol. 6: *Papers of the Governors, 1832–1845*, ed. George Edward Reed (Harrisburg: State of Pennsylvania, 1901), pp. 384–86.

[87] Merk, "Eastern Antecedents of the Grangers," pp. 1–2; Van Metre, *Early Opposition*, pp. 57–59; Meyer, *History of Transportation*, p. 395; Howard Ward Schotter, *The Growth and Development of the Pennsylvania Railroad Company: A Review of the Charter and Annual Reports of the Pennsylvania Railroad Company 1846 to 1926, Inclusive* (Philadelphia: Press of Allen, Lane & Scott, 1927), pp. 7–8; James Pollock, "Annual Message to the Assembly, 1858," in *Pennsylvania Archives*, 4th ser., vol. 7: *Papers of the Governors, 1845–1858*, ed. George Edward Reed (Harrisburg: State of Pennsylvania, 1902), p. 937. The agreement by which the state sold the Main Line to the railroad in 1857 stipulated that the railroad thenceforth be exempt from state taxes, including the tonnage tax, but the state supreme court declared the provision unconstitutional. The tax remained in force until finally repealed in 1861.

as a way of tapping this new source of wealth. Transit taxes applied to passenger or freight traffic that passed through a state and were usually spelled out in company charters. The New Jersey legislature, for example, granted the Camden and Amboy Railroad and connecting lines a monopoly of transportation between New York and Philadelphia in 1832—not an uncommon practice in either country at the time. In exchange, however, it took two thousand shares in the railroad and imposed a tax on all through traffic on the railroad (ten cents per passenger and fifteen cents per ton of freight). The transit taxes remained in effect until the company's monopoly expired in 1869. New Jersey also taxed the traffic of the Camden and Pemberton Agricultural Company, requiring it to pay eight cents for each passenger it carried and ten cents per ton of freight.[88]

The Maryland legislature adopted a similar strategy when it chartered the Washington branch of the Baltimore and Ohio Railroad, which was expected to carry primarily passengers between Baltimore and Washington. Initially, a legislative committee had recommended that the line be constructed by the state. "The reasons for this opinion are sufficiently obvious," the committee report explained in 1831:

> They consist in the belief, that while such a measure would materially cheapen the transportation of goods and passengers, and thereby render essential service to citizens, both of our own and other states; while it would increase the prosperity of our great commercial emporium, advance the interests of agriculture, and bring home its advantages to the manufacturing and labouring classes of our community, it would also ensure a permanent and valuable revenue to the State.
>
> If this should be the case, every system of revenue burthensome to the citizens of the state, unfair in its operation or injurious to the morals of the community, might at once be dispensed with and abolished.[89]

Although this proposal did not make headway, the legislature incorporated the Washington branch in 1833 in such a way as to obtain the

[88] Merk, "Eastern Antecedents," pp. 2–3; Hsien-Ju Huang, *State Taxation of Railways in the United States* (New York: Columbia University Press, 1928), p. 7.

[89] "Report of the Committee on Internal Improvement, Delivered by Archibald Lee, Esq. Chairman," Maryland House of Delegates, Committee on Internal Improvement, December session, 1830–31 (Annapolis, 1831), p. 5.

revenue without state ownership. It fixed the one-way passenger fare at $2.50 and imposed a transit tax of 20 percent or fifty cents per passenger. In response to stagecoach competition in 1844 the legislature lowered the fare to $1.50, leaving the transit tax at 20 percent. This tax—the "onerous tax imposed by the state," as the company put it—was not repealed until the 1870s.[90] In general, the Maryland legislature drove a hard bargain in the antebellum period—"too hard to be acceded to," as a committee of stockholders of the Baltimore and Susquehanna Railroad concluded in 1839 (although they did accede in the end).[91]

Other state legislatures, meanwhile, sought to generate revenue from the railroads by taxing their net income rather than their gross revenue. These provisions, too, were usually included in railroad charters rather than in general laws, and most often they required the railroads to pay the state a percentage of profits above a specified level. The Reading Railroad's charter, granted in 1833, required it to pay into the Pennsylvania education fund half of all dividends above 12 percent, a provision changed in 1837 to a straight 8 percent of all dividends. New Jersey required the "Swedsboro" Railroad to pay a tax equal to .5 percent of its cost when its net income exceeded 7 percent of its cost. In a charter granted to the Akron and Pennsylvania Railroad in 1836, the Ohio legislature reserved the right to impose taxes on its dividends when they exceeded 6 percent. Virginia passed an act in 1842 requiring at least one railroad to pay a tax on its dividends before disbursing them to the stockholders. In a departure from the usual practice, New Hampshire legislation of 1844 extracted taxes as a specific quid pro quo: it required railroads that made use of the law's provisions regarding eminent domain to pay to the state all receipts exceeding net expenditures by an average of 10 percent.[92]

[90] Merk, "Eastern Antecedents," p. 3; Edward Hungerford, The Story of the Baltimore and Ohio Railroad, 1827–1927, 2 vols. (New York: G. P. Putnam's Sons, 1928), 1:156–57; Twenty-Seventh Annual Report of the President & Directors of the Baltimore and Ohio Rail Road Company (Baltimore: John Murphy & Company, 1853), p. 7. This kind of tax became popular during the Civil War. See Merk, "Eastern Antecedents," pp. 3–4.

[91] Report of a Committee of the Stockholders, p. 21.

[92] Jules I. Bogen, The Anthracite Railroads: A Study in American Railroad Enterprise (New York: Ronald Press, 1927), pp. 22, 25; Huang, State Taxation, pp. 7, 13, 77–78; Gregg and Pond, comps., Railroad Laws, 1: 644, 647. As Huang explains (pp. 77–78), the Virginia tax "was a specific tax on the corporation as such, and was levied not for

The impact of these measures depended, of course, on enforcement and, in the case of taxes on profits, on the company's performance. The latter were necessarily less reliable, but the transit taxes provided substantial income for New Jersey and Maryland, which were in effect taxing traffic on the busy corridor between New York and Washington. For New Jersey, as Frederick Merk writes, a "profitable partnership" between the state and the Camden and Amboy Railroad resulted; the state received more than $2 million in taxes and dividends on the railroad's stock through 1861. Together the transit tax and dividends provided "virtually all" of the government's revenues and obviated the traditional reliance on general property taxes.[93] Similarly, until the transit tax on the Washington branch of the Baltimore and Ohio was repealed in 1878, the state of Maryland, according to Merk, "derived from it a large part of its annual revenue."[94]

The American state legislatures did not routinely impose protective or revenue taxes; as often as not, they treated them like public enterprises and exempted their shares or property from state (though not local) taxes, occasionally in perpetuity but usually for a specified period.[95] For understanding the character of the antebellum American state writ large, however, this does not diminish the significance of the occasions on which the legislatures not only imposed protective taxes but also proved able to sustain them for decades, as New York and Pennsylvania did. In this achievement, their experience proved quite unlike that of the *Vormärz* Prussian ministers, who

---

the purposes of reaching the individual's property. The latter was taxed by the general property tax."

[93] Merk, "Eastern Antecedents," p. 2. Lucrative though it was, the Camden and Amboy's monopoly generated endless controversy. For criticism of the veracity of the returns on which the Camden and Amboy's transit taxes were paid, see [Henry C. Carey], *Beauties of the Monopoly System of New Jersey. By a Citizen of Burlington* (Philadelphia: C. Harron, 1848); *Address of the Joint Board of Directors of the Delaware and Raritan Canal and Camden and Amboy Railroad Companies, to the People of New Jersey, June—1848* (Trenton: Sherman and Harron, 1848); [Henry C. Carey], *Review of an Address of the Joint Board of Directors of the Delaware and Raritan Canal and Camden and Amboy Railroad Companies, to the People of New Jersey. By a Citizen of Burlington* (Philadelphia: C. Sherman, 1848).

[94] Merk, "Eastern Antecedents," p. 3. The annual payments were reported in the company's annual reports. During the 1840s, for example, they fluctuated around $40,000 per year.

[95] Meyer, *History of Transportation*, p. 563; Taylor, *Transportation Revolution*, p. 89.

never even proposed taxing traffic to generate new state revenues and whose efforts to levy protective taxes generally foundered on the opposition of the railroad companies.

Like some American state legislatures, Prussian officials sought to shield state investment from railroad competition, but they worried about investment in roads and postal revenues rather than investment in canals. When the railroad era opened in the late 1820s, Prussia, like Britain, possessed a considerable network of state-controlled canals and improved waterways that had been built up during the eighteenth century. Unlike the United States, therefore, Prussia did not experience a canal-building "mania" after the Napoleonic Wars. Instead, the bulk of state investment went into road construction. By 1830 Prussia had more than 6,300 kilometers of state-maintained roads. This represented a doubling in the size of the road system since 1816 at an estimated cost of some $4 million, about a quarter of which had come from tolls (*Chausseengelder*).[96] To the extent that the railroads would divert passenger or freight traffic from state roads, therefore, they threatened the viability of the state's toll roads. Even more worrisome to some officials, however, was the potential impact on Prussian postal revenues from passenger-coach traffic.[97] The Post Office not only moved the mail (letters and packages) but also pas-

[96] Richard H. Tilly, "Capital Formation in Germany in the Nineteenth Century," in *Cambridge Economic History of Europe*, vol. 7: *The Industrial Economies: Capital, Labour, and Enterprise*, pt. 1, *Britain, France, Germany, and Scandinavia*, ed. Peter Mathias and M. M. Postan (Cambridge: Cambridge University Press, 1977), pp. 411–12. The density of roadways varied greatly between East and West; the two western provinces claimed about 40 percent of the total in 1831, while the provinces of East and West Prussia had few state-maintained roads and as late as 1826 Posen had none. C.F.W. Dieterici, *Der Volkswohlstand im Preußischen Staate* (Berlin: Ernst Siegfried Mittler, 1846), p. 260; J. H. Clapham, *The Economic Development of France and Germany, 1815–1914*, 4th ed. (Cambridge: Cambridge University Press, 1963), p. 108; and Friedrich-Wilhelm Henning, *Die Industrialisierung in Deutschland 1800 bis 1914*, Wirtschafts- und Sozialgeschichte, vol. 2, 6th ed. (Paderborn: Ferdinand Schöningh, 1984), pp. 80–84.

[97] Passenger-coach traffic was not an issue for the federal government in the United States, since it depended almost exclusively on import duties for revenues and since the Post Office contracted with stagecoach proprietors to carry the mail. Davis Rich Dewey, *Financial History of the United States*, 12th ed. (New York: Longmans Green & Company, 1934; reprint ed., New York: Augustus M. Kelley Publishers, 1968), p. 168. In one instance, however, the federal government had entered the passenger coach business. Frustrated with the poor service provided by private lines between Philadelphia and Baltimore, Postmaster General Joseph Habersham set up a government-owned stagecoach line along the Atlantic Coast in 1799 and operated it until 1818 when it was sold to a private party. Oliver W. Holmes and Peter T. Rohrbach, *Stagecoach East: Stagecoach Days in the East from the Colonial Period to the Civil War* (Washington, D.C.: Smithsonian Institution Press, 1983), pp. 119–20.

sengers, and since 1804 it had enjoyed a virtual monopoly of passenger traffic on post roads. During the Napoleonic Wars, the system had been reduced to shambles, but Postmaster General Karl von Nagler, promoted to the position in 1823, moved quickly to rejuvenate it. He expanded and improved service, more than doubling net postal revenues, which grew from some $500,000 in 1821 to more than $1 million annually by 1840. Officially, postal service was not supposed to produce a surplus, but in practice it served as a valuable means of supplementing general state revenues. Since most observers in Prussia, as elsewhere, expected passenger traffic to constitute the more lucrative side of the railroad business, von Nagler quickly perceived in railroad development an imminent threat to state revenues.[98]

During the 1830s, consequently, von Nagler quarreled repeatedly with the railroads and his fellow ministers as he fought with "extraordinary tenacity," as one writer put it, to protect his revenue base. Anticipating a decline in revenues as railroad projects got underway, he came to the conclusion in 1835 that the railroads should be allowed to compete with the Post Office in transporting passengers and small freight, but he was determined that the Post Office should receive full compensation for giving up its monopoly rights.[99]

Initially, von Nagler enjoyed a modicum of success. The *Allgemeine Bedingungen* of 1836 required the railroads to pay to the Post Office "appropriate compensation" for taking over postal functions and gave the Post Office the right to use the railroads to transport passengers or mail, either on a contractual basis (the terms to be arranged through negotiations with the individual companies) or by running its own equipment. At this time in both countries, it should be noted, many still thought that different companies or individuals would run their own equipment on the railroads; following prevailing practice on turnpikes and canals, they would pay tolls to the owners of the road. From the standpoint of operations, therefore, the proposal

---

[98] H. Stephan, *Geschichte der Preußischen Post von ihrem Ursprunge bis auf die Gegenwart* (Berlin: Verlag der Königlichen Geheimen Ober-Hofbuchdruckerei [R. Decker], 1859), pp. 399–400; Enkling, *Die Stellung des Staates*, pp. 9–10, 28, 52; Paul, "Die preußische Eisenbahnpolitik," pp. 260, 268–70; Klee, *Preußische Eisenbahngeschichte*, pp. 56, 99. Postmaster General von Nagler was a state minister who reported directly to the king and sat in the Council of State, but he was not a member of the Council of Ministers.

[99] Paul, "Die preußische Eisenbahnpolitik," pp. 269–70.

did not seem unreasonable at the time (although by 1836 von Nagler himself no longer thought that competition on the rails would be practical).[100] But the railroads, needless to say, viewed the twin prospects of compensation and competition with much alarm and did not hesitate to voice their concerns. Nonetheless, von Nagler concluded agreements on compensation with at least two companies in the spring of 1837. The Berlin-Potsdam Railroad agreed to pay a fixed sum of $3,500 (5,000 *Taler*) per year; a similar accord with the Magdeburg-Leipzig Railroad would have brought the state $2,100 (3,000 *Taler*) per year.[101] But the railroads lodged strenuous objections to this arrangement. As that most vocal of critics, David Hansemann, wrote that year:

> In North America, the reimbursement that the railroads receive from the postal administration constitutes a more or less substantial portion of [their] revenue. . . . What is a source of income there is supposed to be an expense here. Everyone knows that this makes a powerful difference in the accounts, namely, that 10,000 Thaler of income turned into 10,000 Thaler of expenses causes a 20,000 deficit.[102]

Particularly vexing was the way that the level of "compensation" depended neither on the financial condition of the railroad nor on the actual level of postal revenues.

As the railroads continued to lobby for changes in the policy, von Nagler held fast to his demand for compensation but gradually gave way in other respects. In 1837 he agreed to pay the Rhenish Railroad's public rates, rather than negotiate special rates as the provisional guidelines empowered him to do. The following year, he capitulated altogether and agreed to relinquish all rights to passenger transportation on the line. By then, it had become clear that safety and manage-

[100] For contemporary views, see *Evidence Showing the Manner in Which Locomotive Engines Are Used Upon Rail-Roads: And the Danger and Inexpediency of Permitting Rival Companies Using Them on the Same Road* (Boston, 1838); Hansemann, *Die Eisenbahnen und deren Aktionäre*, pp. 80–82 (who noted that the American state-owned Philadelphia and Columbia Railroad had adopted the practice, which he opposed). On von Nagler's view of competition, see Paul, "Die preußische Eisenbahnpolitik," pp. 290–91.

[101] Enkling, *Die Stellung des Staates*, pp. 45–47. For the calculations on which the agreement with the Berlin-Potsdam Railroad was based, see ibid., pp. 78–79.

[102] Hansemann, *Die Eisenbahnen und deren Aktionäre*, p. 86.

rial efficiency would not allow multiple carriers on the railroads. Technical considerations thus foreclosed this method of protecting postal revenues.[103]

As the railroads continued to protest postal policy over the next year or so, state officials first retreated, then reasserted what they saw as their rights, then staged a partial retreat. After extensive ministerial deliberations in the spring of 1837, according to a newspaper report, the king announced that the Post Office would no longer demand compensation and that it would deal with the railroads as any private party would.[104] Yet about the same time another report indicated that the most important question remaining in negotiations between the railroads and state officials concerned the level of compensation. State officials were reported to be willing to drop all other matters of dispute, if the railroads would pay the "postal compensation" and agree that the resulting funds be used to purchase the railroads over the next twenty years.[105] When the new railroad law was made public in 1838, however, it reasserted von Nagler's demand for compensation, although in the form of a compromise. The law required the railroads to pay compensation in the form of an annual tax (*Abgabe*), which varied with their net profit. It went further, moreover, in requiring the railroads to carry the mail free of charge.[106]

Within four years, however, state officials again retreated on the issue of compensation. The tax provision of the 1838 law was not to take effect immediately; rather, the level of compensation would be set when Prussia's second railroad had been in full operation for three years. But under the weight of the railroads' renewed protests, this tax never took effect at all. In 1840, von Nagler was still quarreling with the Berlin-Potsdam Railroad about compensation, for the company refused to recognize the principle at stake and refused to pay what the postmaster general demanded. The postal administration was not likely to push the issue further, Hansemann observed, because it had changed its views and developed "such a gratifying predilection for railroads that, as everyone knows, it is pursuing the collosal plan of

---

[103] *Allgemeine Zeitung* (Augsburg), Beilage no. 70, March 11, 1837, p. 559; Enkling, *Die Stellung des Staates*, pp. 49–53.

[104] "Eisenbahnen, III. In Rheinpreußen," *Allgemeine Zeitung* (Augsburg), Außerordentliche Beilage, no. 161/2, April 8, 1837, p. 642.

[105] "Preußische Eisenbahnen," *Allgemeine Zeitung* (Augsburg), Außerordentliche Beilage, no. 168–69, April 12, 1837, p. 673.

[106] "Gesetz über die Eisenbahn-Unternehmungen," §38.

using postal surpluses to build a railroad from Halle through Kassel to Cologne." Then as the time approached for the payments to begin, a royal decree in April of 1842 did away with them. The requirement that the railroads carry the mail free of charge remained on the books, but collection of a railroad tax did not actually begin until a new law was passed in 1853. In the meantime, the Post Office's revenues, after two decades of steady increase, leveled off between 1840 and 1845, and its net income declined by 30 percent.[107]

Compared to the measures taken by some American state legislatures to protect canal revenues during the antebellum period, the *Vormärz* Prussian state's efforts at protection must be judged less effective. In their efforts to impose a tax on the railroads, Prussian officials proved unable to overcome resistance from the railroads. The Prussian ministers, moreover, never sought to use railroad development to shift or enlarge the state's revenue base. The closest they came was the tax on profits (one-third of profits above 5%) that the Prussian state imposed in exchange for an interest guarantee. Some of the American state legislatures, in contrast, seized on the emergence of the new transportation technology to generate new sources of state revenue. In essence, they used their charter-granting powers as leverage to appropriate a portion of railroad revenues for public ends. Again, not all state legislatures pursued such policies, but in this

[107] Hansemann, *Kritik des Preußischen Eisenbahn-Gesetzes*, pp. 93n-94n; Enkling, *Die Stellung des Staates*, pp. 47–48; *Geschäfts-Bericht des Directoriums der Magdeburg-Cöthen-Halle-Leipziger Eisenbahn-Gesellschaft für die Zeit vom 15ten Mai 1842 bis zum 7ten April 1843*, in ZStAM, Rep. 77, Tit. 258a, no. 2, vol. 1, p. 170r; Bessel and Kühlwetter, *Das Preussische Eisenbahnrecht*, 2:223; Henderson, *The State and the Industrial Revolution*, pp. 179–80; Stephan, *Geschichte der Preußischen Post*, p. 728. On von Nagler's plans, see Sautter, "General Postmeister von Nagler," pp. 223–38. Whether the companies actually carried the mail free of charge is not clear; at least one company was receiving payment from the Post Office for "wagon use" in 1846 (Röll, *Entstehungsgeschichte*, pp. 33–34), and Enkling, *Die Stellung des Staates*, p. 75, implies that this provision, like most others, was not strictly observed in practice. For insight into the endless controversies over "mail-pay" in the United States, where the federal government lacked the leverage that came with the power to incorporate, see *History of the Railway Mail Service; George Bliss, Reply to a Late Letter of the Post-Master General, and Report of the First Assistant Post-Master General* (Springfield: Wood and Rupp, 1842); *Report of a Committee of the Joint Board of Directors of the Delaware and Raritan Canal and Camden & Amboy R. R. & Transportation Co's, on the Subject of the Transportation of the Mails Between New York and Philadelphia, October, 1846* (Trenton: Arnold and Brittain, 1847); *Reply of the Executive Committee of the Delaware and Raritan Canal and Camden and Amboy Railroad and Transportation companies, to a Letter Addressed to the Hon. G. W. Hopkins, Chairman of the Committee of Post Offices and Post Roads of the House of Representatives of the U.S.*

respect, nonetheless, the interventionist tendencies of the American state legislatures exceeded those of Prussian state officials, who diverted relatively little capital from early railroads.

Rate Regulation

Prussian and American policy regarding that most familiar of regulatory problems—the rates that the railroads offered to the public—also developed along divergent lines until the late 1840s. In both countries, state officials sought to regulate railroad rates in the way that they had traditionally regulated transportation prices—by setting maximum tolls for use of the "highway" or at least reserving the right to lower them. In the United States, these provisions were sometimes so generously construed that they did not have much effect; in other cases, however, they in fact constrained the railroads' ability to set rates. In Prussia, in contrast, the national law of 1838 gave the state considerable power over rates, but those provisions were simply not enforced before the 1850s.

In both countries, prevailing regulatory practice reflected two characteristics of traditional forms of transportation: the road- or waterway itself was owned by one party who set tolls (*Bahngelder*) for its use under noncompetitive conditions, while competition prevailed among the various parties (e.g., boatmen or stage companies) who collected a carrying charge (*Transport-Preis* or *Personen- und Warentarif*) for transporting passengers and freight. Under the common assumption, noted earlier, that competing carriers would also use the same railroad tracks, the American legislatures and the Prussian ministers initially regulated tolls for the use of the track, but relied on competition among carriers to keep carrying charges at reasonable levels. This assumption went by the wayside after 1840. As the British railroad expert Dionysius Lardner observed in 1850:

> It soon became apparent . . . that this new means of transport was attended with qualities which must exclude every indiscriminate exercise of the carrying business. A railway, like a vast machine, the wheels of which are all connected with each other, and whose movement requires a certain harmony, cannot be worked by a num-

---

by the Hon. *Cave Johnson, Post Master General* (Trenton: Arnold and Brittain, 1847); and chap. 4 of this book.

ber of independent agents. Such a system would speedily be attended with self-destruction.[108]

But when the Prussian national law was formulated and when the major American railroads received their charters, the railroad was still viewed as simply another form of highway, one on which the public would run its own vehicles, and it was regulated accordingly.

The Prussian state's authority to regulate rates derived from the 1838 railroad law (§29–35), and most of its regulatory powers concerned tolls rather than transportation charges.[109] For the first three years of operation, each railroad had the exclusive right to provide transportation and the company was free to determine both tolls and transportation charges itself. After the three years expired, the state would periodically regulate tolls so that the company's net profits (income minus expenses and reserve funds) would neither exceed 10 percent nor fall below 6 percent. The law reserved less authority for the state over carrying charges, since these, unlike the tolls, were expected to be kept in line by competition. The companies were allowed to set their initial carrying charges on their own, although an increase required state approval; the state also reserved the right to lower them, if the company's net income exceeded 10 percent; and the law prohibited rate discrimination. But none of these provisions regarding carrying charges were to take effect until the state began to regulate tolls. This meant that it had no powers to set rates during the first three years of operations.

After the three years elapsed, state officials made two tentative moves to exercise their legal powers, but with little practical effect. In 1843, Finance Minister von Bodelschwingh used the leverage that the new policy of state promotion gave him to reconstitute the state's authority over one company, the Upper Silesian Railroad. When the company received the first state interest guarantee, he required it to accept a charter amendment that gave the state (among other wide-ranging powers) control over its fares, rates, and schedules.[110] Then in 1846 Finance Minister Flottwell instructed the railroads to submit

---

[108] Lardner, *Railway Economy*, p. 503.

[109] "Gesetz über die Eisenbahn-Unternehmungen." For contemporary discussion of tolls and carrying charges, see Hansemann, *Die Eisenbahnen und deren Aktionäre*, p. 21.

[110] *Zur Feier des Fünfundzwanzigsten Jahrestages der Eröffnung des Betriebes auf der Oberschlesischen Eisenbahn*, pp. 60–67; Enkling, *Die Stellung des Staates*, pp. 55–56. The charter amendment is reprinted in Rapmund, *Die finanzielle Betheiligung*, pp.

the annual reports that the law also required, another provision that had not been enforced until then.[111] Since §34 of the law explicitly described these as essential for the state to exercise its powers to regulate tolls and rates, his action implied a renewed effort to strengthen the state's powers.[112] This was the railroads' interpretation, at least, and as chapter 4 suggests they quickly took defensive action, forming a national association of Prussian railroads. Now facing organized opposition, the finance minister did not press the request. Through 1848 and for some time afterward, state officials, in practice, left the determination of rates to the railroads. As two experts in railroad law noted in the mid-1850s, "the royal Trade Ministry has not yet, so far as is known, regulated the tolls (*Bahngeld*) of any Prussian railroad" (although there had been talk of doing so in early 1853, they reported).[113] Even the prohibition on rate discrimination the railroads apparently found ways of circumventing.[114]

In the United States, the state legislatures regulated rates on antebellum railroads initially through provisions inserted in railroad charters and later through general legislation. "It would probably be safe to say," George H. Miller observes, "that most of the railroad mileage in the United States in the year 1850 was subject to some form of statutory rate restriction." Charter provisions either set maximum rates; reserved the legislatures' right to reduce rates, if cash dividends exceeded a specified maximum; or simply reserved the state's right to change charter provisions at will. The charters of the South Carolina, Philadelphia and Reading, Pennsylvania, and Wilmington and Raleigh railroads, to cite a few examples, set rates directly, but as time passed dividend or profit ceilings superseded the setting of maximum rates. New York's general railroad incorporation laws of 1848 and 1850 adopted both strategies, for they set a maximum rate for passengers (three cents per mile) and reserved the right

50–56. This seems to have been the only time (before 1848) that the state forced such provisions on the railroads.

[111] Many American states required railroads to file annual reports, Massachusetts and New York specifying more than one hundred accounts each by 1850. For details, see Goodrich, *Government Promotion*, p. 98; Gregg and Pond, comps., *Railroad Laws*, 2:639, 651–55, 1158; Laws of New York (1848), chap. 140, §28, and (1850), chap. 140, §31.

[112] *Festschrift*, p. 393; "Gesetz über die Eisenbahn-Unternehmungen."

[113] Enkling, *Die Stellung des Staates*, 49–54; Bessel and Kühlwetter, *Das Preussische Eisenbahnrecht*, 2:191–200 (quotation from p. 200).

[114] Enkling, *Die Stellung des Staates*, pp. 54–55.

to alter tolls if profits exceeded 10 percent. The act authorizing consolidation of the companies that formed the New York Central Railroad in 1853 also set a maximum fare for local passengers of two cents
per mile. Massachusetts charters sometimes used a combination of
the two strategies, but by the 1840s they routinely reserved the legislature's right to reduce tolls every five or ten years if profits exceeded
10 percent. Yet, whatever the specific formulation, "the point to be
remembered," Miller emphasizes, "is that legislative regulation of
rates was a normal practice of the early railroad era. . . . The power to
alter railroad tolls, barring the existence of a legislative contract to
the contrary, was taken for granted."[115] In this regard, the American
states—with considerable variation, as usual—pursued a policy like
that spelled out in the Prussian law of 1838.

But how effective did these measures prove in the United States?
The consensus has been that they had little impact. "Limitations on
railroad charges," George Rogers Taylor writes, "were usually so generously drawn as to impose no burden or, as in Ohio, were simply
ignored." Miller concludes that "few of the existing limitations had
any practical effect" in 1850. Few lines earned profits above 10 percent, and those that did generally found ways to circumvent legal
limitations, issuing stock dividends instead of cash, for example, or
increasing their capital in order to enlarge the absolute value of legal
dividends. The dividend cap proved effective in Massachusetts where
the railroads could not legally issue stock dividends, but that is usually regarded as an exceptional case.[116] Yet misconceptions about
antebellum American railroad regulation extend as far back as
Charles Francis Adams's writings in the late nineteenth century, as
Edward Chase Kirkland once noted.[117] In view of long-standing tendencies to discount the significance of state activity in the United
States, the consensus bears reevaluation.

---

[115] Miller, *Railroads and the Granger Laws*, pp. 30–31. For examples, see *Charter. . . South-Carolina Rail Road Company*, p. 71; *By-Laws . . . with the Charter of the
Pennsylvania Railroad*, p. 21; *Laws of New York* (1848), chap. 140, §9, §30, and (1850),
chap. 140, §28/9, §33; Bishop, *General Rail Road Law*, p. 110; Gregg and Pond, comps.,
Railroad Laws, 2:3–598; Salsbury, *The State, the Investor, and the Railroad*, pp. 85–
88. For discussion, Taylor, *Transportation Revolution*, pp. 88–89, 379; Meyer, *History
of Transportation*, p. 558.
[116] Taylor, *Transportation Revolution*, pp. 88–89; Meyer, *History of Transportation*,
pp. 558–59; Miller, *Railroads and the Granger Laws*, p. 30.
[117] Kirkland, *Men, Cities, and Transportation*, 2:231–32.

In practice, the impact of such provisions depended on circumstances, for it mattered a great deal whether the railroads encountered significant competition. In its absence, railroads claimed an effective monopoly of transportation, and then a legislated ceiling on rates or dividends, set sufficiently low and enforced, could present real constraints. And through the 1830s and early 1840s, most railroads did not (yet) face significant competition. Railroad rates, as a result, remained high by later standards. The Austrian railroad expert, Franz Anton Ritter von Gerstner, concluded during his travels in the United States in the late 1830s that passenger fares averaged five cents a mile and freight rates, seven and a half cents. The directors of the Baltimore and Ohio Railroad, defending the performance of their company in 1836, reported that other roads around the country, unlike their own, enjoyed the benefits of rates that ranged from three and a half to six cents per passenger-mile and seven to ten cents per ton-mile.[118] Four years later, the directors of the Boston and Worcester Railroad claimed that their rate of three and a half cents per passenger-mile "is lower than is taken on any road in the United States."[119]

Given a paucity of competition and the prevalence of relatively high rates in the 1830s and early 1840s, a number of lines bumped up against the maximum rates that the legislatures set. In New Jersey, the Camden and Amboy Railroad qualified quite literally as a monopoly, for it enjoyed a state-sanctioned (and controversial) monopoly of transportation between New York and Philadelphia throughout the antebellum period. And, as Taylor himself notes, the Camden and Amboy Railroad was forced, at least once, "to refund overcharges."[120] The directors of the Baltimore and Ohio Railroad explained their company's relatively poor performance in 1836 by noting, among other problems, that their state-mandated rates were too low. When their road had been chartered in 1826, they explained,

> it was the first rail road for general purposes that had been projected in the country—and so sanguine of profits were its friends, that the

[118] *Tenth Annual Report of the President and Directors to the Stockholders of the Baltimore and Ohio Rail Road Company* (Baltimore: Lucas & Deaver, 1836), p. 16; Fishlow, *American Railroads*, pp. 323–24.

[119] *Report of a Committee of Directors of the Boston and Worcester Rail-Road Corporation*, p. 6.

[120] Taylor, *Transportation Revolution*, pp. 88–89.

charge for passengers was deemed ample at three cents per mile, and for merchandize and produce, four cents eastward and six cents westward, making an average, as experience shews, of about four and an half cents. Experience has since shewn, that, upon a costly road, through a difficult country, these rates are too low . . . and there are but few rail roads in the union on which the charges are not higher.

They had just been allowed to raise their passenger rate one cent per mile, but this had come at a price: they promised within three years to begin paying the state a 6 percent dividend on the $1 million of stock that it subscribed that year.[121]

The directors of the South Carolina Railroad were also allowed an increase in their rates in 1838. Five years earlier, they had noted with optimism that, as they put it, "the Legislature in granting the Company a very liberal Charter, took good care of their constituents. The charges were in every case reduced to half the usual rates for the benefit of the citizens." Happily, this had seemed to stimulate travel. In 1838, however, under financial pressure, they proposed "with great deference" a rate increase sufficient to produce profits of 7 percent. The legislature accommodated by raising fares from five to seven and a half cents per passenger-mile and increasing freight rates by 40 percent.[122]

Two years later, the Cumberland Valley Railroad also pressed the Pennsylvania government for higher rates, but without success. Running southwest from the state works near Harrisburg to Chambersburg, it is not likely to have faced much competitive pressure, and that year it sought authorization from the legislature to set rates at a level that would yield a minimum net income of 9 percent. Legislation to that effect was passed, but only to be vetoed by the governor. "Why does this company fear to trust to the wisdom and justice of the Legislature?" Governor David Rittenhouse Porter questioned. The Cumberland constituted "an essential link" in the chain of transportation between Philadelphia and Pittsburgh, he declared; it should be

[121] *Tenth Annual Report . . . of the Baltimore and Ohio Rail Road Company*, pp. 6, 16; Fishlow, *American Railroads*, p. 323.

[122] *Semi-Annual Report of the Direction of the South-Carolina Canal and Rail-Road Company, to July, 1838* (Charleston: Burges & James, 1838), p. 4; *Semi-Annual Report of the South-Carolina Canal and Rail-Road Company, Accepted Jan. 18th, 1839* (Charleston: A. E. Miller, 1839), p. 11; Fishlow, *American Railroads*, pp. 321, 323.

subject to "the same general control of the law" as the connecting lines.[123] These railroads did not find the rate-setting provisions of their charters "generously drawn," and others that faced little or no competition presumably felt similarly constrained.

If rate regulation did ultimately prove ineffective in the United States, the failure came mainly after the 1840s. As the rail network became denser in the late 1840s and as the trunk-line railroads reached completion in the early 1850s, competition began to push down rates on through traffic (although rail transportation remained more expensive than water transportation throughout the nineteenth century).[124] In those radically new circumstances, the intractable problem of nineteenth-century rate regulation—the *structure* rather than the level of rates—emerged in its full dimensions. Then the legislatures' traditional methods of regulation, which focused on maximum rates, proved an inadequate remedy for the problem of rate structures on through traffic, particularly when it crossed state lines.[125]

But legislative controls still did not prove entirely irrelevant, for the rates that competition pushed down were those on through, not local (or way), traffic, and local traffic remained important to the railroads. "It has been found to the surprise of every one," a committee of Charleston citizens remarked in 1847, "that the way freight and passage money of Rail-Roads, passing through a populous country, taken at intermediate points, exceed that taken at the ends of the road. The experience of the South-Carolina Rail-Road, even upon the apparent desert between Charleston and Hamburg, is a very extraordinary one on this point."[126] Even as the trunk-line railroads encountered strenuous competition from 1851 onward, they still, as a rule,

[123] *Report of William Milnor Roberts, Chief Engineer of the Cumberland Valley Rail Road Company, Made to the Board, on the 23d October, 1835* (Annapolis: Jeremiah Hughes, 1836); David Rittenhouse Porter, "To the Assembly Vetoing a Bill Entitled 'A Further Supplement to the Act to Incorporate the Cumberland Valley Railroad Company,'" signed January 9, 1840, in *Pennsylvania Archives*, 4th ser., vol. 6, p. 654.

[124] For comparison of rates for different modes of transportation, see Douglass C. North, Terry L. Anderson, and Peter J. Hill, *Growth and Welfare in the American Past: A New Economic History*, 3d ed. (Englewood Cliffs, N.J.: Prentice-Hall, Inc., 1983), pp. 103–4.

[125] See chap. 6.

[126] *Proceedings of a Meeting of Citizens of Charleston City and Neck, and Report of Committee in Relation to Charlotte Rail-Road* (Charleston: Walker and Burke, 1847), p. 9.

maintained a near-monopoly of local traffic. Indeed, under the new competitive conditions, local traffic took on added importance, for the road that broke even or lost money on its through traffic could make up the difference on local rates. As the president of the Lafayette and Indianapolis Railroad, located in the crossfire of trunk-line competition, stressed in 1851: "The best and surest anchorage of a road . . . is its *local* business."[127] Or as the directors of the Philadelphia, Wilmington, and Baltimore Railroad emphasized in the mid-1850s,

> No Rail Road can ever succeed in a long run, which does not cultivate and increase its local business. It is that which generally pays better than the business from other Roads, and it is that only which may not at some time or other be cut off or affected by rival lines. . . . The through business so called of any Road, is small compared with the constant and ever increasing tide of local trade.[128]

In the altered conditions that emerged during the 1850s, the state legislatures were hard-put to maintain regulatory control, as the fate of the Granger laws showed later in the century, but this does not diminish the significance of the degree to which they were able to control rates through the 1840s. In comparative perspective, the antebellum state legislatures shared with the Prussian state a propensity to regulate rates, but through the 1840s they also showed what the Prussian state did not: a greater ability to do so.

On the whole, these contrasting patterns of promotion and regulation suggest that the American state—largely but not exclusively through the state legislatures—pursued more "interventionist" policies than Prussian officials did. The state governments' investment in railroads, state and private, far outpaced that of the central state in Prussia through the 1840s; the federal government provided technical assistance on a larger scale than the Prussian central state; some of the state governments, unlike the Prussian state, exploited the new technology to generate new sources of revenue or instituted more

---

[127] *Exhibit of the Lafayette and Indianapolis Railroad Company* (New York: Oliver & Brother, 1851), p. 8 (original emphasis).

[128] *Nineteenth Annual Report of the President and Directors to the Stockholders of the Philadelphia, Wilmington and Baltimore Rail Road Company, for the Year Ending November 30, 1857. Made January 12th, 1857* (Philadelphia: James H. Bryson, 1857), pp. 16–17.

effective protection for their existing investments; the American state legislatures also proved, until the late 1840s at least, somewhat more adept at regulating rates. In this sense, it seems reasonable to conclude that "economic liberalism" better characterized Prussian railroad policies than it did American policies. Despite conventional images of the United States as "the land of private enterprise *par excellence*; the place where 'State interference' has played the smallest part, and individual enterprise has been given the largest scope," one scholar observed nearly a century ago, "it is a fact that this country was one of the first to exhibit this modern tendency to extend the activity of the State into industry."[129] The Prussian state, in contrast, largely abstained. Broadly speaking, the two political economies, viewed through the lens of railroad development, looked like mirror images of each other: Prussia, with its illiberal political structure, adopted more liberal railroad policies; the United States, with a more liberal political structure, adopted less liberal railroad policies. The next chapter considers why this was so.

[129] Callender, "Early Transportation and Banking Enterprises," p. 111.

3

Interpreting Early Railroad Policies

WHAT ACCOUNTS for these striking patterns of political structure and railroad policy? Why did the more liberal American state intervene more extensively and effectively in early railroad development, while the less liberal Prussian state proved less willing or at least less able to intervene? One possibility is that the configuration of interests—social, political, or economic—differed in the two countries. Were interests, in other words, arrayed in ways that encouraged intervention in one country but abstention in the other? Or did these contrasting policies reflect differences in prevailing ideas about the proper relationship between government and business? Did most Americans simply believe that the railroads should be subjected to a large measure of government promotion *and* regulation, because tradition or party ideology dictated such policies? And did Prussians tend to look askance at both forms of intervention on similar grounds? Or was policy divergence, in fact, linked intimately to differences in the two political structures?[1]

This chapter considers each alternative in turn and concludes that differences in the two political structures ultimately mattered the most, that it was these—in a capitalist context—that pushed early railroad policy in opposite directions. In comparative perspective, the two patterns of railroad policy reveal the underlying complexities that drove policy-making in each country, highlighting two critical features of industrial policy-making in a capitalist context: they accentuate the causal links that ran from the political structure through the policy-making process to the content of policy itself; and they show how the state's regulatory power depended critically on its ability to promote capitalist enterprise (which in turn depended on its political structure). In a nutshell, the contrasting stories of American intervention and Prussian abstention in the 1830s and 1840s underscore the way that the nature of the political structure shaped the

[1] For discussion of alternative variables, see the sources cited in chap. 1, notes 22 and 23.

state's power to promote capitalist enterprise—enhancing it in the United States and diluting it in Prussia—and therefore determined, as well, the capability of each state to sustain regulatory initiatives.

The Configuration of Interests

As an explanation for differences in the intensity of state efforts to promote railroad development, the configuration of interests that supported and opposed early railroad projects deserves serious consideration. It is possible that railroad promoters faced substantially greater opposition in Prussia, while their counterparts in the United States encountered widespread enthusiasm. Divergent state policies, then, would have reflected such differences.

But this line of argument, familiar in treatments of Prussian railroad history and implicit in American histories as well,[2] does not withstand comparative scrutiny. As it turns out, the configuration of interests looked much the same in the two countries. In both, commercial and political (including military) considerations generated considerable enthusiasm for railroad development—in the abstract. But, when attention turned to concrete proposals, the new technology generated some of the stormiest public debates in these years. Unlike the constitutional questions that they raised in both countries, these debates reflected pervasive disagreement of a more mundane kind: either about the merits of particular projects or about the value of the new technology itself.

Although conflict over railroad projects played out along similar lines in the two countries, it deserves some emphasis here, for by underestimating it we risk seriously misunderstanding the process of industrial change. The history of railroad development, in particular, has been plagued by the almost reflexive assumption that the new technology was obviously and inevitably a superior technology. In both countries, however, contemporaries understood that this new and peculiar form of transportation brought its own special problems. Like other episodes in the history of technology, railroad develop-

[2] On its power in Prussian railroad history, see Rolf Peter Sieferle, *Fortschrittsfeinde? Opposition gegen Technik und Industrie von der Romantik bis zur Gegenwart* (Munich: C. H. Beck, 1984). On the United States, see, for example, Taylor, *Transportation Revolution*, p. 75.

ment had its "dark side," even in the United States. As one scholar observed in the early years of this century:

> When one considers how great a factor the railroad has been in the development of the United States, one would hardly suppose that this great instrument of progress was introduced in this country only with the greatest difficulty and came into general use in the face of the most bitter opposition. Yet such was the case.[3]

In this respect, Americans were not as different as some like to believe. In practice, the only point of consensus in either country was that "improvement" meant change. Whether it would bring a change for the better long remained a topic of heated debate. To explore this essential similarity, the following sections survey the general attractions of internal improvements in both countries, the reasons for opposing particular railroad projects, and the objections lodged against the new technology itself.

Patterns of Support

Regardless whether discussion turned to canals and turnpikes or to railroads, the arguments advanced in favor of internal improvements in both countries generally fell into one of three categories. Some stressed the *commercial* benefits to be gained from improved transportation; others emphasized the *political* advantages to be derived from more extensive contacts among the citizens of each nation; still others focused on the *military* significance of internal improve-

[3] Van Metre, *Early Opposition*, p. 9. Over the past two decades, historians have discovered considerable resistance to technological change, evidence that the process of industrial change seldom proceeded smoothly. For a sampling of the literature, see John Kasson, *Civilizing the Machine: Technology and Republican Values in America, 1776–1900* (New York: Penguin Books, 1976); Smith, *Harpers Ferry*; Sieferle, *Fortschrittsfeinde*?; Gary Kulik, "Dams, Fish, and Farmers: Defense of Public Rights in Eighteenth-Century Rhode Island," in *The Countryside in the Age of Capitalist Transformation: Essays in the Social History of Rural America*, ed. Steven Hahn and Jonathan Prude (Chapel Hill: University of North Carolina Press, 1985), pp. 25–50; Joel Mokyr, "Technological Inertia in Economic History," *Journal of Economic History* 52 (June 1992): 325–38. Two studies that explore the ideological dimensions of resistance to industrial change in the late nineteenth-century United States are Berk, "Constituting Corporations," and Hattam, *Labor Visions*. For criticism of studies that focus on the "dark side" of history, see Brooke Hindle, "'The Exhilaration of Early American Technology': A New Look," in *The History of American Technology: Exhilaration or Discontent?*, ed. David A. Hounshell (Greenville, Del.: Hagley Papers, 1984), pp. 8–9, 12–13.

ments. Although a particular group of advocates might attach special importance to one or the other argument, appeals to all three frequently interlaced the rhetoric of internal improvements supporters.

Thus the General Survey Act of 1824, under which successive American presidents dispatched the army engineers, directed the president to aid those projects that he considered "of national importance, in a commercial or military point of view, or necessary for the transportation of the public mail."[4] In 1832 a Whig congressman from Pennsylvania used similar language to defend the National Road, which some saw as the first step toward a national system of internal improvements: "It is, sir, *a great commercial, military, mail, national work.*"[5] Maj. Gen. Edmund P. Gaines, lobbying in the 1830s for construction of a national system of railroads by the military, also saw the three aspects as intimately related: his railroads would

> contribute greatly, incalculably, to the national defense during a state of war; and then, on the return of peace, . . . our railroads . . . may be turned to commercial purposes, in which they will yield an income sufficient to replace in the Treasury . . . every dollar expended in their location and construction; and though last, not least, they will form *ligaments*, inflexible in strength and endless in duration, to render our beloved Union indissoluble and perpetual.[6]

A Senate committee employed the same equation in abbreviated form in 1838: in its judgment, the Alabama, Florida, and Georgia Railroad's "claims [to federal aid] are equally strong in a political, commercial, or military aspect."[7]

In Prussia commentators employed similar language. After the change of state policy, Friedrich Wilhelm Freiherr von Reden, who had served as special director of the Berlin-Stettin Railroad and became known as the father of German statistics, noted the broader implications: "About the political, military, and commercial value of

---

[4] Quoted in Hill, *Roads, Rails, and Waterways*, p. 47.

[5] Thomas M. T. McKennan, quoted in Thomas B. Searight, *The Old Pike: A History of the National Road* (Uniontown, Pa.: By the Author, 1894), p. 107 (original italics); *A Biographical Congressional Directory, 1774 to 1903* (Washington: Government Printing Office, 1903), p. 672.

[6] [Edmund P. Gaines], *To the Young Men of the States of the American Union, Civil and Military* (n.p., n.d.), p. 38 (original italics).

[7] "Report [To accompany Senate bill No. 260]," Senate Doc. No. 294, 25th Cong., 2d sess., 1837–38.

[the] railroad lines [chosen for state aid] there can be no doubt."[8] Through much of the *Vormärz* period, moreover, the nationalist political economist Friederich List took an expansive view of internal improvements in general and of the railroads in particular. List knew the railroad business firsthand, since he had been instrumental in founding the Little Schuylkill Navigation, Railroad and Coal Company in Pennsylvania during a period of political exile in the late 1820s. As a result of his American experience, List became a committed railroad enthusiast. When he returned to Germany in 1832, by then a naturalized American citizen, he campaigned with such ardor for a national network of railroads that historians regard him as the "father of German railroads."[9] Although he is perhaps best known for the emphasis that he placed on their political benefits, List also stressed, time and again, the railroads' strategic and commercial implications.[10]

The commercial benefits of internal improvements attracted greatest attention in urban areas, and in both countries urban rivalry—competition among trading centers—drove that enthusiasm. As George Rogers Taylor has shown, the eastern seaboard cities' rivalry for commercial prominence generated agitation for internal improvements that would better their position, especially after the opening of the Erie Canal in 1825. As attention shifted from canals to railroads in the late 1820s and early 1830s, "there developed a sort of metropolitan mercantilism," Taylor writes, "in which railroads, rather than merchant fleets, were the chief weapons of warfare."[11] As the

[8] Friedrich Wilhelm Freiherr von Reden, *Die Eisenbahnen Deutschlands*, 1. Abt., 1. Abschnitt: *Allgemeines über die deutschen Eisenbahnen* (Berlin: Ernst Siegfried Mittler, 1843), p. 306.

[9] On Frederick List's railroad work in the United States as well as Germany, see W. O. Henderson, *Frederick List: Economist and Visionary, 1789–1846* (Totowa, N.J.: Frank Cass, 1983), pp. 124–42; and Colleen A. Dunlavy, "Der 'Vater der deutschen Eisenbahnen' in den Vereinigten Staaten von Amerika: Friedrich List und Früheisenbahnbauweisen," *Wissenschaftliche Zeitschrift* (Dresden), Sonderheft 54, *Friedrich List—Leben und Werk* (1990): 51–60.

[10] See, for example, List's most influential work, a pamphlet published while he was serving as American consul in Leipzig: *Über ein sächsisches Eisenbahn-System als Grundlage eines allgemeinen deutschen Eisenbahn-Systems und insbesondere über die Anlegung einer Eisenbahn von Leipzig nach Dresden* (Leipzig: A. G. Liebeskind, 1833), which is reprinted in *Friedrich List: Schriften, Reden, Briefe*, vol. 3: *Schriften zum Verkehrswesen*, pt. 1: *Einleitung und Text*, ed. Erwin V. Beckerath and Otto Stühler (Berlin: Reimar Hobbing, 1929), pp. 155–95. Among later works, see "Auszüge aus Lists Beitrag zum Staats-Lexikon: Eisenbahnen and Kanäle, Dampfboote und Dampfwagentransport," in ibid., pp. 39–78. Hereafter, this volume is cited as FL3/1.

[11] Taylor, *Transportation Revolution*, pp. 98–99. See also Harry N. Scheiber and

country expanded to the west, cities up and down the coast sought to capture trade from the hinterlands, and improving internal communication seemed a necessary requirement. Thus the Massachusetts Board of Directors of Internal Improvement in 1829 deemed a railroad to the Hudson "an essential element in metropolitan greatness" because of the western trade that it would secure for Boston. Further south, the port cities of Baltimore and Charleston endorsed this view, joining Boston as railroad-building pioneers. Construction of the earliest lines, in turn, spurred a new round of competition.[12]

In Prussian towns and cities the commercial argument also drew many adherents after the Napoleonic Wars. In this case, however, the new technology had an additional attraction, for it offered a promising means of circumventing burdensome tolls on river traffic. The opening of the tiny Nürnberg-Fürth Railroad in Bavaria in 1835, followed by a section of the Leipzig-Dresden Railroad in Saxony in 1837, prompted commercial and political elites in cities throughout Prussia to scramble to improve their transportation facilities as well. These early lines had a "demonstration" effect much like the Baltimore and Ohio or South Carolina railroads a decade earlier in the United States. In the late 1830s, cities and towns throughout Prussia turned decisively to railroads as the best means of preserving or enhancing their commercial importance.[13]

One of the most virulent episodes of urban rivalry came during debates about the location of the Berlin-Hamburg Railroad in the early 1840s. Urban rivalry fairly bristled, as town after town petitioned the king to be included in its route. As the Salzwedel city council (*Magistrat*) and city delegates (*Stadt-Verordneten*) wrote in August 1840, the decision whether the Berlin-Hamburg Railroad

---

Stephen Salsbury, "Reflections on George Rogers Taylor's *The Transportation Revolution, 1815–1860*: A Twenty-five Year Retrospect," *Business History Review* 51 (Spring 1977): 82.

[12] Kirkland, *Men, Cities, and Transportation*, 1:108; Taylor, *Transportation Revolution*, pp. 77–78, 98–99.

[13] See Peter Beyer, *Leipzig und die Anfänge des Deutschen Eisenbahnbaues: Die Strecke nach Magdeburg als zweitälteste deutsche Fernverbindung und das Ringen der Kaufleute um ihr Entstehen, 1829–1840* (Weimar: Verlag Hermann Böhlaus Nachfolger, 1978), pp. 138–49; Röll, *Die Entstehungsgeschichte der Thüringischen Eisenbahn*, pp. 5–18; Steitz, *Entstehung*; and Klee, *Preußische Eisenbahngeschichte*, pp. 20–67, for numerous instances in which urban rivalry stimulated railroad construction in western and eastern Prussia. As Steitz shows, urban rivalry was not always productive; the rivalry ("war of the cities" or *Städtekrieg*) between Cologne and Aachen hindered construction of railroads in that area.

would run through the Old Mark or along the right bank of the Elbe vitally affected the city and its environs. On it depended "not only the existence of our city, but the prosperity of the entire Old Mark." They were already having trouble competing with neighboring areas that had acquired better means of communication, they explained, "and it would no doubt completely impoverish the Old Mark in a very short time, if the railroad connection between Your Majesty's capital cities and the city of Hamburg now also ran along the right bank of the Elbe and not through the Old Mark."[14] The estates (*Stände*) of the Ruppin district expressed similar concerns early the next year. The direction of the Berlin-Hamburg line was of the utmost importance, they explained, since the district was suffering from increased competition with neighboring areas that had developed better connections with Berlin. "If the railroad cuts through our area," they argued,

> then we can expect from it the most propitious consequences not only for the trade of our cities but also for the sales of our agricultural products; but if it does not pass through [our] district, [we] will become more and more isolated and the above advantages will be replaced by disadvantages, all the greater and more permanent since we cannot now count on another railroad ever running through our region.[15]

Petition after petition framed the question as one of life or death for the communities concerned.[16] Although the agitation generated by the Berlin-Hamburg controversy reached unusual proportions, the phenomenon was not unique to either country.

Besides commercial attractions, many saw in internal improvements a means of creating physical links among the various sections of the two countries, which would enhance political unity. In the United States, the westward-expanding frontier continually threatened to upset the delicate political balance between North and South,

---

[14] Magistrat und Stadt-Verordneten [to the king], Salzwedel, August 18, 1840, in ZStAM, Rep. 93E, No. 3305/1, vol. 2, p. 49v.

[15] Die Stände des Ruppinschen Kreises, Neu-Ruppin, January 20, 1841, in ibid., pp. 131r–v.

[16] In addition to correspondence with the two committees directly backing the competing left and right bank projects in ibid., see the fifteen petitions in the same volume, pp. 2r–22v, 46r–48v, 57r–59v, 67r–68v, 71r–v, 107r–v, 131r–v, 150r–152v, 162r–163v, 169r–72r, 174r–v, 197r–200r, 225r–239v, and 252r–53r. Another six petitions can be found in ZStAM, Rep. 77, Tit. 258a, no. 30, vol. 1, pp. 21r–22v, 33r–34r, 60r–v, and 63r–68r.

if not split away altogether as it developed its own sectional inter-ests.[17] The era of internal improvements opened, as James A. Ward notes, just as the country underwent its "first great political convul-sion over slavery." To the French traveler, Michel Chevalier, the polit-ical utility of internal improvements in the new and fragile nation seemed obvious in the 1830s. "These numerous routes, which are traversed with so much ease and speed, will contribute to the mainte-nance of the Union more than regularly balanced national represen-tation," he thought (rather optimistically, as it turns out). "Distance will be annihilated, and this colossus, ten times greater than France, will preserve its unity without an effort." Amid widespread doubt about the political viability of the Union, others shared his view; in Ward's words, railroad promoters painted "railways as the country's best hope for achieving a much desired national unity."[18]

In Prussia, the railroad took on a dual political significance. On the one hand, it became intimately associated with German aspirations for national unity. Friedrich List laid great weight on this point, par-ticularly in conjunction with the German Customs Union (Zoll-verein), established in 1834: "The railroad system and the customs union are Siamese twins," he wrote in 1841; together they would create "a rich, powerful, and inviolable nation."[19] For Prussia itself, on the other hand, the railroad had great practical significance, for the western territories, newly acquired at the Congress of Vienna in 1815, presented political problems analogous to those posed by the westward-moving American frontier. They had long been economi-cally more advanced than most of the other Prussian provinces, a difference exacerbated by the Napoleonic Wars. Moreover, a corridor of other German principalities separated them physically from the rest of Prussia, including its capital, Berlin (fig. 1). Some railroad visionaries, therefore, foresaw as grand a result in Prussia as their counterparts did in the United States. As Prussian Finance Minister von Bodelschwingh pointed out during the debates about railroad aid in 1842, railroads would promote closer ties among the Prussian citi-

---

[17] Frederick Jackson Turner, "The Significance of the Section in American History," in idem, *Frontier and Section: Selected Essays of Frederick Jackson Turner* (Englewood Cliffs, N.J.: Prentice-Hall, Inc., Spectrum Books, 1961), pp. 116–23.

[18] James A. Ward, *Railroads and the Character of America, 1820–1887* (Knoxville: University of Tennessee Press, 1986), pp. 12–27 (quotations from pp. 12, 13); Chevalier, *Society, Manners and Politics*, p. 275.

[19] Friedrich List, "Das deutsche Eisenbahnsystem III" (1841), in FL3/1, p. 347.

zenry and strengthen their feelings of national identity.[20] In both countries, internal improvements generally—and the railroad in particular—held out the promise of a technological means of knitting together the nation politically as well as commercially.

Yet, the political and the commercial interacted in different ways in the two countries. Both countries showed deep regional differences, but other factors in the United States—the nature of the political system and the perpetual instability produced by an advancing frontier—combined with regional divisions to give the internal-improvements question a special potency along the Atlantic seaboard. At stake was not only regional prosperity, but ultimately national political power. In a representative political system, regional power in national politics depended critically on population; a region's ability to retain its population hinged on prosperity; and regional prosperity was precisely what transportation improvements promised to enhance.[21] Ultimately at issue, then, was the political power not merely of cities and states, but of sections. A "contest for empire," as William Grayson put it at the Virginia ratification convention in 1787, characterized union relations from the outset. "This contest of the Mississippi involves the great national contest," Grayson continued; "that is whether one part of this continent shall govern the other." As Frederick Jackson Turner wrote, citing Grayson's words:

> rival societies, free and slave, were marching side by side into the unoccupied lands of the West, each attempting to dominate the back country, the hinterland, working out agreements from time to time, something like the diplomatic treaties of European nations, defining spheres of influence, and awarding mandates, such as in the Missouri Compromise, the Compromise of 1850, and the Kansas-Nebraska Act. Each Atlantic section was, in truth, engaged in a struggle for power; and power was to be gained by drawing upon the growing West.

This was the context, he argued, in which "rival Eastern cities and states, the centers of power in their respective sections, engaged in

[20] "Die Verhandlungen," pp. 7–8.
[21] Kirkland, *Men, Cities, and Transportation,* 1:96–97.

contests for the commercial control of the Mississippi by transportation lines."[22]

Thus concerns about Southern power in national politics echoed in speeches delivered at southern railroad conventions in the 1830s. The Western and Atlantic Railroad Convention in 1832 drew delegates from Tennessee, South Carolina, and North Carolina to discuss a railroad project from the Atlantic to the navigable waters of the West. The railroad would be advantageous, Gen. Alexander Anderson of Tennessee pointed out, "not less in a political than commercial point of view, so indissolubly connecting the Southern and Western interests, strengthening the bonds of Union, and thereby perpetuating all the blessings of our valuable institutions."[23] A few years later at the Knoxville Convention, which drew 380 delegates from nine states, former Senator Robert Y. Hayne closed the proceedings with a toast to the impending "marriage" between the two sections that the Louisville, Cincinnati, and Charleston Railroad would effect: "The South and West.—We have published the banns—if any one know aught why these should not be joined together, let him speak now, or forever after hold his peace."[24] Shortly thereafter Hayne returned to the theme. The commerce generated by the railroad would not only increase the wealth of both sections, he argued; it would create a "golden chain, which is to bind these states together in a 'Perpetual Union,' founded on mutual harmony and affection and a community of feeling and of interest."[25] Another writer, also urging Charleston to support the proposed Louisville, Cincinnati, and Charleston Railroad, framed the issue more explicitly in 1836:

[22] Turner, "The Significance of the Section," pp. 118, 122. For an illuminating discussion of the way that territorial expansion combined with the federal political structure to escalate the slavery issue into a constitutional crisis, see Arthur Bestor, "The American Civil War as a Constitutional Crisis," in *American Law and the Constitutional Order: Historical Perspectives*, ed. Lawrence M. Friedman and Harry N. Scheiber (Cambridge: Harvard University Press, 1978), pp. 219–36.

[23] Elias Horry, *An Address Respecting the Charleston & Hamburgh Rail-Road; and on the Rail-Road System as Regards a Large Portion of the Southern and Western States of the North-American Union* (Charleston: A. E. Miller, 1833), p. 21. The convention unanimously adopted a preamble to that effect. See also Meyer, *History of Transportation*, pp. 427–37.

[24] Quoted in Samuel Melanchthon Derrick, *Centennial History of South Carolina Railroad* (Columbia, S.C.: The State Company, 1930), pp. 150–51.

[25] Robert Y. Hayne, *Address in Behalf of the Knoxville Convention to the Citizens of the Several States Interested in the Proposed Louisville, Cincinnati and Charleston Railroad* (1836), quoted in Derrick, *Centennial History*, p. 153.

The connection with Cincinnati, from a political point of view, meant [sic] detaching a powerful confederate from the East, as far as commercial and social relations could do it, and might keep Ohio a friend to the South on the slavery question, as she would receive all the benefits of slave labor, indirectly, without any of its evils. If the road ended at Louisville in a slave State, it would not be attended with so many advantages.[26]

Commercial control through railroad connections, in other words, seemed doubly important, promising not only to increase Southern prosperity, thus preserving numbers—and congressional representation—at home, but also to strengthen political ties with the West. Both in turn would enhance sectional power in national politics at a time when the first fractures in Southern control of the federal government were appearing.

Westward expansion—and American railroad lines—did indeed run largely along east-west lines during the antebellum years. The French observer, Michel Chevalier, remarked on the phenomenon during his travels in 1834. "The great flood of civilisation, which has poured over the vast regions of the West, in the south and the north, . . . has flowed on with a wonderful power and an admirable regularity," he reported. "Emigration has taken place, along the whole line of march, from east to west," the New England states and Virginia giving rise to two great "columns of migration."[27] Railroad construction, like internal migration, also tended to proceed along straight east-west lines. By the 1850s, four trunk-line railroads had crossed the Alleghenies to unite the northeastern and northwestern sections of the country. As they did so, they defined more sharply the lines of sectional conflict. In the end, as John F. Stover writes, "Iron rails and puffing locomotives helped the Northwest decide it would support the Union."[28]

Sectional rivalry for control of the expanding West thus overlay urban rivalry in the United States, for the degree of urban rivalry

[26] Blanding, *Address to Citizens on the Louisville, Cincinnati, and Charleston Railroad* (Columbia, S.C., 1836), quoted in Meyer, *History of Transportation*, p. 427.

[27] Chevalier, *Society, Manners and Politics*, pp. 109–11. Cf. Richard H. Steckel, "The Economic Foundations of East-West Migration during the 19th Century," *Explorations in Economic History* 20 (1983): 14–19.

[28] John F. Stover, *American Railroads* (Chicago: University of Chicago Press, 1961; Midway Reprint, 1976), pp. 42, 54.

depended partly on sectional location and it placed limits on the quest for national unity. It was no doubt in this spirit that Elias Horry, president of the South Carolina Railroad, sent words of encouragement to a railroad promoter in Savannah, despite the fact that his own railroad represented the culmination of Charleston's long-standing efforts to capture Savannah River trade. "You may be assured that Charleston has no jealousy as to the prosperity of Savannah," he wrote, for "she is a Southern city, important to a large portion of South-Carolina, and her interests should be fostered; and whenever these contemplated Rail-Roads shall be made and completed, there will be ample and sufficient commerce for *all*." Railroads along either of the proposed routes warranted support, he concluded, for both "will promote the prosperity of our Southern country."[29] In the dynamic context created by a federal-legislative political structure and an expanding frontier, sectional divisions transformed "metropolitan mercantilism" and even "state mercantilism"[30] into sectional mercantilism.

In *Vormärz* Prussia, East differed from West arguably as much as South from North in the antebellum United States, but absent a national legislature, the political power of provinces and sections depended less on numbers. There internal improvements took on a different kind of urgency, for inter-German and international rivalry augmented urban rivalry within Prussia. In this regard, German "particularism" and variations in the economic policies adopted by German states served, much like American federalism, to generate competition, which, in turn, prompted emulation or innovation.[31] Central European rivalry, moreover, overlay inter-German competition and made railroad construction all the more imperative. As Friedrich List summed up the complexities of the Prussian situation in 1834: "The French force the Belgians, the Belgians force the Dutch, all of them together force the Germans to build railroads; [and] the

---

[29] Elias Horry to James A. Meriwether, June 21, 1831, in Horry, *Address*, pp. 33–37 (original emphasis). On Charleston's efforts to divert trade from Savannah, see Derrick, *Centennial History*, pp. 8–9.

[30] On "state mercantilism," see Scheiber, "Federalism and the American Economic Order," pp. 97–100.

[31] Hardach, "Some Remarks on German Economic Historiography," p. 77. Hardach notes the positive effects of particularism on railroad construction, banking, and technical education. On "federal effects" in the American case, see Scheiber, "Federalism and the Economic Order," pp. 97–100.

Germans . . . force one another to build railroads."[32] Prussian Finance Minister von Bodelschwingh took explicit note of international rivalry in addressing the standing committees from the provinces in 1842: the experience of neighboring countries already showed the commercial advantages of railroads, he pointed out; if Prussia did not keep up with its neighbors, it would soon be outstripped by them.[33] Just as sectional rivalry augmented urban and state rivalry in the United States, so inter-German and international rivalry overlapped with urban rivalry in Prussia to make railroad construction seem as urgent in that country as it did in the United States.

In both countries, finally, observers offered a different take on the political arguments in favor of internal improvements, one that stressed their military significance. Indeed, the policy of loaning state engineers to the railroads, common to state policy in both countries, rested on an understanding that the railroads were likely to enhance national defense. The unsettled state of international relations in the decades following the Congress of Vienna made practically any transportation improvement attractive on both sides of the Atlantic.

For Prussia, a country situated at the crossroads of central Europe and lacking natural borders, the centrality of such concerns after the Napoleonic Wars needs little elaboration. The addition of the western provinces in 1815, moreover, split the nation in two parts and altered its strategic orientation. "At the stroke of a pen," writes William Carr, "the population doubled, the centre of gravity of the kingdom moved from Poland to Germany, and Prussia became the guardian of Western Germany against France."[34] Any transportation improvement took on heightened significance in those circumstances, for the ability to assemble the militia and mobilize troops would prove critical to the viability of a divided Prussia.[35] Several

[32] Friedrich List, National-Magazin, 1834, p. 35, quoted in Beyer, Leipzig und die Anfänge des Deutschen Eisenbahnbaues, p. 140.

[33] "Die Verhandlungen," pp. 7–8. For similar thoughts five years earlier, see "Eisenbahnen, III. In Rheinpreußen," Allgemeine Zeitung (Augsburg), Außerordentliche Beilage, nos. 161–62, April 8, 1837, p. 642. On the role of competition in stimulating German railroad development, see the excellent discussion in Beyer, Leipzig und die Anfänge des Deutschen Eisenbahnbaues, pp. 138–49, and the evidence in Klee, Preußische Eisenbahngeschichte, pp. 20–67.

[34] William Carr, A History of Germany, 1815–1945, 2d ed. (New York: St. Martin's Press, 1979), pp. 7–8.

[35] On the Prussian militia, a product of the earlier reform era, Petter, "Militär und Militarisierung," pp. 59–65; Heinrich Heffter, "Der nachmärzliche Liberalismus: die

treatises on the railroad's military significance appeared between 1833 and 1842, one of the most influential coming from a commission appointed by the crown in 1836. Its members, civilian and military, welcomed the railroad as an improvement in communication, but cautioned that it would have limited utility for offensive purposes and appeared more suitable for transporting infantry than for moving cavalry. In 1837 the Prussian Council of Ministers decided that military authorities should review applications for railroad charters, just as they had always scrutinized plans for highways. The same year, Friedrich List emphasized the value of canals and railroads in defending Germany from the east as well as the west. In subsequent years, railroad promoters took up the theme.[36]

In the United States, railroad construction also began at a time of continuing anxiety about the new nation's security. This point, though often passed over, seems obvious in view of the United States' strategic position in the antebellum years. As Lt. H. Wager Halleck of the Corps of Engineers observed in an 1845 report on national defense, since the time of George Washington, "we have once been plunged, without preparation, into a costly and desolating war, and thrice upon the very brink of hostilities with two of the most powerful nations of Europe." At no point in the antebellum years could it have been said with certainty that a permanent peace had finally been achieved in Europe. At home, moreover, the United States' borders remained relatively vulnerable in several ways. The War of 1812 had shown all too clearly the inadequacies of the nation's inland transportation network, while the development of steam-powered warships in Europe made the nation's coastal defenses seem increasingly inadequate. As conflict with American Indians continued to rage on its

---

Reaktion der fünfziger Jahre," in *Moderne deutsche Sozialgeschichte*, ed. Hans-Ulrich Wehler, 5th ed. (Cologne: Kiepenheuer & Witsch, 1976), pp. 194–96.

36 Edwin A. Pratt, *The Rise of Rail-Power in War and Conquest, 1833–1914* (London: P. S. King & Son, 1915), pp. 2–6; Dennis E. Showalter, *Railroads and Rifles: Soldiers, Technology, and the Unification of Germany* (Hamden, Conn.: Shoe String Press, 1975; Archon Book, 1986), pp. 19–35; Bernhard Meinke, "Die ältesten Stimmen über die militärische Bedeutung der Eisenbahnen, 1833–1842," *Archiv für Eisenbahnwesen* 41 (1918): 921–34 and 42 (1919): 46–74; Udo von Bonin, *Geschichte des Ingenieurkorps und der Pioniere in Preußen*, 2 vols. (Berlin, 1877–78; reprint ed., Wiesbaden: LTR-Verlag, 1981), 2:250; List, "Auszüge aus Lists Beitrag zum Staats-Lexikon," pp. 54–55; Das Comité zur Begründung eines Actien-Vereins für die Eisenbahn-Verbindung zwischen Berlin und Hamburg to the king, December 27, 1840, Berlin, in ZStAM, Rep. 93E, Nr. 3305/1, vol. 2, pp. 42r–45v.

frontiers, and as the frontiers themselves continued to move, defense became more and more difficult. Like Prussia, moreover, the United States relied in part on a militia for its defense, which hampered speedy mobilization of the troops.[37]

Thus railroad promoters from Florida to Boston, in and outside military circles, cited the military value of railroads, especially when they sought the patronage of the federal government, where "national importance" became the catchword. As the promoters of the South Carolina Railroad explained in 1828, "In time of War,—the security arising from the certainty of immediate succour, will be increased. Two locomotive engines will convey 1,000 troops one hundred miles in twelve hours! Can we in time of Peace fully appreciate the value of this advantage?"[38] In this view, railroad promoters received considerable encouragement from the War Department itself. As Secretary of War James Barbour explained in 1827, when he dispatched army engineers to the Baltimore and Ohio Railroad:

> The successful introduction of Rail-Roads, into this country, is viewed by the Department as of great national importance, and especially any practicable mode of connecting the Atlantic States with the Western; whether by Rail-Roads or Canals, so that the commodities to be found in either can be conveniently and cheaply conveyed to the other, across the barriers which divide them, and which communications, while aiding in the advancement of commercial enterprise, offer the most sure and economical means to the Government to convey, to the different parts of the Union, the means of defence, in the transportation of men and munitions to the seat of war, wherever it shall exist.[39]

[37] H. Wager Halleck, Lieutenant of Engineers, "Report on the Means of National Defense," Senate Doc. 85, 28th Cong., 2d sess., 1844–45; E. G. Campbell, "Railroads in National Defense, 1829–1848," *Mississippi Valley Historical Review* 27 (December 1940): 361; Ward, *Railroads and the Character of America*, pp. 41–55.

[38] *Report of a Special Committee Appointed by the [Charleston] Chamber of Commerce to Inquire into the Cost, Revenue and Advantages of a Rail Road Communication between the City of Charleston and the Towns of Hamburg & Augusta* (Charleston: A. E. Miller, 1828), p. 20. See also William Howard, U.S. Civil Engineer, *Report on the Charleston and Hamburg Rail-Road* (Charleston, 1829), p. 17; and for an example from the North, "Survey of Connecticut River, &c.," *House Reports*, Doc. 294, 21st Cong., 1st sess., vol. 2, 1829–30.

[39] Secretary of War James Barbour to P. E. Thomas, June 25, 1827, in National Archives, R.G. 77, Office of the Chief of Engineers, Miscellaneous Letters Sent by the Chief of Engineers, 1812–1869, Microcopy 1113, vol. 4, p. 224, also quoted in Hill, *Roads, Rails, and Waterways*, p. 102.

By the 1830s, enthusiasm had spread in some quarters of the military. "[S]uch is the progress and probable extent of the new system of intercommunication," Secretary of War Lewis Cass reported to President Andrew Jackson in 1833, "that the time will soon come when almost any amount of physical force may be thrown, in a few hours, upon any point threatened by an enemy. . . . This wonderful capacity of movement increases, in effect, some of the most important elements of national power."[40] Most energetic of military enthusiasts was Maj. Gen. Edmund P. Gaines, who, as noted earlier, favored federal construction of railroads and lobbied first the War Department and then Congress for more than a decade on behalf of his plan. He wanted the military to build seven railroads radiating from Kentucky and Tennessee. Totaling more than four thousand miles in length, the system would cost, according to his estimate, $64 million (his critics predicted twice this amount).[41] "I recommend with all my heart, and with all my mind, and with all my strength, the construction and employment of RAILROADS with steam-power . . . for the supply of every military post of the United States," he wrote in 1838.[42] Even the short and seemingly inconsequential Boston and Lowell Railroad—"this great work," in the eyes of Col. Stephen Long in 1836—formed a critical link in a system of national defense.[43]

Yet, even though many Americans saw the military value of railroads almost from the start, the subject did not elicit heated debate—except perhaps for Major General Gaines's ambitious plans—because few questioned the urgent need to improve the nation's transportation network. Even the National Road had great military

[40] "Military and Naval Defenses," House Exec. Doc. 243, 24th Cong., 1st sess., 1835–36, p. 18.

[41] "Memorial of Edmund P. Gaines, Proposing a system of national defense, and praying its adoption by Congress," Senate Doc. 256, 26th Cong., 1st sess., 1839–40; "Letter from the Secretary of War, Transmitting . . . a system of national defence and the establishment of national foundries," House Exec. Doc. 206, 26th Cong., 1st sess., 1839–40; Campbell, "Railroads in the National Defense," pp. 369–73. See also Gaines's letter of September 10, 1834, quoted in Richard George Wood, *Stephen Harriman Long, 1784–1864: Army Engineer, Explorer, Inventor* (Glendale, Calif.: Arthur H. Clark Co., 1966), p. 163.

[42] [Gaines], *To the Young Men*, p. 36.

[43] Col. Stephen H. Long to Governor Isaac Hill of New Hampshire, "Report on the New Hampshire and Vermont Divisions of the Boston and Ogdenburg Rail-road," November 26, 1836, p. 39, in National Archives, Record Group 77, Entry 250, Reports on Internal Improvements, 1823–39.

importance. As one member of Congress put it to his colleagues in 1832:

The facilities afforded by such a road in time of war for transportation of the munitions of war, and the means of defence from one point of the country to another, need scarcely be noticed; they must be palpable and plain to every reflecting mind, and I will not take up the time of the House in detailing them.[44]

Such arguments applied at least with equal force to railroads by the mid-1830s, but as Col. William Howard said of the South Carolina Railroad, its strategic advantages were "too obvious to require to be insisted on."[45] From the earliest years, then, railroad partisans in the United States and Prussia—in civilian and military circles alike—highlighted the military value of railroad projects.

Sources of Opposition

But internal improvements generated as much opposition in some quarters as they did support in others, for conflict erupted when projects began to take on concrete form. Then enthusiasm tended to fracture under the weight of pragmatic opposition, which sprang from one of two broad sources: either it centered on the impact that such projects would have on local interests, or it reflected pervasive doubts about the value of the new technology itself.

Conflict involving local interests followed a pattern that has become familiar in times of large-scale industrial change. Those who defended specific projects usually answered their critics by stressing the general, long-term benefits of technological change (although they might actually have their own short-term interests at heart). Those who opposed specific projects generally did so because they feared the short-term effects of a change either in the mode of transportation or in existing trade patterns. They were reluctant, in other words, to sacrifice the current advantages that they enjoyed. The two views of technological change were not mutually exclusive, for an individual could advocate internal improvements in the abstract but

[44] Speech of Hon. T.M.T. McKennan, delivered in Congress, June 6, 1832, quoted in Searight, *The Old Pike,* p. 108.
[45] Howard, *Report on the Charleston and Hamburg Rail-Road,* p. 17.

oppose specific projects or ways of carrying them out.[46] Nonetheless, the inherent disjunction between the long-term, general benefits of internal improvements and their short-term, disruptive effects on the local economy inevitably generated conflict.

One source of opposition in both countries encompassed all those with a stake in the existing modes of transportation. When railroads entered the debate, their opponents included those whose livelihood was bound up in one way or another with roads or canals: wagoners; canal boatmen; stagecoach operators and their provisioners; as well as tavern owners and bridge, turnpike, and canal proprietors. Although they may have favored internal improvements in the abstract, such groups "often fought bitterly," in George Rogers Taylor's words, once they realized the threat posed by specific projects.[47] This sometimes meant direct action. When J. Edgar Thomson set out in 1835 to survey the Georgia Railroad between Augusta and Atlanta, he and his party planned to board in private homes along the way. But, as his biographer reports, "they soon found the inhabitants so hostile and insulting, fearing that the railroad threatened their profitable business of provisioning wagoners, that Thomson, the Quakers' son, was forced to arm the entire group and purchase camping equipage to live in the field."[48] In Pennsylvania, boatmen on the Schuylkill Canal who were losing freight traffic to the Reading Railroad in the 1840s employed similar tactics: they burned railroad bridges over the canal. Rather than continuing to pay "[t]he expense of keeping up a large force of watchmen to protect our bridges from the incendiaries of the

[46] Attitudes toward railroad development could also change as the circumstances changed. The citizens of Worcester, Massachusetts, for example, initially favored construction of the Boston and Worcester Railroad, but later they opposed plans to extend the railroad to the Hudson, fearing that Worcester would be reduced from an important terminal city to a mere way station. Bliss, *Historical Memoir*, p. 23n; Kirkland, *Men, Cities, and Transportation*, 1:128; Meyer, *History of Transportation*, p. 328.

[47] Taylor, *Transportation Revolution*, p. 75; Meyer, *History of Transportation*, pp. 316–18. The civil engineer Alexander Gordon sympathized with similar concerns in England: "The prevailing disposition,—I had almost said *mania*—for general edge rail-way communication, must be viewed with no little anxiety by landowners, road trustees, innkeepers, postmasters, carriers, and others interested in the existing lines of turnpike road, and also by those who value this important branch of our inland intercourse, threatened as 'these good old ways' are with extinction, or at least some great alterations, by speculators in what, in the opinion of many, is still an unproved system of rail-way intercourse." Alexander Gordon, *The Fitness of Turnpike Roads and Highways for the Most Expeditious, Safe, Convenient and Economical Internal Communication* (London: Roake and Varty, 1835), p. 6 (original emphasis).

[48] James A. Ward, *J. Edgar Thomson: Master of the Pennsylvania* (Westport, Conn.: Greenwood Press, 1980), p. 27.

Canal," the Reading's engineer explained, the company constructed one of the first iron railroad bridges in the United States.[49] In Prussia a few years later, wagoners who had long but unsuccessfully sought state protection from railroad competition destroyed a section of the Taunus Railroad during the revolution of 1848. As Rolf Peter Sieferle notes, the railroad quickly became "a symbol for the hated industrial freedom and the machine system" among the working classes.[50]

More often, however, opponents of particular projects sought to defend their interests through conventional political channels, and those who drew their livelihood from the roads and highways stood at the forefront of opposition. An opponent of the Baltimore and Ohio Railroad marshaled graphic evidence to show the array of interests bound up with the National Road, which the railroad paralleled. As Thomas B. Searight recounts:

> In one of his characteristic speeches on the subject, [the congressman] furnished a careful estimate of the number of horse-shoes made by the blacksmiths along the road, the number of nails required to fasten them to the horses' feet, the number of bushels of grain and tons of hay furnished by the farmers to the tavern keepers, the vast quantity of chickens, turkeys, eggs and butter that found a ready market on the line, and other like statistical information going to show that the National Road would better subserve the public weal than a steam railroad. This view at the time, and in the locality affected, was regarded as correct.[51]

Tavern owners proved particularly energetic in their political opposition, for example, on the Conestoga wagon trail in Pennsylvania, but turnpike owners also did their best to block legislative approval of railroad charters. Failing that, they had provisions inserted in railroad

[49] Quoted in Emory L. Kemp and Richard K. Anderson, "The Reading-Halls Station Bridge," *Industrial Archaeology*, 13 (1987): 24. See also David Rittenhouse Porter, "Proclamation of Reward for the Apprehension of Incendiaries who have Set Fire to Certain Reading Railway Bridges," [October 1, 1842], in *Pennsylvania Archives*, 4th ser., vol. 6, pp. 913–14; idem, "To the Assembly Concerning the Claimants of a Reward Offered for the Apprehension of Certain Incendiaries," [February 6, 1844], in ibid., pp. 1033–34; Jay V. Hare, *History of the Reading* (Philadelphia: John Henry Strock, 1966), pp. 19–20.

[50] Sieferle, *Fortschrittsfeinde*, pp. 99–100.

[51] Quoted in Searight, *The Old Pike*, p. 15. The speaker was Gen. Henry W. Beeson, Democrat from Pennsylvania, who served in the House from 1841 to 1843. *Biographical Congressional Directory*, p. 385.

charters that required the railroad to buy the turnpike or to pay damages.[52]

In the United States, political coalitions sometimes helped an otherwise diverse array of interests to defeat chartering legislation, at least temporarily. In Massachusetts in 1830, for example, a projected railroad between Boston and Worcester threatened to take business away from stage lines, some sixty of which served Boston at the time. The railroad's opponents, therefore, included stagecoach operators, tavern owners, and the farmers who supplied stagecoach lines. Allied with them were canal investors as well as representatives from inland and coastal towns that stood to gain little from the railroad line.[53]

In Prussia, threatened interests also sought to exert political pressure, but, given the differences in the two political structures, they did so by other means. As early as 1826 mine owners petitioned the minister of the interior to deny a concession for a horse-powered mining railroad, because they feared its competitive effects. During the 1830s and 1840s, some of the most vocal opponents were those who made their living from road transportation. In 1840, for example, freight haulers on the Leipziger Road petitioned the Prussian king to prevent the Magdeburg-Leipzig Railroad from carrying freight. During the revolution, a ship owner plying his trade on the Elbe River also petitioned the minister of the interior for protection from the Berlin-Hamburg Railroad, which paralleled the Elbe.[54] What Thurman W. Van Metre notes of the United States held for Prussia as well. In each case, the grounds for opposition were familiar ones: "The railroad was

[52] Van Metre, *Early Opposition*, pp. 44–51; Meyer, *History of Transportation*, pp. 317–18, 326. For another variation, see the charter of the Eastern Railroad, [Massachusetts] Laws of 1836, chap. 232, An Act to establish the Eastern Railroad Company, Sect. 6, in Gregg and Pond, comps., *Railroad Laws and Charters*, p. 260, which reserved a quarter of the railroad's stock for the Salem Turnpike and Chelsea Bridge Corporation.

[53] Meyer, *History of Transportation*, pp. 317, 326; Kirkland, *Men, Cities, and Transportation*, 1:105–11; Salsbury, *The State, the Investor, and the Railroad*, pp. 70–75; Holmes and Rohrbach, *Stagecoach East*, pp. 178–79. The question of state aid for the Boston and Worcester complicates interpretation of the legislative battle over its charter, but Salsbury (p. 75) concludes that the resounding defeat of the bill reflected antipathy to that particular railroad rather than to state aid in general.

[54] Henning, *Industrialisierung*, p. 160; Bösselmann, *Entwicklung*, p. 87; Enkling, *Die Stellung des Staates*, p. 21; Gastwirthe C. Hüttenrauch und Genossen [to the king], September 9, 1840, Magdeburg, in ZStAM, Rep. 2.2.1, no. 29485, pp. 4r–6v; [Friedrich Wilhelm IV] to Minister von Alvensleben, October 31, 1840, in ibid., pp. 1r–v; Votum, Ministry of the Interior to the Finance Ministry, March 26, 1848, in ZStAM, Rep. 77, Tit. 258a, no. 30, vol. I, pp. 328r–v.

ing their business, and they were suffering, just as skilled workers suffer when they are displaced by machines."[55]

Joining these interests was another group, who defended the comparative market advantage that they enjoyed under the old transportation regime. Farmers in western Massachusetts, for example, formed the "center of hostility" to state aid for a railroad from Boston to the Hudson because they feared Western competition. As Kirkland explains, "To stress the future importation of whisky, livestock, lumber, and grain from the American West was hardly a way to endear a project to the landowners and farmers of Franklin or Worcester."[56] In the South, planter opposition apparently forced the directors of the South Carolina Railroad to abandon plans to run the line along the valley of the Edisto River, for planters with good access to water transportation, as one writer explains, saw railroads as a threat to their market advantage.[57] Just as the capital for the Boston and Worcester came largely from Boston, the first stock offering for the South Carolina Railroad found takers only in Charleston. That fact alone, as the South Carolina Railroad's historian put it, suggested "a feeling of hostility or indifference to the movement in the interior." [58]

In Prussia, opposition arose from similar sources and ran along analogous lines. Some Junkers (nobles on large estates east of the Elbe River) actively opposed railroad construction—indeed, they are famed in Prussian railroad history for doing so—but they did so, like Southern planters and western Massachusetts farmers, largely because they feared that it would change trade patterns to their disadvantage. As Dietrich Eichholtz writes, "one surely cannot speak of a principled opposition of the Junkers to railroad construction," since they had turned increasingly to production for the market in the decades before 1848.[59] If they did not object to the amount of compensation the railroad companies offered for their land, then they worried about losing their market advantage. When a county magistrate sur-

---

[55] Van Metre, *Early Opposition*, p. 50.

[56] Kirkland, *Men, Cities, and Transportation*, 1:95–96, 106.

[57] Trenholm, *South Carolina Handbook* (1883), p. 634, quoted in Derrick, *Centennial History*, p. 34.

[58] Derrick, *Centennial History*, pp. 33–35, 116–18 (quotation from pp. 33–34).

[59] Dietrich Eichholtz, *Junker und Bourgeoisie vor 1848 in der preußischen Eisenbahngeschichte*, Deutsche Akademie der Wissenschaften zu Berlin, Schriften des Instituts für Geschichte, ser. 1, vol. 11 (Berlin: Akademie-Verlag, 1962), p. 42.

veyed views of a proposed railroad to Berlin, he got this response from Herr von Ribbeck on the Ribbeck estate near Berlin:

> I . . . believe, where the profitable sale of so many products is concerned, that danger threatens the estates that lie near Berlin, which have easy and certain communication with the capital—as, for example, Ribbeck—because of the railroad and the increased competition from more removed regions that will result.[60]

Von Ribbeck possessed "a monopoly of profitable communication," Eichholtz points out, and "[w]hoever possessed [such a monopoly] usually had no interest whatsoever in a further development of the means of transportation and was decidedly against it if [his monopoly] would be diminished as a result." Even the most extreme opponent of Prussian railroads, who fought a "paper war" with the Berlin-Hamburg line for several years, did so only after the company refused his offer to donate land if the company would establish a station on his land "forever" and leave the tavern business to him.[61] In this context, it is not surprising to find that the 1842 meeting of standing committees from the provincial assemblies, where the nobility had a large voice, endorsed by a vote of 90 to 8 a resolution characterizing a national railroad network as "an urgent need" (*ein dringendes Bedürfniss*).[62] Although welcome in the abstract, railroad projects disturbed local interests in both countries, and they did so in comparable ways.

Meanwhile, the characteristics of the new technology itself also generated a good deal of debate.[63] In both countries, some objected to the monopolistic aspects of railroads. As Taylor notes of the United States, "considerable popular suspicion of the corporate form as being a monopolistic device prevailed, especially in rural districts,"[64] and most railroads in the two countries quite literally received monopoly rights in their charters. But critics also saw monopolistic tendencies

---

[60] Ibid., pp. 55–56.
[61] Ibid., pp. 50–51, 52n, 57.
[62] "Die Verhandlungen," p. 10.
[63] On the novelty of the railroad, see especially Wolfang Schivelbusch, *The Railroad Journey: The Industrialization of Time and Space in the 19th Century* (orig. pub. New York: Urizen Books, 1979; Berkeley: University of California Press, 1986). The book first appeared in German as *Geschichte der Eisenbahnreise* (Munich: Carl Hanser Verlag, 1977).
[64] Taylor, *Transportation Revolution*, p. 88.

in the way that railroad officials, rather than individual shippers or travelers, determined the conditions of travel.[65] Josiah White, acting manager of the Lehigh Coal and Navigation Company, offered his views in 1830 (still under the assumption that multiple carriers would use a railroad's tracks):

> Railroads are a great improvement on turnpikes; but, in my opinion, are vastly inferior (particularly as a public work, and *in a republican country*) to canals, both as to convenience as well as to economy. A canal is accessible anywhere, a railroad nowhere (without interrupting the current of traffic) except by an arrangement for turning out; and the more turn outs are made, the greater the casualties. By canal every boatman may choose his own motion, within the maximum motion; by railroad every traveller must have the same motion, or be subject to turn outs; which, as I have said, have their casualties.[66]

In 1836, one representative's outburst in Congress, although in defense of a proposal to make the National Road a railroad, indicated the nature of public dissatisfaction:

> nothing is more surprising to me than the strange determination manifested by intelligent gentlemen of this floor, to throw dust into each other's eyes, in relation to this very important project. A railroad is a monopoly!—not so democratic! They are willing that gentlemen of wealth and aristocrats, should build railroads, and travel on them if they choose! But their constituents are all democratic republicans—plain men—and want a road on which they can all travel together; no toll, no monopoly, nothing exclusive—a real "people's road."[67]

Disgruntlement intensified in the 1830s, when steam locomotives became the preferred means of locomotion and the viability of competition on the rails began to appear questionable, for this implied even tighter control over operations. Pennsylvania farmers peti-

[65] For an illuminating discussion of the politics of technologies, see Winner, *The Whale and the Reactor.* For an English engineer's criticism along these lines, see Gordon, *The Fitness of Turnpike Roads,* p. 24.

[66] Extract of a letter in "Chesapeake and Ohio Canal Company," House Exec. Doc. 18, 22d Cong., 1st sess., 1831–32, quoted in Van Metre, *Early Opposition,* p. 36 (emphasis added).

[67] *Register of Debates of Congress,* 1836, p. 4498, quoted in Van Metre, *Early Opposition,* p. 25. See also Meyer, *History of Transportation,* p. 593.

tioned their legislature repeatedly to have locomotives removed from the state-owned Philadelphia and Columbia Railroad and the line made a public highway.[68] An 1833 amendment to a North Carolina railroad charter *empowered* the company to require passengers to get off only at regular stops, and Virginia's generic railroad law of 1837 carried a similar provision.[69] In Prussia, state engineer August L. Crelle acknowledged the popular view that railroads had "disadvantages" (*Nachtheile*) compared with highways, because conventional wagons could not be used on them and access could not be had as freely. The projected railroad from Frankfurt/Oder to Breslau, he promised in 1839, would have plenty of stations.[70]

At the same time, the performance of the new technology gave abundant grounds for skepticism, especially when locomotives first came into wider use in the 1830s.[71] Experience with imported locomotives quickly showed how troublesome the process of technology transfer could be. The first American locomotives, imported and assembled at the West Point Foundry for the Delaware and Hudson in 1829, could not be used because the company's track was too light.[72] Four years later, Friedrich List's railroad imported two machines, but both ran off the tracks during a trial run, doing considerable damage in the process.[73] Once in service, moreover, early locomotives performed erratically, and for years they routinely had to be supplemented with horses in rainy weather or in winter. Indeed, some of the early northern lines initially planned to close down during the winter, which, of course, undercut a major—some said, the only—reason for building them in the first place. American construction techniques, such as the use of wooden rails capped with strap iron, also created safety problems, for the iron strap sometimes came crashing

---

[68] Van Metre, *Early Opposition*, pp. 24–25.

[69] Weaver, *Internal Improvements*, p. 80; "An Act, Prescribing certain general regulations for the incorporation of railroad companies," in *Charter of the Richmond and Ohio Railroad Company*, p. 20.

[70] A. L. Crelle, "Einiges über die Ausführbarkeit von Eisenbahnen in bergigen Gegenden," *Journal für die Baukunst* 13 (1839): 128; "Zum überschläglichen Entwurf einer Eisenbahn zwischen Frankfurt an der Oder und Breslau," *Journal für die Baukunst* 13 (1839): 12.

[71] Van Metre, *Early Opposition*, p. 22; Kirkland, *Men, Cities, and Transportation*, 1:100.

[72] John W. White, Jr., *A History of the American Locomotive, Its Development: 1830–1880* (New York: Dover Publications, Inc., 1968), pp. 7, 239–41.

[73] Hare, *History of the Reading*, pp. 231–32.

through the floor of a passing wagon.[74] Broken axles caused added problems. In 1832, the South Carolina Railroad's directors apologized for a serious accident involving a number of townspeople. "The whole system of rapid travelling," they acknowledged, "has undoubtedly given rise to great destruction of life. . . . [I]f rail roads do not now, they very soon *will* offer not only the most easy, rapid and convenient, but the safest of all known modes of locomotion." Although Prussian railroads generally seem to have had a better record, they were not immune to such problems. Ten years later, the Berlin-Stettin Railroad had its own problems with broken axles.[75]

Not only were early railroads often unreliable and dangerous, but travel could also be unpleasant in other ways and not nearly as rapid as promoters claimed. John Parsons of Virginia voiced complaints on all accounts after a railroad journey from Petersburg to Richmond and Fredericksburg in 1840:

> The method of travelling, a new one to me, is in the main very pleasant, but the rumbling, tremulous motion of the cars is not very agreeable, and after the novelty has worn off, the pleasure of it is diminished by the fumes of the oil, the hissing of the steam, and the scorching of the cinders which are falling around you.

He was not impressed with the speed of travel either: "I noted that we did not go beyond seven or eight miles an hour."[76] The fastest American stagecoaches had already attained comparable speeds more than a decade earlier, while trains ran appreciably faster in Europe. Average speeds did improve in the 1840s and even more so with the increasing competition of the 1850s, but throughout the nineteenth century average freight train speeds seldom exceeded 10 mph (16 kph).[77]

[74] Taylor, *Transportation Revolution*, pp. 81–83; Meyer, *History of Transportation*, pp. 311, 317, 555.

[75] *Annual Report of the Board of Directors of the South Carolina Canal & Rail Road Company to the Stockholders, with Accompanying Documents, Submitted at their Meeting, May 7, 1832* (Charleston: William S. Blain, 1832), pp. 6–7 (original emphasis); *Dritter Jahresbericht des Directorium der Berlin-Stettiner Eisenbahn-Gesellschaft*, p. 12. See also "Report of H. Allen" in *Semi-Annual Report of the Direction of the South-Carolina Canal and Rail-Road Company, to the Stockholders, October 31, 1834* (Charleston, 1834), pp. 6–7; Robert B. Shaw, *A History of Railroad Accidents, Safety Precautions and Operating Practices*, 2d ed. (Robert B. Shaw, 1978); Eugene Alvarez, *Travel on Southern Antebellum Railroads, 1828–1860* (University, Ala.: University of Alabama Press, 1974), pp. 68–106.

[76] Quoted in Van Metre, *Early Opposition*, p. 30.

[77] "Abstract of a Plan of a Rail-Road, Peculiarly adapted to facilitate the operations of

Meanwhile, the public put pressure on the railroads to run passenger trains faster—which the English locomotive manufacturer Robert Stephenson advised doing in the early 1830s "not from considerations of economy or durability, but solely to gratify the public in their wishes for rapid travelling." Promoters of the Berlin-Hamburg Railroad acknowledged similar pressures in Prussia in 1840. Passengers already complained of "a bad trip," they reported, if the one-hour trip from Berlin to Potsdam took fifteen or twenty minutes longer than usual. "And nevertheless," they exclaimed, "it is a race-track speed."[78]

Given prevailing uncertainties about the new technology, some observers advocated alternative technologies. Plank roads continued to have their advocates, such as Robert Dale Owen in the United States. On the Michigan frontier, petitions to the federal government in the 1830s suggested a greater popular demand for common roads than for canals or railroads. In Prussia, a delegate representing Posen at the 1842 meeting of standing committees thought highways should be built instead of railroads.[79] Others defended the utility of canals, sometimes joining forces with those who saw a viable alternative in the development of steam carriages for common roads. In England, considerable work was being done on steam carriages in the 1830s, in part by canal owners who hoped to develop steamboats for use on canals (and thereby fend off railroad competition). By 1835, the British civil engineer Alexander Gordon claimed to have traveled "upwards of 3,000 miles" by steam carriage and thought they were

the Mail, with an Estimate of the Cost of one between the City of Washington and the City of New Orleans, in a letter from Robert Mills, Engineer and Architect, to the Post Master General of the United States," in *Three Papers on Rail-Roads* (1826–27, from the *American Farmer*), p. 5 (Smithsonian Institution, National Museum of American History, Dibner Collection); "Deutsche Eisenbahnen," *Allgemeine Zeitung* (Augsburg), Außerordentliche Beilage, no. 101, March 18, 1835, p. 400; *Berliner Gewerbe-, Industrie- und Handelsblatt*, July 20, 1842, p. 93; White, *History of the American Locomotive*, pp. 73–74. The speeds at which trains traveled bore a close relationship to both the cost of construction and operating costs. See chap. 5.

[78] *Report of the Committee on Cars, to the Direction of the South-Carolina Canal & Rail-Road Company Submitted to the Stockholders on Wednesday, 20th November 1833*, p. 11 (also quoted in White, *History of the American Locomotive*, p. 73); Das Comité zur Begründung eines Actien-Vereins für die Eisenbahn-Verbindung zwischen Berlin und Hamburg to the king, December 27, 1840, in ZStAM, Rep. 93E, no. 3305/1, vol. 2, p. 43v.

[79] Robert Dale Owen, *A Brief Practical Treatise on the Construction and Management of Plank Roads* (New Albany: Kent and Norman, 1850); Robert J. Parks, *Democracy's Railroads: Public Enterprise in Jacksonian Michigan* (Port Washington, N.Y.: Kennikat Press, 1972), p. 43; "Die Verhandlungen," p. 8.

better suited for use on common roads than on railways, which he considered "commercially, agriculturally, and politically hurtful."[80] Steam carriages on common roads had also attracted sufficient support in the German states that the Bavarian mining engineer-turned-railroad expert Joseph Ritter von Baader felt compelled to publish a tract attacking the notion.[81] "It is a shame that the governments of northern Europe no longer give highway steam carriages active attention," opined a newspaper writer from Hamburg in 1837.[82]

All of these complaints and reservations underscore the extent to which opinions remained divided in the early years of railroad construction. In this respect, Robert W. Fogel was surely right to emphasize that "the railroad was not born with the distinction attributed to it by later generations."[83] In the earliest years, railroads could plausibly claim a decisive advantage only in their comparative freedom from geographical constraints, for this not only freed them from reliance on nature for an adequate supply of water; it allowed them to be built parallel to an existing canal. Support for this view may be gleaned from the histories of the Boston and Lowell and the Philadelphia and Reading railroads, two American lines that were constructed parallel to canals. For all the rhetoric of their promoters, the fundamental motivation in both cases seems to have been to break the monopoly of the canals that they paralleled. The directors of the Chesapeake and Ohio Canal, themselves under threat from a parallel railroad (the Baltimore and Ohio) in 1830, cited evidence that the railroad's monopoly-breaking power constituted its principal appeal even in the land that had given birth to the new technology: "Here is the true secret of the imputed superiority of railroads, to canals, in England," they exclaimed.[84]

---

[80] "Chesapeake and Ohio Canal Company," House Exec. Doc. 18, 22d Cong., 1st sess., 1831–32, pp. 163–217, which marshaled evidence in defense of canals; Gordon, *Fitness of Turnpike Roads*, pp. 5, 19–21, 32.

[81] Joseph Ritter von Baader, *Die Unmöglichkeit, Dampfwagen auf gewöhnlichen Strassen mit Vortheil als allgemeines Transportmittel einzuführen, und die Ungereimheit aller Projekte, die Eisenbahnen dadurch entbehrlich zu machen* (Nürnberg: Riegel und Weißner, 1835), pp. xiv, 1–2.

[82] *Allgemeine Zeitung* (Augsburg), Außerordentliche Beilage, no. 64, March 5, 1837, p. 512.

[83] Fogel, *Railroads*, p. 1.

[84] "Chesapeake and Ohio Canal Company," p. 193. The story regarding the two railroads may be pieced together from *Report of a Committee on the Boston and Lowell Rail Road* (Boston, 1831), pp. 7–8; Taylor, *Transportation Revolution*, pp. 80, 111–12; Bogen, *Anthracite Railroads*, pp. 11, 15, 23, 26, 29, 35–36, 44, 44n, 111–12, 186; Hare,

If the efforts and apprehensions of those who resisted the coming of the railroad—those often disparaged as "vested interests, timid individuals, and conservative communities fearful of change"[85]—appear misguided, this is only because hindsight and subsequent history lend an aura of inevitability to the process of technological change. The 1830s and 1840s represented what some authors term "branch-points" and another calls "critical moments, or points of *bifurcation* in the dynamic process of technical change."[86] In those years, the direction of change remained clouded in uncertainty, much as it does in our own time.

Yet, on the whole, neither the prevailing pattern of support for early railroad development nor the varied sources of opposition differed much in the United States and Prussia during these years. Attending to the configuration of interests illuminates the political context in which early railroad policy was made, but it provides little leverage in understanding why that policy took a more interventionist turn in the United States than it did in Prussia.

The Force of Ideas

Another avenue of approach to this puzzle centers on the power of ideas in shaping patterns of regulatory policy: ideas either deriving from the tenets of particular political ideologies or growing out of prior experience, that is, out of traditional practice in the sphere of government-business relations. As one might surmise from what has been said already, however, the two countries did not differ markedly on this score either.

In both countries, ideological divisions marked public discourse during the 1830s and 1840s. In the United States, as John Ashworth shows, real differences separated Whigs and Democrats, and pro-

---

History of the Reading, pp. 16, 23; [Philadelphia and Reading Railroad], *Report from the Friends of This Improvement* (Philadelphia? 1833), p. 4; Examiner (pseud.), *The Reading Railroad Company: Their Policy and Prospects. Being a Series of Articles published in the Pennsylvanian, in January, February, and March, 1844* (Philadelphia, 1844).

[85] Taylor, *Transportation Revolution*, p. 75.

[86] See, respectively, Sabel and Zeitlin, "Historical Alternatives to Mass Production"; and Paul A. David, "Heroes, Herds and Hysteresis in Technological History: Thomas Edison and 'The Battle of the Systems' Reconsidered," *Industrial and Corporate Change* 1 (1992): 129–80.

grammatic disagreements regarding internal improvements helped to mark out that division. A central tenet of "the Democratic crusade against governmental intervention and partial legislation [i.e., conferring special privilege]," Ashworth writes, was opposition to government promotion of internal improvements. Whig policy, in contrast, favored a strong government role. The Democrats' platform consistently carried a resolution that denied the constitutional power of the federal government "to commence and carry on, a general system of internal improvements"; other party platforms were generally silent on the matter.[87] Although Prussia lacked formal political parties, ideological divisions nonetheless marked policy debates there, too. Conservatives vied with liberals, and liberals contended among themselves, with Smithian liberals advocating free-trade policy and nationalist liberals, such as Friedrich List, favoring protectionism and a stronger state role. Even the ministers held different views of appropriate economic policy—hence, a good deal of interministerial wrangling went on before and after the 1838 law was issued. Only at the end of the 1860s, writes Hans Jaeger, did "economic liberalism and free-trade thought, in particular, seem finally to have gained wide acceptance in Germany."[88] During the *Vormärz* period, no single view predominated.

Yet, these ideological divisions, with one exception, had little effect on the tenor of railroad policy in either country. In the United States the Democrats consistently opposed government support for internal improvements on paper, but in practice they held to this policy only loosely and then mainly at the federal level. At the state level, they were as likely to support internal improvements as Whigs were. And Whigs could sometimes be found in opposition. "In most cases," as Goodrich explains, "programs of state action [regarding internal improvements] had at their inception wide popular support regardless of party; the differences that developed were more often traceable to conflicts of local and sectional interests than to differences in party doctrine."[89] Or as James N. Primm concluded in one of

[87] John Ashworth, *'Agrarians' and 'Aristocrats': Party Political Ideology in the United States, 1837–1846* (Cambridge: Cambridge University Press, 1987), pp. 42, 78; Donald Bruce Johnson, comp., *National Party Platforms*, vol. 1: *1840–1956*, rev. ed. (Urbana: University of Illinois Press, 1978).

[88] Jaeger, *Geschichte der Wirtschaftsordnung*, p. 68.

[89] Goodrich, *Government Promotion*, p. 266. See also Taylor, *Transportation Revolution*, p. 382.

the pioneering, state-level studies, an activist state policy was no more hampered "by laissez-faire or non-intervention theories" in Missouri than in Massachusetts, Pennsylvania, or New Jersey.[90]

In Prussia, evidence that ideological divisions had little bearing on railroad policy may be found by recalling two episodes. One was the meeting of the standing committees that produced a new railroad policy in 1842. Since the delegates came from provincial assemblies across the country, they comprised a reasonably good cross-section of the nation's elites and, therefore, of the ideological divisions among elites. The landed nobility was well-represented, but so were the "economic liberals" from the western provinces. Although the ministers' agenda for the meeting omitted the subject of state construction, the delegates took up the subject on their own initiative. The results of their discussions, led by the merchant August von der Heydt from Elberfeld, revealed strong, though divided, opinions about the value of *state* construction (47 in favor, 50 against), but widespread support for railroad development in general (90 in favor, 8 against). State construction did not win approval, and the provincial delegates went on to approve by a wide majority the state's plans to provide aid to selected railroads.[91] If ideology drove Prussia's abstemious railroad policy, it found, at best, weak expression in this forum. Other evidence against this view may be seen in Postmaster General von Nagler's change of views by 1839. The epitome of the conservative bureaucrat,[92] he initially led opposition to railroad development among the ministers and remains best known for that. But by 1839 he had reversed his position, dropping his opposition to railroad construction and pursuing plans for the Post Office to build and run a railroad from Halle to the western provinces.[93] The rapidity with which he changed course implies that pragmatic concerns underlay his thinking all along. Together the two episodes suggest that political ideology had little to do with Prussian policy.

[90] Primm, *Economic Policy*, p. 124.

[91] "Die Verhandlungen," pp. 7, 10, 15–16. The final vote was 83 in favor and 14 opposed. The latter included the eight who opposed railroad construction altogether and three who apparently voted against interest guarantees because they favored state construction.

[92] Paul, "Die preußische Eisenbahnpolitik," p. 269.

[93] Substantial portions of his plans are reprinted in Sautter, "General-Postmeister von Nagler," which indicate that, even as he battled with the private railroads, he had also favored construction of at least one railroad before the Halle-Kassel line.

If ideology had any impact in the two countries, then an exception might be discerned in the formulation of federal-government policy in the United States. As Primm observed of antebellum Missouri, "[i]nsofar as negative ideas found expression, they tended to be directed at federal, rather than state economic activity."[94] Throughout the antebellum period, the question of federal support for internal improvements raised difficult constitutional issues.[95] At the national level, the Democrats adhered to their opposition to government support for internal improvements more consistently, and this produced a virtual stalemate that confined federal action to the dispatching of army engineers and to occasional grants of land before 1850. But one must be cautious about attributing even this stalemate solely to ideology. Antebellum Democratic ideology, Richard Bensel argues, was at bottom a "pragmatic political program" that served a "tactical role."[96] This became fully apparent during and after the Civil War, as he shows, but it also lay at the root of the ideological inconsistency inherent in antebellum Democratic support, in practice, for government promotion of internal improvements at the state level. Despite the federal stalemate, moreover, events at the national level made clear that ideological predilections did not rule out a strong federal role. Earlier in the century, when President James Madison vetoed the Bonus Bill, which would have used fees from chartering the Bank of the United States to finance federal internal improvements, he did not object to the *principle* of state intervention. He, like Jefferson before him and Monroe and Jackson later, merely wanted a specific constitutional amendment so that the proposed activities would not entail a broad construction of the Constitution (and thus would not inflame conflict over slavery).[97] "Despite a great parade of constitutional scruple," moreover, as Taylor points out, "successive chief executives and congresses actually approved grants

[94] Primm, *Economic Policy*, p. 124.

[95] Harry N. Scheiber, "The Transportation Revolution and American Law: Constitutionalism and Public Policy," in *Transportation and the Early Nation*, Indiana American Revolution Bicentennial Symposium (Indianapolis: Indiana Historical Society, 1982), pp. 1–29.

[96] Bensel, *Yankee Leviathan*, p. 13. See also Mark W. Summers, *Railroads, Reconstruction, and the Gospel of Prosperity: Aid under the Radical Republicans, 1865–1877* (Princeton: Princeton University Press, 1984).

[97] Scheiber, "Transportation Revolution," pp. 5–6; David J. Russo, "The Major Political Issues of the Jacksonian Period and the Development of Party Loyalty in Congress, 1830–1840," *Transactions of the American Philosophical Society*, n.s. 62, pt. 5 (1972): 9–10; Bestor, "American Civil War."

to aid in building specific roads, canals, and railroads." Even President Andrew Jackson, known for his hostility to federal action, spent nearly twice as much each year on internal improvements as John Quincy Adams, "the great champion of internal improvements," had. This is consistent with David J. Russo's finding in a study of the major political issues in the 1830s: congressional debates over internal improvements were the least likely to break down along party lines.[98] Even at the federal level in the United States, then, it is difficult to see that political ideology shaped railroad policy.

In both countries, moreover, the past provided ample precedent for both promotion and regulation of railroad enterprise. In the United States, the canal-building "mania" that peaked as railroad construction began set a strong precedent in this regard. The most prominent models were the great state canal sytems of New York, Pennsylvania, and Ohio. Between 1815 and 1860, Goodrich estimates, 62 percent of some $195 million invested in canals went into public works. Taking into account state investment in private canals, the states' share rises to 70 percent. Even the federal government took part in the movement, after President Madison impressed upon Congress in 1815 "the great importance of establishing throughout our country the roads and canals which can best be executed under national authority." Although it never undertook systematic planning on the large scale envisioned by Albert Gallatin and others, it sent its engineers out to do road and canal surveys, built the National Road, and subscribed $1 million of stock in the Chesapeake and Ohio Canal.[99] Thus, traditional American practice carried over into the railroad era, although in more limited form at the federal level (despite the wishes of men such as Major General Gaines).

In Prussia, too, the railroad era came at the end of—but in this case departed from—a long tradition of government support for transportation improvements. Prussian peasants were required to build and maintain local roads, much as American citizens did in lieu of paying highway taxes. But responsibility for canal construction fell to the state, a tradition that extended back as far as the fourteenth century,

[98] The Jackson administration averaged $1.3 million annually, while the Adams administration had spent $702,000 per year. Taylor, *Transportation Revolution*, pp. 20–21; Russo, "The Major Political Issues of the Jacksonian Period," pp. 9–13, 47–49.
[99] Goodrich, *Government Promotion*, p. 270. For an overview of the federal government's activities before the railroad era, see also Hill, *Roads, Rails, and Waterways*, pp. 3–95.

and highway construction had also begun to absorb considerable state resources by the late eighteenth century. Even though state officials had made important moves in the early nineteenth century to liberalize the Prussian economy, it would be too much to say that such ideas applied to transportation as well. Indeed, throughout the decades when private capital was building the railroads, the state continued to provide highways itself. Between 1830 and 1852, the length of state-owned and maintained roads (which accounted for more than three-quarters of the road system) doubled from 6,400 km to 12,800. Richard H. Tilly estimates that the state road system between 1831 and 1853 absorbed more than $12 million, of which about $3 million came from tolls.[100] Prussian railroad policy flew in the face of tradition.

Much the same can be said of regulation, as should be clear by now. State officials in both countries initially viewed the railroads merely as a new kind of highway. Accordingly, they set out to regulate them closely in time-honored fashion. From the start, the American state legislatures maintained their traditional prerogatives to regulate; and the provisions found in most railroad charters leave little doubt that the tradition remained vibrant. In Prussia, too, the national law of 1838 made abundantly clear the state's intent to regulate in the traditional fashion, for it reserved broad powers over the private corporations—hence, the great outpouring of protest from the private companies. As one student of railroad policy concludes, Prussian railroads *would have* amounted to "mixed enterprises" from the outset, "*if* [the law's provisions] had been strictly followed in practice."[101] But most of the provisions on the books were simply not enforced before 1848. Neither ideology nor tradition, then, explains why railroad policy took quite different directions in the two countries.

Political Structure and Policy-Making

A more satisfying explanation must be sought elsewhere. It might begin with the observation that interests—whether material, ideo-

[100] Tilly, "Capital Formation," pp. 411–12.
[101] Enkling, *Die Stellung des Staates*, p. 75. See also Gleim, "Zum dritten November 1888," *Archiv für Eisenbahnwesen* 11 (1888): 804–6.

logical, or social—and their effective expression in politics are two, quite distinct matters. Between them stand particular political structures, which shape and mold the expression of interests. Attention to the way that the American and Prussian political structures shaped the conflict that surrounded railroad construction shows how they molded that conflict into contrasting railroad policies. The more liberal American political structure offered more latitude for the expression of opposing interests; this is why the American state promoted early American railroads with greater energy; and, because it promoted, it was able to regulate. Prussian officials, in contrast, could not foster railroad development in a comparable manner without yielding to demands for political liberalization. Constrained to rely to a greater extent on private capital to build the railroads, they yielded to cries of "alarmed capital" and moderated the regulatory thrust of state policy.

In Prussia the prospect of railroad development, in a nutshell, forced *Vormärz* state officials to choose between political and economic liberalism, and they opted for the latter in order to stave off the former. Two factors converged to force the choice. On the one hand, central state officials' interest in promoting railroad construction had crystallized by the late 1830s and, indeed, as we have seen, was supported by considerable public sentiment in favor of outright state construction. The high cost of railroad construction, on the other hand, militated against the more interventionist (hence, less liberal) solution—state construction—since the task required far more capital than the monarchy had at its disposal. In theory, the Prussian state could have financed construction through taxation or borrowing, but not in practice. Following a protracted recovery from the Napoleonic Wars, the state budget had only just been put in sufficient shape by the early 1840s to allow a long-awaited reduction of taxes. The ministries were thus hardly in a position to press for additional taxes of the magnitude required to finance railroad construction. Even if they had, however, they would have run up against the restrictions of the national debt law of 1820, which effectively prevented recourse both to new taxes and to borrowing. In the aftermath of the Napoleonic Wars, the king had agreed not to impose new (direct) taxes or expand the national debt without parliamentary approval. This was a concession—a "credible commitment," as Douglass North and Barry Weingast would put it—apparently extracted by the monarchy's cred-

itors after the Napoleonic Wars. State officials had found ways to live
with (and occasionally circumvent) it, until the coming of the railroads with their unprecedented capital needs and high visibility.
Then the issue stood clearly posed. In order to finance construction
itself, the crown would have to convene a parliament: marshaling the
financial means to pursue a policy defined here as economically less
liberal would require political liberalization.[102] In the eyes of the
Vormärz crown, the price was simply too high. To be sure, convening
delegates from the provincial assemblies in 1842 signaled a small
concession by the king to liberal demands, but in reality little
changed. The Prussian state retained its illiberal characteristics and
railroad construction proceeded under the aegis of private enterprise.

Having made that choice, state officials then found it necessary to
cede to the railroads' demands for a measure of freedom from government supervision, if the much-desired railroads were to be built at all.
The railroad men, with cries of "alarmed capital," quickly turned the
government's difficult position to advantage and used it to good effect
in fending off regulation.[103] Time and again, they warned that state
efforts to regulate the industry would scare off investors. If the postmaster general persisted in his plans to pay below-market rates for the
railroads' services, officials of the Magdeburg-Leipzig Railroad
warned the king in 1836, it would imperil the entire enterprise.
"[R]elations with the Post Office must be placed on a better footing,"
declared the stockholders of the Elberfeld-Wittenberg Railroad in
1836, "if any railroad project is to be undertaken by a stockholders'
association in Prussia." The board of directors of the Rhine-Weser
Railroad raised similar concerns in 1838, warning the postmaster
general that concern among monied interests about the "postal question" threatened the viability of their project. If a state preferred
private capital to build the railroads, as seemed to be the case in
Prussia, wrote a railroad supporter in reviewing the new railroad law

---

[102] North and Weingast, "Constitutions and Commitment," and for details on these
widely known circumstances: von Reden, *Die Eisenbahnen Deutschlands*, 1. Abt., 2.
Abschnitt, pp. 303–4; "Die Verhandlungen," pp. 4, 14–15; Henderson, *The State and
the Industrial Revolution*, pp. 124, 163, 164–65; Tilly, "Political Economy," pp. 487–
89; Klee, *Preußische Eisenbahngeschichte*, pp. 10–11. As Thomas Nipperdey writes,
the 1820 agreement became "quite central" to Prussian politics in the *Vormärz* period.
Nipperdey, *Deutsche Geschichte*, p. 278.

[103] See also Gleim, "Zum dritten November 1888," pp. 291–96. I have borrowed the
term "alarmed capital" from Miller, *Railroads and the Granger Laws*, who draws it
from the mid-nineteenth-century American context. See chap. 6.

of 1838, then it had no choice but "to facilitate in every way" the business of private capital.[104]

David Hansemann, himself an advocate of state railroads, a director of the Rhenish Railroad, and briefly a "liberal" minister in 1848, was particularly vocal on the subject. He first raised the specter of a capital flight when the state issued its preliminary General Stipulations to govern the chartering of railroads in 1836,[105] and he elaborated on it in subsequent publications. "It cannot be emphasized enough," he wrote in his critique of the 1838 railroad law, "if the state wants to satisfy the great desire for railroads through private industry, then it must also give prospective capital all possible guarantees of lucrative and secure investment; this is the best means of attracting and keeping capital."[106] At the heart of the matter, as he saw it, lay a compromise:

> Since one does not presently want to apply this principle [state construction] and expects the construction of railroads by private enterprises without substantial aid from the state, then at the very least no burdens or obstacles should be imposed on the private entrepreneurs that are not absolutely necessary for the public good; on the contrary they should be granted all possible assistance in the construction and operation of railroads.[107]

Railroads plainly had political and military utility, Hansemann pointed out, and the state acknowledged their value. If, despite this fact, it wanted private parties to build them, then "the least that the state must do," he argued, "is to prescribe good statutory regulations for the railroad system that will infuse not only native but also foreign capitalists with lasting trust and in that way attract capital to the larger railroad projects as well."[108] In short, private capitalists would build the railroads but they would extract a price for their services. Even after the change of state policy in 1842, Hansemann urged state officials to regulate with a light hand, although he acknowledged that

---

[104] [Minutes], General-Versammlung der Elberfeld-Wittenbergischen Eisenbahn-Gesellschaft, July 29, 1836, in MA Nachl. 5, VIII; Enkling, *Die Stellung des Staates*, pp. 43, 51–52; "Das preußische Eisenbahngesetz," *Allgemeine Zeitung* (Augsburg), Außerordentliche Beilage, nos. 694–95, December 30, 1838, p. 2777.

[105] Hansemann, *Die Eisenbahnen und deren Aktionäre*, pp. 71, 98–100, 131.

[106] Hansemann, *Kritik des Preußischen Eisenbahn-Gesetzes*, pp. 110–11.

[107] Ibid., pp. 26–27.

[108] Ibid., pp. 24–25.

the new policy of aiding private railroads would entitle the state to regulate them more extensively.[109]

In a sense, then, the railroad era carried forward for a time the distinctive compromise between state and capital that had prevailed in Prussia since 1815. As Wolfgang Klee writes, "Economic progress had to take place, had to show entrepreneurs (especially in the Rhineland) that the desired economic conditions, which made other western countries seem like a liberal economic paradise to the capitalists, could also be achieved without a parliament or constitution."[110] As others observed at the time, it was a common conundrum in the age of internal improvements, and state construction offered one means of resolving it. Michel Chevalier mused over the dilemma during his American travels in 1835:

> The partisans of the monarchical principle maintain, that it is as powerful in promoting the greatness and welfare of peoples, and the progress of the human race, as the principle of independence and self-government, which prevails on this side [of] the Atlantic. For myself, I believe them to be in the right; but it is necessary that some tangible proofs of the correctness of their opinion should be given, if we do not wish that the contrary doctrine should make proselytes. It is by the fruits that the tree must be judged.[111]

Thus he admonished European sovereigns to divert their monies from war to internal improvements. "By putting off the day of these useful works, do not the sovereigns give countenance to the reasonings of those, who assert that the cause of kings is irreconcilable with the cause of nations?"[112] But the Prussian monarchy did not have the financial resources to seize the initiative and could not obtain them without liberalizing its polity. Hence, it found itself forced to concede a large measure of freedom in the economic sphere in order to promote "the greatness and welfare of peoples," as Chevalier put it, while resisting "the principle of independence and self-government."

In the United States, too, the pattern of railroad policy in the 1830s and 1840s reflected constraints imposed by the political structure itself. In a federal-legislative system, sectional conflict translated

---

[109] Hansemann, *Über die Ausführung des Preußischen Eisenbahn-Systems*, pp. 38, 49.

[110] Klee, *Preußische Eisenbahngeschichte*, p. 100.

[111] Chevalier, *Society, Manners and Politics*, p. 275.

[112] Ibid., p. 276.

into constitutional conflict in Congress, which effectively reduced the national government's powers over internal improvements from the early 1830s on. The state governments, therefore, stepped into the breach. And because greater formal representation and more distinct separation of powers allowed the state legislatures to dominate the policy-making process, a different dynamic drove the policy-making process in the United States, for the state legislatures proved, above all, more receptive to competing political demands.

A quick look at the fate of groups that sought protection from railroad competition through conventional political channels provides a sense of the critical differences in the two policy-making processes. In Massachusetts, the stagecoach companies that opposed construction of the Boston and Worcester Railroad and a wide array of their allies formed a political coalition in the legislature. In this way, they achieved a "smashing defeat," as Stephen Salsbury puts it, for they managed to block legislative approval of the charter in early 1830 (although they were defeated the next year).[113] If turnpike companies could not prevent legislative approval of a railroad charter, as noted earlier, they often salvaged something by having provisions inserted in railroad charters that required the railroad to buy the turnpike or to pay damages. Canal owners, too, engaged in lengthy legislative and legal battles to preserve their business. In each case, relatively easy access to the legislature and the utility of log-rolling made the difference.

In Prussia, in contrast, the structure of the state gave state officials not only an overriding interest in resisting pleas for protection, but also the capability to do so, for it offered railroad opponents fewer "veto points" at which to apply pressure.[114] Such groups, accordingly, met with less success than their counterparts in the United States. The mine owners, who, as noted above, petitioned the minister of the interior in 1826 to deny a charter to a competing mine for a horse-powered railroad, learned early on that central state officials would not lend a sympathetic ear to pleas for protection. State officials turned aside their protests and granted the concession.[115] Fourteen

---

[113] Salsbury, *The State, the Investor, and the Railroad*, pp. 70–75.

[114] On the concept of veto points, see Ellen Immergut, "The Rules of the Game: The Logic of Health Policy-Making in France, Switzerland, and Sweden," in *Structuring Politics*, ed. Steinmo, Thelen, and Longstreth, pp. 57–89.

[115] Enkling, *Die Stellung des Staates*, p. 21.

years later, when the freight haulers on the Leipziger Road petitioned the Prussian king for protection, the ministers sent an unambiguous signal that they meant to encourage railroad construction. Finance Minister Albrecht Graf von Alvensleben recommended that the king reject their petition. "A claim to compensation . . . is clearly not warranted," he argued,

> since the advantageous circumstances that have obtained until now have served them well, not as a result of a vested right (*eines wohlerworbenen Rechts*), but merely because of the propitiousness of actual conditions, and any change resulting from the loss of [their current advantages] entails no infringement of rights.[116]

Customary rights, in other words, would not be recognized. Although he acknowledged the plight of those facing railroad competition, Minister von Alvensleben refused to intervene. Much like Supreme Court Chief Justice Roger B. Taney three years earlier in the Charles River Bridge case,[117] von Alvensleben feared that a grant of protection would create financial obstacles to technological progress:

> If one were to acknowledge a right to compensation on the part of the tavern owners or other tradesmen who are suffering as a result of the railroad construction, such as shipowners, wagoners, forwarding agents, it would give rise to undeniable claims, the settlement of which would make the development of this new means of communication impracticable.[118]

The king agreed, in this as in other cases.[119] Pragmatic concerns, rather than economic ideology, drove the monarchy's response, and petitioners had as yet no recourse to a national legislature. Even in the midst of the 1848 revolution a few years later, the shipowner who sought to protect his business on the Elbe encountered indifference, for the interior minister merely referred his complaint to the finance minister and suggested that, if river traffic on the Elbe was declining

---

[116] Minister von Alvensleben to [Friedrich Wilhelm IV], November 23, 1840, in ZStAM, Rep. 2.2.1, no. 29485, p. 2r.

[117] Kutler, *Privilege and Creative Destruction*, p. 93.

[118] Minister von Alvensleben to [Friedrich Wilhelm IV], November 23, 1840, in ZStAM, Rep. 2.2.1, no. 29485, pp. 2r–3r.

[119] [Friedrich Wilhelm IV] to Gastwirthe C. Hüttenrauch und Genossen zu Magdeburg, December 21, 1840, ZStAM, Rep. 2.2.1, no. 29485, p. 7r. For other examples, see ibid., pp. 8r–22r.

because of railroad competition, the shipper might be advised to try the Oder River instead.[120]

In short, the effective expression of interests depended on the nature of the political structure. In the context of a unitary-bureaucratic state, railroad opponents had far fewer avenues through which to defend their interests. As a result, the Prussian ministries resisted such demands more easily than American legislatures did. American railroad promoters, in contrast, could usually marshal the political strength to obtain railroad charters, but their critics or opponents, equally empowered by the franchise, often proved capable of imposing constraints on them. Log-rolling in the legislatures, combined with the competitive pressures of federalism, made obtaining a railroad charter relatively easy in the United States. As Dionysius Lardner observed in 1850:

> Nothing could be more simple, expeditious, and cheap than the means of obtaining an act for the establishment of a railway company in America. A public meeting is held, at which the project is discussed and adopted. A deputation is appointed to apply to the legislature, which grants the act without expense, delay, or official difficulty. The principle of competition is not brought into play, as in France; nor is there any investigation as to the expediency of the project . . . as in England. No other guarantee or security is required from the company than the payment by the shareholders of a certain amount constituting the first call.[121]

Log-rolling, meanwhile, encouraged the chartering of a multiplicity of railroads, for the practice entailed the passage of packages of railroad (or other) charters, each of which individually catered to a particular section of the state and which as a package garnered enough votes to ensure passage.[122] Together, these aspects of the American politi-

---

[120] Votum, Ministry of the Interior to the Finance Ministry, March 26, 1848, ZStAM, Rep. 77, Tit. 258a, no. 30, vol. 1, pp. 328r–v.

[121] Lardner, *Railway Economy*, p. 413.

[122] Scheiber, "Federalism and the American Economic Order," p. 89; Hartz, *Economic Policy*, pp. 44–45. Log-rolling also produced packages of state aid for existing projects. This is how the Baltimore and Ohio Railroad, in coalition with interests in the western part of the state, overcame opposition in the Maryland legislature and obtained a $1 million state stock subscription in 1835. *Tenth Annual Report . . . of the Baltimore and Ohio Rail Road Company*, p. 5. Log-rolling also involved banks as well as transportation projects and sometimes linked the two. Pennsylvania's 1835 charter for the second Bank of the United States, for example, required it to subscribe to the stock of ten transportation companies (mainly railroads and canals) and to make

cal structure encouraged early and rapid railroad construction and they explain why the United States built so much mileage so early. But when opposition to particular projects reached sufficient proportions, the corollary came into play: log-rolling also generated regulatory measures.

Two incidents involving competing railroad projects in the United States and Prussia during the 1840s provide deeper insight into this essential difference in the two policy-making processes. The first concerns the origins of the transit tax on the Pennsylvania Railroad and illustrates the way that legislative policy-making itself encouraged interventionist economic policies. In 1846 the Baltimore and Ohio Railroad applied to the Pennsylvania legislature for a charter to extend its road from Cumberland, Maryland, to Pittsburgh. At the same time, however, Philadelphia interests backed the proposed Pennsylvania Railroad, which would run parallel to the state works between Harrisburg and Pittsburgh. With the western and southwestern counties of Pennsylvania solidly behind the Baltimore and Ohio, and the eastern region lobbying for the Pennsylvania Railroad, the rival railroad projects unleashed political conflict of tremendous proportions. At one point, twenty-two western counties threatened to secede from Pennsylvania if the Baltimore and Ohio Railroad did not receive a charter.[123]

The Pennsylvania legislature ultimately resolved the conflict with a three-part compromise. First, it provisionally granted both charters, thus accommodating both east and west. Then, to the satisfaction of Philadelphia interests, it made the Baltimore and Ohio's charter contingent on the Pennsylvania Railroad's progress in raising capital and getting construction underway; if it failed to do so within a specified period, the Baltimore and Ohio's charter would take effect. Finally, the legislature inserted the provision in the Pennsylvania Railroad's charter that required it to pay a transit tax on freight. This was, in effect, the price of consent from the western counties. They not only stood to gain little from construction of the Pennsylvania Railroad but also feared higher taxes if traffic declined on the state canals. The

---

"grants of financial assistance" to another eleven turnpikes and roads. Hartz, *Economic Policy*, pp. 46–47. For a contemporary criticism of the practice, see [Henshaw], *Remarks Upon the Rights and Powers of Corporations.*

[123] Hungerford, *Story of the Baltimore & Ohio Railroad*, pp. 241–42; John F. Stover, *History of the Baltimore and Ohio Railroad* (West Lafayette, Ind.: Purdue University Press, 1987), pp. 66–67; Hartz, *Economic Policy*, pp. 42–44.

railroad's promoters advocated the tax themselves, Louis Hartz notes, "as a polemical weapon for breaking opposition in the west." The railroad transit tax served, in effect, as a consolation prize.[124]

In short, because the liberal structure of the American state empowered conflicting interests at the level of the state governments, the Pennsylvania Railroad received its charter but also labored under a transit tax. Noting how the Prussian state, once it had committed itself to private construction, stepped in to protect the railroads from competing interests, German historian Thomas Nipperdey concludes that "[i]n a fully democratic order the railroad would scarcely have been built."[125] But the American experience in the antebellum state legislatures suggests differently. Not only would more railroads have been built in Prussia; more of them would have paid canal tolls, transit taxes, and the like.

In Prussia, the competing projects for a line to connect Berlin with Hamburg not only inflamed urban rivalry but touched off a similar controversy in the early 1840s. In the context of a different political structure, however, the controversy took a different course. At issue in this case was whether the railroad should run along the right (northern) or left (southern) bank of the Elbe River. The right-bank project would mainly cross territory belonging to Prussia and Mecklenburg; the route along the left bank would pass through Hannover. The decision regarding the railroad's location took on extra importance for the cities on either side of the river, because, as was well understood at the time, bridging the Elbe would be difficult. Hence, the cities on the opposite side of the river from the railroad would effectively be denied access to it for some time to come. This was true even for a city as far away as Magdeburg, which lay to the southwest of Berlin. Businessmen there urgently desired a connection with Hamburg and a railroad located on the right bank of the Elbe would hinder their access to it.[126]

One of the two principle contenders to build the Hamburg line was the Berlin-Potsdam Railroad, a short line whose directors wanted to build an extension along the left bank of the Elbe to Hamburg, so that

---

[124] Hungerford, *Story of the Baltimore & Ohio Railroad*, pp. 242–44; Stover, *History of the Baltimore and Ohio Railroad*, p. 68; Hartz, *Economic Policy*, pp. 43, 52–53, 267–68. Had the Baltimore and Ohio's charter taken effect, it would have borne a tax on both passengers and freight. *By-Laws of the . . . Pennsylvania Railroad Company*, p. 26.

[125] Nipperdey, *Deutsche Geschichte*, p. 192.

[126] Klee, *Preußische Eisenbahngeschichte*, p. 59.

they could make a connection south to Magdeburg as well. The other was a committee composed mainly of merchants and bankers from Berlin, who proposed building along the right bank.[127] The Berlin-Anhalt Railroad, meanwhile, joined forces with the right-bank committee in opposing the Berlin-Potsdam Railroad's plans to extend its road to Magdeburg. The Berlin-Anhalt had earlier ceded to the state's request that it run its line from Berlin to a junction on the Magdeburg-Leipzig Railroad rather than to the Leipzig-Dresden Railroad in Saxony, and it viewed the projected Potsdam-Magdeburg Railroad as a competing line that should not be allowed under the monopoly provisions of the 1838 railroad law.[128] The Berlin-Anhalt directors insisted, moreover, that they had been offered the route to Magdeburg "as *compensation*" for giving up the route to the Leipzig-Dresden Railroad.[129] State officials did not agree, but in late 1840 they nonetheless held confidential discussions "with two especially influential members" of the Berlin-Anhalt's board, during which they offered to let the company build a line to the Leipzig-Dresden Railroad after all, if its directors would only drop their opposition to the Berlin-Potsdam's plans. They refused.[130]

Caught between competing interests, the Prussian ministers reached an interim solution much like the Pennsylvania legislature's. They notified the right-bank committee informally in early 1841 that it would receive the charter, but only if negotiations with Mecklenburg over its precise location reached a successful conclusion and if the committee demonstrated the project's technical viability and raised the necessary capital within six months. If not, then the southern route would be taken. They informed the Berlin-Potsdam Railroad, however, that, even if it obtained a charter for the Berlin-Hamburg line, it should not count on obtaining one for the Magdeburg connection.[131] They likewise notified the Berlin-Anhalt Rail-

---

[127] Ibid., p. 59. Cf. *Bericht des Comité zur Begründung eines Actien-Vereins für die Eisenbahn-Verbindung zwischen Berlin und Hamburg* (Berlin, 1842), to which is appended a thirty-page report by the Berlin banker, Georg Ferdinand Oppert, on the advantages of a right-bank location. Hamburg did not initially show much interest in the project. Von Reden, *Die Eisenbahnen Deutschlands*, 1. Abt., 2. Abschnitt, p. 352.

[128] Board of Directors of the Berlin-Anhalt Railroad to the king, July 25, 1840, and October 25, 1840, in ZStAM, Rep. 93E, no. 3305/1, vol. 2, pp. 29r–32v, 34r–35v.

[129] Board of Directors of the Berlin-Anhalt Railroad to the Finance Minister, February 16, 1841, in ZStAM, Rep. 93E, no. 3305/1, vol. 2, p. 88v (original italics).

[130] Friedrich Wilhelm to Finance Minister von Alvensleben, December 7, 1840, in ZStAM, Rep. 93E, no. 3305/1, vol. 2, p. 28r.

[131] Friedrich Wilhelm to Finance Minister von Alvensleben, December 10, 1840, in

road that, although it had no right to contest the chartering of a line from Potsdam to Magdeburg, it could rest assured that no charter would be granted for the time being.[132]

Since the location of the road was still not definitively settled, the petitions discussed earlier poured in from the towns and provincial governments on both sides of the river, and the Berlin-Potsdam Railroad undertook an extensive lobbying campaign on behalf of a left-bank railroad. Before state officials had given the nod to the right-bank project, the Berlin-Potsdam's technical director, Baron (and Captain) von Puttkammer, had mobilized local governments to petition the finance minister on behalf of the southern route. He had also tried to interest the minister of the interior in a stock subscription and asked him to intervene with the king on behalf of the project. He urged the minister to help, he explained, because he feared "the influence of the Berlin-Anhalt road and of Minister Rother, who has an interest in it on behalf of the Overseas Trading Company (*Seehandlung*)."[133] Von Puttkammer did indeed have cause to worry. August Bloch, a high-ranking official at the *Seehandlung*, sat on the Berlin-Anhalt's board of directors and may have been one of the two "influential" members with whom the ministers had held confidential discussions; after the right-bank project finally got official approval, its stockholders expressly thanked Bloch for his assistance.[134] Meanwhile, when state officials decided provisionally to support the right-bank project, von Puttkammer's efforts intensified. Now he took it upon himself to seek support from the Hannover government, a fact that the minister for foreign affairs found "remarkable" (*auffallend*), since it was public knowledge that the state had given the rival project

ZStAM, Rep. 93E, no. 3305/1, vol. 2, p. 37r; Friedrich Wilhelm to Finance Minister von Alvensleben, January 14, 1841, in ibid., pp. 41r–v, and in ZStAM, Rep. 90a, K.III.3, no. 7, vol. 1, pp. 15r–v; and Finance Minister to the Comité zur Begründung eines Actien-Vereins für die Eisenbahn-Verbindung zwischen Berlin und Hamburg, January 28, 1841, in ZStAM, Rep. 93E, no. 3305/1, vol. 2, pp. 62r–63r.

[132] Finance Minister to Board of Directors of the Berlin-Anhalt Railroad, January 28, 1841, in ZStAM, Rep. 93E, no. 3305/1, vol. 2, p. 60r. The state finally granted a charter for the line in 1846 to a separate company which then purchased the Berlin-Potsdam line.

[133] Baron von Puttkammer to Minister of the Interior, August 27, 1840, in ZStAM, Rep. 77, Tit. 258a, no. 30, vol. 1, pp. 52r–53r.

[134] *Protocoll der ersten Generalversammlung der Actionairs der Berlin-Hamburger Eisenbahn-Gesellschaft nebst Bericht des Ausschusses an dieselben* (Berlin: E. S. Mittler, 1845), pp. 4, 10, 12.

its sanction.[135] The company also went ahead and solicited stock subscriptions, raising five million *Taler* in five days.[136]

By the end of 1841, the Prussian state had made official its support for the right-bank project, it had negotiated an agreement with the governments whose territory the road would cross, and the entire line had been surveyed.[137] But Baron von Puttkammer and the Berlin-Potsdam Railroad still did not give up. In late 1842, public controversy over the merits of the right- and left-bank routes resurfaced when the standing committees met in Berlin to debate railroad policy.[138] Now von Puttkammer and his allies attempted to circumvent the finance minister by taking their case directly to this quasi-representative body. But to no avail. The marshal presiding over the meeting merely referred the matter to the minister of the interior, who referred it back to the finance minister.[139] With that, the controversy finally came to a close. The right-bank committee received a charter for the Berlin-Hamburg Railroad and opened its books for stock subscriptions on January 1, 1843.[140]

The Prussian state's solution to the controversy over the Berlin-Hamburg line superficially resembled the compromise reached in the Pennsylvania legislature. In both cases, one project received the go-ahead and the other was put on hold until it became clear whether the first road would materialize. But it also differed in important respects. Missing, apparently, was opposition from those who moved goods on the river. Or perhaps they realized that state officials would not inter-

[135] Minister of Foreign Affairs to Finance Minister von Alvensleben, March 6, 1841, in ZStAM, Rep. 93E, no. 3305/1, vol. 2, pp. 140r–v.

[136] Board of Directors of the Berlin-Potsdam Railroad Company to Finance Minister von Alvensleben, July 16, 1841, in ZStAM, Rep. 93E, no. 3305/1, vol. 2, pp. 207r–23r and in ZStAM, Rep. 77, Tit. 258a, no. 30, vol. 1, pp. 87r–100r. The subscribers were only required to pay in one-quarter percent immediately, however. *Circular*, Berlin, Potsdam, and Brandenburg, August, 1840, in ZStAM, Rep. 77, Tit. 258a, no. 30, vol. 1, pp. 54r–55r.

[137] *Königlichen privilegierten Berlinischen Zeitung*, Außerordentliche Beilage, no. 301, December 24, 1841, in ZStAM, Rep. 90a, K.III.3, no. 7, vol. 1, pp. 13r–v; von Reden, *Die Eisenbahnen Deutschlands*, 1. Abt., 2. Abschnitt, p. 361. The governments involved were those of Mecklenburg-Schwerin, Denmark, and the free cities of Lübeck and Hamburg. The treaty, signed November 8, 1841, was published in the *Gesetzsammlung*, no. 2564, and is described in von Reden, *Die Eisenbahnen Deutschlands*, 1. Abt., 2. Abschnitt, pp. 353–59.

[138] Von Reden, *Die Eisenbahnen Deutschlands*, 1. Abt., 2. Abschnitt, p. 363.

[139] Minister of the Interior Graf von Arnim to Finance Minister von Bodelschwingh and to the Board of Directors of the Berlin-Potsdam Railroad, November 29, 1842, in ZStAM, Rep. 77, Tit. 258a, no. 30, vol. 1, pp. 123r–v.

[140] Von Reden, *Die Eisenbahnen Deutschlands*, 1. Abt., 2. Abschnitt, p. 364.

vene on their behalf, for the ministers, as we have seen, generally declined to do so. Supporters of the Berlin-Potsdam's plans, moreover, despite their apparent numbers, did not extract a *quid pro quo* for acquiescing to construction of the Berlin-Hamburg Railroad on the right bank of the Elbe, as supporters of the Baltimore and Ohio did with respect to the Pennsylvania Railroad. Despite their impressive efforts to pressure or circumvent the ministers, the political resources that they brought to bear proved largely ineffectual in the Prussian political context. Von Puttkammer's efforts cannot be faulted, but log-rolling and coalition-building did not work well without the independent points of access—and, therefore, political leverage—offered by a legislature. Prussian officials did not have unlimited room to maneuver, but, once the right-bank project had received official sanction, the Berlin-Hamburg Railroad, unlike the Pennsylvania Railroad, went ahead unencumbered, even though it missed several deadlines for raising the necessary capital.[141]

When federalism is given proper weight, the early years of railroad development suggest that economic liberalism prevailed to a lesser extent in the United States than in Prussia, precisely because of the different constraints imposed by the two political structures on policy-making in a capitalist context. Because both economies were largely capitalist, private interests, through their control over the allocation of resources, set limits on the exercise of state power; as a consequence, the Prussian central state and the American state legislatures, each in their own way, engaged in a process of negotiation with private interests as the first railroads were built. But the fundamental weakness of the unitary-bureaucratic Prussian state became apparent when it encountered the new demands of industrial capitalism, for the peculiarities of the Prussian situation—a largely illiberal state seeking to preserve itself in an industrial capitalist context—hindered promotion and, therefore, discouraged regulation. The American state governments, in contrast, entered the fray firmly empowered by a tradition of state promotion *and* regulation, precisely because of the United States' more liberal structure. Behind the veil of

---

[141] *Protocoll der ersten Generalversammlung der Actionairs der Berlin-Hamburger Eisenbahn-Gesellschaft*, p. 9. The company had difficulty raising the necessary capital (8 million *Taler*) until Mecklenburg and Hamburg finally subscribed to 1.5 million *Taler* each; typically, Prussia did not invest in the line. The company did not open stock subscriptions to the general public, which probably contributed to its problems. Von Reden, *Die Eisenbahnen Deutschlands*, 1. Abt., 2. Abschnitt, p. 365.

federalism lay a moderately "statist" pattern of industrialization, driven by the exigencies of legislative policy-making and interstate competition. This serves as a clear warning not to assume that economic and political liberalism necessarily come as a package. Neither myth—neither antebellum laissez-faire nor *Vormärz* étatism—obtained in practice and, when the policy-making consequences of the two political structures are understood, there is no longer any reason to think that either should have.

This is one way in which appreciating the subtle, yet pervasive, influence of the ambient political structure enriches historical (and, therefore, contemporary) understanding of the process of industrial change. But the story does not end here. The following chapters show how the American and Prussian structures penetrated even deeper, shaping the organizational and technological foundations of the industry itself.

4

Organizing Railroad Interests

FROM the outset, as American and Prussian railroad men grappled with the new and rapidly evolving technology, they sought to address common problems collectively. Beginning in the late 1840s, railroad men in both countries set about to give permanence to their informal efforts by establishing formal associations. But their achievements differed radically, for Prussian railroads organized a permanent national association some forty years earlier than American railroads. Prussian railroad men launched a national association in 1846, and within a year it had extended membership to all German railroads. By the early 1850s, it was busily standardizing the operations and technology of German railroads, and it retained its vitality through the remainder of the century. In the United States, in contrast, railroad men organized a number of associations for the same purposes, but throughout the antebellum period their efforts foundered. Indeed, as chapter 6 affirms, the pattern delineated here held for nearly forty years. Not until 1886 did American railroads prove able to build and *sustain* a national association.

Understanding why Prussian railroad men proved more adept than their American counterparts at building interfirm institutions is important, because organized interests historically have been potent forces both politically and economically. In the realm of politics, conflict over the organization of interests delineates the boundary between state and society and, therefore, helps to define at any given moment what counts as "state" and what as "society."[1] Where the state-society boundary lies on the social landscape matters, in turn, in the economic realm, for it shapes the institutional underpinnings of economic performance. In practical terms, the historical result of

[1] On the contested nature of state-society or public-private boundaries, see Graham K. Wilson, *Interest Groups* (Oxford: Basil Blackwell, 1990), pp. 1–23; Timothy Mitchell, "The Limits of the State: Beyond Statist Approaches and Their Critics," *American Political Science Review* 85 (March 1991): 77–96; John Bendix, Bertell Ollman, Bartholomew H. Sparrow, and Timothy P. Mitchell, "Controversy: Going Beyond the State?" *American Political Science Review* 86 (December 1992): 1007–21.

this ongoing conflict in the nineteenth century was the varying degrees of organization that characterized industrial capitalism in different countries.

For the economic performance of the railroads (indeed, of industrial capitalism, generally), interfirm relations mattered a great deal. The multitude of railroad companies constituted the first distinctively modern technological system, and by definition, the manifold parts of large-scale, capital-intensive systems had to be coordinated and made coherent—systematized—if they were to yield economies of scale. For private railroads, this entailed not only the now-familiar process of creating managerial hierarchies within the corporation;[2] it also meant agreeing on construction norms, so that traffic could flow from one line to the next, and setting up procedures for handling through traffic. These tasks required cooperation among companies, usually carried out through regional, national, or international associations. But capital intensity, manifested in high fixed costs, made cooperation more difficult (see chapter 1). Under the new competitive conditions, the railroads responded to hard times by slashing prices and fighting to capture even more traffic from their competitors. The nature of the business, in short, made interfirm cooperation more critical, yet more difficult to achieve.

But the new institutionalism in business and economic history has proven better at chronicling the emergence of economic institutions and explaining their function, once in place, than it has at showing why they emerged in the first place. Indeed, the common assumption is that the function of economic institutions, once filtered through marketplace competition, explains their origins. As Tolliday and Zeitlin write, "most analyses of business behaviour . . . regard the conduct of the firm as a more or less functional response to changing environmental pressures."[3] By this line of reasoning, the few historians who have explored the emergence of trade associations portray

---

[2] See Chandler, *The Visible Hand*, pp. 81–197; Kocka, "Eisenbahnverwaltung."

[3] Tolliday and Zeitlin, "Introduction: Employers and Industrial Relations," p. 1. See also Gordon, "Critical Legal Histories," p. 84; Smith, "Political Jurisprudence," pp. 96–99; Marc Schneiberg and J. Rogers Hollingsworth, "Can Transaction Cost Economics Explain Trade Associations?" in *The Firm as a Nexus of Treaties*, ed. Masahiko Aoki, Bo Gustafsson, and Oliver E. Williamson (London: Sage Publications, 1990), pp. 320–46.

it as a response to the changing demands of the business environment. As Louis Galambos writes in one such study:

> To the cotton manufacturer [in the early twentieth century], the
> new forces creating modern America and transforming his own
> industry posed a serious threat. They were changing the political
> and economic world with which he was familiar and in which he
> had been able to achieve some success. Ideas that had seemed per-
> fectly reasonable in an earlier context now seemed out of date.
> Institutions that had solved his problems before now proved to be
> weak and unreliable.
>
> Responding to these difficulties the cotton manufacturers cre-
> ated a new type of trade group, the "service association."[4]

Relying implicitly on an evolutionary paradigm, he conveys the im-
pression that businessmen responded without fail to environmental
demands, doing so automatically, appropriately, and successfully.

But this paradigm provides little guidance in understanding why
Prussian railroad men succeeded so early in building a national association and why forty years elapsed before American railroad men
followed suit. Given the close parallels in American and Prussian
railroad development, it is not at all obvious that functional requirements in the industry differed dramatically enough to account for the
forty-year difference or that they varied sufficiently in time and place
to account for the diversity of associations created in the United
States. The greatest difference lay in the scale of construction, but
when American railroads did organize in the 1880s, it must be emphasized, the industry was not only much larger than in these years
but also labored under much greater competitive pressure. If American railroad men, moreover, did not actually need any of these associations until they succeeded in forming one that lasted, this merely
raises a new question: how could they have been so mistaken in their
impressive efforts to form associations earlier? Since the work of
Mancur Olson, moreover, it is well understood that economic associations do not form spontaneously—not even in countries such as
the U.S. and the Germanies, whose citizens have traditionally displayed a propensity to form associations (*Verbände*), and not even

---

[4] Louis Galambos, *Competition and Cooperation: The Emergence of a National
Trade Association* (Baltimore: Johns Hopkins University Press, 1966), p. 55.

when the benefits to be gained are apparent to all, as they were to early railroad men in both countries. In one form or another, there were always collective-action problems to overcome.[5]

The Prussians' early success and the Americans' manifold difficulties reveal another way in which political structure mattered, for the type of structure they dealt with—federal or unitary—and the governmental level at which policy was made, this chapter argues, were critical. Efforts to organize antebellum American and *Vormärz* Prussian railroad interests actually followed a remarkably similar dynamic, one distinguished in both countries by two phases of associational activity. In the first phase, cooperative relations developed informally among the pioneer railroad companies in both countries, as they turned to one another for advice and as state officials called them together for collective discussions of railroad operations. In a few instances, these experimental efforts produced the first functional or regional institutions in the industry. During the second phase, however, the American and Prussian paths diverged, for the two distinctive state structures and the thrust of state policy, as we have seen, differed markedly at any moment in time. Prussian railroad companies built a permanent national association much earlier, this chapter argues, because they dealt with a unitary state that began to turn interventionist in the mid- to late 1840s. As a consequence, they also standardized technology and operations much earlier. Antebellum American railroad men likewise sought to derive strength from unity, and they organized an impressive number of associations to fend off or reshape interventionist policies. But their efforts, in contrast, repeatedly foundered, for no single institution could meet all of their needs simultaneously. When federal officials occasionally abandoned their customary practice of proceeding consensually, political expedience required building national institutions. As the railroads crossed state lines with increasing frequency from the 1850s on, their operational needs called for regional associations. Yet,

---

[5] Mancur Olson, *The Logic of Collective Action: Public Goods and the Theory of Groups* (Cambridge: Harvard University Press, 1965; reprint ed., 1971); Claus Offe and Helmut Wiesenthal, "Two Logics of Collective Action: Theoretical Notes on Social Class and Organization Form," *Political Power and Social Theory* 1 (1980): 67–115; North, *Structure and Change*, pp. 10–11; Wolfgang Streeck, "Interest Heterogeneity and Organizing Capacity: Two Class Logics of Collective Action," Centro de Estudios Avanzados en Ciencias Sociales, Working Paper 1990/2, June 1990.

through the 1870s, the most troublesome policies came from the state legislatures and, for the task of defending railroad interests in this quarter, state-level associations seemed most suitable. In the fragmented American political structure, in other words, a multitude of state legislatures wielded more (but not exclusive) power over more (but not all) aspects of railroad policy than the federal government did. This made it inordinately difficult to sustain any association.

To highlight the political incentives that drove association-building is not to deny, of course, that industry problems increasingly demanded cooperation from the late 1840s on. By the mid-1840s, as noted in chapter 1, regional concentrations of railroads had emerged in Prussia around Berlin and Cologne and in other German states. Where the density of track was relatively high, some competition was beginning to be felt. To the south of Berlin, for example, the Magdeburg-Leipzig Railroad lowered its rates in 1845 because of competitive pressure from its neighbor, the Berlin-Anhalt Railroad.[6] Then between 1845 and 1850 new construction bound together these regional fragments and a Prussian—indeed, a German—system began to emerge. As that occurred, through traffic increased and competition intensified.

During the same years, American railroads also entered a new stage of maturity. After the economic hard times of the late 1830s and the early 1840s, the pace of railroad construction picked up nationwide in the late 1840s. With completion of the four great east-west trunk-line railroads between 1851 and 1854 and construction in the Midwest, increased opportunities for through traffic intensified competition, at the same time introducing unprecedented operational problems. The strong market for railroad securities in the early 1850s, meanwhile, prompted the more conservative of American railroad men to warn against speculation and overconstruction.[7] To-

[6] *Geschäftsbericht des Directoriums der Magdeburg-Cöthen-Halle-Leipziger Eisenbahn-Gesellschaft für die Zeit vom 8.4.1844 bis zum 7.4.1845,* in StA Magdeburg, Rep. C20Ib, no. 2851, vol. 3, pp. 19v–19/11.

[7] Alfred A. Chandler, Jr., *Henry Varnum Poor: Business Editor, Analyst, and Reformer* (Cambridge: Harvard University Press, 1956), pp. 103–27. The suddenness with which trunk-line competition arrived may be gauged from the railroads' annual reports; see, for example, *Twenty-Fifth Annual Report of the President and Directors to the Stockholders of the Baltimore and Ohio Rail Road Company* (Baltimore: John Murphy & Co., 1851), pp. 3–4, 18–23. For comments on the dangers of speculation and overconstruction, see *Twenty-Fifth Annual Report of the Directors of the Boston and*

gether, financial scandals and safety lapses put the industry squarely in the public eye.[8] Railroad associations in both countries, accordingly, sought to promote "harmony," as the Americans put it, which meant either standardizing railroad technology and operations or dampening competition.

But the general condition of the industry during these decades does not explain why railroad men tackled the problems of harmony precisely when they did, why they organized at one level—state, regional, or national—rather than another, or why their efforts succeeded or failed. Answering these questions requires due attention to the political context in which they acted. What helped the railroad men to surmount the obstacles to collective action and to standardize railroad technology and operations was government action or the threat of it—the "gun behind the door," in Thomas McCraw's apt phrase,[9] and what defined the scope of their efforts was the structure of the state or, more precisely, the level at which policy was made in that structure. That Prussian railroad men succeeded so quickly, while the Americans found it impossible to maintain their associations, reflected the special incentives and obstacles to collective action inherent in the two political structures.

Yet, even the most advantageous political structure did not empower the railroads to solve all of their problems collectively. American and Prussian railroads alike pursued the second kind of harmony, seeking to dampen competition through collective action. But in neither country were regional or national associations able to deal effectively with the new competition that marked the era of industrial capitalism. The centripetal force of interventionist policymaking at the national level, in other words, enabled the railroads to harmonize their technology and operations, but it did not prove strong enough to overcome the centrifugal pressures of competition.

Worcester Railroad Corporation, for the Year Ending November 30, 1854 (Boston: David Clapp, 1855), p. 14.

[8] John K. Towles, "Early Railroad Monopoly and Discrimination in Rhode Island, 1835–55," *Yale Review* 18 (November 1909): 307–19; Merk, "Eastern Antecedents," pp. 7–8; Kirkland, *Men, Cities, and Transportation,* 2:233–35.

[9] Thomas K. McCraw, *Prophets of Regulation: Charles Francis Adams, Louis D. Brandeis, James M. Landis, Alfred E. Kahn* (Cambridge: Harvard University Press, Belknap Press, 1984), p. 35.

The First Stirrings of Interfirm Cooperation

In both countries, informal relations developed quickly, as early railroad men turned to their colleagues in the industry for advice. A good deal of information could, of course, be obtained in printed form. As the next chapter shows, the first books devoted to railroads appeared in Europe in 1825, and the pool of printed sources—books and specialized periodicals—expanded rapidly over the next two decades. But published accounts could not convey a hands-on sense of a new technology, and even the most up-to-date editions quickly became outdated, because technological practice was changing so rapidly. The early works, moreover, had little to say about the *business* of running a railroad. Thus the novelty of the technology and the complexity of its operation encouraged railroad promoters to develop an extensive network of personal contacts.

In both countries, the earliest long-distance lines quickly became "schools of practice" that drew railroad men from far and wide to discuss the latest methods of construction and operation.[10] The directors of Prussia's first long-distance line, the Magdeburg-Leipzig Railroad, relied heavily on the first major German line, the Leipzig-Dresden Railroad in neighboring Saxony, for operating advice and practical training, as they prepared to open their line in the late 1830s.[11] One of their directors, *Stadtrath* (City Councilor) Costenoble, toured the Leipzig-Dresden in 1836, and the following year he notified its directors that the Magdeburg-Leipzig's treasurer (*Rendant*) would be visiting them as well: He is coming, "just as I did, to attend school" on the Leipzig-Dresden Railroad, Costenoble ex-

10 I have borrowed the term "school of practice" from Hill, *Roads, Rails, and Waterways*, p. 105. See below.

11 The two companies necessarily enjoyed close relations, for they constructed and operated jointly a small piece of the Magdeburg-Leipzig Railroad that lay in Saxony. For details on that aspect of their relationship, see Board of Directors (Directorium), Magdeburg-Cöthen-Halle-Leipzig Railroad (hereafter, BD/ML), signed Francke, Chairman, to Board of Directors, Leipzig-Dresden Railroad (hereafter, BD/LD), March 5, 1838, in Staatsarchiv Dresden (hereafter cited as StA Dresden), RBD Dresden, no. 7657, pp. 156r–v; BD/LD, signed Gustav Harkort, Chairman, and F. Brusse, General Agent, to District Director Dr. von Falkenstein, State Railroad Commissioner, June 6, 1838, in StA Dresden, [Finance Ministry], Loc. 37544, no. 386a, p. 26r. On early relations between the two companies, see von der Leyen, "Entstehung der Magdeburg-Leipziger Eisenbahn," pp. 215–83; Beyer, *Leipzig und die Anfänge des deutschen Eisenbahnbaus.*

plained. "We must, of course, learn everything from you."[12] The same
year another director, the state engineer Friedrich Mellin who later
moved to the finance ministry, sought advice from the Leipzig-
Dresden Railroad's chief engineer.[13] As their project neared completion in the late 1830s, the Magdeburg-Leipzig directors solicited information from the Leipzig-Dresden on a range of subjects: their
experience in importing English locomotives; their operating rules;
and their coke-manufacturing techniques. After sending a man to
train at their facilities and borrowing coal for their own experiments,
the Magdeburg-Leipzig directors decided to make their own coke for
locomotive fuel: "we intend, as we already have in so many things, to
follow your example."[14] Many times, the Magdeburg-Leipzig obtained experienced locomotive engineers from the Leipzig-Dresden
and exchanged information about employees and on the status of
negotiations with postal authorities.[15] By 1842, the Magdeburg-
Leipzig had transcended its status as a novice. In that year it loaned
the Leipzig-Dresden Railroad one of its English locomotives, together
with a locomotive engineer to make trial runs. The Magdeburg-
Leipzig refused payment for the favor, a gesture reflecting not only
gratitude for a copy of the test report but more generally, one sus-
pects, for all that it had learned from the Leipzig-Dresden Railroad.[16]

Relations between the two railroads were unusually close, but they
were by no means unique. During the 1830s and the early 1840s,
other prospective railroad promoters or builders borrowed the expertise of the two lines by correspondence, and they also became regular
stops on the "learning journey" (*Entdeckungsreise*) that many novice

[12] Costenoble to [BD/LD], April 3, 1837, in StA Dresden, RBD Dresden, no. 7657, pp.
57r–v.

[13] Gruson to Tenner, Agent (*Bevollmächtiger*) of the Leipzig-Dresden Railroad, February 23, 1837, in StA Dresden, RBD Dresden, no. 7657, p. 28r.

[14] BD/ML to BD/LD, December 23, 1837, and BD/LD to BD/ML, December 27, 1837, in
StA Dresden, RBD Dresden, no. 7657, pp. 126r–27v; BD/ML to BD/LD, February 13, 1839,
and BD/LD to BD/ML, February 20, 1839, in StA Dresden, RBD Dresden, no. 7658, pp. 8r–
9r; BD/ML, signed Francke, Chairman, to BD/LD, October 17, 1839, and BD/LD to
BD/ML, October 26(?), 1839, in ibid., pp. 62r–v, 64r; and BD/ML to BD/LD, November 3,
1840, in ibid., p. 163r.

[15] See the correspondence on employees in StA Dresden, RBD Dresden, no. 7658, pp.
22r–24r, 36r–37v, 82r–83r, 125r, and 140r, and in StA Dresden, RBD Dresden, no. 7657,
pp. 204r, 205r, 212/11r–v, 231r–32r, 253r–54r, 265r–266v; and on postal matters in ibid,
pp. 144r–49r, 154r–166v, 178r, 179r–80r.

[16] BD/LD to BD/ML, March 5, 1842; BD/ML to BD/LD, March 11, 1842; BD/LD to
BD/ML, May 20, 1842; and BD/ML to BD/LD, May 26, 1842, in StA Dresden, RBD Dresden, no. 7659, pp. 41r, 46r, 77r, and 79r, respectively.

railroad men made. This was the term that the engineer in charge of surveying the Upper Silesian Railroad used to describe his visit to the Leipzig-Dresden Railroad in 1837, his first stop on a tour that included railroads in southern and western German states and in Belgium.[17] In late 1836 or early 1837, meanwhile, promoters of the Berlin-Stettin Railroad had sent their chief engineer to inspect other railroads before deciding on a construction style, a tour that would certainly have included the Magdeburg-Leipzig and Leipzig-Dresden railroads.[18] In 1841, moreover, when the Berlin-Stettin directors approved a major change in construction style, they reported to their stockholders that they had prudently sent their engineers to the Leipzig-Dresden and Magdeburg-Leipzig railroads (and to England) before making that decision. By mid-1841 the Berlin-Stettin also had several prospective locomotive engineers training on the Leipzig-Dresden Railroad.[19] When the time came to set up their own operating and administrative procedures, the Berlin-Stettin directors solicited advice from existing railroads and sent their depot inspectors, cashiers, and conductors to the Leipzig-Dresden and Magdeburg-Leipzig railroads for training.[20]

In the United States, early railroad promoters also turned to their colleagues for advice that had stood the test of experience. The directors of the South Carolina Railroad, one of the first long-distance roads, tried a variety of methods to overcome the difficulties of obtaining sound advice at a time when the railroad remained very much a novelty. They took pains "to procure at their respective sources, a variety of information, which will proximately or remotely, be very valuable to the Company." This meant sending "letters to a number of gentlemen, whose acknowledged talents and general information, would furnish to their inquiries, answers replete with valuable matter" and dispatching one of their members to England and France in 1828.[21] Five years later, still experiencing the embarrassing diffi-

[17] Poschinger, ed., *Erinnerungen aus dem Leben von Hans Viktor von Unruh*, pp. 46–49.

[18] *Bericht des Comité's an die Actionairs der Berlin-Stettiner Eisenbahn* (Stettin, February, 1837), p. 3.

[19] [Berlin-Stettin Railroad, Annual Report of the Directors], May 15, 1841. For details on the Berlin-Stettin's change of plans, see chap. 5.

[20] *Zweiter Jahresbericht des Direktorii der Berlin-Stettiner Eisenbahngesellschaft über den Fortgang des Unternehmens im Jahre vom Mai 1841 bis 1842, vorgetragen in der General-Versammlung der Aktionaire am 26. Mai 1842* (n.p., n.d.), p. 3.

[21] *First Semi-Annual Report, to the President and Directors of the South-Carolina Canal and Rail-Road Company, by their Committee of Inquiry* (Charleston: A. E. Miller, 1828), pp. 4–5.

culties with locomotives and inexperienced engineers that seemed endemic to the new business, the directors acknowledged that, "where their circumstances were peculiar," they too had "been obliged to purchase experience, as all others had done before them." When they encountered problems common to the early railroads, however, they had "availed themselves of the experience dearly bought by others, and ha[d] profited by it."[22] While the directors were deliberating in 1829 whether to use horses or locomotives, for example, their chief engineer, Horatio Allen, visited the Delaware and Hudson Canal to see its new English locomotives, and he corresponded with the Baltimore and Ohio Railroad, which was then using horses on its sixteen miles of track.[23]

When the promoters of the Baltimore and Ohio Railroad began work in the late 1820s, they, too, gathered advice not only through contacts in England but also from the nascent community of American railroad builders. When Baltimore merchants and bankers first met to discuss the railroad project in early 1827, they already had at their disposal information collected by two of the merchants' brothers, who resided in England.[24] A few months later, they obtained advice on construction styles from an English engineer, Jesse Hartley of Liverpool, and from Thomas Perkins, one of Boston's "merchant-princes." Hartley was the engineer in charge of Liverpool's docks, who had built the Bolton and Manchester railroad and canal; while Perkins, together with an engineer-partner, had built the United States' first horse railroad in Quincy, Massachusetts, and a few years later became a stockholder in the Boston and Worcester Railroad.[25]

The Baltimore and Ohio Railroad, moreover, quickly emerged as a clearinghouse of information in the industry. Like its German coun-

---

[22] *Annual Report of the Board of Directors of the South-Carolina Canal & Rail-Road Company to the Stockholders, with Accompanying Documents submitted at their Meeting May 6, 1833* (Charleston: A. E. Miller, 1833), p. 5.

[23] Derrick, *Centennial History*, p. 43.

[24] Hungerford, *The Story of the Baltimore & Ohio Railroad*, pp. 18–20; [Smith], *History and Description of the Baltimore and Ohio Rail Road*, pp. 10–11; J. Thomas Scharf, *History of Baltimore City and County* (Philadelphia: Louis H. Everts, 1881), pp. 474–75.

[25] Jesse Hartley to William Brown, April 2, 1827, Liverpool, and "Extract of a Letter from Thomas H. Perkins Esq. dated Boston, April 25, 1827," in Smithsonian Institution, National Museum of American History, Division of Engineering and Industry, Baltimore and Ohio Railroad Collection; *Dictionary of National Biography* 9:71; Salsbury, *The State, the Investor, and the Railroad*, pp. 45–46, 96. On Perkins's career,

terparts, this company, with its brigades of military engineers in the late 1820s and civilian engineers in the 1830s, served as an American "school of practice" for railroad builders.[26] The company also circulated information freely and widely. The advice that it had obtained from Jesse Hartley in 1827, for example, quickly made its way into the hands of the South Carolina Railroad's directors, who summarized it in a report to their stockholders the following year.[27] Among the stream of visitors to the Baltimore and Ohio, meanwhile, were engineers from the Boston and Worcester Railroad, who toured the road in 1832, and travelers from Europe in the late 1830s and early 1840s.[28] In 1835, the *American Railroad Journal* designated the Baltimore and Ohio Railroad "the *Rail Road University* of the United States": "Their reports have in truth gone forth as a text-book, and their road and work-shops have been a lecture-room to thousands who are now practising and improving upon their experience."[29] A few years later, the Austrian observer Franz Anton Ritter von Gerstner concurred. Even though the company initially made many mistakes in construction and operation, he noted, it nonetheless performed "a great service" by publishing detailed annual reports and other pamphlets. "[S]ince its engineers and officials always shared the results of their experience with the greatest liberality and the enterprise itself employed more and more engineers," he concluded, "it has become, so to speak, a practical school for railroad construction in America."[30]

Out of these informal contacts, no national association emerged in either country, but early railroad men in both countries moved to address common problems more systematically in the late 1830s and the 1840s. This was not yet because of pressing industry needs. As a

---

see Carl Seaburg and Stanley Paterson, *Merchant Prince of Boston: Colonel T. H. Perkins, 1764–1854* (Cambridge: Harvard University Press, 1971).

[26] Hill, *Roads, Rails, and Waterways*, p. 105.

[27] *First Semi-Annual Report*, pp. 13, 20. By 1833, the South Carolina Railroad was also contracting for imported iron through Liverpool merchants, who were brothers of George Brown, a member of the Baltimore and Ohio Railroad's board of directors. *Annual Report . . . May 6, 1833*, p. 4.

[28] *Report of the Directors of the Boston and Worcester Rail-Road Corporation to the Stockholders* (Boston: Steam Press, 1832), pp. 26–27; Carl Ghega, *Die Baltimore-Ohio-Eisenbahn über das Alleghany-Gebirg* (Vienna: Kaulfuß Wwe, Prandel & Co., 1844); von Gerstner, *Die innern Communicationen*, 2:199–220.

[29] *American Railroad Journal*, November 28, 1835, p. 737, quoted in [Smith], *History and Description of the Baltimore and Ohio Rail Road*, p. 33n (original emphasis), and partially quoted in Chandler, *Henry Varnum Poor*, p. 38.

[30] Gerstner, *Die innern Communicationen*, 2:199.

rule, problems associated with through traffic and interfirm competition would not trouble the industry in either country until the mid- to late 1840s. Rather, in both countries, it was government policies in the early 1840s that prompted the first collective attention to railroad technology and operations.

In the United States, the first deliberations occurred in 1842 at the invitation of the postmaster general.[31] From 1838, when Congress declared all railroads to be post roads, through much of the nineteenth century, successive postmasters general engaged in a running battle with the railroads. At issue was not only the rates that the railroads received for the service but also the mail agents that the postmaster general wanted to accompany the mail and the scheduling of through traffic. Among his other initiatives in the early 1840s, Postmaster General Charles A. Wickliffe undertook to persuade the railroads along the Atlantic seaboard to coordinate their through traffic in order to expedite mail delivery—at reasonable rates—between Boston and Charleston. But, even though he was prepared to offer extra compensation for running night trains, he had not been able by the fall of 1841 to convince the companies to embrace his plans.[32] The general state of relations between the railroads and the Post Office during this period may be gauged from a public protest by the Western Railroad's agent, George Bliss, that postal officials adopted a "rather authoritative and dictatorial" tone in their dealings with the railroads.[33]

In an effort to resolve the impasse, the postmaster general sent out invitations to railroads that held mail contracts, asking them to come to Washington for a meeting on January 1, 1842. Postal officials represented it to the railroads, in Bliss's words, as "an opportunity . . . to arrange our differences."[34] Postmaster General Wickliffe proposed two topics for discussion: not only the question of schedules and rates but also, as James Gadsden of the Louisville, Cincinnati, and Charleston Railroad put it, "graver subjects of consideration," namely, a plan to have the federal government purchase the right of perpetual transportation for the mails and for military personnel and

---

[31] I am much indebted to Richard R. John for bringing these events to my attention and for generously sharing sources.

[32] *History of the Railway Mail Service*, pp. 41–42.

[33] Bliss, *Reply to a Late Letter of the Post-Master General*, p. 13. See also *American Railroad Journal*, June 15, 1841, pp. 353–56.

[34] Bliss, *Reply to a Late Letter of the Post-Master General*, p. 9.

equipment. Given the railroads' precarious financial position, the postmaster general's initiative "received general approbation," the *American Railroad Journal* reported. "I think you have it in your power . . . (from the peculiar circumstances of the Money Markets)," the president of the Philadelphia, Wilmington, and Baltimore Railroad responded, "to secure one of the most beautiful Mail arrangements that ever existed in this Country." President Gadsden of the Louisville, Cincinnati, and Charleston also welcomed the meeting (to which he sought an invitation): "It is the i[n]terest of the Roads as well as the Government that they should move in concert."[35]

The convention met for two days, but ultimately to no avail, for Congress showed little interest in their ambitious scheme. During 1842 and 1843, Wickliffe continued his efforts to convince Congress to buy the rights that the Post Office needed. Since the federal government had not chartered the corporations, it had no leverage to exercise direct control. The competition among carriers that had traditionally kept mail pay at lower levels, moreover, simply did not obtain on most of the railroad routes. Postal legislation ought to be changed, Wickliffe argued in 1843, "to dispense with the idle ceremony and useless expense of advertising for the lowest bids on those roads, where there is and can be no competition." But Congress remained unresponsive, so Wickliffe worked on his own to obtain favorable rates and to entice the companies into closer cooperation with each other.[36]

In Prussia, the shift in state policy in 1842 stimulated two meetings of railroad men in the capital city and emerging rail center, Berlin.[37] Just a week before the standing committees were scheduled

[35] M. Newkirk to C. A. Wickliffe, Philadelphia, November 22, 1841, and James Gadsden to the Postmaster General, Charleston, December 22, 1841, in Letters Received (Entry 4, Box 1), Post Office Department, Record Group 28, National Archives; *American Railroad Journal*, January 1, 1842, p. 13. The latter (pp. 13–15) includes Wickliffe's explanation of the plan. For additional details, see "Report of the Postmaster General," in Senate Doc. 1, 27th Cong., 2d sess., 1841–42, pp. 461–62.

[36] Bliss, *Reply to a Late Letter of the Post-Master General*, p. 5; "Report of the Postmaster General," in Senate Doc. 1, 27th Cong., 3d sess., 1842–43, pp. 725–26; "Report of the Postmaster General," in Senate Doc. 1, 28th Cong., 1st sess., 1843–44, p. 596.

[37] An earlier but much more limited move toward organization came from the directors of the Leipzig-Dresden Railroad in Saxony, who proposed forming a so-called cartel (*Cartell*) in 1838. They had in mind bilateral contracts with nine Central European railroads, including the Magdeburg-Leipzig Railroad, in which each would agree not to hire the other's employees without a letter of recommendation and release from the previous employer. For details, see Leipzig-Dresden Railroad to BD/ML, July

to consider the ministers' proposal to provide more systematic railroad aid, Berlin railroad men and others with an interest in the business assembled in Berlin to discuss railroad technology and operations. They did so at the invitation of the Berlin-Potsdam Railroad's
general superintendent, von Puttkammer, and of Dr. O. von Mül-
mann of the Berlin police. The meeting, attended by eighteen men,
took place at the Berlin-Stettin Railroad's depot. Out of their deliberations grew the first formal institution associated with the railroad
industry, the *Verein für Eisenbahn-Kunde* (VfEK) or Association for
Railroad Science, which survived at least long enough to celebrate its
fiftieth anniversary.[38]

The Berlin association, however, did not represent industry interests exclusively. Individuals, not corporations, counted as members,
and they had to be nominated and elected by their colleagues. This
was also a regional association: residence in Berlin qualified one for
regular membership; those outside the city could become corresponding members. The VfEK's founders, moreover, included, together with distinguished railroad men, a number of others with a
personal or professional interest in railroad technology. Thus,
alongside railroad figures such as state engineer Georg Neuhaus, who
was building the Berlin-Stettin Railroad, and the banker Georg Ferdinand Oppert, who had been instrumental in bringing the Berlin-
Hamburg Railroad into existence, sat August Borsig, one of the
VfEK's most enthusiastic supporters. Borsig owned a Berlin machine
works and had built his first locomotive the previous year; he would
soon dominate the industry in Prussia. One of his competitors, Franz
Anton Egells, who was then experimenting with locomotive construction, also joined the VfEK, which claimed sixty-three members
within three weeks. Besides other railroad men, the roster of early
members listed a number of middle-level state officials, including a
handful of military men. Although the association insisted on receiving official state approval of its statutes, it was intended merely to

---

17, 1838, in StA Dresden, RBD Dresden, no. 7657, pp. 204r–v; "Vertrag," July 17, 1838,
in ibid., p. 205r; BD/ML, signed Francke, Chairman, to BD/LD, July 23, 1838, in ibid., pp.
212/11r–v; and [BD/LD] to [BD/ML], August 18, 1838, in ibid., pp. 231r–v. See also the
correspondence on employees cited in note 15 above.

[38] *Der Verein für Eisenbahnkunde zu Berlin, 1842 bis 1892, Festschrift zur Feier des
fünfzigjährigen Bestehens des Vereins am 11. Oktober 1892* (n.p., n.d.), pp. 43–44. I
have translated *Kunde* as "science" to reflect nineteenth-century usage of the latter
term.

provide a learned forum for discussing practical aspects of railroad construction and operation, not to generate uniform operating or technological standards or to address the problem of competition. Indeed, to avoid any misunderstanding about its function, it quickly changed its original name, *Eisenbahn-Verein* or Railroad Association, to the *Verein für Eisenbahn-Kunde*. The VfEK established its own library, and its members met monthly in Berlin to hear a lecture or two, followed by discussion and a dinner. Borsig himself gave the first lecture on a spark catcher that he had developed.[39] Thus the VfEK brought together a diverse group of Berliners who had a special interest in railroad technology and operations, but its purview was limited to that sphere, while its membership extended beyond the railroads.

Once the Prussian crown had approved the policy of aiding private railroads, however, ministry officials, like American Postmaster General Wickliffe, quickly developed a special interest in railroad operations and sought to encourage collective deliberations. A few months after the first meeting of the VfEK, Ernst von Bodelschwingh, who had recently been appointed finance minister and thus had responsibility for railroad policy, convened another meeting of railroad men in Berlin. Minister von Bodelschwingh may have called the meeting preemptively for fear that the newly formed VfEK would exert undue influence over railroad affairs, but it seems even more likely that he hoped that the meeting, together with the recent change of state policy, would deflect the railroads' demands for a revision of the 1838 national railroad law. The private companies, as we have seen, had been highly critical of the law from the beginning, and the state had done little to ease their concerns in the interim. The railroads still wanted changes in most features of the law, especially the provisions regarding liability. By February of 1843, moreover, Minister von

[39] *Der Verein für Eisenbahnkunde*, pp. 4–5, 7–8, 43–44, 47–49, 114–15; and correspondence in ZStAM, Rep. 77, Tit. 258, no. 7, pp. 4rv, 6rv. On Neuhaus, see chap. 5 and the two-part obituary in the *Deutsche Bauzeitung*, August 18, 1877, p. 328, and August 25, 1877, p. 338. On Oppert, see a memorandum by von Pommer Esche II, February 24, 1841, in ZStAM, Rep. 93E, no. 3305/1, vol. 2, p. 110r; and *Protocoll der ersten Generalversamlung der Actionairs der Berlin-Hamburger Eisenbahn-Gesellschaft*, p. 7. On Borsig, see Dieter Vorsteher, *Borsig: Eisengießerei und Maschinenbauanstalt zu Berlin* (Berlin: Siedler Verlag, 1983); and on Borsig, Egells, and other German locomotive builders, Horst Wagenblass, *Der Eisenbahnbau und das Wachstum der deutschen Eisen- und Maschinenbauindustrie 1835 bis 1860: Ein Beitrag zur Geschichte der Industrialisierung Deutschlands* (Stuttgart: Gustav Fischer Verlag, 1973), pp. 88–108.

Bodelschwingh had let it be known that a revision of the law would be undertaken, and he had solicited the railroads' comments for consideration.[40] Yet, when the Ministry informed the provincial governors of plans for the conference, the official notice described it merely as concerning technology and operating procedures, with a special emphasis on public safety and through traffic. Indeed, the Ministry specifically requested that the railroads send representatives who had an intimate knowledge of their company's operations.[41] At best, then, the meeting represented a partial response to their concerns. The attention devoted to public safety might well have represented a sincere effort to alleviate the railroads' fears about the law's provisions regarding liability—not by changing the law but by enhancing the safety of operations. This would have been consistent with what David Hansemann saw in railroad affairs as a tendency on the part of state officials to behave reactively rather than to seize the initiative.[42] In any event, the railroads' key demand, reform of the railroad law, remained off limits.

The meeting, which did indeed concern only railroad technology and operations, brought together representatives of seven railroads for collective deliberation. Held in the Finance Ministry's offices in Berlin in late March and early April of 1843, it was chaired by Adolph von Pommer Esche II, an official in the Finance Ministry. In attendance were also one official each from the Ministry of the Interior and the Police Department in Berlin as well as two railroad commissioners.[43] As von Pommer Esche acknowledged at the outset, operating problems had not prompted the conference; indeed, accidents had not been a problem. He assured the railroad men, moreover, that the

[40] Kühlwetter, Quadflieg, and Mevissen, "Zusammenstellung von Grundsätzen für ein neues Eisenbahn-Gesetz, unter Berücksichtigung der bisherigen Erfahrungen," October 1, 1847, in Staatsarchiv Hamburg (hereafter, StA Hamburg), Senat, Cl.VII, Lit. Kª, no. 11, vol. 7, Fasc. 8ᵇ, Inv. 1 (Anlagen zum Brief vom 27.7.1848), no. 2; Geschäfts-Bericht des Directoriums der Magdeburg-Cöthen-Halle-Leipziger Eisenbahn-Gesellschaft für die Zeit vom 15ten Mai 1842 bis zum 7ten April 1843, ZStAM, Rep. 77, Tit. 258a, no. 2, vol. 1, p. 170r; Hansemann, Über die Ausführung des Preußischen Eisenbahn-Systems, p. 72.

[41] Finance Minister to [the Provincial Governors], January 18, 1843, in ZStAM, Rep. 93E, no. 1092, vol. 1, pp. 1r–2v; Festschrift, p. xiii.

[42] Hansemann, Über die Ausführung des Preußischen Eisenbahn-Systems, p. 83.

[43] [Railroad Conference Minutes], Berlin, April 5, 1843, in ZStAM, Rep. 93E, no. 1127, vol. 1, p. 71; Festschrift, pp. xiii–xiv. One railroad, the Düsseldorf-Elberfeld, had indicated in advance that it would not be able to send a representative.

state did not intend to inhibit their "free activity" with oppressive regulations. Instead, the idea was merely to arrive at comprehensive guidelines regarding railroad technology and operations.[44] Thus, over the course of seven days, they agreed on guidelines regarding the obligations of the traveling public; the condition, maintenance, and supervision of the roadbed; design and condition of rolling stock; safety regulations; signaling systems; the conduct of operating employees; and procedures to facilitate through traffic.[45] The companies did not have to adopt these word for word; they were merely to provide guidance when the companies drafted or revised their own operating procedures, although state officials reserved the right to approve their final form.[46] Although it reportedly had no practical impact on through traffic, this initial foray into collective action, like the meeting of American railroad men in Washington the previous year, clearly set a precedent for industry-wide consultations.[47] Yet it did not automatically evolve further, for state officials were still proceeding in a largely consensual (though evasive) fashion.

In both countries, then, early railroad men, of necessity, cultivated close relations with their colleagues, as they struggled to master the new technology. The early long-distance roads constituted critical nodes in impressive networks of personal contacts that sprang up in both countries. These networks, in turn, created the basis for more formal methods of cooperation, as the pace of railroad construction picked up and as the density of the railroad network increased. In both countries, moreover, the state stepped in and encouraged the railroads to cooperate with one another. Yet, no national organization sprang up to represent industry interests in either country. In the late 1840s and early 1850s, however, the American and Prussian paths diverged. While Prussian railroad men quickly forged what proved to be a permanent national association, American railroad men made extraordinary efforts to organize an assortment of associations but uniformly failed to sustain them.

[44] [Railroad Conference Minutes], April 5, 1843, p. 7v.

[45] For details, see ibid., pp. 8r–37v.

[46] Ibid., p. 7v; *Dritter Generalbericht der Direction der Berlin-Hamburger Eisenbahn-Gesellschaft* (Berlin: E. S. Mittler, 1846), p. 13. Hansemann, *Kritik des Preußischen Eisenbahn-Gesetzes*, p. 67, had argued two years earlier that they should not be compulsory.

[47] *Festschrift*, pp. xiii–xiv.

Organizing Prussian Railroad Interests

A decade before the first moves to organize a national association
in Prussia, a telltale sign emerged of the organizational incentives
generated by the structure of the Prussian state. In April of 1836,
Joseph Mendelssohn, a private banker in Berlin and one of the principal promoters of the Berlin-Stettin Railroad, reported to his partner in
the project, Senior Mayor (*Oberbürgermeister*) Masche of Stettin,
that members of the Düsseldorf-Elberfeld railroad committee were in
town to negotiate charter terms with the ministries. "All of these
negotiations . . . are still highly chaotic," he complained,

> and neither side has brought a hard and fast principle to the matter.
> I think we would not do wrong at all, if we hold back a little with
> our negotiations, so we do not make things even more complicated.
> Without a doubt it would be highly beneficial for all railroads in the
> country if every committee sent a delegate here and these delegates
> then got together for joint negotiations with the authorities. [Illegi-
> ble] . . . unity and order in the affair. What do you think of this
> proposal?[48]

What Mendelssohn's suggestion implicitly recognized, in other
words, was the political reality of dealing with a unitary, bureaucratic
state. All of the railroads had to negotiate charter terms with the
same small group of individuals in the ministries. It made sense,
therefore, to do so collectively. It was this aspect of policy-making in a
unitary state structure that generated incentives for a corresponding,
unitary organization of railroad interests. Nothing seems to have
come of Mendelssohn's proposal at that time, although the VfEK held
its organizational meeting in his company's depot and his company
called the first national meeting of railroads ten years later. Still, the
distinctive incentives of the Prussian structure had made themselves
felt.

When Prussian policy turned more interventionist in the mid-
1840s, those incentives exerted greater force and a national association rapidly began to take shape. The process began when, as noted in
chapter 2, the finance minister gave a clear signal that he might
enforce provisions of the Prussian railroad law pertaining to rates. In

---

[48] Joseph Mendelssohn to *Oberbürgermeister* Masche, April 4, 1836, in MA Nachl.
5, VIII.

August of 1846, he ordered all Prussian railroads to submit the annual reports required by the 1838 law.[49] The railroads took this to mean that regulation might be incipient and they moved collectively to defend their interests. As events unfolded, however, the extent of the railroads' dissatisfaction with the 1838 railroad law emerged in full force. What followed was a battle of wills between the railroads and the finance minister that produced a *German* railroad association, leaving the Prussian railroads with a mixed victory at best.

Mendelssohn's Berlin-Stettin Railroad responded to the minister's order by inviting the other sixteen Prussian railroads to Berlin for a meeting that November. Representatives of ten companies attended the meeting and promptly appointed committees not only to draw up a common system of accounting (*Etat*) in response to Minister von Bodelschwingh's order but also to formulate principles for a new railroad law. Clearly dissatisfied with the finance minister's response to their concerns thus far, the delegates agreed to petition for a conference with state officials to discuss a thorough-going revision of the railroad law. To the discretion of the individual members they left the question whether to ask their respective provincial assemblies to lobby the ministers on their behalf. This meeting made clear, moreover, that the railroad men took particular issue with §25 of the law, which held the corporations responsible for nearly all damages or injuries resulting from railroad operation. As Hansemann had argued several times in print, this section of the law gave the railroads *less* protection than other carriers enjoyed. Individual railroads, they decided, might also petition their provincial assemblies for help in obtaining its immediate nullification. The day's business finished, the meeting ended with a motion by Dr. Rhades of the Berlin-Stettin Railroad to establish a permanent organization, the *Verband Preußischer Eisenbahn-Direktionen* or Association of Prussian Railroad Administrations, in order to give "unanimity" (*Einmüthigkeit*) to the railroads' efforts.[50]

[49] *Festschrift*, p. 393.

[50] Ibid., pp. xii–xiii, 403; *Rückblick auf die Thätigkeit des Vereins Deutscher Eisenbahn-Verwaltungen in technischer Beziehung, 1850–1900* (Berlin: Felgentreff and Co., 1900), pp. 5–6 (hereafter cited as *Rückblick*); [VDEV Minutes], Cologne, June 28–29, 1847, in StA Hamburg, Senat, Cl. VII, Lit. Kª, no. 11, vol. 7, Fasc. 8ᵇ, Inv. 1 (Anlagen zum Brief vom 18.9.1847, no. 205), no. 1; "Gesetz über die Eisenbahn-Unternehmungen," §25; Hansemann, *Kritik des Preußischen Eisenbahn-Gesetzes*, p. 68; idem, *Über die Ausführung des Preußischen Eisenbahn-Systems*, p. 74; Kühlwetter et al., "Zusammenstellung von Grundsätzen."

Before the next meeting of the new association, scheduled for late June of 1847, the finance minister responded to its petition in a way that suggested a two-pronged offensive, once again, to diffuse agitation for changes in the Prussian law. First, he duly announced plans for another conference, probably to be held in the late fall, but this one to include railroad representatives from other German states as well. Second, the finance minister restricted the agenda to a variety of technical questions, especially procedures to facilitate free circulation of rolling stock over the various railroad lines; he made no mention of the railroad law.[51] Again, he responded to the railroads' demands but hardly acceded to them.

When the Prussian association went ahead with its second meeting in Cologne that June, the delegates decided, in effect, to respond in kind to the minister's apparent attempt to diffuse agitation. Other matters remained on hold, since the finance minister had not yet set a date for the conference and the committee appointed at the Berlin meeting had not had time to formulate principles for a new law. Again the subject of §25 came up, but the delegates put off a full discussion of changes in the law to their next meeting in the fall. In the meantime, they agreed to call an extraordinary session to prepare for the conference, if the finance minister convened it before their next meeting. Then, in the final hours of the meeting, the delegates moved unanimously to open the association to all German railroads.[52]

This action reflected several considerations. According to a knowledgeable observer, two concerns prompted the move. On the one hand, it reflected nationalist and even internationalist sentiment, the railroad men (especially from the western provinces) voicing "a general desire that the railroads not become the cause of segregation of the German tribes [*Stämme*]." This was "a task of the times," as one speaker put it, "a patriotic duty." They hoped to promote closer international relations and "thereby contribute actively to the great

[51] Oesterreich, for the Finance Minister, to Ministry of Foreign Affairs, June 6, 1847, in ZStAM, Rep. 93E, no. 1127, vol. 1, pp. 40r–42r. The other German states were Hannover, Hesse, Saxony, and Braunschweig. [VDEV Minutes], Cologne, June 28–29, 1847, indicates that a royal communication dated February 3, 1847, obviated the need to petition the provincial assemblies for help; this presumably was an official notice that a conference would be called.

[52] [VDEV Minutes], Cologne, June 28–29, 1847; von Reden, *Eisenbahn-Jahrbuch*, p. 316.

goal of humankind, the accommodation of hostile nationalities." On the other hand, the move registered the understanding that the association, after dealing with issues of importance primarily to Prussian lines, would address problems common to all German railroads.[53] A pan-German association had obvious attractions for Prussian railroads, since other German countries separated the eastern and western provinces of Prussia. But, in view of their persistent demands for revision of the railroad law, the timing of the decision points to a third consideration as well. Taken just three weeks after the finance minister's action, it suggests a more pragmatic political purpose: by transforming their organization into the *Verein Deutscher Eisenbahn-Verwaltungen* (VDEV) or Association of *German* Railroad Administrations, the Prussian lines hoped to preserve unity among the railroads at the finance minister's conference.

There the matter rested until early 1848. Late in October of 1847, as the time had approached for the newly expanded VDEV's third meeting, the Finance Ministry had reaffirmed plans to call a conference—the agenda unchanged—but it still could not or would not set a date.[54] Finally, in early January of 1848, as political tension reached crisis proportions throughout central Europe, the finance minister sent notice that the conference would begin on March 14. To be presided over by Councilor Mellin, who had represented the Magdeburg-Leipzig Railroad at the 1843 conference but had since gone to work for the Finance Ministry, it would take as its starting point the minutes from the 1843 conference. Discussion would be confined to technical matters, despite efforts by the Hannover government to expand the agenda.[55]

---

[53] [VDEV Minutes], Cologne, June 28–29, 1847; and von Reden, *Eisenbahn-Jahrbuch*, pp. 316–17. In a spirit of internationalism, von Reden reported, a French railroad association sent its greetings and a copy of its bylaws to this meeting. These indicated, he commented cryptically, that the "need for such associations" had arisen from similar sources in the two countries. Von Reden, *Eisenbahn-Jahrbuch*, p. 317. The author has not been able to learn anything about a French association.

[54] Finance Minister to Minister of Foreign Affairs, October 26, 1847, in ZStAM, Rep. 93E, no. 1127, vol. 1, pp. 49r–v.

[55] See the letters from the Finance Minister to all railroad commissioners, to the Minister of Foreign Affairs, and to officials in Saxony, Hesse, and Brunswick, all dated January 8, 1848, in ibid., pp. 54r–56r. Regarding Mellin's role in the 1843 and 1848 conferences, see [Railroad Conference Minutes], April 5, 1843, p. 7r; and Finance Minister to Minister of the Interior von Bodelschwingh, February 25, 1848, in ZStAM, Rep. 93E, no. 1127, vol. 1, p. 65r. Hannover officials wanted to discuss termination of customs duties and taxes on railroad freight, the high freight rates on some German lines, and adoption of the *Zollcenter* as the weight standard. Von Falcke to the Prussian

As it turned out, however, the revolution handed the railroads a victory of sorts. Twenty-eight representatives did indeed travel to Berlin for the conference, but only to find the barricades going up on the eve of the "March Days" of the 1848 revolution. In the circumstances, they prudently agreed that the matter would best be taken up at another time.[56] More than two years passed before the state again contemplated intervening to improve through traffic, and the VDEV, in the meantime, was able to consolidate its control over technical matters. This time, the Thüringian Railroad, through its commissioner, Count (*Graf*) von Keller, brought problems with through traffic to the attention of the Ministry for Trade, Commerce, and Public Works, which now held responsibility for railroad policy. Citing problems with car accounting procedures and the like, von Keller asked permission to draw up appropriate regulations not just for Prussian but for all German railroads.[57] But the Ministry's inquiries revealed a consensus that the railroads could take care of such problems themselves. "In our judgment," the railroad commissioner in Cologne replied, the problem "requires no intervention by the state." The commissioner in Berlin agreed: the present, private arrangements obviated any need for state action.[58] Where technical matters were concerned, the Prussian state's attempt to orchestrate relations among Prussian railroads never quite recovered the momentum that it lost during the revolution. In that sense, the railroads emerged the victor by a slight margin.[59]

If the German railroads won a partial victory, however, the Prussian railroads lost in important respects. For the tactic that the Prussian state had adopted in preparation for the conference—extending invi-

---

Legation (*Gesandtschaft*), Hannover, January 21, 1848, and Finance Minister to Minister of Foreign Affairs, February 24, 1848, in ibid., pp. 60r–64v.

[56] Mellin and [?], Berlin, March 3, 1848, in ibid., p. 100r, and [Railroad Conference Minutes], Berlin, March 14, 1848, in ibid., pp. 101r–102v.

[57] Board of Directors of the Thüringian Railroad Company to Railroad Commissioner Count von Keller, August 8, 1850, Erfurt, and Royal Railroad Commissioner Keller to the Ministry for Trade, Commerce, and Public Works, II. Abt., August 27, 1850, Erfurt, in ibid., pp. 103r–105v.

[58] Royal Railroad Commissioner von Moeller (?) to Minister for Trade, Commerce, and Public Works, Cologne, November 21, 1850, and Royal Railroad Commissioner von Noitiz (?) to Minister for Trade, Commerce, and Public Works, Berlin, December 12, 1850, in ibid., pp. 112r–19v.

[59] By 1850 Prussian officials had begun to court the association, staging a banquet at its annual meeting that year at a cost of more than $900 (1,316 *Taler*). By 1853 it had become the practice for the government of the host country to stage similar events at VDEV meetings. See the correspondence in ZStAM, Rep. 2.2.1, no. 29497, pp. 11–61, 81.

tations to other German railroads—eventually succeeded in dividing their ranks and heading off demands for reform of the Prussian railroad law. Once the association had been opened to all German railroads, some of its Prussian members, apparently recognizing that the tactic might dilute their force, sought to regroup around specifically Prussian issues. But it was a losing battle.

The first attempt to restore Prussian strength within the organization came at the VDEV's third meeting in November of 1847. A proposal to create a separate Prussian section within the VDEV met with defeat, and the VDEV adjourned after four days without addressing the strictly Prussian items on the agenda—a report on the petition presented to the finance minister; a proposal to request immediate nullification of §25 of the railroad law, if the finance minister failed to respond to the petition; and a report from the committee appointed to formulate principles for a new railroad law.[60] Finally, just as the meeting came to a close, the chairman of the Berlin-Hamburg's board of directors, Costenoble, made a last attempt to refocus the association on Prussian problems. He proposed that the VDEV notify the Prussian ministries of its existence, so that state officials might henceforth deal directly with it as the representative of the Prussian railroads. This idea reportedly "found support" among the delegates and was sent to a committee for further discussion.[61]

But, when the VDEV met again in September of 1848, altered political circumstances derailed the initiative. Further deliberations on the railroad law took place at this meeting in Dresden, but, in the meantime, the founding of new (though short-lived) representative institutions reinforced tendencies inherent in the pan-German composition of the association. Already that spring Costenoble of the Berlin-Hamburg Railroad had changed his earlier proposal and recommended instead that the new German national assembly represent the railroads in their dealings with the Prussian state. Then, in July, the Economics Committee of the Frankfurt Parliament had writ-

---

[60] "Tagesordnung für die am 29th November 1847 zusammentretende General-Versammlung der Abgeordneten des Verbandes der Deutscher Eisenbahn-Directionen," in StA Hamburg, Senat, Cl. VII, Lit. Kᵃ, no. 11, vol. 7, Fasc. 8ᵇ, Inv. 1 (Anlagen zum Brief vom 13.11.1847, no. 205ᵃ), no. 1.

[61] [VDEV Minutes], Hamburg, November 29–December 2, 1847, in ibid., Inv. 1 (Anlagen zum Brief vom 20.12.1847, no. 321). Although it did not have an opportunity to report at the meeting, the commission on the Prussian railroad law had prepared a report; see Kühlwetter et al., "Zusammenstellung von Grundsätzen."

ten to the VDEV, inquiring what changes in railroad legislation had been suggested in their meetings. The delegates interpreted this as equivalent to the official recognition that Costenoble had wanted to elicit from the Prussian government, and consequently they turned their attention to the possibility of a German railroad law. Unable to arrive at a consensus that such a law would indeed be desirable, they sent the matter back to committee.[62]

The Prussian railroads never did achieve either the separate status within the VDEV or the legal reforms that they desired. The question of railroad law came up for discussion one last time at the VDEV's annual meeting in Vienna in the fall of 1849, but by then the issue had become largely moot with the success of counterrevolution and as a moderate rebellion occurred within the committee appointed to prepare a report for the 1849 meeting. One committee member, District President von Möller of the Cologne-Minden Railroad, argued that its task was not actually to draft a law but rather to consider "the unity of the entire German railroad system" and how it might be enhanced. "[M]any of these matters," he contended, "could be settled through voluntary agreement among the railroad administrations, without requiring regulation through a state law." As a compromise, the committee broke up into groups to decide which matters might require legislation and which would not.[63] One group again considered whether the VDEV should create regional sections, as had been proposed at the meeting in the fall of 1847.[64] But the matter never made much progress. When the committee presented its report to the VDEV at the 1849 meeting, the minutes dryly noted, "A general discussion was not desired." Although the committee was instructed to continue its work, this effectively put an end to agitation for legal changes, Prussian or German.[65] Whether *Vormärz* Prussian officials

[62] [VDEV Minutes], Dresden, September 11–13, 1848, and Anlage X, "Commissions-Vorschläge zu Nr. 4 der Tagesordnung für die General-Versammlung des Vereins Deutscher Eisenbahn-Verwaltungen vom 11. September 1848," in StA Hamburg, Senat, Cl. VII, Lit. Kᵃ, no. 11, vol. 7, Fasc. 8ᵇ, Inv. 1 (Anlagen zu den Brief des Vereins Deutscher Eisenbahn-Verwaltungen).

[63] "Sitzung der Commission zur Bearbeitung des Entwurfes eines allgemeinen deutschen Eisenbahngesetzes," Cologne, October 11, 1848, in *Protokoll der zu Wien vom 15. bis 19. October 1849 abgehaltenen Generalversammlung des Vereins Deutscher Eisenbahnverwaltungen*, Anlage XIII.A, pp. 38–39; *Festschrift*, p. 43.

[64] "Bericht und protokollarische Verhandlung der Commission zur Bearbeitung des Entwurfs eines allgemeinen deutschen Eisenbahn-Gesetzes," Vienna, October 13, 1849, in *Protokoll*, Vienna, October 15–19, 1849, Anlage XIII, p. 36.

[65] *Protokoll*, Vienna, October 19, 1849, p. 6; *Festschrift*, p. 43; *Rückblick*, pp. 6–7.

had intended it or not, the pan-German composition of the VDEV ultimately debilitated the movement to revise the Prussian railroad law.

As an all-German organization devoted primarily to the technical and organizational problems of creating a unified railroad system, however, the VDEV flourished. Between 1846 and 1852, the railroad men worked out the basic rules to govern its operation. The bylaws adopted at the Vienna meeting in 1849 spelled out its purpose: to promote the interests of the railroads as well as the public interest "through collective discussions and united action." All railroads in Germany (*Deutschland*) were eligible for membership, a provision later changed to widen membership. Each member was initially entitled to one vote, a simple majority sufficing to approve resolutions; in 1852, however, voting rights were changed to reflect differences in the members' size. From the outset, dues were apportioned among the members according to their length, and this principle was retained. Originally the railroad men had planned to meet twice a year, but they decided to meet annually when membership was extended to all German railroads at the June 1847 meeting. Management of the association's affairs, finally, was to rotate among the members every two to three years, but in practice virtually no rotation occurred. The Berlin-Stettin Railroad, which had initiated the first meeting, managed the association's affairs until 1854; then the Berlin-Anhalt Railroad took over and continued as manager until the road was nationalized in the 1880s.[66]

The critical question, of course, was how it would enforce compliance with its decisions if, as the bylaws provided, regulations could be passed by a simple majority. In fact, its resolutions were not binding. Adoption of regulations governing through freight and passenger traffic remained a voluntary matter. From the start, this naturally hindered attempts to bring about uniformity. At the annual meeting in 1852, an amendment to the bylaws was proposed that would have made resolutions passed by three-fourths of the members binding on all members. But this proposal succumbed to critics who argued that the association had been created to foster cooperation, not coercion. There the matter rested for a quarter of a century. Only in 1875, after

---

[66] For the bylaws adopted in 1849 and subsequent changes, see *Festschrift*, pp. 3–14. On the 1847 decision to switch to annual meetings, see [VDEV Minutes], Cologne, June 29, 1847.

prolonged discussion, did the VDEV adopt a rule that certain resolutions approved by nine-tenths of the members were binding on all members. Resolutions regarding internal administrative matters apparently continued to require only a simple majority, and at the other extreme those regarding rates could be made only by unanimous agreement.[67]

Despite the fact that dissenters could simply decline to follow VDEV policies, the association held together. By late 1847, after membership had been opened to all German railroads, forty of fifty eligible railroads belonged to the association, and it had begun to publish its own newspaper.[68] By 1850 its membership had grown to forty-eight lines, representing nearly seven thousand kilometers of track in operation; and by 1860, to sixty-one lines with more than fifteen thousand kilometers.[69]

Once the national association had taken shape, associational activity snowballed for a brief time.[70] The first ancillary organization, the Association of German Railroad Employees (*Verein Deutscher Eisenbahn-Beamten*), had formed by late July of 1848. Through the Berlin-Hamburg Railroad's directors, it presented a list of demands at the VDEV's annual meeting that fall and requested permission to have a delegate present when the petition came up for discussion. The railroad employees' demands centered on two concerns: job security and retirement benefits. But the association concluded that petitions of this sort did not fall within the purview of the VDEV and that such matters should be left up to the individual railroads. Whether the employees' association retained its integrity after being rebuffed by their employers' association remains unclear.[71]

[67] *Festschrift*, pp. xiv, 12–13.

[68] The VDEV became the official sponsor of the *Eisenbahn-Zeitung*, which had begun publication in 1844 under the auspices of the Württemberg state railroads. [VDEV Minutes], Hamburg, November 29–December 2, 1847; Anlage VIII in StA Hamburg, Senat, Cl. VII, Lit. Kᵃ, no. 11, vol. 7, Fasc. 8ᵇ, Inv. 1 (Anlagen zum Brief vom 20.12.1847, no. 321).

[69] *Festschrift*, pp. xii–xvi, 34. For a brief summary of later developments, see chap. 6.

[70] On this general pattern, see Suzanne Berger, "Introduction," in *Organizing Interests*, ed. idem, p. 15.

[71] [VDEV Minutes], Dresden, September 11, 1848; [Committee Report], Dresden, September 9, 1848, in ibid., Anlage III. The latter refers to a letter from the board of directors (*Vorstand*) of the employees' association, dated July 29, 1848. Presumably these were salaried employees such as resident engineers, locomotive engineers, conductors, and workshop foremen. The VDEV Minutes suggest that the Berlin-Hamburg directors were rather more sympathetic to the employees' demands than most of their colleagues in the association. See ibid., September 11 and 12, 1848. For the lengthy

A second organization, the Association of German Railroad Engineers (*Verein Deutscher Eisenbahn-Techniker* [VDET]), held its first meeting in 1850. This association actually grew out of the discussions of railroad law at the VDEV's 1849 meeting, for the committee that had declined to draft a general German railroad law proposed instead that German railroad engineers meet to draw up regulations that would enhance the unity of German railroads. At the 1850 meeting in Berlin, the engineers (i.e., technical directors, chief engineers, and master machinists) decided that they were meeting not as representatives of their companies but as individuals, and they even allowed the locomotive manufacturer Borsig to participate as a voting member. Over the course of the eight-day meeting, they voted to form their own society, which would meet annually and admit individuals as members. In practice, however, the VDET served mainly as a technical advisory body to the VDEV, meeting irregularly whenever called upon by the latter association and preparing recommendations for its decision. Out of this meeting came procedures for handling through traffic as well as a comprehensive set of guidelines to encourage uniformity in all aspects of the construction and operation of German railroads. The VDEV approved these at its July 1850 meeting, distributed copies to the membership, and recommended their adoption as soon as possible.[72]

Meanwhile, as these associations were getting underway, Prussian railroads also confronted, as noted earlier, the thorny problem of trunk-line competition for the first time in the late 1840s. The Prussian national association initially tackled this issue as well, but it failed to reach (unanimous) agreement on a common rate schedule. Instead, regional groups of connecting railroads set up *Tarifverbände* or rate associations that worked closely with the VDEV but set rates

---

report prepared for the meeting on behalf of the employees, see Neuhaus, Technical Director of the Berlin-Hamburg Railroad, September 6, 1848, in StA Hamburg, Senat, Cl. VII, Lit. Kª, no. 11, vol. 7, Fasc. 8ᵇ, Inv. 1 (Anlagen zum Brief vom 28.9.1848, no. 259), no. 5. His report is also included in [VDEV Minutes], Dresden, September 11–13, 1848, Anlage VI.

[72] *Protokoll*, Vienna, October 19, 1849, p. 6; "Bericht und protokollarische Verhandlung," in ibid., pp. 36–37; *Festschrift*, pp. 43–45; *Rückblick*, pp. 6–8, 13, 53, 63, 67–70. The latter contains the minutes of the 1850 engineers' meeting (pp. 47–74). The regulations drawn up there may be found in *Rückblick*, pp. 75–98; in *Festschrift*, pp. 47–66, 257–64; and in translation in Royal Commission on Railways, 1865–67, *Report*, Appendices CA and CB, British Parliamentary Papers, 1867, 38, ii, pp. 202ff. I am indebted to Carlene Stephens for the latter reference.

autonomously. The earliest was the *Norddeutsches Eisenbahn-Verband* or North German Railroad Association, which had organized by the fall of 1848. It drew up a freight classification scheme and set rates for through traffic between Berlin, Hamburg, Cologne, and Leipzig, and it also proposed most of the early regulations governing freight traffic that the VDEV adopted in 1849. Within a few years, a number of such associations had been created in the northern and central German states. Since they overlapped geographically, however, they could not avoid rivalry with each other and did not succeed in eliminating competition.[73]

By mid-century, then, Prussian railroads had organized an impressive set of institutions to manage interfirm relations. Although no peak association emerged to oversee both technical and competitive problems, all of these associations were national in scope and all (with the exception, apparently, of the employees' association) proved durable. Because the highest levels of the state made railroad policy from the outset, the resulting incentives for a national organization of railroad interests were felt just as early. For reasons suggested in chapter 3, however, the state did not initially enforce many provisions of the 1838 railroad law, and it often tempered its demands when the railroads found them unduly burdensome. But, when the state stepped in to promote private railroad development in 1842 and then began to experiment with the leverage to regulate that a modicum of promotion gave it, the railroads quickly mobilized to defend their interests. This, rather than the railroads' own business needs, served as the "special incentive" (*besonderer Anlaß*) to organize.[74] The tactics adopted on both sides in the ensuing conflict between the railroads and the state produced a permanent national association, which, with its engineering arm, encompassed all German railroads before there existed any German state—or German railroad system—to speak of. This diluted Prussian strength within the organization and effectively diffused agitation for changes in the Prussian railroad law, which remained in force and, as chapter 6 indicates, served the

---

[73] "Sitzung der Commission"; and "Tages-Ordnung für die am 15. Oktober 1849 zu Wien zusammentretende General-Versammlung des Vereins Deutscher Eisenbahn-Verwaltungen," in *Protokoll*, Vienna, October 15–19, 1849, Anlage II, pp. 9–11; *Die Tätigkeit des Deutschen Eisenbahn-Verkehrs-Verbandes in den ersten 25 Jahren seines Bestehens 1886–1911* (Hannover: Gebrüder Jänecke, Hof-Buch- und Steindruckerei, 1911), p. 3.

[74] *Festschrift*, p. 410.

Prussian state well when officials finally moved to assert control over the railroads after the revolution. In the meantime, the railroads, once organized, turned their attention firmly to the task of creating a unified system of railroads.

Fruitless American Efforts

From the late 1840s through the early 1850s (and beyond), American railroad men also sought to form interest associations and they did so for similar reasons, but their exertions yielded a diversity, rather than a unity, of action and they invariably proved fruitless. All told, a half dozen railroad associations coalesced, flourished briefly, and then disappeared. The fate of some organizations remains sketchy, but the general pattern is clear: antebellum associational activity began at the state and regional level in the late 1840s and culminated in abortive efforts to form national associations in 1854. These endeavors, moreover, followed a dynamic much like the Prussian: it was the threat of regulatory action at one or another level of government that prompted the railroads to pursue collective action. But, operating in the context of a radically different political structure, they, unlike their Prussian counterparts, encountered inordinate difficulties in acting collectively.

By the time the first signs of national activity appeared in the early 1850s, American railroad men had already acquired more than a passing acquaintance with the problems of collective action. On their own initiative (rather than the postmaster general's), American railroad men first met for collective discussions in New England, where a dense railroad network had been laid down by the late 1840s. In the spring of 1848, Boston railroad men launched the New England Association of Railway Superintendents, which counted members from twenty-four roads among its founders and over its lifetime attracted members from fifty-nine lines as well as a handful of individual members. As in the VfEK, membership was individual, not corporate, and required nomination and (unanimous) election by the current membership. But "immediate members" had to hold the position of railroad superintendent in New England; others joined as associate members. Like the VfEK, the New England association established its own library, met monthly, and was designed to promote "the increase and diffusion of knowledge upon scientific and practical subjects connected with rail roads."[75]

But its constitution indicated a second objective: "the promotion of harmony among the rail road companies of New England." As far as the minutes of its monthly meetings reveal, "promotion of harmony" meant mainly standardizing operating rules and technology rather than dampening competition. Over the years, the association devoted most of its time to such problems: it agreed on a variety of rules to govern passenger behavior, lost baggage, and the forwarding of freight, for example; it adopted a standard time for New England railroads; it proposed "a uniform method for certifying the discharge of men from the different roads"; and it devoted a great deal of attention to patent matters.[76] Thus, the New England association functioned like a combined, regional version of the VfEK and the VDEV (with its engineers' association) at this time.

Meanwhile, a second group, to which many of the superintendents also belonged, held two meetings in Boston in late 1850 and early 1851 to tackle the other aspect of railroad "harmony," ameliorating competition. The Convention of the Northern Lines of Railway drew delegates from the twenty-one railroads that handled traffic between Boston and Lake Champlain. Its principal purpose was to devise ways of regulating competition so that passenger fares and freight rates might be increased, for competition had already become intense in this part of the country. The railroad men would have preferred simply to consolidate the mainline railroads and their feeders into a smaller (and more manageable) number of corporations, it seems, but were loath to apply to their legislatures for the necessary statutory permission. They also proved unable to reach agreement on a revenue

[75] *Records of the New England Association of Railway Superintendents* (Washington, D.C.: Gibson Brothers, 1910), pp. 8, 97–98, 101–3. Only three of the fifty-nine lines extended outside of New England, and they connected New England states with New York and New Jersey.

[76] *Records of the New England Association; Reports and Other Papers of the New-England Association of Railroad Superintendents* (Boston: Stacey, Richardson & Co., 1850); Meyer, *History of Transportation*, p. 565. On the adoption of standard time, see Carlene Stephens, "'The Most Reliable Time': William Bond, the New England Railroads, and Time Awareness in 19th-Century America," *Technology and Culture* 30 (January 1989): 1–24. A New York legislative committee included in its report excerpts from the association's reports. *Report of the Committee Appointed to Examine and Report the Causes of Railroad Accidents, the Means of Preventing their Recurrence, &c. Transmitted to the Legislature January 14, 1853* (Albany: C. Van Benthuysen, 1853), pp. 152–56.

pool. Instead, they produced a set of advisory resolutions to govern through traffic and excursion trains, and they set up central boards to act collectively on behalf of each of the mainlines and their feeders.[77] In its broad outlines, the Convention of Northern Lines resembled the rate associations that began to coordinate through traffic and rates in Prussia about the same time.

In both of these cases, the industry's emerging problems with competition and through traffic in New England seem to have called forth appropriate associations. Yet the political context in which they occurred must also be borne in mind, for it seems quite likely that hostility in the state legislatures in the 1840s actually moved the railroad men to act in self-defense, to address their problems collectively, in order to ward off regulation. Public outcry over a series of accidents on the Western Railroad (which later merged with the Boston and Worcester to form the Boston and Albany Railroad) had prompted the Massachusetts legislature to investigate its operations in the early 1840s. More recently, the Western Railroad had drawn the legislature into its battles with the Boston and Worcester Railroad over joint rates and fares, a dispute that festered until the two lines merged after the Civil War. In 1845, moreover, the legislature had gone so far as to create a railroad commission. Although it repealed the act the following year, the legislature generally regulated its railroads more closely than most of the state governments did, requiring them to submit detailed annual reports, fixing rates, and so on.[78]

Discussions at the Convention of Northern Lines in 1850 left little doubt that New England lines perceived hostility in the state legislatures. During a lull in the proceedings one afternoon, the conversation turned to common-carrier liability—one of the Prussian railroads' concerns, it will be recalled—and it became clear that the railroad men would have liked the legislatures to clarify the issue. But Thomas Hopkinson, president of the Boston and Worcester Railroad,

[77] *Proceedings of the Convention of the Northern Lines of Railway, held at Boston, in December, 1850, and January, 1851* (Boston: J. B. Yerrinton & Son, 1851), esp. pp. 28, 85, on the question of consolidation and the environment in the legislatures; *Records of the New England Association*, p. 55; Meyer, *History of Transportation*, pp. 566–69. On the legal issues involved in consolidation, see Chandler, *The Visible Hand*, pp. 135–36; Friedman, *History of American Law*, pp. 454–55; Porter, *Rise of Big Business*, p. 56.

[78] Cf. Handlin and Handlin, *Commonwealth*, pp. 222–24; Salsbury, *The State, the Investor, and the Railroad*, pp. 251–59; Gregg and Pond, comps., *Railroad Laws*, 2:598–660.

stressed the danger of taking railroad problems to the legislature: "If anyone should go before the Legislature . . . for an explanatory law [the minutes reported], he greatly feared that the burdens would be rather increased than diminished." The Boston and Lowell's representative concurred: "It would doubtless be very desirable to have the Legislatures define these and other points, but he much feared that, if they undertook it, they would do the Railroads more harm than good."[79] The railroad men, unwilling to call on the legislatures for help and perhaps fearing that they might intervene of their own accord, set out to solve the industry's problems themselves.

But neither association retained its vitality very long, a pattern that proved typical throughout the antebellum period. By late 1851, the superintendents' association was having trouble attracting a quorum and the number of meetings had dwindled to a half dozen or less per year. Despite periodic efforts to revive it, the association finally dissolved in 1857.[80] Meanwhile, the Convention of Northern Lines considered holding further meetings; Judge Timothy Follet of Vermont "thought they were beneficial, and hoped they would be frequent." But the delegates adjourned indefinitely, leaving it to the central boards to call conventions as necessary.[81]

If the "gun behind the door" must be inferred in the New England context, it need not be in the case of a state-level railroad association that appeared further to the west in the early 1850s, for this one—up to a point—fit the Prussian pattern very closely. This was an association of Ohio railroads that convened because of concerns about a new state tax law. After an initial meeting in late 1851, nineteen railroads sent delegates to a convention in Columbus the following May. There they appointed a committee to contact the state's auditor and attorney general and to obtain their "construction of the law taxing railroad companies." The legislation, following principles set out in Ohio's new constitution, had changed the basis of taxation from a percentage of dividends or an assessment on capital stock to a tax on all real and personal property, and they wanted to clarify the procedures for reporting property values. Once they received a satisfactory response—one that apparently left the procedure up to them—the

[79] Proceedings of the Convention of the Northern Lines, p. 85.
[80] Records of the New England Association, pp. 66, 84–85, 87, 92, 95.
[81] Proceedings of the Convention of the Northern Lines, p. 124.

railroad men proceeded to draw up "a uniform method of listing and returning property for taxation."[82]

But, having formed to handle a political problem and evidently encouraged by their success, the Ohio railroad men decided to form a permanent association. Much like the VDEV in Prussia, it would bring together the presidents of Ohio railroads and connecting lines and would provide a forum for "mutual consultation, and for producing *uniformity of action* in regard to railways in this State." They resolved to meet annually and recommended that the superintendents of the member railroads "form an organization similar to that of the New England Association of Superintendents, and for similar purposes."[83]

The Ohio Railroad Convention held three more meetings over the next two and a half years and took on a range of issues, although it concentrated mainly on competition. The railroad presidents devoted a good deal of their discussion to rules regarding free tickets and passes but also endorsed minimum freight and passenger rates; less contentious issues—that is, unrelated to competition—they resolved with greater dispatch (e.g., recommending the adoption of Columbus time as standard time for Ohio railroads). Like the Convention of Northern Lines, they considered—but found "inexpedient"—the idea of securing state legislation to back up company regulations. They also deemed it "inexpedient to run trains on Sunday" and resolved "that the Postmaster General be respectfully requested to discontinue the transportation of the mails on that day."[84]

Clearly, the state legislature's action mobilized Ohio railroads to pursue "unity of action and intimate association," as a committee

---

[82] *Report of the Proceedings of a Convention of Delegates from Railroad Companies, Held in Columbus, May 4, 1852* (Columbus: Scott and Bascom, 1852), pp. 1–7. For the next ten years, the railroads prepared their own reports on the value of their property and its distribution among districts; state officials generally accepted them at face value. Huang, *State Taxation of Railways*, p. 16.

[83] *Report of the Proceedings . . . May 4, 1852*, p. 7 (emphasis added). Within a year, they were apparently taking steps in that direction, for the New England Association's minutes duly noted a communication from "the Ohio Association" in March of 1853. *Records of the New England Association*, p. 76.

[84] *Report of the Proceedings . . . May 4, 1852*; *Report of Proceedings of the Ohio Railroad Convention, Held in Columbus, December 7th and 8th, 1852* (Columbus: Scott and Bascom, 1852), pp. 5–9; *Report of the Proceedings of the Ohio Rail Road Convention, Held in Columbus, on the 18th Day of January, 1854* (Columbus: Ohio State Journal Office, 1854), pp. 4–7; and *Proceedings of a Convention of the Rail Roads of Ohio and Indiana: Held at Columbus, Ohio, on the 21st and 22d of September, 1854* (Columbus: Ohio State Journal Company, 1854).

report put it, and, once mobilized, they built an association that dealt with a much broader range of political and business issues. It is worth noting also that the political climate in Ohio had recently turned decidedly hostile. The new state constitution of 1851 explicitly prohibited a variety of practices that had previously been used at the state or local level to promote railroad development, and, like others elsewhere, it forbade any state debt for internal improvements. Legislation passed just three days before the association's first official meeting in 1852, moreover, prohibited long haul–short haul rate discrimination as well as the variety of means by which the railroads offered discounts on their published rates.[85] By analogy with the Prussian case, therefore, one might have expected this turn of events to have provided ample incentive for the railroads to hold their new association together.

But, in the American political context, the Ohio association did not survive as a state-level association. Events at its last recorded meeting in September of 1854, in the context of developments elsewhere, provide tantalizing clues to its fate. On the one hand, by its last meeting, industry interests had pulled the association across state lines, and it had formally expanded to include Indiana railroads. In the fall of 1854, Ohio railroads met separately during the Ohio and Indiana Railroad Convention, much as Prussian lines had wanted to do in the VDEV. On the other hand, the September meeting was held off-schedule, three or four months earlier than it should have been, for reasons not explained in the proceedings. It followed by one month, however, a meeting of the eastern trunk-line presidents in New York, and the Ohio and Indiana delegates certainly knew about that meeting, for they considered and then adopted at their September meeting the same freight classification scheme that the trunk-line presidents had drawn up in August. The trunk-line presidents' meeting itself, moreover, represented one step along the path to formation of a national association that included Ohio and Indiana railroads (see below). It may be inferred, therefore, that the Ohio association fell victim to the centrifugal force inherent in the American political structure, first expanding across state lines and then joining what would turn out to be a short-lived national association.

[85] *Acts of a General Nature Passed by the Fiftieth General Assembly of the State of Ohio*, vol. 51 (Columbus: Osgood and Blake, 1853), pp. 17, 24; Scheiber, *Ohio Canal Era*, pp. 286–87, 296.

In the meantime, while Ohio railroads were organizing, regional associations also sprouted in the Northeast, as the industry came under increasing public pressure in the early 1850s. In 1852, the New York and New Haven Railroad took the initiative in convening the first of several self-styled "general" associations. This one was initially called the General Railroad Convention (GRC) and later the General Railroad Association. Invitations went out to all railroads in New England as well as to selected lines in New York and New Jersey. This organization, which also drew delegates from railroads in the British provinces adjacent to New England, held two meetings in 1852, both presided over by Thomas Hopkinson, president of the Boston and Worcester.[86]

As the New York and New Haven's directors explained in their circular, the railroad association was intended to "give to each Company the benefit of the experience of all." Explicit agreement on "proper regulations," they hoped, would prove "perfectly effectual," certainly more so than regulations adopted "without such general concurrence."[87] Thus railroad men representing thirty-some lines addressed the question of technological and operational harmony, setting up a series of committees and tending to settle on broad statements of policy rather than on specific regulations (neither of which were legally binding anyway). They also agreed to "a concert of action" regarding patents: the association would negotiate terms with patentees on behalf of all its members and would spread out over the membership the cost of defending individual roads against "unjust claims." For technical advice regarding patents, they relied on the New England superintendents' association (as the VDEV relied on the VDET in Prussia), because they had too many other questions of "vital moment" to consider. One of those vital questions—the perennial problem of competition—proved intractable once again, however. The relevant committees found it impossible to formulate "general principles" to fight the downward pressure on fares and rates. They merely concluded that current passenger fares were "entirely too low" and freight rates, "entirely inadequate." At the second meeting,

---

[86] *Journal of the Proceedings of the General Railroad Convention, Held at Spring-field, August 24th and 25th, 1852* (New Haven: T. J. Stafford, 1852), pp. 3–7; *Journal of the Proceedings of the General Railroad Association, at their Second Convention, Holden at Springfield, November 10th, 1852* (New Haven: T. J. Stafford, 1852), pp. 3–4.

[87] *Journal of the . . . General Railroad Convention . . . August . . . 1852*, p. 3.

a committee appointed to "define by geographical lines the legiti-
mate business that belongs to each Railroad Company" and to consider plans to apportion gross receipts at points of competition reported the results of its deliberations. After a lengthy discussion, the
convention merely affirmed the need for "a more harmonious action
and friendly coöperation among all the lines of Railway throughout
the country," urged competing lines to practice "mutual for-
bearance," and recommended that a third party mediate disputes.[88]

Again, railroad men in the Northeast seemed merely to be respond-
ing in a timely fashion to the internal pressure of industry problems,
but this time the "gun behind the door" had become more visible. In
their circular invitation, the New York and New Haven directors
warned that the industry would suffer the consequences, if it did not
take action to solve its own problems: "The Railroad interest has
become one of very great importance to the public, as well as to the
Stockholders," they declared, "and it is apparent that *united action*
alone, can secure to it the influence it ought to have."[89] Indeed, a
committee report described the association's formation explicitly as
a defensive move "for the protection and prosperity of the Railroad
Corporations interested."[90] In 1849 and 1850, it will be recalled, the
Connecticut General Assembly had established a commissioner system, appointing three commissioners for every railroad and giving
them a mandate to improve public safety. This reflected concern
about the increasing number of railroad accidents. "We can hardly
look into an exchange paper, of late," observed the *American Railroad Journal* early in 1851, "without meeting an account of some
dreadful accident on railroads."[91] By this time, financial scandals also
were beginning to plague the industry. This was the background

---

[88] Ibid., pp. 14, 19, 23; *Journal of the . . . General Railroad Association . . . November . . . 1852*, pp. 5, 10. The New York and New Haven's superintendent, George W.
Whistler, had been elected a member of the New England superintendent's association
that spring. *Records of the New England Association*, p. 67. The GRC committees dealt
with construction, rules and regulations, freight rates, passenger fares, mail compensation, "free lists" (i.e., lists of individuals who had been given the privilege of traveling
without charge), ticketing and payment of fares to conductors, and connection of
trains.
[89] *Journal of the . . . General Railroad Convention . . . August . . . 1852*, p. 3 (emphasis added).
[90] *Journal of the . . . General Railroad Association . . . November . . . 1852*, p. 5.
[91] *American Railroad Journal*, February 15, 1851, quoted in *Report of the Committee Appointed to Examine and Report the Causes of Railroad Accidents*, p. 145.

against which the New York and New Haven issued its call for an association to defend industry interests.

Since the industry had interstate interests, the association had an interstate membership—indeed, it opened membership to all railroads in the country—but state policy continued to be made largely at the state-government level. The GRC, now renamed the General Railroad Association, scheduled another convention for Saratoga Springs in June of 1853, but it does not seem to have met again.[92] The most persistent regulatory threat continued to come from the state legislatures, but the industry in this part of the country had clearly achieved interstate dimensions—hence, the rather extravagant move to open membership to all railroads in the country. Yet, absent a credible threat of sustained regulation from above, the railroad men could not sustain a national—or any other—association in a fragmented regulatory context.

Efforts to promote harmony nonetheless intensified in the banner year 1854 and, with an inadvertent boost from the federal government, culminated in the first (nearly) national meetings of American railroads. This was the year in which the last of the great eastern trunk-lines was completed, a year also marked by nationwide economic troubles and turmoil in the industry. "The year just passed," the directors of the Philadelphia, Wilmington, and Baltimore Railroad reported in early 1855, "has been marked by an unparalleled stringency in the money market, affecting all branches of business, and none more severely than that of rail roads."[93] Exacerbating the industry's troubles, as the directors of the Boston and Worcester Railroad noted frankly, was "a series of disasters, follies and crimes in railway management."[94] These events threw the industry into turmoil, heightening the need for collective action, and they help to account for the multiplicity of railroad meetings that year. But only in part, for what pushed the railroad men to the point of action was something quite different: the United States postmaster general's

---

[92] *Journal of the . . . General Railroad Association . . . November . . . 1852*, p. 13. The New England Association of Railway Superintendents, it might be noted, also held no meetings between April of 1853 and January of 1854. *Records of the New England Association*, pp. 76–77.

[93] *Seventeenth Annual Report of the Philadelphia, Wilmington, and Baltimore Rail Road Company . . . made January 8, 1855* (Philadelphia: John C. Clark and Son, 1855), p. 5.

[94] *Twenty-Fifth Annual Report of the Directors of the Boston and Worcester Railroad Corporation*, p. 13.

sudden departure (as the railroads saw it) from cooperative methods of negotiation with the railroads.

This dispute, like its predecessor in 1841–42, began when Postmaster General James Campbell initiated a new campaign to adjust the railroads' "mail pay." This, the rate that the Post Office paid the railroads to transport mail, had been a constant source of irritation on both sides, since the railroads first began to carry the mail in the 1830s. In this instance, according to the railroad men, the postmaster general had moved—without prior consultation with the railroads— to have a bill introduced in Congress that would have mandated a maximum of $75 (per year per mile of track) for one daily first-class mail, when the current maximum of $300 for two daily mails, as they saw it, was "barely adequate."[95]

Representatives from twenty-two railroads throughout the country gathered in Baltimore in May of 1854 to protest the postmaster general's action. The convention drew delegates not only from the four trunk-lines but also from other northeastern and mid-Atlantic railroads, from the Ohio Central, and from several roads in Virginia, North Carolina, and Georgia. After a preliminary meeting of the lines between New York and Montgomery, Alabama, in April, the call for "a General Rail Road Convention" had come from the Philadelphia, Wilmington, and Baltimore Railroad. The purpose of the meeting being to persuade Congress to reject the proposed legislation, the delegates appointed a distinguished committee to prepare a memorial.[96]

As emerged forcefully in the memorial, one of their principal objections centered on the unilateral manner in which the federal government, to which the railroads owed little, had proceeded. On the one hand, they had actually hoped for an increase in the mail rates, the memorial explained, "and expected to be met in a spirit of candor and

[95] "Report of the Committee" in *Proceedings of a Convention Held in the City of Baltimore, May 19th, 1854, on the Recommendation to Reduce the Pay for Mail Service to Rail Road Companies. Together with the Report of the Committee Appointed on That Occasion* (Baltimore: John Murphy and Co., 1854), pp. 11, 15–16. On the 1845 legislation that governed postal contracts at the time, see *History of the Railway Mail Service*, p. 110.

[96] *Proceedings of a Convention Held in the City of Baltimore*, pp. 3–5. The committee members were Nathan Randall of the New York Central; J. Edgar Thomson, president of the Pennsylvania Railroad; Samuel M. Felton, president of the Philadelphia, Wilmington, and Baltimore Railroad; George W. Hughes of the Baltimore and Susquehanna; John H. Done, Baltimore and Ohio's Master of Transportation; and John P. King, president of the Georgia Railroad. Ibid., p. 9.

fairness by the Department."[97] Instead, the postmaster general had "startled" the railroads by attributing his own difficulties in meeting expenses to the "exhorbitant [sic] amounts" paid to the railroads: "The Committee cannot conceal the surprise with which the recommendation of the Postmaster General [to reduce mail pay] has been received by the Rail Road interests throughout the country." The postmaster, they fairly exclaimed, had formulated the proposed legislation "[w]ithout consultation with any of the great lines of communication—whose co-operation must be sought in any plan which the Government in its wisdom may think proper to adopt in the transportation of the mails." Such a manner of proceeding, they declared, was "entirely without precedent in the previous history of the Government."[98]

That the *federal* government, on the other hand, should demand what they considered to be special, low rates made the whole affair intolerable:

> The Rail Road interest has grown up, as is well known, under every species of embarrassment, and is indebted exclusively to the States in which these various enterprises have originated, and the public spirited individuals whose capital has contributed to their development and support. From the General Government they have received no aid. At times when capital was almost indispensable in the accomplishment of those important results which have contributed so largely to the public convenience, they have been left to their own unaided exertions. The policy of the Government towards these works, has been one of passive indifference. While it has deemed it unwise to aid in this great effort on the part of the States, and individuals, to secure by a moderate investment in the beginning, the perpetual transportation of their mails, it has been among the first to throw itself upon these improved facilities, and has at no time failed to claim greater privileges than are allowed to the public at large. Such had been the policy of the Post Office Department for years past, and the Committee refer to it in the present connection, more as a matter of history than in any spirit of crimination [sic] or complaint.[99]

[97] "Report of the Committee" in *Proceedings of a Convention Held in the City of Baltimore*, p. 13.
[98] Ibid., pp. 11, 14.
[99] Ibid., p. 12. "Perpetual transportation" was an allusion to proposals, such as that

Feeling no special debt to the federal government, they could not but object forcefully to the postmaster's initiative. The railroads, they concluded, "believe that something is due to the States, corporations and individuals, to whom they owe their existence." But the federal government had no such claims to special consideration; the railroads would "serve the Government *upon terms as advantageous as those extended to any other interest, whether public or private.*"[100]

At issue, however, was far more than the matter of adequate compensation. The postmaster general's action contravened basic democratic principles, they contended, and it was this conviction that had prompted their convention. "An attempt had been made, by the aid of Congress, to subject [the railroads] to the absolute control of the Post Office Department," they maintained:

> They were to be brought under an arbitrary standard of rates for the service required by the Government *without their consent*—and . . . in violation of every principle of justice and fair dealing.
>
> The rights of corporations, as well as of individuals, are sustained alike by law and public sympathy. The Rail Road Companies. . . . assembled in convention for no purpose of intimidation or monopoly. They had no desire to take advantage of the dependence of Government upon the facilities which their own capital had supplied. They have been willing at all times to submit to a fair and impartial arbitration, as between the department and themselves, upon all questions of disagreement. The Companies could do no more without an absolute and slavish submission to the will of the Post Office Department.[101]

The committee expressed the companies' faith that Congress would not endorse "the attempt to coerce them." To force the railroads to carry the mail at below-market prices, they contended, would "vio-

under discussion in 1842, that the federal government subsidize railroad development by buying perpetual rights of transportation. For other examples, see Report of the Committee on the Post Office and Post Roads, *American State Papers*, vol. 4, 1835–36, Doc. 291; "Documents Showing the value of railways for the defence of the country, and for the speedy and cheap transportation of the mails," Senate Doc. 327, 27th Cong., 2d sess., 1841–42; Duff Green, *Circular to the Presidents of Railroad Companies*, Washington City, December 10, 1851.

[100] "Report of the Committee" in *Proceedings of a Convention Held in the City of Baltimore*, pp. 20–21 (original emphasis). The postmaster general believed that the Post Office was paying higher rates than private parties in 1854. See *History of the Railway Mail Service*, p. 53.

[101] "Report of the Committee" in *Proceedings of a Convention Held in the City of Baltimore*, pp. 12–13 (original emphasis).

late one of the fundamental principles of our Government, viz: *that private property shall not be taken for public use, without full compensation.*" If events proved them wrong, then they would have no recourse but "to retire from all connexion with the Mail service." And in that case, they cautioned, the postmaster general, facing public wrath over "a derangement of the Mail service of the country,—a result certain to take place," would have "to justify the Department in an act, as extraordinary in its character, as it would be unjust and oppressive in its effects." The Post Office would do better to make up its deficit by limiting the franking privilege, they warned. "Certain it is, that the Companies represented in the late Convention understand their rights, and will never consent to be driven from the impregnable ground which they occupy."[102]

After the convention had endorsed a series of resolutions to this effect and appointed the committee that prepared this memorial, it adjourned indefinitely. But it left open the possibility of further meetings, empowering the Baltimore and Ohio and Philadelphia, Wilmington, and Baltimore railroads to call another convention whenever they thought it necessary.[103] The postmaster general apparently returned to the consensual relations that generally characterized the antebellum period.[104] A decade later, the president of the Virginia Central Railroad, encountering a Confederate postmaster general who used the same powers much more aggressively, yearned for the relatively amicable relations of the past: "powers which might have been claimed [in the antebellum period]," he recalled, "had lain dormant under the old Government."[105]

Once prompted to action by the federal government, however, the trunk-lines sought to capitalize on their experience, as Prussian roads had eight years earlier. Three months after the Baltimore convention, representatives of the four trunk-line railroads held their first meeting in New York City. Present when deliberations began on August 15, 1854, were officials from the New York Central, New York and Erie, Pennsylvania, and Baltimore and Ohio railroads as well as from

[102] Ibid., pp. 14, 19–20 (original emphasis).

[103] *Proceedings of a Convention Held in the City of Baltimore*, pp. 7–9.

[104] Between 1845 and 1867, the legislation governing mail pay as well as Post Office contracting practices remained largely unchanged. *History of the Railway Mail Service*, p. 110.

[105] *Address of the President of the Va. Central Railroad Co., to the Stockholders, on the Subject of Withdrawal of the Mails by the Postmaster General* (Richmond: MacFarlane & Ferguson, 1864), p. 4. On the policies and activities of the Union and Confederate states, see Bensel, *Yankee Leviathan*.

two railroads and a steamboat line that connected the trunk-lines. The first item of business: "the subject of Mail Pay." The remaining issues on the agenda concerned freight and passenger rates, the desirability of joint advertising and a common sales office for through tickets in New York, and other measures to dampen nonrate forms of competition. Over the course of four days, the railroad men accepted a committee report that set out their views on the proper principles to guide the setting of mail-pay rates. The committee then proceeded to adopt some twenty resolutions regarding operations and rate-making. They also agreed on a freight-classification scheme as well as on a detailed enumeration of passenger and freight rates. Their business concluded, the railroad men adjourned, leaving all other matters for the collective decision of the trunk-line superintendents.[106]

Within six months American railroad men resumed their efforts to form national associations, but in the American context diversity rather than unity prevailed, for not one but two overlapping groups of railroad men determined to form (nearly) national associations that year. Pursuing a common strategy of private regulation to stabilize the industry, but adopting fundamentally different tactics, neither of them survived very long.

One association grew directly out of meetings of the trunk-line superintendents that followed the trunk-line presidents' meeting in August. After a series of meetings in Buffalo, Philadelphia, Columbus, Dayton, and elsewhere, the superintendents met in Cleveland on November 28, 1854. This meeting began as a routine assembly, it seems, attended by representatives from the four trunk-lines, two New England lines, and some twenty other railroads in the Midwest. Most of the delegates were top-level managers—general superintendents, chief engineers, general freight and ticket agents. A handful of railroad presidents also attended, but none from the trunk-lines, although those lines were amply represented on the committee appointed to prepare an agenda for the meeting.[107]

---

[106] *Proceedings of the Railroad Convention Held at the St. Nicholas Hotel, New York. August 15, 1854* (New York: New York and Erie Railroad Company's Printing Office, 1854). The dollar amounts of the agreed-upon fares and rates were omitted in the published proceedings, however. See also Chandler, *The Visible Hand*, p. 125; idem, *Henry Varnum Poor*, pp. 150–51. Among those attending were J. Edgar Thomson, Herman Haupt, William G. Harrison, and Erastus Corning, who was elected president of the convention.

[107] *Proceedings of a Meeting of Representatives of the Several Railroad Companies Between New York, Boston, Philadelphia and Baltimore, Chicago, Cincinnati, and*

Over three days of deliberations, the railroad men reached agreement on a wide range of issues that addressed both aspects of harmony (although in the domain of standardization those issues that pertained strictly to railroad technology—as opposed to operations—received minimal attention). The first item of business concerned rates and the classification of freight. The delegates adopted resolutions establishing minimum rates and fares, delineating a freight-classification scheme, and prohibiting nonrate means of competing for freight and passengers (such as rebates and drawbacks, the indiscriminate use of free passes, and "the employment of Runners and solicitors of passengers"). They also agreed to share the cost of an agent to protect the railroads from the "litigations and annoyances" arising from patent disputes.[108] Enforcement relied, as in the VDEV, on the "good faith" of the member companies. "[N]o company shall be at liberty to feel itself morally absolved from any obligation imposed upon it by the proceedings of this Convention," they agreed, "without at least giving thirty days notice."[109]

In a departure from its more mundane agenda, however, the convention also took several steps to secure the larger interests of the industry. First, the delegates appointed a committee to draw up a public statement "setting out the position of the general Railroad Interest in the United States, and stating the reasons why higher rates of compensation should be obtained for the carriage of Passengers, Mails and Freight." In its report, accordingly, the committee expounded at length on the harmful effects of competition and on the need for higher rates and fares. They did not propose to obtain all of "the increased revenue which Railroad companies require" from the

---

the Ohio and Mississippi Rivers, Held at Cleveland, November 28th, 1854 (Cleveland: Sanford and Hayward, 1854), pp. 3–6.

[108] Ibid., pp. 9–12, 19–23. The distribution of an excessive number of free passes (especially to politicians and journalists) absorbed at least some—and often a good deal—of attention in all railroad meetings. "Until a general reform shall take place in reference to the issue of these passes," one committee of railroad men concluded in 1855, "it is not probable that any single Company will undertake to abolish the practice entirely." Report of a Committee Appointed January 4th, 1855, by the Directors of the New York Central Railroad Company, at the Request of the Stockholders, Authorizing Certain Examinations to Be Made of the 'Acts and Doings of the Directors and Treasurer,' Subsequent to the Consolidation (Boston: J. H. Eastburn's Press, 1855), p. 28. The practice also troubled Prussian railroads; see [VDEV Minutes], Cologne, June 28–29, 1847.

[109] Proceedings of a Meeting of Representatives of the Several Railroad Companies, p. 23.

public alone. "The object of the Convention has not been to destroy but to regulate competition," and "reforms commenced at home" would also improve the railroads' balance sheets. But their central point was clear enough: the railroads needed higher fares and rates. In this connection, they also returned to the subject of mail pay, quoting several paragraphs from the proceedings of the trunk-line presidents' meeting in August. "It is upon the principles exhibited in this report, that Railway companies propose to act," they concluded.[110]

Second, the delegates did what earlier conventions had declined to do: they endorsed the idea of approaching their state legislatures for help. Two issues stood at the forefront. Having themselves agreed to foreswear use of soliciting agents as a competitive device, they advocated "the abolition of all laws licencing [sic] Runners or Bookers" and the enactment of legislation to make those activities illegal. They also wanted legal penalties on employees who neglected or disobeyed operating regulations, causing accidents "by which life is taken or imperiled, and property destroyed." Indeed, it would be "most beneficial," they maintained, if railroad employees were generally held legally accountable "for the violation of the laws of the road."[111]

Finally, as the meeting came to a close, the railroad men deemed it "expedient and proper" to adopt "a permanent organization of an association" that would hold semiannual meetings. This association —the General Railroad Association of the Eastern, Middle, and Western States (GRAEMWS)—not only would look after the problems of passenger safety and freight service but would attend more generally to "the mutual interests of the Railroad Companies." In their final action, the delegates prepared an agenda for the first meeting of the new association by creating seven committees to report on subjects running the gamut from police and management of the roads to passenger comfort and freight traffic to "the principle which should govern the distribution of joint receipts."[112]

At its first official meeting, the strategic emphasis of the GRAEMWS took on sharper definition. This meeting drew an even better turnout—sixty-three delegates from thirty-eight railroads—but a sufficient number of delegates had resigned or were unable to partici-

---

[110] Ibid., pp. 6, 17–18.
[111] Ibid., p. 11.
[112] Ibid., pp. 23–24.

pate that those in attendance decided to reconstitute the committees set up at the previous meeting.[113] As the dust settled and they proceeded with substantive discussions, it became clear that the GRAEMWS would focus principally on plans for a revenue pool. On behalf of the committee appointed to consider the distribution of joint receipts, Herman Haupt of the Pennsylvania Railroad presented a report that dwelt at length on the "intricate and diversified" problems to be addressed, if the railroads were "to secure the desired concert of action." An equitable scheme for the distribution of joint receipts, the committee concluded, could not be achieved through calculation: "in fact, concessions must form the foundation of any arrangement that will not prove to be in practice a rope of sand." In the end, they proposed a set of (still quite complex) rules to cut "the Gordian knot," which the convention unanimously endorsed.[114]

In other business, the railroad men endorsed a strategy of private regulation regarding railroad operations. They returned to the question of the companies' liability for their employees' work-related injuries, but now they had evidently decided not to pursue state legislation after all. Instead, the reporting committee noted that federalism made it difficult to standardize employee rules:

> the various laws and somewhat conflicting decisions of the courts of different States, impose a greater necessity of providing against these evils in some States than in others, and renders [sic] it difficult to adopt a system of rules, or a form of contract between railroad companies and their employees that will be equally well adapted to all cases and situations.[115]

The delegates settled for the committee's recommendation that railroads that were located in states where their liability for employee injuries was "not clearly defined" should require their employees to sign contracts absolving the company of liability.[116] Thus by the end

---

[113] *Proceedings of the General Railroad Association of the Eastern, Middle, and Western States; Also of the General Ticket Agents' Association, Convened at the Monongahela House, Pittsburg, March 13, 1855* (Philadelphia: T. K. and P. G. Collins, 1855), pp. 6–9.

[114] *Proceedings of the General Railroad Association of the Eastern, Middle, and Western States*, pp. 10–16 (quotations from pp. 11, 14).

[115] Ibid., p. 17. On the development of the fellow-servant rule in tort law, see Friedman, *History of American Law*, pp. 261–64, 409–27.

[116] Before adjourning to meet again in November, the delegates also adopted resolutions regarding ticketing, which had been hammered out at a concurrent meeting of

of its first official meeting the GRAEMWS delegates had settled on a strategy of private rather than state action to stabilize the industry, and they chose a revenue pool as their preferred tactic to eliminate competition.

The associational dynamic was remarkably "Prussian": the United States postmaster general's unilateral effort to reduce the railroads' mail pay, like Minister von Bodelschwingh's hint that he might enforce the rate provisions of the 1838 railroad law, initially prompted the railroads to act collectively. Once moved to action, American railroads turned their attention, as Prussian lines had a few years earlier, to other problems common to the industry. Completion of the last of the trunk-line railroads in 1854 and the attendant increase in competition clearly coincided with the first meetings of trunk-line representatives, but industry developments alone did not provide the initial impetus to overcome the barriers to collective action. The postmaster general did that.

In typical American fashion, however, this association yielded neither a truly national nor a permanent nor a unitary association. From the outset, this new and most ambitious association did not include southern lines, presumably because the trunk-lines (with the exception of the Baltimore and Ohio) shared so few connections with southern lines. Even as a northern association, the GRAEMWS itself apparently did not survive to meet again in November as planned. To complicate matters, furthermore, another self-styled "general" association had sprung up simultaneously in the Northeast, intent on pursuing private regulation with different tactics.

The General Railroad Association (GRA) held its first meeting in New York City in November of 1854, five days before the Cleveland meeting that produced the GRAEMWS. The three monthly meetings of this more modest association (later called the General Railroad Convention) attracted top-level managers—again, superintendents, general agents, and the occasional president—from twelve to thirteen roads in New England, New York, and New Jersey as well as from the Michigan Southern and Northern Indiana Railroad. It may well have represented an effort to revive the 1852 organization of the same name, since its meetings were chaired by John P. Jackson of the

---

general ticket agents, and after some dissension agreed to maintain the prevailing fares and rates for the summer. Ibid., pp. 17–18.

New Jersey Railroad and Transportation Company, who had served as a vice-president of the earlier association and was elected president of this association at its last recorded meeting. But Jackson himself characterized the GRA as "a new organization," and delegates to the third meeting, accordingly, adopted rules of permanent organization.[117]

Why this parallel association formed is not immediately evident. It certainly reflected renewed concern, as Chairman Jackson emphasized in his remarks at the first meeting, that the railroads put their affairs in order, lest they invite attempts by the "public"—that is, the state legislatures—to do so. Pressing problems included not only competition and profits but railroad safety. The previous year the New York and New Haven Railroad had experienced one of the worst railroad accidents in New England history, prompting the Connecticut legislature to appoint a railroad commission (in addition to the system of commissioners for each railroad). The New York legislature had also turned its attention to the "causes of railroad accidents" in 1853, and its investigating committee had reached "the opinion that the public safety and welfare would be enhanced by placing railroads under the rigid supervision of the State."[118] In addition, the industry found itself under pressure, Jackson acknowledged, because of "the stupendous frauds which have lately produced such deep distrust."[119] One of the more spectacular events had occurred earlier that year, when the New York and New Haven Railroad went bankrupt and its president fled to Europe.[120] In the circumstances, a rail-

---

[117] Journal of the . . . General Railroad Association . . . November . . . 1852, p. 2; Journal of the Proceedings of the General Railroad Association, at their Meeting Holden in New York, November 23d, 1854 (Newark: Daily Advertiser Print, 1855), pp. 3, 9–10, 25–30. The latter includes minutes for the meeting named as well as for subsequent meetings on December 12, 1854, and January 16, 1855. A report on the last meeting in the trade press referred to it as the General Railroad Convention. American Railroad Journal, January 27, 1855, pp. 58–59.

[118] Kirkland, Men, Cities, and Transportation, 2:235; Report of the Committee Appointed to Examine and Report the Causes of Railroad Accidents, p. 20. From 1831 through 1852, 32 railroad accidents had claimed 73 lives, an average of 1.5 accidents and 3.3 deaths per year. But in the year 1853 alone the number of fatal accidents suddenly jumped to 11, in which 121 people were killed. In 1854, the incidence of fatal accidents declined—there were only 2—but those 2 alone resulted in 81 deaths. Shaw, History of Railroad Accidents, pp. 453–54. For insight into the industry's financial position in the mid-1850s, see Chandler, Henry Varnum Poor, pp. 129–44; Fishlow, American Railroads, pp. 112–18.

[119] Journal of the . . . General Railroad Association . . . November . . . 1854, pp. 6–7.

[120] Fishlow, American Railroads, p. 113.

road association would provide a forum for "mutual improvement
and protection," Jackson reasoned. Echoing a theme stressed by the
American Railroad Journal from late 1852 on, Jackson urged his fellow railroad men to pursue "a general retrenchment and reform, [so]
that our railroads may be regarded as permanent institutions."[121] He
returned to the theme in his closing remarks at the last recorded
meeting in January of 1855, acknowledging managerial deficiencies
and alluding to the threat of unilateral public action to correct them.[122]
Lurking in the background, the threat of legislative action lent added
urgency to efforts to address industry problems collectively.

Like the GRAEMWS and previous associations, moreover, the GRA
considered and then rejected a strategy of state action to bring order to
industry operations. Resolutions to have maximum train speeds and
operating regulations fixed in state law were sent to committee, but
in the end the delegates decided against the strategy. As before, the
railroads feared that the legislatures would impose additional burdens on them. Thomas Hopkinson of the Boston and Worcester Railroad disapproved of the idea for the same reasons that he had outlined
at the Convention of Northern Lines: he deemed it "a bad policy to be
bringing to bear directly on railroad corporations so much of the kind
attention of legislators." Also, changes in the industry—especially
the increasing frequency with which the railroads crossed state
lines—made state-level legislation less attractive. Hopkinson voiced
reservations on this score, too. On the one hand, he warned, variations in the operating conditions from one company to another pre-
cluded a universally applicable speed limit; and, on the other, state
legislation would complicate interstate operation, because it would
be difficult to secure "united and uniform laws in the various States
through which some railroads run."[123] Consequently, the GRA, like
the GRAEMWS, opted for a strategy of private regulation of railroad
operations.

Yet, on closer inspection, the policies of the two associations di-

---

[121] *Journal of the . . . General Railroad Association . . . November . . . 1854*, pp. 6–7;
Chandler, *Henry Varnum Poor*, p. 103. The passage regarding "general retrenchment
and reform" along with other sections of Jackson's opening speech were incorporated
into the articles of association adopted at the January 1855 meeting. Ibid., p. 27, and
American Railroad Journal, January 27, 1855, p. 58.

[122] *Journal of the . . . General Railroad Association . . . November . . . 1854*, pp. 30–
32.

[123] Ibid., pp. 9, 17–18, 20 (quotations from pp. 17–18).

verged in a fundamental way: the GRA advocated different tactics in its pursuit of private regulation of competition. Like other railroad men in other forums, the GRA delegates saw "adequate remuneration" as indispensable, and they agreed that passengers should normally be charged no less than three cents per mile. But they failed to adopt explicit means of attaining "just compensation." Their discussions of competition frequently centered on train speeds, for competition had driven up speeds and costs were known to increase disproportionately with speed. Having rejected the idea of seeking help from the legislatures in restraining speeds, however, the GRA's Committee on Speed simply recommended in a lengthy report that the public be made to pay the extra cost of the express trains that it demanded. It also urged competing lines, "the bane of railroad interests," to resolve their differences in ways that would "leave each the proper enjoyment of its facilities, and reasonable compensation for their respective traffic." But it had nothing to say about how this might be accomplished, and it offered no resolutions for consideration. In the long discussion that ensued, the railroad men adopted a general resolution affirming as "reasonable" express passenger fares 20–25 percent higher than regular fares. But they shied away from concerted action. One delegate considered the resolution "too indefinite," but Hopkinson's response made clear that the GRA operated under a more limited mandate than the GRAEMWS: "It could not be expected of this convention to make any resolutions of a definite character," he retorted, "inasmuch as each of the Boards of Directors of the many railroads are in no way bound to the decision of the convention."[124] Instead, GRA discussions centered mainly on technical, rather than cooperative, means of reducing costs. The delegates agreed to step up efforts to economize on fuel by substituting coal and coke for wood, for example, and they heard a report on the Norwich and Worcester Railroad's experience with a bituminous coal-burning locomotive. They also resolved to bolster profits by eliminating "all perquisites received by employees, and all other abuses which deprive companies of their rightful earnings, and much abate their revenues."[125] The GRA's emphasis on

[124] Ibid., pp. 6–7, 16–19; *American Railroad Journal*, January 27, 1855, p. 58. The committee report on speed is reprinted in the former source, pp. 11–17, and indicates that express trains had been introduced only in the previous ten years (p. 11).

[125] *Journal of the . . . General Railroad Association . . . November . . . 1854*, pp. 6–7, 19–20, 26–27; *American Railroad Journal*, January 27, 1855, p. 58.

economy rather than interfirm agreement as a way of improving profits contrasted sharply with the proceedings in the GRAEMWS.[126]

Thus the two associations seem to have represented alternative conceptions of the appropriate methods that the industry should use to defend its interests. Both drew high-level railroad officials, up to but not including the trunk-line presidents. Their membership overlapped and fluctuated over their brief existence, possibly indicating a good deal of indecision about appropriate tactics among the mass of railroad officials. Six roads, including three of the trunk-lines, sent delegates to at least one meeting of each association, while two lines—the New York and Erie and the Michigan Southern—sent representatives to all meetings of both associations.[127] Both associations debated the value of state legislation before electing reluctantly to pursue private action. But they parted ways in their choice of tactics to address the prickly problem of competition, the GRAEMWS opting for a revenue pool and the GRA for individual economy.

Such discrepancies aside, a larger point emerges from this confusion of associations: the way that the fragmented American political structure tended to pull the attention of railroad men in several directions at once. The fate of the antebellum associations surely reflected the difficulties of collective action under conditions of trunk-line competition. But the Prussian experience, as well as the success that American railroads would enjoy later in the century, suggests that the locus of railroad policy in the antebellum American political structure presented special obstacles of its own. Despite occasional troubles with the postmaster general, the locus of policy-making remained largely in the hands of the state legislatures—hence, the repeated discussions of state legislation. The necessity of keeping an eye on a multitude of increasingly hostile legislatures surely hindered cohesion across state lines. But, as the railroads' interests be-

[126] This was also Henry Varnum Poor's preferred strategy for dealing with trunk-line competition. Chandler, *Henry Varnum Poor*, pp. 151–52.

[127] For details, see the proceedings cited above. In the GRA, John B. Jervis, president of the Michigan Southern, appears to have been a pivotal member: he headed several committees, including the one that drew up plans for a permanent organization, and would probably have been its president, had he not declined the position. But his road also sent representatives to both meetings of the GRAEMWS. On Jervis's railroad work, see Neal Fitzsimons, ed., *The Reminiscences of John B. Jervis, Engineer of the Old Croton* (Syracuse: Syracuse University Press, 1971), pp. 85–108, 176–82. During these same years, it should be remembered, the New England Association of Railway Superintendents still officially existed, although it had grown rather moribund.

came regional in scope, the common problems of interstate traffic demanded cohesion across state lines. Collective action on a regional scale thus promised to yield economic benefits, but in the antebellum context it offered limited political rewards. The postmaster general's threat from "above," which had precipitated this flurry of activity in 1854, proved neither adequate to sustain a "general" association nor sufficiently menacing to force the railroads to resolve their differences regarding tactics. Mail pay constituted merely one of a multiplicity of issues that the railroads faced in a multiplicity of policy-making arenas. In a political structure without a clear center, the GRA met the same fate as all the other antebellum associations: after adopting rules for a permanent organization and opening membership to all American railroads,[128] it quietly disintegrated.

After 1854 the trunk-line presidents continued to meet regularly, occasionally seeking again to reach interregional agreement on rates and fares, but they achieved a measure of success only when increased traffic during the Civil War dampened competition. Southern railroads, meanwhile, held intermittent conventions of their own.[129] No permanent, national association emerged until later in the century.

Political Structure and System-Building

As these contrasting stories suggest, careful attention to the structure of national political institutions exposes new dimensions to the process of organizing interests. At any given moment, the American and Prussian political structures each embodied distinctive incentives that encouraged railroad interests to organize differently in the two countries. Because policy emanated from the Prussian central state from the outset, Prussian railroads succeeded much earlier in forming a permanent, (inter)national association that enabled them to draw on their collective strength in dealing with state officials. The unitary-bureaucratic structure of the Prussian state helped to offset the centrifugal pressures of competition, thus encouraging the kind of interfirm cooperation that became the hallmark of late nineteenth-century German industrialism. American lines initially

---

[128] *Journal of the . . . General Railroad Association . . . November . . . 1854*, pp. 26–28; *American Railroad Journal*, January 27, 1855, pp. 58–59.

[129] On subsequent antebellum meetings and later developments, see chap. 6.

faced a mosaic of fragmented state policies, and they organized valiantly but unsuccessfully during the antebellum years. The federal-
legislative structure of the American state, in effect, worked in tandem with competition to inhibit coordination of interfirm relations.
This divergence, it should be noted, confirms Chandler's finding that
the pattern of interfirm relations marked a critical point of difference
between the American and German experiences with managerial
capitalism. *Vormärz* Prussian railroad men, like German industrial
capitalists later in the century, proved better able to achieve cooperation than their American counterparts.

But it is difficult to see that the causal forces to which Chandler
points—differences in the way that American and Prusso-German
law treated combinations, which reflected, in turn, differences in
shared beliefs about the value of competition and cooperation—had
much impact in this industry during these years.[130] The VDEV could
have made adoption of its policies mandatory for all members, but it
declined to do so, as noted earlier, and held to the policy for nearly
thirty years. Legal differences, therefore, cannot account for the durability of the German association or for the ephemeral nature of antebellum American associations. The repeated efforts of American railroad men to build a comparable association, moreover, suggest that
they, too, placed a high value on cooperation. And in neither country
did either the law or shared beliefs enable railroad men to deal effectively with interfirm competition. Instead, the story of railroad associations highlights an alternative explanation for the competitive
nature of managerial capitalism in the United States and its cooperative nature in Germany: the exceptional American and Prussian political structures. An institutionalist perspective on business and
economic history not sufficiently expansive to encompass the structure of national political institutions misses the culprit responsible
for the generally weak organization of economic interests in the
United States and for their comparative strength in Prusso-Germany.

The economic consequences also deserve notice. Because of their
repeated failures to sustain railroad associations, it seems reasonable
to think, American railroads operated less efficiently as a national
system than they might have. Since they labored under high fixed
costs, their cost efficiency depended critically on the volume of traffic

---

[130] Chandler, *Scale and Scope*, pp. 395, 501.

and the distance that it traveled. Railroad men in both countries understood this as early as 1840.[131] At a minimum, efficient through traffic required a uniform gauge so that wagons and cars could range freely over the system. But it also called for uniform construction of rolling stock and for standardized procedures to handle traffic as it moved from one line to another. In all respects, the Prussians— together with their colleagues in the other German states—moved ahead earlier than American lines.[132]

Standardized gauge, for example, had become a reality in the German states by the mid-1850s. In this respect, choices made in neighboring countries—Saxony, Bavaria, Belgium—constrained the options open to Prussian railroad men. Once the Leipzig-Dresden Railroad in Saxony, for example, adopted the English gauge, neighboring Prussian lines followed suit, and this in turn increased the economic advantages of doing so for subsequent companies.[133] As the directors of the Berlin-Stettin Railroad explained in 1841, they had originally planned to install a broader gauge but had now decided to follow the lead of other lines; with a broader gauge, they feared that they would be forced to pay more for rolling stock.[134] By 1842, as Finance Minister von Alvensleben saw it, Prussian railroads no longer had much choice in the matter.[135] At the 1843 meeting with state officials in Berlin, Prussian railroad men endorsed the English gauge (4' 8-1/2" English or 1.435 meters), which was already the only gauge in use on Prussian lines.[136] A few months later, Peter Beuth, acting for the finance minister, sent a copy of the proceedings of the meeting to the minister of foreign affairs with the request that the importance of a uniform gauge be impressed upon officials in neigh-

---

[131] See chap. 1.

[132] In addition to the activities discussed below, the German association also, as noted earlier, sponsored the *Eisenbahn-Zeitung*, and it published increasingly comprehensive railroad statistics (*Deutsche Eisenbahn-Statistik für das Betriebs-Jahr . . . , 1851–1877*). [VDEV Minutes], Hamburg, November 29–December 2, 1847; *Festschrift*, pp. 393–94.

[133] Zeschau to Jordan, Dresden, October 10, 1847, in ZStAM, Rep. 93E, no. 1127, vol. I, pp. 511–521.

[134] [Berlin-Stettin Railroad, Annual Report of the Directors], May 15, 1841.

[135] Graf von Alvensleben to the Ministry of Foreign Affairs, February 7, 1842, in ZStAM, Rep. 93E, no. 1127, vol. I, pp. 1r–6v. The ministries advocated a uniform gauge for commercial as well as military reasons, a viewpoint also expressed in the United States. Von Bonin, *Geschichte des Ingenieurkorps*, 2:251; George Rogers Taylor and Irene D. Neu, *The American Railroad Network, 1861–1890* (Cambridge: Harvard University Press, 1956), p. 13.

[136] [Railroad Conference Minutes], April 5, 1843, p. 34v.

boring states.[137] When the engineers' association met for the first time in 1850, it too declared the English gauge to be the standard on German railroads. Four years later, the one major deviant, the Baden state railroads, finally relented and changed its broad gauge to fit the German system.[138]

American lines, in contrast, adopted a wide diversity of gauges. To be sure, a measure of uniformity obtained within regions or states. Many southern lines had adopted a 5' gauge, while New England lines tended to follow English practice. To ensure uniformity with its state works, the Pennsylvania legislature required the railroads in that state to adopt the standard gauge after 1852.[139] But in some parts of the country little uniformity obtained—sometimes this was even by design, as when the New York legislature required the New York and Erie Railroad to adopt a gauge that would prevent through traffic to Pennsylvania and New Jersey—and nowhere did it obtain entirely. Once a fragmented network had been laid down, moreover, standardization became more difficult, for local interests —those who derived a living from transshipping freight or boarding travelers—did their best to prevent the development of through traffic. A widely discussed incident of this sort occurred in Erie, Pennsylvania, in 1854, which brought condemnation from the Ohio Railroad Convention.[140] Thus, on the eve of the Civil War, only 53 percent of the country's railroad track had been constructed with the English gauge (or a width close to that); the rest had broader gauges that ranged from 4' 10" to 6'. Competition for through traffic encouraged progressive uniformity in the two decades after the Civil War, but a

[137] Beuth for the Finance Minister to the Minister of Foreign Affairs, July 30, 1843, ZStAM, Rep. 93E, no. 1127, vol. 1, pp. 38r–39v. On Beuth's career, which was then near an end, see Henderson, *The State and the Industrial Revolution*, pp. 96–118; Brose, *Politics of Technological Change*, pp. 98–132.

[138] *Festschrift*, p. 48; *Rückblick*, p. 51; Karl Müller, *Die badischen Eisenbahnen in historisch-statistischer Darstellung: Ein Beitrag zur Geschichte des Eisenbahnwesens* (Heidelberg: Heidelberger Verlagsanstalt und Druckerei, 1904), pp. 72–75; Hippel et al., *Eisenbahn-Fieber*, pp. 234–37.

[139] Taylor, *Transportation Revolution*, p. 82.

[140] Meyer, *History of Transportation*, p. 368; *Journal of Commerce* (New York), January 18 and 20, 1854, p. 2; *Report of the Proceedings of the Ohio Rail Road Convention. . . January, 1854*, pp. 7–8. During the "Erie outrages," according to the *Journal*, an estimated one hundred of the city's "leading ladies," armed with axes and saws, destroyed several railroad bridges. I am indebted to Elizabeth Blackmar for alerting me to this episode.

(nearly) uniform national gauge was not adopted until 1886, the year that the American Railway Association formed.[141]

Through its engineers' association, moreover, the VDEV moved ahead rapidly with comprehensive guidelines to facilitate through traffic. One of the earliest sets, approved at the 1847 VDEV meeting and periodically revised, spelled out procedures for handling passengers, baggage, and livestock.[142] The VDEV took longer to arrive at acceptable regulations regarding through freight, but this was finally achieved in 1850, in part through the lengthy meeting of engineers in Berlin that year, and resulted in three sets of regulations. One concerned the technical requirements of through traffic, that is, not only the construction and layout of the railroad itself but also the construction of rolling stock. A second set established uniform procedures for the handling of through freight traffic. A third set of regulations spelled out very general principles to be adhered to by the companies that engaged in the interchange of cars (avoiding transshipment, allowing foreign cars to use one's lines, and so on). These were substantially expanded in 1855 and subsequent years to include specific provisions setting fees for the use of cars and apportioning responsibility for damage and repairs. A uniform bill of lading was also adopted in 1856.[143] Finally, an overlapping but far more comprehensive set of guidelines set forth norms to cover practically every aspect of the railroad business from the building of the track to the construction of locomotives and wagons to signal systems and safety regulations. These were formulated at the engineers' meeting in 1850, even though the companies did not then expect to run their own locomotives or use their own personnel on each others' lines— indeed, they initially eschewed a common signal system for this reason.[144] With these various agreements as a foundation, the VDEV and its engineers' association pursued its goal of instituting sufficient uniformity that German railroads, as they put it, would appear to be

[141] See chap. 6.

[142] *Festschrift*, pp. 190–92, 248–51.

[143] Ibid., pp. 47–66, 136–85, 192–94, 257–65.

[144] The initial guidelines (proposed by a Hannover state railroad official), contemporary debates, and subsequent revisions may be tracked in *Festschrift* and *Rückblick*. Regarding the assumption that through traffic would not require the interchange of passenger cars or locomotives for the foreseeable future, see *Rückblick*, pp. 41–42, 45–46, 60.

operated by a single management. Not all railroads agreed to adopt every set of agreements, which hindered progress, but substantial compliance appears to have been achieved by the late 1850s.[145]

In the United States, progress in standardizing railroad technology and operations—and, therefore, in handling through freight and passengers—proceeded more slowly. State legislation sometimes encouraged or even forced the railroads to permit through traffic,[146] and numerous state, regional, or "general" associations, as we have seen, tackled the problem in the late 1840s and early 1850s. The relatively long-lived New England superintendents' association clearly served as the model in this regard, but it had already begun to lose its momentum by the early 1850s, and none of the other associations seems to have survived long enough to have had much effect. As a partial alternative perhaps, American companies quickly came to rely on so-called fast freight companies to handle through traffic in light, valuable freight, unlike Prussian railroads, which provided the service themselves. Fast freight companies handled local deliveries almost from the beginning of American railroad development and in the mid-1850s the trunk-line railroads began to establish alliances with the express companies on a contract basis.[147] This presumably took some of the pressure off American railroad men to organize through traffic themselves. It was not until after the Civil War that they gave sustained attention to the coordination of through traffic. As Alfred Chandler writes, American "railroad managers were by 1861 only beginning to develop organizational procedures to permit the movement of freight cars over the tracks of several different railroad companies."[148]

By then, Prussian railroads had enjoyed for more than a decade the benefits of a national association that attended to questions of organizational and technical unity—not because they had greater need of such an association, or because Germans as individuals were somehow better at forming organizations, or because German law em-

---

[145] *Festschrift*, pp. 12, 189–90.

[146] Edward C. Kirkland, *Industry Comes of Age: Business, Labor, and Public Policy, 1860–1897* (New York: Holt, Rinehart and Winston, 1961), p. 50; Massachusetts legislation of 1845 in Gregg and Pond, comps., *Railroad Laws and Charters*, 2:648–49.

[147] Chandler, *Visible Hand*, p. 127. On express freight in Prussia, see, for example, *Geschäfts-Bericht des Directoriums der Magdeburg-Cöthen-Halle-Leipziger Eisenbahn-Gesellschaft für das Jahr 1847*, in ZStAM, Rep. 90a, K.III.3, no. 1, vol. 1, p. 211.

[148] Chandler, *Visible Hand*, p. 122.

powered them to do so, but because the early Prussian railroad men responded quite rationally to the incentives generated by the distinctive Prussian political structure. American railroads took much longer to reach the state of economic maturity that the German system had achieved by the late 1850s—not for lack of effort, but because of the fragmented American political structure. The events that gave rise to the GRAEMWS and the GRA foreshadowed what, as chapter 6 shows, became clearer after the Civil War: when the locus of power shifted from the state to the national level (under the impetus of railroad development itself), American railroads, like the Prussian lines, did not hesitate to act nationally. Then the standardization movement finally made headway. Throughout the antebellum period, however, the American political structure fractured efforts to organize railroad interests, leaving American railroads to cope with greater diversity in their system.

5

National Styles of Railroad Technology

BECAUSE of differences in the two political structures, the foregoing chapters suggest, American railroad builders faced a greater diversity of more interventionist state policies than their Prussian counterparts did. At the same time, the fragmented American structure, unlike the more centralized Prussian, hindered cooperative efforts to reduce the diversity that inevitably marked a national railroad system-in-the-making. These circumstances help to explain the qualities in the Prussian system—its uniformity, solidity, and harmony—that an American railroad man would have envied in 1847. But there is more to the story, for the two political structures also imparted a distinctive character to the American and Prussian engineering communities, which, in turn, compounded the problem of diversity in the United States and minimized it in Prussia. By the late 1840s, in other words, important stylistic differences marked the two railroad networks—due largely, this chapter argues, to the subtle workings of the two political structures.

For the task of understanding why different national styles of technology emerge, the railroads offer a number of attractions.[1] As Joachim Radkau observes, "the more a technology is subject to political influences, the more it takes on the character of a system, the weightier the security problems, the clearer becomes the national character of the technology."[2] Railroad technology surely met those conditions in the early nineteenth-century context and was arguably the first technology to do so. It was also the first major technology to be adopted nearly simultaneously by the industrializing powers, unlike innovations in, say, textile manufacturing or machine-tool making.

---

[1] For an early suggestion to this effect, see Thomas P. Hughes, "A Technological Frontier: The Railway," in *The Railroad and the Space Program: An Exploration in Historical Analogy*, ed. Bruce Mazlish (Cambridge: M.I.T. Press, 1965), pp. 53–73. Among the most thoughtful of recent contributions to the literature on technological style, see Hughes, "The Evolution of Large Technological Systems"; and Joachim Radkau, *Technik in Deutschland: Vom 18. Jahrhundert bis zur Gegenwart* (Frankfurt/Main: Suhrkamp, 1989).

[2] Radkau, *Technik in Deutschland*, p. 23.

The fact of near-simultaneity, in effect, holds international background conditions more or less constant, thus making it (somewhat) easier to discern why different styles emerged. Yet another attraction concerns the intellectual context of early railroad development, for the railroad was the first major technology whose contours were hammered out differently in different countries, yet on the basis of an international pool of knowledge. This commonality, explored in the next section, also provides a means of gauging differences in technological style across countries. With that information at hand, the remainder of the chapter explores the parameters that shaped the thinking of early American and Prussian railroad men about the choices that they faced.

International Colloquy on Technological Styles

As means of communication improved, it is not surprising to learn how extensively technical information circulated in international engineering circles in the late nineteenth century.[3] But already a half century earlier, a surprisingly vibrant international colloquy on the new railroad technology took place. Information circulated by a variety of means. Within each country, as chapter 4 indicated, the railroads maintained close contact with one another, and by the late 1840s institutions such as the Association for Railroad Science in Berlin and the New England Association of Railway Superintendents in Boston provided an important forum. The flow of information also extended across national borders, however, both through the personal travels of railroad men and in printed form.

The engineer's expedition or "learning journey" often entailed travel not only at home but abroad. Indeed, a trip to England to view the latest developments firsthand became almost obligatory for engineers in both countries. "More than a dozen American civil engineers," reports Darwin H. Stapleton, "visited Britain from 1825 to 1840 to learn more about their profession, and in doing so acquired the knowledge and skill to build railroads."[4] The Baltimore and Ohio

---

[3] Hughes, *Networks of Power*, esp. pp. 47–78; Hans-Joachim Braun, "The National Association of German-American Technologists and Technology Transfer between Germany and the United States, 1884–1930," *History of Technology* 8 (1983): 15–35.

[4] Darwin H. Stapleton, "The Origin of American Railroad Technology, 1825–1840," *Railroad History*, no. 139 (1978): 65. On the "learning journey," see pp. 152–53.

Railroad, as we saw, sent its engineers—the civil engineer Knight and two of its borrowed army engineers, Capt. McNeill and Lt. Whistler— to England in the late 1820s. The South Carolina Railroad sent one of its engineers, a German by the name of Christian Detmold, to England in 1835 both to buy railroad iron and to catch up on the latest technology. After working on several American railroad surveys, J. Edgar Thomson, who later headed the Pennsylvania Railroad, toured English railroads on his own initiative, shortly before becoming chief engineer of the Georgia Railroad. Moncure Robinson, one of the best-known American railroad engineers, ranged further abroad, not only touring British canals and railroads but also studying engineering in France.[5]

Engineers on the Continent undertook similar journeys, either on their own account or at the behest of their governments or companies. Michel Chevalier, who formed a close friendship with Moncure Robinson, toured American public works in 1834 at the request of the French government.[6] An Austrian railroad official, Carl Ghega, toured Belgian and English railroads in 1836–37, and his government sent him to the United States in 1842.[7] Another Austrian engineer, Franz Anton Ritter von Gerstner, the first railroad expert on the Continent and in Russia, toured all European railroads on his own initiative, before embarking on an extensive tour of the United States in the late 1830s. He inspected almost all American canals and railroads, completed or under construction, before his untimely death in Philadelphia.[8] Prussian companies also sent representatives off to

[5] Roenne to the Ministry of Foreign Affairs, Washington, July 23, 1840, in ZStAM, Rep. 2.4.1, Abt. II, no. 7694, vol. 1, p. 26; *Dictionary of American Biography* 5:258 (on Detmold); Burgess and Kennedy, *Centennial History*, pp. 45–46; and on these as well as other individuals and industries, Darwin H. Stapleton, *The Transfer of Early Industrial Technologies to America* (Philadelphia: American Philosophical Society, 1987).

[6] Darwin H. Stapleton, "Neither Tocqueville nor Trollope: Michel Chevalier and the Industrialization of America and Europe," in *The World of the Industrial Revolution: Comparative and International Aspects of Industrialization*, ed. Robert Weible, Essays from the Lowell Conference on Industrial History, 1984 (North Andover, Mass.: Museum of American Textile History, 1986), pp. 21–34.

[7] Ghega, *Die Baltimore-Ohio-Eisenbahn*, pp. ix–x.

[8] Von Gerstner, *Die innern Communicationen*, 1:iv. On von Gerstner's career, see Frederick C. Gamst, "Franz Anton Ritter von Gerstner, Student of America's Pioneering Railroads," *Railroad History*, no. 163 (1990): 13–27. On his work in Russia, see Anton Ritter v. Gerstner, "Ueber die Vortheile einer Eisenbahn von St. Petersburg nach Zarskoe-Selo und Powlowsk," *Eisenbahn-Journal*, no. 23 (1836): 36–43 and no. 24 (1836): 54–59; Christopher Kreeft, *First Russian Railroad From St. Petersburg to Zarscoe-Selo and Powlowsk . . .*, trans. from the German (London: Charles Skipper and East, 1837). The Russian line constituted the first link of the St. Petersburg-Moscow

England and Continental countries. A member of the committee formed to build the Magdeburg-Leipzig Railroad, for example, went to England, France, and Belgium in 1835. The following year the promoters of the Upper Silesian Railroad hired state waterways inspector Hans Viktor von Unruh to do surveys and draw up cost estimates in 1836 and then promptly sent him off to tour railroads in Germany and Belgium. A few years later, the Berlin-Stettin Railroad sent its new chief engineer, state highway inspector Georg Neuhaus, to England before they reached a definitive decision on a construction style.[9]

Through personal contacts and travels, information no doubt moved somewhat idiosyncratically, but an impressive amount of technical material was also circulated in published form. The earliest books devoted to railroad construction appeared in the mid-1820s, when the practicality of locomotives remained quite uncertain. The year 1825 saw the publication of Nicholas Wood's *A Practical Treatise on Railroads* and Thomas Tredgold's *A Practical Treatise on Rail-Roads and Carriages...*, both of which appeared in London and went through several editions. In Munich the following year, the Bavarian railroad enthusiast Joseph Ritter von Baader published a slim volume on the latest improvements in the construction of railroads.[10]

On the heels of these early volumes came a flood of published information that circulated widely in translation in the 1830s. The French engineer F.M.G. de Pambour, who considered even the newest editions of Wood and Tredgold out-dated by the mid-1830s, published his own book on locomotives in French in 1835. This was followed by an English translation in 1836, and both quickly became widely

---

Railroad, the construction of which was superintended by the American army engineer George W. Whistler. William Harrison, Jr., manufactured its rolling stock. See Merritt Roe Smith, "Becoming Engineers in Early Industrial America," Program in Science, Technology, and Society Working Paper No. 13, Massachusetts Institute of Technology.

[9] Von der Leyen, "Entstehung der Magdeburg-Leipziger Eisenbahn," pp. 256, 259–60; *Allgemeine Zeitung* (Augsburg), Ausserordentliche Beilage, no. 235/6, May 20, 1837, p. 839; *Zur Feier des Fünfundzwanzigsten Jahrestages der Eröffnung des Betriebes auf der Oberschlesischen Eisenbahn*, pp. 17–18; [Berlin-Stettin Railroad, Annual Report of the Directors], May, 15, 1841. Several years earlier Berlin-Stettin directors had also corresponded with Benjamin H. Latrobe (Jr.) and other American engineers. *Bericht des Comité's an die Actionairs der Berlin-Stettiner Eisenbahn*, pp. 9–10.

[10] Nicholas Wood, *A Practical Treatise on Rail-Roads* (London: Knight and Lacey, 1825); Thomas Tredgold, *A Practical Treatise on Rail-Roads and Carriages...* (London: J. B. Nichols and Son, 1825); Joseph Ritter von Baader, *Über die neuesten Verbesserungen und die zweckmäßige Einrichtung der Eisenbahnen* (Munich: A. E. Fleischmann, [1826]).

known. In 1836 the Prussian state engineer August L. Crelle, who edited a civil engineering journal (*Journal für die Baukunst*), published a German translation of de Pambour's English edition in its entirety in his journal, praising the way that de Pambour treated his subject "practically and scientifically at the same time." The following year, the Prussian railroad promoter David Hansemann cited de Pambour's French edition as an authoritative source, while two American army engineers, William Gibbs McNeill and William G. Williams, echoed Crelle's sentiment: In their judgment, "[n]o author has yet treated the subject of power in locomotive engines with the science and practical experiment of De Pambour."[11] Also well known in the international engineering community were the works of another French engineer, Maj. G. Tell-Poussin, who had served with his compatriot, Gen. Simon Bernard, in planning internal improvements with the U.S. Board of Engineers. Poussin published his observations on American public works in French-language books in 1834 and 1836. In 1836, Crelle published extracts in translation in the *Journal für die Baukunst*, and the following year a full-length translation of Poussin's volume on American railroads was published in Germany.[12]

To German engineers, Crelle's journal, which had a large circulation, provided a wealth of information on the latest developments in other countries. It frequently carried extracts from the journal published by the French civil engineering corps (*Journal du génie civil*) and from the *Annales des ponts et chaussées*. These included in 1836 a translation of lectures on railroads given by the engineer Minard at the *École des ponts et chaussées* in 1833–34. Other reports went through multiple translations. In 1833, for example, Crelle published what seems to have been a German translation of a French

[11] "Praktische Abhandlung über Dampfwagen auf Eisenbahnen, von Herrn Chev. F.M.G. de Pambour," *Journal für die Baukunst* 10 (1836): 27–83, 183–206, 256–301, 363–413; Hansemann, *Die Eisenbahnen und deren Aktionäre*, pp. 4n–5n; "Joint Report of the Chief and Associate Engineers of the Louisville, Cincinnati and Charleston Railroad," Senate Doc. 157, 25th Cong., 2d sess., 1837–38, p. 27. See also *First Report of Edward Miller, Engineer in Chief of the Sunbury and Erie Railroad, to the Managers. January 12, 1839* (Philadelphia: John C. Clark, 1839), p. 29. Hereafter, the *Journal für die Baukunst* is cited as *JfdBK*.

[12] "Einige technische Nachrichten über die Constructions-Art der Nord-Amerikanischen Eisenbahnen," *JfdBK* 10 (1836): 207–55; G. Tell-Poussin, *Oeffentliche Bauwerke in den Vereinigten Staaten von Amerika*, pt. 2: *Eisenbahnen*, trans. H. F. Lehritter (Regensburg: Friedrich Pustet, 1837). Hansemann (see note 11) also cited Poussin's work as authoritative in 1837.

translation of an English report on the Liverpool and Manchester Railroad. The mid-1830s also brought an extended series of reports on French and Belgian railroads, including this time a German translation of an English translation of an official Belgian report. These European reports sometimes provided scattered information on American railroads, but other times Crelle offered his readers news directly from the United States, for example, a summary of William Norris's reports on experiments with locomotives in 1839.[13]

In the late 1830s, moreover, published reports from the Austrian engineer von Gerstner kept the international engineering community apprised of developments in the United States. During his year-long tour, Gerstner sent reports back to Germany that were published first in newspapers and then in book form in 1839. Excerpts also appeared in the *Journal für die Baukunst* and the *Journal of the Franklin Institute*. Even American railroad men relied on von Gerstner's report for information about railroads in their own country in the early 1840s.[14] During his American tour, moreover, von Gerstner published in English a brief comparison of American and Belgian railroads for the benefit of the American railroad managers and engineers who had graciously opened their doors and books to him. ("The comparison" of Belgian and American railroads, he concluded, "speaks evidently in favor of the first.") Posthumously, his two-volume report on American internal improvements and banks was published in German in 1842–43, and it remains one of the best sources on early American canals, railroads, and banks.[15] In short,

13 "Nachrichten von der neuen Eisenschienen-Strasse zwischen Liverpool und Manchester," *JfdBK* 6 (1833): 178–98, 215–75; "Vorlesungen über Eisenbahnen. Gehalten in der École des ponts et chaussees zu Paris in den Jahren 1833 und 1834 von Herrn Minard," *JfdBK* 9 (1836): 101–200; "Gesammelte technische und statistische Nachrichten über die Eisenbahnen von St. Etienne nach Roanne und von St. Etienne nach Lyon," *JfdBK* 7 (1834): 214–80, 299–355; "Nachrichten von der Belgische Eisenbahn," *JfdBK* 8 (1835): 268–310, 367–411, 9 (1836): 33–48, 381–402; A. L. Crelle, "Einiges über die Ausführbarkeit von Eisenbahnen in bergigen Gegenden," *JfdBK* 13 (1839): 142–45. The first volume of the journal, published in 1829, listed some one thousand subscribers, mostly individuals but also including governmental bodies from the local level to the Finance and War ministries.

14 *Report of a Committee of Directors of the Boston and Worcester Rail-Road*, p. 18; *Proceedings, at a Meeting of the Stockholders of the Central Rail Road and Banking Company of Georgia, on the 9th. and 11th. Days of March, 1843* (Savannah: Thomas Purse, 1843), p. 16.

15 Franz Anton Ritter von Gerstner, *Berichte aus den Vereinigten Staaten von Nordamerica, über Eisenbahnen, Dampfschiffahrten, Banken und andere öffentliche Unternehmungen* (Leipzig: C. P. Melzer, 1839); idem, *Railroads in the Kingdom of Belgium Compared with Those in the United States* (Cincinnati, 1839); idem, *Die innern*

even in the German states, which were seldom included in international tours to inspect railroads, engineers and investors easily kept up-to-date on new developments elsewhere.

Out of this international colloquy came a common understanding of the universe of technological possibilities by the late 1830s. This common frame of reference was bounded on one end by the English paradigm of railroad construction and, on the other, by the so-called American system; while the Belgian style occupied the middle of the spectrum. Each differed on two essential points: the principles that should guide location of the roadbed (i.e., grades and curves); and those governing construction of the track (i.e., the rails and their supports). These differences, in turn, directly affected both the cost per kilometer of railroad construction and the maximum speed at which trains could safely and profitably be run.[16]

Briefly, the English paradigm—what Friedrich List disparaged as "the English engineers' catechism"—called for a straight and level roadbed. Attaining sufficiently low grades and easy curves often meant a great deal of embankment and excavation. The English paradigm also called for a heavy track, constructed with all-iron rails and iron "chairs" to hold the rails, all of which rested on stone blocks or sills. These aspects of the English style, together with the English propensity for extravagantly appointed depots and carriages, required large amounts of capital. In a play on the German word for railroad (literally, iron road), Friedrich List once observed, "people say, and not just in jest, that with the money that an iron road costs [in England] one could build a silver road [in Germany]."[17] On the other hand, as List and other observers well recognized, the sturdy and expensive English style of construction allowed speedier travel.[18]

Communicationen. For excerpts in translation from von Gerstner's *Berichte,* edited by Frederick C. Gamst, see *Railroad History,* no. 163 (1990): 28–73. The Railroad and Locomotive Historical Society has a project underway to publish translations of the two volumes of *Die innern Communicationen* and of his wife's travel memoir. See Gamst, "Franz Anton Ritter von Gerstner," pp. 13–14, for details.

[16] They also affected locomotive construction, producing in the American case a distinctive style of locomotive that could cope with higher grades and sharper curves. See White, *History of the American Locomotive,* pp. 3–4.

[17] "Die Zukunft des Eisenbahntransports. 1. Über mögliche Verminderung der Anlagekosten," *Allgemeine Zeitung* (Augsburg), Ausserordentliche Beilage, no. 418, August 7, 1838, p. 1669. See also Stapleton, *Transfer of Early Industrial Technologies,* p. 124.

[18] On the relationship between speed and costs, see ibid., p. 1670. List recommended lower speeds in order to minimize construction costs. See also Hansemann, *Die Eisenbahnen und deren Aktionäre,* p. 7; A. L. Crelle, *Einiges allgemein Verständliche über*

Defining the other end of the spectrum was the "American system" of railroad construction, another manifestation of a distinctive style of technology that was rapidly becoming associated with the United States.[19] Those who built according to its precepts followed the natural terrain as much as possible, avoiding the excavation and embankment that could be so labor-intensive and expensive. Where possible, they also used abundant and cheap wood for structural purposes, avoiding the use, and hence the expense, of iron. Perhaps best known—in some quarters, infamous—was the American technique of constructing the rails of wood and capping them with thin iron strips (*Plattschienen* or strap-iron rail).[20] The American system, in essence, minimized the initial outlay of capital, although the sharp curves, high grades, and light superstructure were understood to increase operating costs and to limit the speed at which trains could run.

Eisenbahnen, insbesondere als Privat-Unternehmungen (Berlin: G. Reimer, 1835), pp. 38–49; von Gerstner, *Berichte*, pp. 18, 20. Crelle's work was also published in the *Journal für die Baukunst* 9 (1836): 277–87.

[19] As European observers frequently noted, Americans were not only quicker to substitute machines for human labor; their machines tended to be lightweight and made of wood wherever feasible—thus saving both labor and capital. See Peter Temin, "Labor Scarcity and the Problem of American Industrial Efficiency in the 1850's," *Journal of Economic History* 26 (September 1966): 277–98; Nathan Rosenberg, *Technology and American Economic Growth* (New York: M. E. Sharpe, Inc., 1972), pp. 87–116; Brooke Hindle, ed., *America's Wooden Age: Aspects of Its Early Technology* (Tarrytown, N.Y.: Sleepy Hollow Press, 1975); idem, ed., *Material Culture of the Wooden Age* (Tarrytown, N.Y.: Sleepy Hollow Press, 1981); Harlen I. Halsey, "The Choice Between High-Pressure and Low-Pressure Steam Power in America in the Early Nineteenth Century," *Journal of Economic History* 41 (December 1981): 723–44; Alexander James Field, "Land Abundance, Interest/Profit Rates, and Nineteenth-Century American and British Technology," *Journal of Economic History* 43 (June 1983): 405–31.

[20] For descriptions in the 1830s, see Chevalier, *Society, Manners and Politics*, pp. 270–72; von Gerstner, *Berichte*; idem, *Die innern Communicationen*; Ghega, *Die Baltimore-Ohio-Eisenbahn*; List, *Über ein sächsisches Eisenbahnsystem*, in FL3/1, pp. 155–95; *Vierter Bericht des Eisenbahnkomitees zu Leipzig: Die verschiedenen Arten und die Kosten des Oberbaues der Eisenbahnen betreffend*, Leipzig, September 24, 1834, reprinted in *Friedrich List: Schriften, Reden, Briefe*, vol. 3: *Schriften zum Verkehrswesen*, pt. 2: *Textnachlese und Kommentar*, ed. Alfred von der Leyen, Alfred Genest, and Berta Meyer (Berlin: Verlag von Reimar Hobbing, 1931), pp. 605–34; Eduard Wiebe, *Einige Mängel der bestehenden Eisenbahnen nebst Andeutungen zu deren Abhülfe* (Potsdam, 1838); Charles F. Zimpel, *Das Eisenbahnwesen von Nordamerika, England und anderen Ländern* (Vienna, 1840). This List volume is cited hereafter as FL3/2. For later descriptions, see Friedrich List, "Das deutsche Eisenbahnsystem IV," 1843, in FL3/1, especially pp. 389–91; Lardner, *Railway Economy*, pp. 396–402. See also Stapleton, *Transfer of Early Industrial Technologies*, pp. 147, 154.

The Belgians, finally, marked out the midsection of the spectrum in building their small but early system of state railroads in the mid-1830s. Their engineers tolerated higher grades and sharper curves than English practice called for. As two Belgian engineers observed in 1833, "The straightest line is not always the most advantageous. In order to avoid unevenness in the terrain, some roundabout routes can be better than the direct line." Therefore, they endorsed moderate grades (1:300), where these would allow the length of the line to be shortened or would reduce the amount of embankment and excavation. The track in the Belgian system consisted of iron rails of moderate weight, which rested in cast-iron chairs, which were fastened, in turn, to wooden cross-ties. Recognizing the relationship between construction style and train speeds, the Belgians explicitly adopted a policy of moderate speed.[21]

Yet, despite a common pool of knowledge about early railroad technology, and despite a common framework for evaluating alternative styles of technology, railroad men built railroads differently, and this common frame of reference—more particularly, the relationship between cost and speed that these styles took for granted—provides a way of gauging gross, national differences in style. By the late 1840s, according to British observer Dionysius Lardner, railroad construction costs (table 5-1) ranged from $125,000 per kilometer in the United Kingdom to less than $25,000 per kilometer in the United States. Average passenger-train speeds (including stops) varied accordingly from 39 kph in the United Kingdom to an estimated 24 kph in the United States. As figure 3 shows, the relationship between speed and capital invested per kilometer held rather consistently across countries.[22]

[21] "Nachrichten von der Belgische Eisenbahn," *JfdBK* 8 (1835): 286 and 9 (1836): 399. The rails installed in 1835 weighed 12 kg per meter (8 *Pfund per Fuß*), but the Belgian Minister of the Interior reported that rails weighing up to 18 kg per meter would be used in the future. Von Gerstner reported in 1839 that rails on the Belgian system weighed 23 kg per meter (45 lbs. per yard). Von Gerstner, *Railroads in the Kingdom of Belgium.*

[22] The relatively small difference between the German speeds including and excluding stops can perhaps be attributed to the formation of the national railroad association in 1846–47. See chap. 4. In 1846 39 American railroads were reported to be running passenger trains at an average of 16.6 mph (or 26.6 kph). This presumably included stops. *Address of the Directors of the Camden and Amboy Rail Road and Delaware and Raritan Canal Companies, to the People of New Jersey* (Trenton: Press of the Emporium, 1846), p. 22. The American speed excluding stops on the graph is my own "guesstimate," derived by adding to Lardner's estimated speed including stops the average difference between the two speeds in Belgium, France, and the United Kingdom.

TABLE 5-1
Comparative Railroad Data
United States and Europe, ca. 1849

Country	Length of Track (Km)	Total Capital ($ Million)	Capital per Km of Track ($)	Average Pass.-Train Speed (Kph)[a]
United Kingdom	8,000	1,000	125,000	39/51
France	2,750	229	83,300	34/43
Belgium	730	40	54,800	29/40
German States	7,270	284	39,100	32/38
Prussia (1850)	2,970	107	36,000	—
U.S.-I	10,500	260	24,800	24/—
U.S.-II (1850)	14,400	301	20,900	—

SOURCES: Dionysius Lardner, *Railroad Economy* (London: Taylor, Walton, and Maberly, 1850), pp. 496, 501, with supplementary data for Prussia and the United States in 1850 from table 1-1. Lardner included Austria, Denmark, and the Netherlands in the German states. I have converted miles to kilometers and pounds sterling to dollars (at $5 per pound). The capital includes rolling stock, etc. His average passenger-train speed including stops for the United States is an estimate.

[a] Including/Excluding stops.

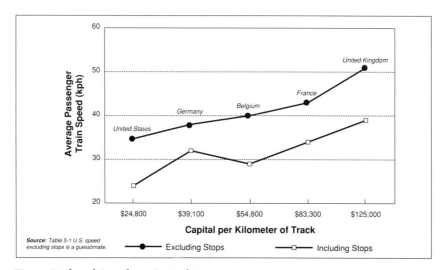

Fig. 3. Railroad Speed vs. Capital, ca. 1849

The question, then, is why construction styles, measured in terms of capital and speed, varied among countries.

National Wealth as a Parameter of Choice

Since differences in the realm of knowledge and understanding may be ruled out, an explanation might be sought in the relative wealth of nations. Data on gross domestic product (GDP) per capita, for instance, produce a nearly identical ranking in 1820, on the eve of the railroad era (table 5-2). Britain and France took the lead, with Britain enjoying by far the largest GDP per capita, a ranking consistent with perceptions at the time. The French state engineers no doubt considered their nation to have a relatively smaller pool of wealth to work with than the British, while the writings of German railroad builders make clear that they saw themselves to be much more constrained in this regard than either the British or the French. The Belgians, again, commanded the intermediate terrain.

But the United States clearly represented an anomaly. It enjoyed a GDP per capita nearly equal to the French. Why, then, did Americans build railroads more cheaply on average than even the Germans, who had the lowest GDP among these nations? The data in table 5-2 permit a direct comparison of American and Prussian conditions, since the German data were based on Prussian GDP estimates. These indicate, then, that American GDP per capita ran about 12 percent higher than the Prussian. This would suggest, in very rough terms, that Prussian railroad builders had less wealth to tap at home than American railroad builders did. If this were the determining factor, then the Prussians should have built railroads as cheaply. But, on average, they did not—a pattern that held even across geographic regions.[23]

Other evidence, however, indicates that American railroads, in practice, had as much, if not more, difficulty in attracting capital than Prussian railroads did.[24] If the practice of paying interest on capital

[23] Dunlavy, "Politics and Industrialization," pp. 237–39.

[24] For theoretical and historical discussion, see Knut Borchardt, "Zur Frage des Kapitalmangels in der ersten Hälfte des 19. Jahrhunderts in Deutschland," *Jahrbuch für Nationalökonomie und Statistik* 173 (1961): 401–21. It would be helpful to have comparative data on domestic capital stock (as in table 1-2) for the years 1830 or 1840, but Hoffmann's do not begin until 1850. Data for 1850 indicate domestic capital stock of $217 per capita in Prussia and $189 in the United States. See the sources cited in table 1-2.

TABLE 5-2
Gross Domestic Product per Capita in 1820
(1985 U.S. Prices)

United Kingdom	$1,405
France	$1,052
United States	$1,048
Belgium	$1,024
Germany	$937

SOURCE: Angus Maddison, *Dynamic Forces in Capitalist Development: A Long-Run Comparative View* (Oxford: Oxford University Press, 1991), pp. 6–7. Madison adjusted exchange rates for differences in the purchasing power of national currencies and constructed the German data on the basis of estimates of Prussian GDP. Germany here, unlike in table 5-1, does not include Austria, Denmark, or the Netherlands.

during construction (i.e., before a railroad generated any income) indicated capital scarcity, for example, then both countries labored under this constraint, since railroads in both countries adopted the practice.[25] American railroads, moreover, generally had to offer higher rates of interest to attract capital. Prussian lines usually issued bonds bearing 4–5 percent interest, 4-percent bonds more common in the 1840s and 5-percent bonds in the 1850s; American roads issued, for example, state-backed bonds bearing 5 percent interest, or they borrowed money on their own credit at 6 percent or more.[26]

How do we reconcile this with the evidence of a higher GDP per capita in the United States, which, coupled with less restrictive bank-

[25] In both countries, a charge for interest during construction usually appeared in the statement of accounts accompanying reports to stockholders. The Pennsylvania Railroad's charter, granted in 1846, specified that its stockholders should receive 5 percent interest until the first hundred miles had been completed, the cost to be charged to construction. Schotter, *Growth and Development of the Pennsylvania Railroad Company*, p. 8.

[26] For Prussian railroads, see Michaelis, *Deutschlands Eisenbahnen;* and Rapmund, *Die finanzielle Betheiligung*, which provide information on the individual bond issues of Prussian railroads through 1853 and 1869, respectively. For American railroads, see von Gerstner, *Berichte*, pp. 23–24; and scattered evidence in idem, *Die innern Communicationen*. The 5 percent interest that the Pennsylvania Railroad's stockholders were to receive during the initial construction phase was raised to 6 percent in 1848 because, as one writer explains, 5 percent "was not deemed sufficient to attract subscriptions to Capital Stock." Schotter, *Growth and Development of the Pennsylvania Railroad Company*, p. 20.

ing policies,[27] should have made capital more plentiful in the United States? By recalling certain features of American railroad development recounted in the preceding chapters. First, Americans built railroads at a faster pace and much earlier than the Prussians. Already by 1839 (table 1-1), construction had been completed on some 4,500 kilometers of track at a cost of some $96 million in the United States; in Prussia, only $5 million had been invested in 185 km by 1840. Then during the decade of the 1840s, Americans added nearly 10,000 km, while the Prussian system expanded by less than 3,000 km. This meant that Americans built railroads in ways that made their ventures riskier—during the 1830s, because the technology remained unproven; and during the 1840s, because the rapid multiplication of railroads threatened the security of investment in other lines. Also, the sheer proliferation of projects, driven by log-rolling, must have put pressure on domestic supplies of capital. The experience of the South Carolina Railroad illustrates the kind of problems that railroad promoters encountered. While the road was still under construction in the summer and fall of 1833, its directors canvassed the eastern seaboard for a loan of $300,000. Initially, they explained, they thought that a third of it "might be obtained in our own State at six per cent per annum, from some of the capitalists, usually investing their funds at or about five per cent." But this effort failed, so they sent a representative north to New York City in hopes that he could negotiate a loan for no more than 6 percent interest. This, too, failed. "The urgent demand for money at that time, to construct other public works of great extent, prevented his success," they reported. Finally, refusing the offer of a second mortgage from an Alabama company, they issued more stock instead. As Friedrich List wrote the same year (having returned from the United States the previous year), "[i]n North America . . . capital is not scarce, but sought after, [and] therefore the rate of interest is high."[28] By making the chartering of railroads so easy, thus generating a surfeit of demand, the American political structure made capital scarcer in relative terms.

---

[27] See, for example, List's comments on paper money in *Über ein sächsisches Eisenbahnsystem*, in FL3/1, pp. 168, 168n–70n.

[28] *Semi-Annual Report of the Direction of the South-Carolina Canal & Rail-Road Company to the Stockholders, November 4th, 1833, With Accompanying Documents* (Charleston: A. E. Miller, 1833), pp. 3–4; List, *Über ein sächsisches Eisenbahnsystem*, in FL3/1, p. 179.

In Prussia, in contrast, railroad promoters dealt with a unitary-bureaucratic state, which meant that they dealt with a handful of central state officials in Berlin. These officials, enjoying greater structural insulation, viewed the new technology with considerable (and well-founded) skepticism during the 1830s, and they scrutinized railroad projects more carefully throughout the period. As a result, the Prussian state granted far fewer railroad charters than the American state legislatures did. Despite a lower GDP per capita, therefore, Prussian railroad builders confronted a scarcity of capital that was certainly no worse and may have been marginally more favorable than in the United States, where the dynamics of policy-making in the American political structure, in effect, compounded the scarcity of capital. Attention to the way that the two political structures shaped distinctive investment environments thus helps to reorder the five nations according to wealth in a manner that is consistent with the data on railroad construction styles in table 5-1.

The American System in Prussia

But constraints on the supply of capital relative to demand are not enough to explain why Americans chose to build railroads as cheaply—or Prussians, as expensively—as they did. Many contemporary observers certainly did not think so. On the contrary, men such as Franz Anton von Gerstner, Friedrich List, and August Crelle thought that such constraints set only very loose boundaries that left railroad builders with considerable room for choice. All three men believed that German railroads could—and two believed that they should—be built according to the American system.

The German national economist Friedrich List not only spent a lifetime advocating railroad construction in Germany; he also became the earliest and most vocal advocate of the American system of construction in the German states. As early as 1829, although he did not yet call it the "American system," List outlined its essentials in a letter that he wrote from Reading, Pennsylvania, to Joseph Ritter von Baader in Munich:

> In our view, those countries, which do not have a surplus of capital and for which a rapid improvement in the ease of transportation is of great importance, should at the outset avoid as much as possible

all expenditures for excavation, tunnels, and complicated machinery and for the time being should make do with the simplest and least expensive methods of executing the work. Even though they are not the absolute best, nonetheless, under the circumstances, they are certainly the best in relative terms.[29]

This view List claimed to have impressed upon his colleagues on the Little Schuylkill Railroad in 1829. By building an inexpensive railroad—what he termed a *wohlfeile Eisenbahn*—they would be "ten times better off," he argued, than if they built a "solid" railroad, for solidity should be defined in financial rather than technical terms. That meant a railroad that served immediate purposes and brought in the greatest profits.[30] Fourteen years later, List remained more convinced than ever of the American system's value:

> What is the American system? It is, in the simplest terms, the system of having no system. It is the system of common sense which is not befuddled by the haughtiness of theory or false ambition, by the arrogance of scientific mystery-mongering and boasting, by supercilious know-it-alls and those who only seek originality, or by a presumptuous concern for the far-too-distant future . . . [the common sense] that, in a word, cuts the coat according to the cloth and not to the same size for all.[31]

The American system, he asserted, was "the simplest, most prudent, most expedient, most advantageous system in the world."[32] Time and again in the intervening years, he had derided engineers—the British-influenced "priests of technology," "the English legislators of railroad mechanics"—who put technical considerations above all else.[33] Conversely, he praised the fundamental pragmatism of the American approach, which, as he saw it, adjusted engineering principles to accommodate economic reality.

[29] Friedrich List, "Entwurf zu einem VI. Brief an Ritter v. Baader [Reading, 1. Juni 1829], nebst einem Anhang: Bruchstücke eines zweiten Entwurfs [Reading, 15. Mai 1829]," in FL3/2, p. 537.

[30] Ibid., p. 545.

[31] Friedrich List, "Das deutsche Eisenbahnsystem IV," 1843, in FL3/1, p. 387.

[32] Ibid., p. 401.

[33] List, "Das deutsche Eisenbahnsystem IV," pp. 386–87. For other samples, see idem, "Die thüringische Eisenbahn," 1840, in FL3/1, pp. 295, 305; idem, "Entwurf zu einem VI. Brief," p. 545; idem, *Über ein sächsisches Eisenbahnsystem*, in FL3/1, p. 162n.

In an outpouring of pamphlets and newspaper articles during the 1830s and early 1840s, List, who returned to Germany in 1832, urged the American system on railroad builders in Bavaria, Baden, Saxony, and Prussia.[34] Repeatedly, he pointed to similarities in the conditions that railroad builders faced in the United States and the German states, arguing that these commonalities made British methods inappropriate in both countries. Land and wood cost more in Germany, he acknowledged; but the total cost of construction would be lower. The slight advantage that the United States enjoyed in its lower land and wood prices, he maintained, would be more than offset by the much higher price of labor. He estimated that Americans paid about $405 less per kilometer of track for land and $270 less for wood, but wage costs four times higher than in Germany would yield a total cost differential of more than $5,000 per kilometer in Germany's favor. "From this it appears," he concluded, "that one must seek the origins of the enterprises of gigantic proportions in North America elsewhere than in the cheapness of the land." He proposed instead that they lay in "the entrepreneurial spirit, commercial freedom, competition, freedom of travel, and the ready co-operation of the governments, wherever any citizens have drafted a plan to improve their situation."[35] He even maintained on a couple of occasions that the American system was *better* suited to German circumstances than it

---

[34] List, *Über ein sächsisches Eisenbahnsystem,* in FL3/1, pp. 161n, 166–68; idem, *Aufruf an unsere Mitbürger in Sachsen, die Anlage einer Eisenbahn zwischen Dresden und Leipzig betreffend* (1834), reprinted in FL3/1, pp. 204–5; idem, "Über die Eisenbahn von Mannheim nach Basel," 1835, in FL3/1, pp. 231–32; idem, "Das deutsche Eisenbahnsystem IV," p. 401. For a bibliography of List's writings in the *Allgemeine Zeitung* (Augsburg) and in his own *Eisenbahn-Journal und National-Magazin,* forty issues of which appeared in 1835–37, see *Mitteilungen der Friedrich List-Gesellschaft e. V.,* no. 6, November 1, 1928, pp. 255–72, and no. 10, February 10, 1930, pp. 315–22, respectively.

[35] List, *Über ein sächsisches Eisenbahnsystem,* in FL3/1, pp. 160n–61n. List's reference to railroads "of gigantic proportions" was rather overblown. Information gleaned from von Gerstner, *Die innern Communicationen,* indicates that in 1840 the length of American lines completed by 124 companies had a mean length of 45 kilometers (with a dot plot trim mean of 40 km); the individual lines ranged in length from 2 to 256 km. By region, mean length varied from 90 km in the Southeast (Va., N.C., S.C., Ga.) to 24 km in the southwestern states (Ala., Fla., La., Miss., Tenn., Ky.). Including the planned mileage that von Gerstner reported for 160 lines yields a national mean of 92 km (trim mean of 74 km). It is also worth noting that, with one possible exception, no American railroad promoters, to my knowledge, ever advocated an inexpensive style for their own line because the country as a whole had to build a lot of mileage. Maj. Gen. Edmund P. Gaines with his plan for the military to build a national system would have been one of the few people to think in national terms.

was to American conditions.[36] As he put it in 1835, the Germans could "do nothing better than to follow in the footsteps of the Americans."[37]

The Austrian railroad man, von Gerstner, voiced similar thoughts during his travels in the United States. In his judgment, construction costs actually ran twice as high in the United States as in Germany. He agreed with List that land costs were higher in Germany[38] and that American wages were much higher than anywhere in Europe. Moreover, wood of a quality suitable for construction (unlike wood for fuel) cost, on average, more than it did in Europe, he observed, and American lines imported rails all the way from England. Nonetheless, American companies *spent* less per mile than European lines did. How did Americans manage to build railroads so cheaply? Von Gerstner, as noted earlier, was a widely traveled man with much hands-on experience in railroad construction. This put him in a better position than List to compare American and European conditions, so his observations are worth exploring in detail.

Midway through his travels, von Gerstner shared his insights in a letter for publication in Germany.[39] American railroad promoters, he observed, showed a greater caution in the planning stages. They put more time and care into locating their railroads, unlike Europeans,

[36] List, "Entwurf zu einem VI. Brief," pp. 544–45; idem, *Über ein sächsisches Eisenbahnsystem*, in FL3/1, pp. 179–81; *Vierter Bericht des Eisenbahnkomitees zu Leipzig*, pp. 620–22; List, "Andeutung der Vorteile eines preußischen Eisenbahnsystems und insbesondere einer Eisenbahn zwischen Hamburg, Berlin, Magdeburg und Leipzig," 1835, reprinted in FL3/1, p. 215n.

[37] "Die Neu-York und Erie-Eisenbahn," *Eisenbahn-Journal* no. 1 (1835): 11.

[38] Given the difference in average construction cost per kilometer in the two countries, it may be inferred that Prussian railroads spent about twice as much on land, since land costs represented about the same proportion of total costs in the two countries. Albert Fishlow estimates that land costs accounted for about 8 percent of the total costs of building American railroads in the 1840s. Walther Hoffmann notes that land cost as a proportion of total railroad construction costs "does not appear to be high and may be about 10% of the total expenditure." This should be viewed as a maximum estimate, however. By 1850, the Berlin-Stettin Railroad, for example, had spent less than 8 percent of its total capital on "land and use damages." By then the Berlin-Hamburg and Cologne-Minden railroads had paid out 9.2 percent and less than 8 percent, respectively. Fishlow, *American Railroads*, pp. 119, 349–51; Hoffmann, *Wachstum der deutschen Wirtschaft*, p. 252; *Jahresbericht des Direktoriums der Berlin-Stettiner Eisenbahn-Gesellschaft für die am 30sten Mai 1851 zusammentretende ordentliche General-Versammlung*, Anlage F; *Siebenter General-Bericht der Direction der Berlin-Hamburger Eisenbahn-Gesellschaft für das Jahr 1849* (Berlin: G. Bernstein, 1850), Anlage O; *Bericht der Direktion der Köln-Mindener Eisenbahn-Gesellschaft über den Bau und Betrieb der unter ihrer Verwaltung stehenden Eisenbahnen im Jahre 1856*, Anlage 1.

[39] The following is based on von Gerstner, *Berichte*, pp. 15–17.

who refused to bear the cost of lengthy deliberations and did not have the patience to do so. "The simple consequence of this," he concluded, "is that there are almost no railroads in Europe, where great mistakes in their location were not committed." American lines, moreover, tolerated a related expense: they frequently hired consulting engineers to assist the chief engineer. Such assistance could be very expensive, he acknowledged, running as high as $5,000 for twenty-four to thirty consulting days a year. Not only did German lines not employ consulting engineers, he charged; they hired the cheapest engineer they could find, worrying more about whether he was a native than about his experience. German lines had not yet learned, he concluded, that spending a few thousand dollars more on the preliminary work could save hundreds of thousands in the end.

But the difference did not come down to cautious planning alone, for von Gerstner pointed to a second set of reasons why Americans built railroads cheaply. First of all, the normal American grade was about thirty feet to the mile (1:176) but as high as ninety feet to the mile (1:58) if necessary. Curves usually had a radius of 2,000 feet (610 m) but could have radii as small as 600 feet (180 m), if the terrain demanded it.[40] This enabled American railroad builders to follow undulating terrain, which meant less excavation and fewer high bridges. Second, wages were certainly very high, he reported, "but nowhere else are so many mechanical devices used as here." As examples he mentioned a steam pile-driver and a steam excavating machine.[41] As a third factor, he pointed to an "entirely new," low-cost method of constructing bridges almost entirely out of wood. Fourth, the superstructure of American lines tended to correspond to operational needs and thus varied with the expected traffic. The weight of rails, he noted, ranged from 29 kg per meter (58 lbs. per yard) to as little as 4 kg per meter (9½ lbs. per yard). Many companies, moreover, lacking the money for heavier rails, initially installed lighter ones and then replaced them as traffic increased, and they tended to construct buildings that served the purpose and no more. They also invested in less equipment, using a much smaller number of locomotives and cars than European lines with comparable traffic

[40] This agreed with what Michel Chevalier reported during his travels. See Chevalier, Society, Manners and Politics, pp. 270–71.

[41] Fishlow, American Railroads, p. 119, regards steam excavators as having been extremely rare.

did; instead of keeping some in reserve, they ran them all constantly. What he singled out in his American travels was surely not the method uniformly adopted by American engineers, but it contained many elements of what List had noted a decade earlier: the method rapidly becoming known as the "American system" of railroad construction.

The difference between the American system and German practice, however, he saw not as a matter of differing resources or different material conditions but of practicality. Here he essentially agreed with List: German railroads, with their lower labor costs, could build railroads just as cheaply as the Americans did, he maintained, if they would just develop "the same practical mentality." This was the "secret" of cheap railroad construction in the United States, von Gerstner claimed, and Germans should learn it.[42]

Even the Prussian state engineer Crelle recognized the attractions of the American system in the German context, although he raised a strong dissenting voice against it. Many were suggesting, he acknowledged in the mid-1830s, that railroads should be built in Germany the way that they often were in the United States—he meant with wooden rails capped with "weak" iron—because the savings would allow more railroads to be built. But "[t]his claim is, as a rule, not correct," he maintained, because, even if wood were cheaper in Germany, the constant need to replace the wooden rails would make such railroads more expensive in the long run.[43] In commentary on Poussin's report on American railroads in 1836, however, he conceded that much could be learned from the Americans' experience, since the conditions that affected the style (*Art*) of railroad construction— terrain and construction materials—differed little between the two countries. But he still urged caution; the American system of construction—again, he meant *die plattierten Bahnen*—would seldom be right for Germany.[44]

---

[42] David Hansemann also viewed German circumstances favorably. In answer to critics who thought traffic would not be sufficient to warrant railroad construction in Germany, he pointed out that it not only had a denser population than the United States but also enjoyed lower costs (especially wages and interest rates). Hansemann, *Die Eisenbahnen und deren Aktionäre*, p. 29.

[43] Crelle, *Einiges allgemein Verständliche über Eisenbahnen*, p. 35.

[44] "Einige technische Nachrichten über die Constructions-Art der Nord-Amerikanischen Eisenbahnen," pp. 207–8.

As these men were publicizing the American system in Europe, several German railroads went ahead and experimented with the American style of construction in the late 1830s.[45] In 1837 the promoters of the Berlin-Stettin Railroad announced that they would install a wooden railroad with strap-iron rails.[46] Acknowledging the controversy surrounding this style of construction, they went to considerable length to explain their thinking to the stockholders. The wooden railroad and the more solid English style of construction each had advantages and disadvantages, they observed, and their own goal was simply to build a railroad that would meet operating requirements at the least cost. (If this sounded very much like List's advice, it was likely no accident, for he had advised them to adopt the American system two years earlier.[47]) "England, which with very few exceptions possesses only solidly built railroads (massive Bahnen), has iron and must obtain wood from us," they reasoned; "we have wood and for the time being must obtain iron from England. That makes a very substantial difference to begin with." For the same reason the United States had the most and the longest wooden railroads, they noted: there, too, wood was cheap and iron was expensive. Contacts with well-known American engineers had also convinced them that wooden railroads were better suited to a northern climate; and the Baltimore and Ohio Railroad's experience (which they learned about from Benjamin H. Latrobe, Jr.) indicated that the wooden rails could be replaced as needed without interrupting traffic. If a wooden railroad meant increased maintenance costs (which they doubted), this would be more than offset by the savings in interest on the initial investment. In any event, they concluded, railroad technology was changing so fast that they might soon be forced to rebuild entirely, in which case it would be better to throw away the investment in a wooden railroad than three times that much.[48]

[45] Ghega, Die Baltimore-Ohio-Eisenbahn, pp. 130–31, reported in the early 1840s that British engineers had also been experimenting with American methods of construction.

[46] Bericht des Comité's an die Actionairs der Berlin-Stettiner Eisenbahn, pp. 3–4.

[47] "Die Eisenbahn von Berlin nach Stettin," Eisenbahn-Journal, no. 5 (1835), pp. 67–70.

[48] Bericht des Comité's an die Actionairs der Berlin-Stettiner Eisenbahn, pp. 9–10. They estimated that 140 km of wooden track with plate rails would cost $520,310 (743,300 Taler) while the solid English style of construction would nearly triple the cost ($1,463,000 or 2,090,000 Taler).

Shortly thereafter, other German railroads opened for operation with at least parts of their lines built according to the American system. The first major line in the German states, the Leipzig-Dresden Railroad, installed wooden rails capped with strap iron on part of its first section, opened in 1838.[49] The Magdeburg-Leipzig Railroad, partially opened by 1840, also adopted a version of the wooden railroad (using bridge rail instead of strap iron) and, according to a contemporary observer, it followed the terrain more than had become the usual practice by the mid-1840s.[50]

Yet, by the early 1840s, a consensus had begun to emerge in Prussia against the American system of construction. The subsequent history of the Berlin-Stettin Railroad helps to pinpoint the timing of the process in Prussia. In 1841, four years after their initial announcement regarding construction style, the Berlin-Stettin's board of directors made their first report to the stockholders. During the intervening years they had had difficulty attracting capital (partly due to their unwillingness to open stock subscriptions to the general public) and the project had nearly fallen victim to conflict between the Berlin and Stettin subcommittees.[51] Having regrouped, the board now announced that they had dropped their plans for a wooden railroad. The company had hired the state engineer Georg Neuhaus to take charge of construction, and he had urged them to install heavier rails, they explained, "in order to avoid continual repairs and to ensure the profitability of the road." At his insistence, therefore, they had decided to reevaluate their plans. First, they sent Neuhaus and two division engineers to visit the Leipzig-Dresden and Magdeburg-Leipzig railroads, where they found considerable dissatisfaction with the wooden, strap-iron construction. In the meantime, reports had also come in from the United States, which indicated similar problems there. But to be absolutely sure they had sent Neuhaus and another engineer-director to visit English railroads. These investigations had convinced Neuhaus that, if anything, they should use even heavier rails than they were considering. So the directors resolved, among

[49] Michaelis, *Deutschlands Eisenbahnen*, p. 123.

[50] Von Reden, *Die Eisenbahnen Deutschlands*, 1. Abt., 2. Abschnitt, pp. 445, 448.

[51] These problems can be followed in the Mendelssohn bank correspondence in MA Nachl. 5.

other things, to dispense with the wooden rails and to install iron rails.[52]

The following year the supervisory board reported general satisfaction with the new construction plans. The company's shares were doing well on the stock exchange, which reflected public confidence, they contended, "in the intelligent leadership of our affairs and in the solid construction of our enterprise." Estimates recently completed by Neuhaus indicated, moreover, that the new construction plans would increase the cost of the enterprise by only 10 percent. These "improvements" would benefit the company, they explained, not only by increasing its assets (*Activ-Vermögen*) but also by reducing operating costs. Among the reasons for the higher construction costs, they listed: the heavier rails; construction of more substantial depots and other buildings; a larger investment in rolling stock; and a change in the location of a section of the line. The latter, they explained, increased initial outlays because the line now passed through more difficult terrain, but it would significantly reduce operating costs.[53]

Soon after Chief Engineer Neuhaus persuaded the Berlin-Stettin directors to build a sturdier (and more expensive) railroad, the other railroads also moved away from the American system. In 1842–43 the Leipzig-Dresden Railroad replaced the section of its line that had been built with wooden rails capped with iron straps.[54] The Magdeburg-Leipzig Railroad began a similar process in 1844, first adding oak cross-ties under the rotting pine rails and then replacing the wooden, iron-capped track with heavy iron rails, a task carried out over several years.[55]

---

[52] [Berlin-Stettin Railroad, Annual Report of the Directors], May 15, 1841. They chose to install rails weighing 17 lbs. per foot (*Fuß*) or 25 kg per meter.

[53] "Jahresbericht des Verwaltungsrathes der Berlin-Stettiner Eisenbahn-Gesellschaft für die am 26. Mai 1842 abzuhaltende General-Versammlung," in *Zweiter Jahresbericht des Direktorii der Berlin-Stettiner Eisenbahngesellschaft*. After the line opened, the directors spelled out their general principles regarding construction and operating costs. See *Dritter Jahresbericht des Directorium der Berlin-Stettiner Eisenbahn-Gesellschaft*, p. 10.

[54] Michaelis, *Deutschlands Eisenbahnen*, p. 123.

[55] Von Reden, *Die Eisenbahnen Deutschlands*, 1. Abt., 2. Abschnitt, p. 448; annual reports of the Magdeburg-Leipzig Railroad for 1845–48 in Staatsarchiv Magdeburg, Rep. C20Ib, no. 2851, vol. 3. The new rails weighed 26 kg per meter (53 *Pfund* per yard). Not all German lines forsook the American style; in 1854 Michaelis described a section of the Bavarian state railroads that opened in 1848 as having been built "according to the American system." *Deutschlands Eisenbahnen*, p. 21.

Neuhaus, meanwhile, also became chief engineer for construction
of the Berlin-Hamburg Railroad in 1843, while he continued to work
for the Berlin-Stettin Railroad, and he prompted a change in their
plans, too.[56] The Berlin-Hamburg would run parallel to the Elbe River
and its promoters expected freight traffic to be their most important
business. This would put them in direct competition with river
freighters. Although for the time being they would receive a measure
of protection from the tolls that river traffic had to pay, they assumed
that the tolls would eventually be reduced or eliminated. In those
circumstances the question of construction style took on added significance.[57] When Neuhaus arrived, the members of the Berlin-
Hamburg's supervisory board reworked their construction plans.[58]
Initially, they had adopted a style approximating the Belgian with a
maximum gradient of 1:300 and a minimum curve radius of 1,900
meters (500 *Ruthen* or 6,230 ft.).[59] Now they established a maximum
gradient of 1:1000 "as a rule" and deviated from it only in two places,
allowing grades of 1:600 and 1:500 in those cases. Although they did
not indicate the maximum curve radius they had adopted, they
pointed out that their road in this respect, too, had substantial advantages over most of the existing lines.[60]

Neuhaus's estimates and plans, together with the experiences of
other railroads, the supervisory board explained to the stockholders,
had convinced them of "the need for a solid, but in no way luxurious,
mode of construction." The result, they argued, would be a road that

---

[56] Nekrologie, *Deutsche Bauzeitung*, August 18, 1877, p. 328; "Bericht des Ausschusses der Berlin-Hamburger Eisenbahn-Gesellschaft an die zur ersten Generalversammlung berufenen Actionairs," in *Protocoll der ersten Generalversammlung der
Actionairs der Berlin-Hamburger Eisenbahn-Gesellschaft*, pp. 12, 18.

[57] *Bericht des Comité zur Begründung eines Actien-Vereins für die Eisenbahn-
Verbindung zwischen Berlin und Hamburg*, p. xx; "Bericht des Ausschusses," in *Protocoll der ersten Generalversammlung der Actionairs der Berlin-Hamburger
Eisenbahn-Gesellschaft*, p. 16; and "Bericht des Ausschusses der Berlin-Hamburger
Eisenbahn-Gesellschaft an die zur zweiten ordentlichen General-Versammlung berufenen Actionairs," in *Protocoll der zweiten Generalversammlung der Actionairs
der Berlin-Hamburger Eisenbahn-Gesellschaft nebst Bericht des Ausschusses an dieselben* (Berlin: E. S. Mittler, 1846), pp. 10–11.

[58] "Bericht des Ausschusses," in *Protocoll der ersten Generalversammlung der Actionairs der Berlin-Hamburger Eisenbahn-Gesellschaft*, p. 15.

[59] *Bericht des Comité zur Begründung eines Actien-Vereins für die Eisenbahn-
Verbindung zwischen Berlin und Hamburg*, p. v.

[60] "Bericht des Ausschusses," in *Protocoll der ersten Generalversammlung der Actionairs der Berlin-Hamburger Eisenbahn-Gesellschaft*, p. 16; "Bericht des Ausschusses," in *Protocoll der zweiten Generalversammlung der Actionairs der Berlin-Hamburger Eisenbahn-Gesellschaft*, p. 11.

was still cheaper than some others but "nonetheless could rightly claim the attribute of great solidity." Even though a solid construction style, like low grades, would increase the initial investment, it would minimize maintenance costs (*Unterhaltungskosten*) in the future. Solidity applied not only to roadbed and track construction, but also to bridges. On first glance, they admitted, it might appear that they could reduce bridge construction costs, but it would only be "at the cost of much greater expenditures in the future"; they would build masonry or iron bridges but not wooden ones, because maintenance and losses due to interruption of traffic during major repairs would be too costly. Low grades and minimal curves together, moreover, would allow them to move loads with less power than any other European railroad could. "Only in this way," they reasoned, would the road be able to minimize costs in the future and carry freight at rates low enough to compete with river freighters if the river tolls were removed or reduced. Thus they had given their stamp of approval both to the principles of construction that Neuhaus had advocated from the beginning and to the increased investment that they required.[61]

In doing so, they were following closely the principles that the state civil engineer Crelle enunciated and articulated throughout the 1830s in his *Journal für die Baukunst*. Neuhaus and many other state civil engineers who worked on early railroads were among his first subscribers in 1829–30.[62] Crelle, himself an engineer with thirty years of experience, argued repeatedly in his own articles and in editorial commentary that the American system of construction would not do for Germany. As noted earlier, he conceded that German railroads *could* be built the same way, but he argued forcefully in the late

---

[61] "Bericht des Ausschusses," in *Protocoll der zweiten Generalversammlung der Actionairs der Berlin-Hamburger Eisenbahn-Gesellschaft*, pp. 12, 17, 18–19. They also planned to use all-iron rails supported by oak cross-ties. Neuhaus's principles are summarized in ibid., p. 18. The stockholders approved an increase in the company's capital from 8 to 13 million *Taler* (i.e., from about $5.6 to $9.1 million), but this also covered other expenses not due to the change of construction style. *Protocoll der zweiten Generalversammlung der Actionairs der Berlin-Hamburger Eisenbahn-Gesellschaft*, p. 5.

[62] See "Subscriptions-Verzeichniß," *JfdBK* 1 (1829): iii–xxii, and "Nachtrag zum Subscriptions-Verzeichniß," *JfdBK* 2 (1830). An autodidact, Crelle enjoyed a long career in state service, during which he was involved in building the Berlin-Potsdam and Berlin-Frankfurt railroads. However, he devoted much of his career to mathematics education. See *Dictionary of Scientific Biography*, 3:466; *Allgemeine Deutsche Biographie*, 4:589–90.

1830s that they should not be, that Germans should take a longer-term view and build more durably. This state civil engineering viewpoint was perhaps best encapsulated in Crelle's general comments in 1831 on economy in the construction of public works. Too often, he argued, economy was confused with the least expenditure, when in reality it was precisely the least expenditure at the outset that would prove more expensive in the long term. Time and again, he returned to the theme: "[b]uild as durably as possible." Crelle endorsed what he viewed as a pragmatic style of construction that sought to build for the long term with limited means. The American system, as he saw it, sought wrongly to build for the short term with limited means. "Everywhere, the principle of building durably and solidly, and not lightly and temporarily," he maintained, "is the right one."[63] When state engineer Neuhaus convinced the Berlin-Stettin and later the Berlin-Hamburg railroads to move away from the American system and toward a more durable style of construction, he argued along practically identical lines.

In 1850, the movement against the American system reached closure, as German railroad engineers acted collectively to endorse a more durable style of construction.[64] Endorsement came in the deliberations of the Association of German Railroad Engineers that had formed that year as an adjunct of the national railroad association. The norms adopted by the parent association endorsed the English gauge and called for maximum curves of twelve hundred feet and rolled iron rails (of a given shape and dimension). They did not specify a weight for the rails but did stipulate that they be capable of withstanding 120 *Zentner* (6,000 kg) on each wheel. Only in setting a maximum grade of 1:200 on level terrain did they depart from a moderately conservative style.[65] Grades and curves were more difficult to alter after the fact, and German railroads still looked very "American" from Lardner's British perspective in 1850. But the wooden rail and strap iron were already gone, as he duly noted.[66]

---

[63] "Über Kosten-Ersparung beim öffentlichen Bauwesen und die Art der Vergleichung mehrere Projecte zu einerlei Werk. Vom Herrn Mondot de Lagorce, Ingénieur en chef des ponts et chaussées. . . . Mit zusätzlichen Bemerkungen des Hrsg.," *JfdBK* 4 (1831): 172–82 (quotations from pp. 179, 182).

[64] On the concept of closure in the social construction of technological systems, see Pinch and Bijker, "The Social Construction of Facts and Artifacts," pp. 44–46.

[65] *Festschrift*, pp. 47–49.

[66] Lardner, *Railway Economy*, pp. 471–76.

Political Structure and Engineering Style

Prussian engineers were not alone in rejecting the American system. A number of American engineers also voiced dissatisfaction with the American system in the late 1830s. The civil engineers Benjamin H. Latrobe, Jr., and Jonathan Knight, for example, explicitly rejected the wooden, strap-iron construction in an 1838 report on construction styles for the Baltimore and Ohio Railroad. Instead, they advocated a moderately durable style of construction entailing all-iron rails and wooden cross-ties (on the Belgian model). "True economy dictates this course," they maintained, words that Crelle and Neuhaus would certainly have endorsed.[67] Another civil engineer, Edward Miller, who had gotten his start in the railroad business on the Pennsylvania state public works and visited Britain, also endorsed a durable construction style for the Sunbury and Erie Railroad in 1839. He recommended that the line "be constructed throughout in the best and most permanent manner; . . . and that heavy iron rails supported by continuous bearings of squared timbers, well bound together by wooden cross-ties, be adopted."[68]

But Miller's comments also made clear that others—as he saw it, too many others—saw attractions in elements of the American system. He began his report on the Sunbury and Erie Railroad by laying out his general principles. "The propriety of this course is more evident than formerly," he explained,

> because the prodigious strides which of late years have been made towards perfection in the mechanism and management of rail roads, have too often excited the naturally ardent imaginations of our countrymen, until misled by the prejudiced and partial statements of ignorant and interested schemers, they have closed their eyes to the plain truths of science, and leapt to conclusions which cannot fail to be disastrous as they are unfounded.

Two alternative strategies for dealing with rough terrain he found "most erroneous": one was the acceptance of steep grades, and the

---

[67] Jonathan Knight and Benjamin H. Latrobe, *Report Upon the Plan of Construction of Several of the Principal Rail Roads in the Northern and Middle States, and Upon a Railway Structure for a New Track on the Baltimore and Ohio Railroad* (Baltimore: Lucas & Deaver, 1838), p. 33.

[68] *First Report of Edward Miller*, p. 22; Stapleton, "Origin of American Railroad Technology," p. 65.

other was the excessive lengthening of railroad routes. "The former of these notions is, of course, adopted only by those who are not conversant with the truths of mechanical science," he asserted; "the latter, I am sorry to say, is held or at least acted upon by professional engineers, and both I conceive to be equally heretical." He favored not the British system of excavation and embankment but the use of inclined planes. (These commonly used stationary steam engines to move trains over a ridge.) Inclined planes had clear disadvantages, he acknowledged, but "[e]xcessive grades and curvatures may be more dangerous, and excessive length may cause more delay, and much great expense, both in construction, annual repairs, and transportation."[69]

In laying out the Sunbury and Erie, therefore, he recommended moderate curves and a maximum grade of 1:1000. The line could be built like the New York and Erie to the north, he admitted, in which case "the first cost of the road would be so small as to astonish every one." But his principles spoke against it:

> I trust . . . that Pennsylvania has by this time learned, that rail roads, if made at all, should be well made. . . . [J]udicious economy dictates that we should rather increase the original outlay, than be cursed by a perpetual and more than equivalent tax, for the increased cost of repairs and transportation, while the history of work ever remains rife with tales of dreadful accidents and vexatious delays.[70]

A diversity of views also prevailed among American engineers, in other words, while Prussian railroads were experimenting with the American system.

But no consensus against the American system emerged as early in the United States, because American engineers lacked the institutional resources that aided the Prussians in arriving at one. That is to say, no central state engineering corps commanded a position of authority in American engineering circles like it did in Prussia. In both countries, state engineers were deeply involved in early railroad construction: in Prussia, as chapter 2 indicated, they were state civil engineers such as Crelle and Neuhaus; in the United States, they

---

[69] *First Report of Edward Miller*, pp. 5, 7.

[70] Ibid., pp. 21–22. Two years later, Miller was appointed chief engineer of the New York and Erie Railroad. He relocated sections of the line to reduce its grade. See Miller's deposition in "Report of the Committee appointed to investigate the affairs of the New York and Erie Railroad Company," New York Assembly, Doc. no. 50, January 18, 1842.

were either army engineers or civil engineers from one of the state systems of public works, where they acquired practical training rather than the "book learning" that distinguished West Point graduates. But the Prussian political structure with its central state engineering corps encouraged a greater homogeneity of experience and sensibility within the Prussian engineering community. The state civil engineers did not necessarily have the same educational background, as engineers did in France, for example.[71] Many state civil engineers received their training at the Academy of Architecture (Bau-Akademie) in Berlin, but others (like Georg Neuhaus and Hans Viktor von Unruh) attended university classes (in Berlin and Königsberg, respectively). Instead, their common tie came from the state engineering examinations that all state engineers had to pass and from the intervening periods of study or unpaid internship with state engineers. As the finance minister acknowledged when the state began to tighten up its restrictions on the engineers' railroad work, the preparation time, as a rule, consumed some fifteen years.[72] During these years, they had ample time to absorb the kind of value system that Crelle propounded through his journal.

The American engineering community, in contrast, encompassed greater diversity, because of the federal political structure. The closest approximation to the Prussian civil engineering corps would have been the War Department's engineers, who were so active in early railroad development.[73] The West Point graduates, in particular, constituted a larger, more homogeneous group of engineers than any other in the country. The abortive efforts of civil engineers to form a national society in 1839, moreover, suggested that the army engineers felt less need to defend their professional status in hard economic times, for it was the traditional civil engineers who responded with greater enthusiasm, while the military engineers displayed a decided lack of interest.[74] It was also indicative of their exclusiveness

---

[71] Smith, "The Longest Run," p. 661.

[72] Minister Flottwell to [Friedrich Wilhelm IV], October 27, 1844, in ZStAM, Rep. 2.2.1, no. 29524, pp. 18r–20. See also Eberhard Grünert, Die Preußische Bau- und Finanzdirektion in Berlin: Entstehung und Entwicklung, 1822–1944 (Cologne: Grote, 1983), pp. 103–4, 128.

[73] See chap. 2.

[74] Calhoun, American Civil Engineer, pp. 182–85; William H. Wisely, The American Civil Engineer, 1852–1974: The History, Traditions and Development of the American Society of Civil Engineers (New York: American Society of Civil Engineers, 1974), pp. 6–10.

that the West Point men initially rebuffed a German immigrant by the name of Albert Fink when he was searching for an engineering position in the United States in the late 1840s. Once Fink had found work on the Baltimore and Ohio Railroad, however, Benjamin H. Latrobe, Jr., introduced him to West Point circles. With the aid of a "gatekeeper," Fink, who enjoyed a long and illustrious career in railroading, reportedly came away from a meeting with Majors Mahan and Clark with assurances "that they wish to keep in close touch with all I am doing."[75]

But the army engineers themselves were a relatively diverse lot. Many were army officers, but others, such as Dr. William C. Howard, who worked on surveys for the Baltimore and Ohio and South Carolina railroads, were not. On the basis of Engineer Department records, Hill reports that about two-thirds of some fifty army engineers who worked for railroads from 1827 to 1840 were army officers; the rest were U.S. civil engineers.[76] Even among the army officers, moreover, important differences in background obtained. Many had received their training at the military academy at West Point, with its mathematics-based curriculum, strongly influenced by French practice after 1817—but not all had.[77] For example, one of the most active of railroad engineers, Col. Stephen H. Long, had graduated from Dartmouth (although he taught mathematics at West Point before beginning his twenty-year railroad career).[78]

And not all railroad engineers were army engineers, let alone West Point graduates. In 1837, army engineers constituted nearly a third of the chief engineers on fifty-two lines, by Daniel Calhoun's count, which means that more than two-thirds came from elsewhere.[79] A number of the better-known engineers got their start on the state governments' public works. John B. Jervis began his career on the Erie Canal, where he worked his way up from axeman to superintending engineer in seven years. Benjamin Latrobe of the Baltimore and Ohio

[75] Quoted from an unidentified letter in Ellen Fink Milton, *A Biography of Albert Fink* (n.p., 1951), p. 34.

[76] Hill, *Roads, Rails, and Waterways*, p. 144n.

[77] On the French influence on the curriculum at West Point during the years when it was producing engineers who worked on railroads, see Molloy, "Technical Education and the Young Republic."

[78] Hill, *Roads, Rails, and Waterways*, p. 145n. On Long's career, see Richard George Wood, *Stephen Harriman Long, 1784–1864: Army Engineer, Explorer, Inventor* (Glendale, Calif.: Arthur H. Clark Co., 1966).

[79] Calhoun, *American Civil Engineer*, p. 52.

Railroad represented a transitional type, who gained his engineering experience by working for the railroad. But his colleague at the Baltimore and Ohio, Jonathan Knight, started out a surveyor in western Maryland and was working on the National Road when the B&O recruited him; in Calhoun's words, he represented "the relatively undifferentiated quasi-engineers of the period before the War of 1812." Edward Miller initially worked on the Lehigh canal and moved to Pennsylvania's Main Line system of public works. Moncure Robinson began his career on the Virginia and Pennsylvania state works.[80] In short, state engineers abounded in early American, as in Prussian, railroad history, but they came from a variety of state services and even those in the military did not necessarily have a uniform training.

Because of this diversity of experience, American railroad engineers, as a whole, favored no particular engineering style. Instead, they worked with a diversity of styles, including but not limited to the American system. Some of the military engineers, for example, displayed a "calculating economy," as Hill puts it, that conflicted with traditional engineering principles. Col. Stephen Long left the Baltimore and Ohio Railroad, for example, after a series of disputes with Caspar Wever, a practically trained engineer, who had come from the National Road. One point of conflict concerned the engineering principles that should govern bridge construction. As Daniel Calhoun relates, "Long's professed object was to build the most economical bridges possible *within the immediately foreseeable needs of the road.*" For Long, that meant using wood instead of stone and employing design principles that reduced the wood to a minimum. As Colonel Long himself explained, in words echoed nine years later by the Berlin-Stettin's directors when they initially endorsed the American system, the "prime cost [of wooden bridges] is so much less than that of stone bridges, that the interest on the additional capital required for the latter, is sufficient to keep wooden bridges in complete repair." But the company's superintendent of construction, Caspar Wever, was not persuaded. A man with practical training rather than a

---

[80] F. Daniel Larkin, *John B. Jervis: An American Engineering Pioneer* (Ames: Iowa State University Press, 1990), pp. 6–15; Calhoun, *American Civil Engineer*, pp. 130–31; "Report of the committee appointed to investigate the affairs of the New York and Erie Railroad Company," p. 31; Stapleton, "Origin of American Railroad Technology," p. 76; idem, *Transfer of Early Industrial Technologies*, p. 128.

formal engineering education, he favored "permanent stone bridges based on traditional architects' rules for arches, rules empirically shown to be safe," and he found powerful backing in the company's president, Philip E. Thomas. This incident revealed a striking difference between the two views of engineering: as Calhoun formulates it, it was a "distinction between two types or attitudes—one mathematical, formal, and professional, the other personal, practical, and conservative." And they implied correspondingly different views of initial costs: the civilian perspective represented by Wever and supported by the board of directors "seemed to favor expensive modes of construction"—building for the long term, Crelle would have said—while Long "favored a calculating economy."[81] Yet this episode symbolized, at best, the stylistic *tendencies* that separated military from civil engineers. Not all army engineers shared Long's preferences. Indeed, those such as McNeill and Whistler who built railroads in New England tended to favor a heavier construction style.[82] And the railroad associations that would have encouraged a technological consensus, as chapter 4 showed, perennially failed to coalesce.

The "American style" of railroad technology thus consisted precisely in a durable *diversity* of styles, a diversity that persisted much longer in the United States than in Prussia.[83] Some railroads enjoyed easy grades and smooth curves from the outset, but high grades and sharp curves—the most difficult features to alter—continued to be found on others well after the mid-century mark. Not even the light iron rails, so closely associated with the American system, had disappeared altogether. "It is notorious," commented Henry Varnum Poor's *American Railroad Journal* in early 1851,

> that . . . a great many of our roads are laid with a very poor iron, entirely unsuitable for its purpose, both as regards true economy and safety. . . . Most of them, for the want of sufficient means, or a

[81] Calhoun, *American Civil Engineer*, pp. 123–30, 138 (quotations from pp. 130, 138). Long's explanation is given in *Report of the Engineers, on the Reconnoissance [sic] and Surveys, Made in Reference to the Baltimore and Ohio Rail Road* (Baltimore, 1828). This line of argument is pushed further in Dunlavy, "Politics and Industrialization," pp. 267–97, 308–15.

[82] For descriptions, see von Gerstner, *Die innern Communicationen*; Knight and Latrobe, *Report Upon the Locomotive Engines*. On the constructing engineers, see Dunlavy, "Politics and Industrialization," appendix.

[83] List, "Das deutsche Eisenbahnsystem IV," pp. 378, 396; Chevalier, *Society, Manners and Politics*, pp. 270–71; von Gerstner, *Berichte*, pp. 15–17.

proper idea of the importance of a liberal expenditure in the outset, or from mistaken ambition of having the reputation of building the cheapest road going, act upon the false principle of economy, of using what cost the least, without any regard to quality. Such are facts too notorious to require proofs.[84]

About this time, some roads were in the process of being reconstructed. The state directors of the Camden and Amboy Railroad reported in 1852, for example, that more than seven miles of track had been relaid with heavier rails (45 kg/m) that year. "Simultaneously with the laying of the heavy rail, the track has been considerably straightened," they explained. "Dangerous curves have been overcome, and the distance shortened."[85] But the obstacles to fundamental change seemed so large that Poor called for government intervention: "We think it should [become the subject of legal interposition], though we are generally opposed to legislative interference with the operations of companies."[86]

In the meantime, one state had already taken steps to rid its railroads of light iron. New York legislation in 1847 authorized all railroads using strap-iron rails to increase their capital or borrow the money to replace them with rails weighing at least 56 pounds per yard (28.3 kg/m). It also specifically required eight railroads to begin doing so by January 1, 1848, and restricted their dividends until they had instituted the improvement. Any that refused or neglected to do so would lose their charter.[87] The New York general railroad incorporation law of 1850 went further, flatly forbidding railroads in the state to lay down rail that weighed less than 56 pounds to the yard (except on sidings, turnouts, and switches).[88]

[84] *American Railroad Journal*, February 15, 1851, quoted in *Report of the Committee Appointed to Examine and Report the Causes of Railroad Accidents*, p. 146. See also Stapleton, *Transfer of Early Industrial Technologies*, p. 154.

[85] *Report of the State Directors of the Delaware and Raritan Canal and Camden and Amboy Railroad Companies to the Legislature of New Jersey* (Trenton: True American Office, 1852), p. 4.

[86] *American Railroad Journal*, February 15, 1851, quoted in *Report of the Committee Appointed to Examine and Report the Causes of Railroad Accidents*, p. 146.

[87] *Laws of New York* (1847), chap. 272, reprinted in Bishop, *General Rail Road Law*, pp. 93–95; Stevens, *Beginnings of the New York Central Railroad*, pp. 293–300. The railroads in question were the Albany and Schenectady (Mohawk and Hudson), the Troy and Schenectady, the Schenectady and Utica, the Utica and Syracuse, the Syracuse and Auburn, the Auburn and Rochester, the Tonawanda, and the Attica and Buffalo, which were consolidated as the New York Central Railroad in 1853.

[88] *Laws of New York* (1850), chap. 140, §27; Bishop, *General Rail Road Law*, p. 54.

National styles of railroad construction in the United States and Prussia, in short, must be seen as twice conditioned by politics: once, in the way that one political structure—the American—encouraged the indiscriminant multiplication of railroads and, hence, put pressure on the supply of capital, while the other did not; and a second time, in the way that one structure—the Prussian—encouraged an early consensus in favor of a more durable construction style, while the other fragmented the engineering community and hindered the building of a consensus. The supply of capital, itself conditioned by politics, thus defined the broad parameters of technological style, locating the United States and Prussia toward the other end of the spectrum from Britain, but early railroad men recognized that they still had weighty choices to make. How quickly those choices coalesced toward consensus in the engineering community depended on the ambient political structure in which they were made. The upshot in Prussia was a decisive shift on the spectrum of technical possibilities, toward a consensus by the early 1840s that railroads should be constructed in a sturdier fashion than the "American system" called for, but not as luxuriously as the British paradigm dictated. The Association of German Railroad Administrations put this in writing in 1850. In the United States, with its fragmented political structure, those who favored sturdier construction represented but one voice among many. In a context of more stringent capital scarcity, this heterogeneity of views served to push down *average* construction costs in the United States. If, as Thomas P. Hughes writes, "[one] of the primary characteristics of a system builder is the ability to construct or to force unity from diversity, centralization in the face of pluralism, and coherence from chaos,"[89] then the antebellum political structure put American railroad builders at a comparative disadvantage.

[89] Hughes, "The Evolution of Large Technological Systems," p. 52.

6

Epilogue: How Industrial Change Structures Politics

THE AMERICAN and Prussian political structures, subtly but ineluctably conditioning railroad development during the 1830s and 1840s, were themselves not fixed and immutable, as subsequent events made clear. Railroad construction moved ahead in both countries from the 1840s on, and as it proceeded it set in motion thoroughgoing changes that ushered in a new industrial order and in the process transformed both political structures. Hints of this transformation were already visible in the early 1840s, when American and Prussian railroad policy began to move in opposite directions. In the hard times of the late 1830s and early 1840s, some of the American state governments began to divest themselves of state railroads—the second stage of what Carter Goodrich calls a "state in, state out" pattern of economic policy; during the same years, the Prussian state began somewhat tentatively to move "in" after it adopted the new railroad aid policy of 1842.[1] These trends not only continued in the 1850s, but gained momentum and took on added dimensions. As Prussian policy took a more interventionist turn, the locus of policymaking in the United States began to shift upward, ultimately creating conditions that finally enabled American railroads to organize a permanent national association.

The Transformation of the 1850s

The transformation in Prussia, begun with the change of state policy in 1842, moved ahead a few years later, when the question of railroad construction forced the crown further down the path toward liberalization. In 1847 the king called a joint meeting of the provincial assemblies (the United Diet) to seek approval of a set of financial measures that included a state loan of some thirty to forty million

[1] Goodrich, "State In, State Out," pp. 365–83.

Taler. Roughly twice what the 1820 debt law allowed the crown to borrow without parliamentary approval, this loan was intended to finance state construction of the great Eastern Railroad, which would run from Berlin to Königsberg in the far northeastern reaches of Prussia. But the members of the provincial assemblies held their ground, insisting that the provisions of the national debt law be abided by, and the king held his, refusing to allow the United Diet full parliamentary powers. Revolution came the following year.[2] In that sense, the new demands of industrial capitalism—the unprecedented amounts of capital that railroad construction demanded—helped to precipitate a transformation of the Prussian political structure.

By no means did a fully liberal regime emerge. The new political structure only took final form after a conservative reaction corrected the "excesses" of the revolution. With the crown in the lead, a coalition composed of *Landtag* conservatives, the bureaucracies, the nobility, the Protestant orthodoxy, and the officers corps of the standing army undid many of the revolutionary reforms between 1848 and 1854, retaining their outward constitutional forms but strengthening the power of the aristocracy, the bureaucracy, and the monarchy within them. At the national level, the attack centered on parliament. Not only was the Council of State revived but, more important, the Upper House was transformed into a House of Lords (*Herrenhaus*) in 1854. This was done in such a way that eligibility for three-quarters of the seats, formerly reserved for the largest taxpayers, was now restricted to an elite among the nobility—those possessing "old" and "established" estates—while the remaining 90 percent of the nobility, including the bourgeois nobles (*bürgerliche Rittergutsbesitzer*), were excluded. Those changes had, in turn, been made possible by replacing manhood suffrage with a three-class system based on wealth. Governmental powers, moreover, remained intertwined, for the executive continued to influence the other branches of government through its ministers, who sat not only in the legislature but also on the final court of appeal (*Ober-Tribunal*). Even the king retained substantial power, since the ministers served at his, rather

---

[2] The railroad loan was one of two financial measures that state officials presented to the United Diet; the other concerned agricultural credit. On these familiar events, see Henderson, *The State and the Industrial Revolution*, pp. 124, 163, 165–68; Tilly, "Political Economy of Public Finance," p. 489; Klee, *Preußische Eisenbahngeschichte*, pp. 110–13.

than the parliament's, pleasure. But bureaucratic control did attenuate somewhat, for the two houses of the Prussian Assembly now influenced policy—including railroad policy—through their powers of approval over state expenditures. Thus the revolution and its aftermath produced a constitutional monarchy in which central-state officials, while still powerful, nonetheless shared policy-making powers with a parliament.[3]

Once a degree of political liberalization had been achieved, the constraints that the old illiberal structure had imposed on economic policy lost their force. The necessity of obtaining parliamentary approval for state loans, as Klee observes, had previously made state railroads too "expensive" from a political standpoint. But now both a parliament and a constitution existed; whatever their deficiencies, the state now had greater latitude to raise the capital that it needed to "cultivate" state railroads.[4] In the early 1850s, August von der Heydt of the Elberfeld banking family, head of the new Ministry for Trade, Commerce, and Public Works now responsible for railroad policy, stopped chartering private railroads for a time and launched a program of state railroad construction. By a variety of means, Minister von der Heydt, who became known as the "state railroad minister" for his enthusiasm to nationalize Prussian railroads, also took over the administration of some of the private lines.[5] Thus the revolution brought, as Tilly notes, "a turning point in Prussian fiscal history."[6] Now that they had the legitimacy that came with parliamentary support, the ministers dramatically increased borrowing and spending to further railroad development.

In the meantime, the political dynamic first manifested in 1842, which coupled regulation with promotion, became more pronounced after the revolution, for Minister von der Heydt also brought the remaining private railroads under control in ways that the state had

[3] Heffter, "Der nachmärzliche Liberalismus," pp. 177–96; Erich Hahn, "Ministerial Responsibility and Impeachment in Prussia, 1848–63," *Central European History* 10 (1977): 3–27; Nipperdey, *Deutsche Geschichte*, pp. 679–83. The constitution resulted only indirectly from popular deliberation. After an assembly elected to deliberate on the subject ended in impasse, the king imposed (*oktroyierte*) the constitution from above.

[4] Klee, *Preußische Eisenbahngeschichte*, p. 118. On relations between the railroads and the state in this period, see especially Brophy, "Capitulation or Negotiated Settlement?"

[5] Henderson, *The State and the Industrial Revolution*, pp. 171–80; Klee, *Preußische Eisenbahngeschichte*, pp. 119–25.

[6] Tilly, "Political Economy of Public Finance," p. 495.

not done before 1848. In 1853, he reasserted the state's authority to tax the railroads by securing passage of a new tax on their net profits.[7] The central thrust of his efforts, however, aimed to reconstitute state control of rates and schedules. This he accomplished by adopting a technique explicitly tying promotion to regulation, the one that had initially been tried out soon after the shift in state policy in 1842: he forced the private companies—when they wanted to increase their capital, for example, or to receive an interest guarantee—to accept charter amendments that gave the state control of rates and schedules.[8] In a related effort, von der Heydt also instituted night-train service on the major railroads in order to facilitate mail delivery, an extensive and ultimately successful campaign known at the time as the "night train affair" (Nachtzugangelegenheit).[9] In another well-known initiative, finally, von der Heydt drove down freight rates for the transportation of coal from Upper Silesia to Berlin.[10] In sum, as the Prussian state undertook an ambitious program to promote railroad development, it also reclaimed its regulatory powers in a variety of ways as the 1850s progressed.

Thus, in Prussia, the railroads' unprecedented capital-intensity— in this case, their sheer demand for capital—pushed events to the point of revolution; the revolution brought a change in political structure, which in turn altered the policy-making process; with a measure of political liberalization came less liberal economic policies. Before 1848, the constrained circumstances had offered little leeway for state action, whether promotional or regulatory. After 1848, the state could borrow virtually at will. The "alarmed capital" argument that the railroads had used to fend off regulation, moreover, lost its force as the major private lines went into operation and as state investment increased. Both trends served to enhance the ministries' leverage. In the 1850s, consequently, Prussian railroad policy

---

[7] Henderson, *The State and the Industrial Revolution*, pp. 179–80, 185; Klee, *Preußische Eisenbahngeschichte*, pp. 122, 124.

[8] Enkling, *Die Stellung des Staates*, pp. 55–56.

[9] Although the railroads contested his action in the courts, von der Heydt had won the battle by the mid-1850s. See Brophy, "Capitulation or Negotiated Settlement?"; and the many documents in the Staatsarchiv Hamburg, especially Bestand Senat, Cl. VII, Lit. K[a], no. 11, vol. 13, Berlin-Hamburger Eisenbahn-Gesellschaft, Fasc. 114a–114d.

[10] Henderson, *The State and the Industrial Revolution*, pp. 182–83; Klee, *Preußische Eisenbahngeschichte*, pp. 126, 129.

came to resemble the more interventionist policy that the American structure had produced earlier, but from the national level.

This, in turn, gave the railroads all the more reason to hold their association together, which they did. Membership in the VDEV grew from 61 lines with more than 15,000 kilometers in 1860 to 109 roads with nearly 50,000 kilometers by 1876. Membership declined thereafter, as consolidations and state purchases reduced the number of railroads. Thus, by the end of the century, the association claimed only 74 members, but they operated more than 80,000 kilometers of track. Amid considerable controversy, meanwhile, the rules governing eligibility for membership had been widened to include roads in neighboring countries, and by 1896 the association drew members from eight nations.[11]

In the United States, meanwhile, the state governments during the 1850s began to find themselves in a position that strangely resembled the Prussian state's predicament before 1848. Having partially divested themselves of railroads in the 1840s, they had lost some of the regulatory leverage that came with promotion. Now the railroads' capital intensity (manifested in high fixed costs) and their geographic sprawl precipitated a virtual revolution that undermined the states' regulatory power and ultimately shifted the locus of policy-making to the national level. Understanding how this came about requires returning to the subject of the legislatures' traditional methods of rate regulation.

Initially, the American state legislatures, as chapter 2 indicated, sought to regulate railroad rates as they had traditionally regulated transportation prices—by setting specific, maximum tolls for use of the highway (or reserving the right to lower them) and assuming that competition among carriers would keep carrying charges at reasonable levels. At first, this approach seemed appropriate for railroads as well, since most of the early railroads did not face significant competition from other roads; like turnpike or canal companies, they enjoyed a monopoly in providing the roadway for use by the public. When it became clear in the late 1830s that safety and managerial efficiency would not allow multiple carriers on the railroads, traditional methods still seemed workable, for now the railroads enjoyed a monopoly in providing both services. The legislatures, therefore,

[11] *Festschrift*, pp. 4–5, 34.

could simply regulate both by setting maximum rates. Tradition, as Miller emphasizes, provided firm support for the legislatures' right to regulate transportation prices under monopoly conditions.[12]

But, from the start, the railroads also presented an unprecedented regulatory problem of another kind: discriminatory rates. This problem first appeared on the railroads, as chapter 1 indicated, because they were the first enterprises to operate under high fixed costs. Because of the incentives inherent in the peculiar structure of their costs, the railroads had a variety of reasons to discriminate among customers. And, as quickly became apparent, traditional modes of regulation had little to say about the railroads' discriminatory rate structures. In writing charters, legislators traditionally focused exclusively on the problem of *high* rates, but the special rates offered to large shippers, those located at points of trunk-line competition, and long-distance shippers were *lower* than the companies' regular rates. Hence, maximum rates fixed in statute law did not address this peculiar new problem. Yet, common sense said that distance-based discrimination, in particular, was unjust, for transportation charges had always been proportional to the distance traveled. Thus a person who shipped goods, say, one hundred miles should have to pay twice as much as someone who shipped goods only half that distance. "It was clear from the outset," Miller observes,

> that many, if not all, of these acts of discrimination were violations of the basic legal principle associated with common carriers: public transportation companies were obligated to treat all their customers fairly and without favor. When they did not do so the courts were supposed to offer remedies. For protection against unequal treatment, therefore, the people first turned to the courts, expecting to find their rights firmly established in the common law.[13]

But they did not. The common law proved equally inadequate, for it, too, traditionally defined the problem in terms of high rates; unjust discrimination occurred only when the rate charged was "higher than the customary or prevailing rate." The courts had no precedent to follow where low rates were concerned. "As long as the higher rate was reasonable in itself," Miller explains, "there was no relief. . . .

---

[12] Miller, *Railroads and the Granger Laws*, pp. 1–41; Levy, *Laws of the Commonwealth*, pp. 135–36.
[13] Miller, *Railroads and the Granger Laws*, p. 23.

The common law provided no protection against the practice of rate cutting." In the late 1840s and early 1850s, therefore, constituents suffering discrimination took the issue back to the state legislatures.[14]

About the same time, new developments in the railroad business completed the legislatures' introduction to the distinctive regulatory problems of the new industrial order and, in doing so, exposed the structural constraints on their power. As the eastern trunk-lines reached completion between 1851 and 1854, the volume of through traffic increased and competition intensified. This, in turn, magnified complaints from small and short-haul shippers as well as from those shippers and communities that were not situated at points of trunk-line competition and, therefore, paid higher rates. When competition among the trunk-lines became the norm, moreover, the premises on which legislative and judicial regulation of rates traditionally rested seemed increasingly irrelevant, for the railroads now enjoyed a monopoly of carriage on their own tracks, but competition prevailed among the various trunk-lines as "highways," thus driving down through rates. The opening of the long-distance trunk-lines also raised that most intractable of questions: the competence of the state legislatures to regulate what was rapidly becoming the first interstate business. Thus, when the issue of rate regulation returned to the legislatures in the 1850s, the long-standing consensus undergirding their right to regulate rates disintegrated under the weight of industrial change. As Miller observes, "railroad reform became a political issue."[15]

In those altered circumstances, the fractures designed into the American political structure in earlier days took on new significance. In the ensuing political battles, which raged from the 1850s into the 1880s, both federalism and separation of powers provided leverage that the railroads used to good advantage. As Harry N. Scheiber argues, the American political structure offered several "routes of escape for business interests that were 'caught' in a particular state's policy of discrimination or stringent regulation."[16] Federalism itself offered two separate avenues of escape from the state legislatures. Using the first, business could take a "lateral" route, in theory at

[14] Ibid., pp. 28, 32.
[15] Ibid., p. 32.
[16] Scheiber, "Federalism and the American Economic Order," pp. 115–16.

least, moving from a "hostile" to a "benign" state. And, indeed, American railroad partisans, like Prussian railroad men, quickly used the "alarmed capital" argument precisely to highlight this threat. Two variants of the argument emerged in the 1850s, both of which exploited the structural constraints of federalism. One closely resembled the argument on which Prussian railroad men had relied: regulation would scare off investors and inhibit further railroad development; the other, uniquely useful in a federal structure once interstate traffic developed, warned that regulation would imperil the capital in existing roads because through traffic would avoid the state that regulated its railroads.

The first major controversy, which erupted in Rhode Island in 1850 when local shippers complained that rates on the New York, Providence, and Boston route discriminated against local traffic, brought both arguments into play. In the mid-1850s, critics of pending legislation to equalize through and local rates charged that it would "alarm capital and crush enterprise." Such regulation, they warned, would "effectually put a stop to any new railroads in our midst." By the late 1850s, as another depression set in and as competition with railroads in neighboring states intensified, the second version of the argument came into play. Now legislators began to worry that regulation would divert traffic away from its own lines. As John K. Towles explains, "the competition of other lines forced the Rhode Islanders to give a free hand to their own roads."[17]

As railroad development progressed, the two versions of the "alarmed capital" argument varied in importance. Where the railroad network was thinner, the "Prussian" variant—stressing the threat to new investment—tended to carry greater weight. In those areas, the communities that had rail service but suffered from rate discrimination tended to support regulation. The railroads, however, drew political support from the "have-not" communities, which feared that they would never obtain rail service if regulation scared off new investment. Then, as the density of the railroad network increased, the "American" variant—the warning that regulation

[17] *Manufacturers' and Farmers' Journal*, January 20, 1854, quoted in John K. Towles, "Early Railroad Monopoly and Discrimination in Rhode Island, 1835–55," *Yale Review* 18 (November 1909): 316–17. Cf. Miller, *Railroads and the Granger Laws*, pp. 33–34.

would divert through traffic to other states—became more pro-nounced.[18] Such considerations lay behind the New York legisla-ture's decision in 1851 to abolish the canal tolls on railroads that paralleled the Erie Canal. Throughout the remainder of the decade, New York state railroads, allied with merchants in New York City, fought off canal tolls and equalized rates by arguing that higher rates for through traffic would divert commerce to other coastal cities and send New York City into decline.[19] Similar arguments were heard in Pennsylvania. Because of the tonnage tax that continued in force on the Pennsylvania Railroad, Governor James Pollock warned in 1858, "the produce of the west is forced upon the competing railroads of other States and to other markets than our own." The Pennsylvania Railroad and its supporters eventually used the same argument a few years later to remove the tonnage tax that its traffic had borne since 1846.[20] Once interstate traffic became a reality, in short, federalism simultaneously undermined the regulatory thrust inherent in the legislative policy-making process and enhanced the leverage to be gained from the American version of the "alarmed capital" argument.

By the 1870s, moreover, the railroads and their critics had both begun to exploit federalism in a second way, this time by moving "upward" to seek national, in place of state, legislation.[21] For the railroads' opponents, this seemed the only way to regulate an indus-try that had become national in scope; for the railroads, it became a means of defense against hostile state legislatures. And once the

[18] Miller, *Railroads and the Granger Laws*, pp. 34–40; Scheiber, "Federalism and the American Economic Order," p. 99. Cf. *Memorial of the Atchison, Topeka and Santa Fe Railroad Company, to the Senate and House of Representatives of the State of Kansas* (Topeka: George W. Martin, 1879). This tract discussed the threat to new construction ("if a stringent tariff law is enacted, *it will be impossible to obtain one dollar of foreign capital for [new railroads]*," [p. 42, original emphasis]) and stressed the company's political support in areas that did not yet have railroads (p. 43) but, given its location in a comparatively thin part of the railroad network, it did not mention the potential diversion of traffic.

[19] Miller, *Railroads and the Granger Laws*, pp. 34–35, 217.

[20] James Pollock, "Annual Message to the Assembly, 1858," in *Pennsylvania Ar-chives*, ed. George Edward Reed, 4th ser., vol. 7: *Papers of the Governors, 1845–1858* (Harrisburg: State of Pennsylvania, 1902), p. 937; Miller, *Railroads and the Granger Laws*, pp. 36–37. The Pennsylvania Railroad did not escape rate regulation altogether in 1861; in a "compromise," the tonnage tax and "other disabilities" were eliminated in exchange for a prohibition against long haul–short haul differentials.

[21] Scheiber, "Federalism and the American Economic Order," pp. 115–16; Tony Freyer, *Forums of Order: The Federal Courts and Business in American History* (Greenwich, Conn.: JAI Press, 1979), pp. 99–120.

railroads crossed state lines, national legislation also suited better their needs. As early as 1854, comments at the railroad conventions on the difficulties "of obtaining united and uniform laws in the various States" implied as much.[22] National legislation had its attractions for both parties.[23]

Once the railroad question had become thoroughly politicized, separation of powers also became a valuable weapon as railroad partisans sought to fend off regulation. In this sense, too, business interests could move laterally—not by threatening to divert traffic to adjacent states but rather by avoiding hostile legislatures in favor of the state courts. Several times in the 1850s, as chapter 4 showed, American railroad men entertained the idea of enlisting the legislatures to help in regulating their industry. But each time they rejected the strategy for fear that the legislatures would do more than asked. Instead, they pursued a strategy of private regulation. As an alternative, however, the railroads also turned to the state courts for aid. At the Convention of the Northern Lines of Railway in 1850, W. R. Lee of the Boston and Providence Railroad deemed "it a doubtful experiment to appeal to legislation, but [thought] each might select particular cases, and test them in Court." The Boston and Maine Railroad's representative reported "that his road was now doing this, in several cases." Another railroad delegate thought this a wise strategy to pursue in his state: "Railroads would have a better chance in New Hampshire Courts, than in the New Hampshire Legislature."[24]

If the state courts also proved hostile, moreover, businessmen could again exploit the opportunities of federalism, moving "upward" by taking their complaints from the state to the federal courts. As through traffic became more important, the railroads resorted to this alternative with increasing frequency on diversity-of-citizenship grounds. Best known are the Granger cases, where the railroads

[22] *Journal of the Proceedings of the General Railroad Association . . . November 23d, 1854*, pp. 17–18.
[23] Cf. Thomas W. Gilligan, William J. Marshall, and Barry R. Weingast, "Regulation and the Theory of Legislative Choice: The Interstate Commerce Act of 1887," *Journal of Law & Economics* 32 (1989): 35–61.
[24] *Proceedings of the Convention of Northern Lines*, pp. 86–87. Mr. Sturgis of the Boston and Lowell Railroad demurred, however: he viewed appeal to the courts as "a good plan, if we looked only to the public good," that is, as a *collectively* rational strategy. "But if the good of the corporation was to be consulted, he thought it would prove most profitable to pay [damages]." Ibid., p. 86.

sought quite explicitly, as Miller puts it, "to find sanctuary in the federal courts."[25]

In the new industrial order, in short, the federal-legislative structure of the American state exacerbated the already substantial difficulties of regulating capitalist enterprise. The expansion of railroads across state lines from the 1850s onward cast the problem in sharp relief: in the altered economic circumstances, the American political structure came to resemble a matrix[26] that offered state-chartered railroads alternative "escape routes," as Scheiber so aptly puts it. As they sought to cope with the novelty inherent in industrial capitalism, the state legislatures' regulatory efforts ultimately foundered, in part because their jurisdiction in a federal structure was simply not adequate to the task and also because they operated in a structure that divided powers among the various branches of government. Conflict over railroad regulation shifted decisively to the national level in 1886 when the Supreme Court declared unconstitutional the states' efforts to regulate interstate rates (*Wabash v. Illinois*). This made it clear that regulation would have to come from Congress. After a decade of stalemate, Congress quickly passed the Interstate Commerce Act (1887), creating the nation's first independent regulatory commission.[27] Neither the interests at stake nor the solution adopted was new; the novelty lay in the way that they were negotiated at the national level. However reluctantly, the Supreme Court and then Congress bowed to the new industrial reality.

Organizing American Railroad Interests

As authority over a substantial portion of railroad policy came to be lodged at the national level in the 1880s, the array of incentives operating on American railroad men changed dramatically. In the meantime, however, the years from 1855 through the 1870s had seen the railroads continue to search for a workable means of private regula-

[25] *Miller, Railroads and the Granger Laws*, pp. 172–93 (quotation from p. 172); Scheiber, "Federalism and the American Economic Order," pp. 76–78, 116.

[26] Cf. Elazar, *Exploring Federalism*, p. 37, for similar usage of this term.

[27] Skowronek, *Building a New American State*, pp. 121–62; Morris P. Fiorina, "Legislator Uncertainty, Legislative Control, and the Delegation of Legislative Power," *Journal of Law, Economics, and Organization* 2 (1986): 33–51; Gilligan, Marshall, and Weingast, "Regulation and the Theory of Legislative Choice."

tion. In the 1850s, the trunk-line presidents met regularly, occasionally seeking again to reach interregional agreement on measures like those that the GRAEMWs had endorsed, while southern railroads held their own conventions.[28] But no permanent, national association emerged. With the coming of the Civil War, however, the actions of the national government began to affect the railroads more extensively and systematically than ever before.[29] When the war came to an end, therefore, the railroads promptly took action on a more ambitious scale than ever before: creation of the National Railway Convention (NRC).[30]

Chaired by J. Edgar Thomson, president of the Pennsylvania Railroad, the NRC held its first official meeting in Philadelphia on the

[28] For details, see *Proceedings of the Rail Road Convention, Held Pursuant to an Adjourned Meeting, at Cleveland, O., October 14, 1857, of the Various Rail Road Companies West of Buffalo, Suspension Bridge and the Ohio River* (Cleveland: Harris, Fairbanks & Co., 1857); *Proceedings of the Convention of Rail Road and Canal Companies of the State of Virginia, Held in the City of Richmond, December 8, 1857* (Richmond: Whig Job Shop, 1857); *Proceedings of a Convention of the Executive Officers of the Rail Road Companies between Augusta and Charleston and the Virginia Springs, Held in Petersburg, April 27th, 1858* (Richmond: Chas. H. Wynne, 1858); *Proceedings of the Rail-Road Convention, Held at the St. Nicholas Hotel, New York. September 25, 1858* (New York: John W. Amerman, 1858); *Proceedings of the Rail-Road Convention, Held at the St. Nicholas Hotel, in New York. July 18, 1860* (Albany: Weed, Parsons and Co., 1860); *Proceedings of the Rail-Road Convention, Held at the United States Hotel. Saratoga, Saturday, July 28, 1860* (Albany: Weed, Parsons and Co., 1860); *Proceedings of an Adjourned Meeting of the Presidents of the Five Atlantic Trunk Lines, Held at Willard's Hotel, Washington City. Monday, January 21, 1861* (New York, 1861); *Proceedings of the Various Conventions Held for the Purpose of Establishing Union Offices in New York & Boston, during April, May, June, July, and August, 1863* (Philadelphia: Crissy & Markley, 1863); *Proceedings of Meetings of General Managers and Passenger Agents of Railroads Forming Lines between New York and Chicago, Held at the St. Nicholas Hotel, New York, on the 18th and 19th November, 1863* (New York, 1863). When a fifth trunk-line attended such meetings, it was the Grand Trunk Railroad in Canada.

[29] On the wider dimensions of this change, see Victor S. Clark, *History of Manufactures in the United States*, vol. 2: *1860–1893* (1929; reprint ed., New York: Peter Smith, 1949), pp. 39–40.

[30] The following discussion relies on *Proceedings of the National Railway Convention, at the Musical Fund Hall, Philadelphia, Pa. July 4th & 5th, 1866* (Philadelphia: E. C. Markley and Son, 1866); *Proceedings of the National Railway Convention, at the St. Nicholas Hotel, New York, October 24 and 25, 1866* (New York: Hosford and Ketcham, 1866); *Proceedings of the National Railway Convention, at the St. Nicholas Hotel, New York, May 8th and 9th, 1867* (New York: Chas. F. Ketcham, 1867). Hereafter, footnotes are used only for quotations; the proceedings are cited as NRC, 7/1866; NRC, 10/1866; and NRC, 5/1867, respectively. The first NRC meeting was preceded by two freight conventions and a meeting of the trunk-line presidents (principally regarding rates). See *Proceedings of the Meeting of the Four Atlantic Trunk Lines, Held at the St. Nicholas Hotel, New York, May 22d and 23d, 1866* . . . (Baltimore: The Printing Office, 1866).

Fourth of July, 1866. Two meetings followed in New York City in October of 1866 and May of 1867, with a fourth meeting scheduled for Altoona, Pennsylvania, in July of 1867. In both size and scope, the NRC represented a signal achievement. The third and largest meeting drew presidents, directors, superintendents, and chief engineers from nearly fifty lines, and for the first time an American railroad association actually attracted delegates not only from the northern tier of states but also from throughout the South. Coming so soon after the Civil War, this was indeed a remarkable accomplishment.

The extent to which national government policies had finally mobilized the industry became clear as soon as the delegates got down to business in 1866. Substantive action at the first meeting concerned the tariff on iron, the delegates drawing up a memorial to Congress and voting to send a committee to Washington to represent their interests. A report on other issues for action, moreover, indicated the full range of federal policies that troubled the railroad men: the railroads' mail-pay; remission of federal taxes on gross freight receipts and on repairs of rolling stock; a reduction in the five-cent stamp on bills of lading; reducing the number of Sunday trains that were being run at the postmaster general's behest; and heading off legislative action to abolish or reduce free passes, something better done "by the voluntary action of the companies—not by legislative inference."[31] Although it was not a topic of public discussion at this meeting, the railroads were surely aware that Congress for the first time had applied the interstate commerce clause to their industry in 1865–66, passing legislation to prevent barriers to interstate railroad transportation. As Lewis Haney notes, "There were predictions of a more extended use of [Congress's constitutional] power over interstate commerce."[32]

Once the NRC delegates had set up committees to address their immediate concerns about government policies, they, like their Prussian counterparts at the initial VDEV meetings forty years earlier, turned their attention to the twin problems of harmony as well. They set up additional committees to deal with technical matters as well as rates and fares. Yet, like earlier associations, they made little headway on the prickly issue of competition. The Committee on Classifi-

[31] NRC, 7/1866, p. 12.
[32] Lewis Haney, *A Congressional History of Railways in the United States*, vol. 2 (New York: Augustus M. Kelley, 1968), pp. 214–30 (quotation from p. 229).

cation, Rates, and Fares declined to offer any resolutions regarding rates and fares, merely suggesting that the roads charge "fair but remunerating prices" and "that competing lines ought not to attempt to work under each other."[33] In this respect, the NRC broke no new ground.

Yet the NRC departed from the typical American pattern in drawing up plans for a permanent administrative arm. For the first time, in other words, the railroad men took steps to arrange their affairs so that collective business could proceed without frequent meetings of the membership. At the NRC's second meeting, a committee was appointed to consider "the necessity and expediency of establishing a 'General Rail Road Bureau,' in which scientific men and able engineers should be employed at liberal salaries, whose duty it would be to collect valuable statistics and information, and to whom all subjects should be referred for thorough investigation."[34] As approved at the third meeting, the functions of the railroad bureau, itself largely the inspiration of the German immigrant Albert Fink, bore a marked similarity to those of the VDEV in Prussia.[35] Its roster of duties included collecting and publishing statistics, devising a system of uniform accounting, investigating the merits of new inventions, publishing a periodical "amply illustrated by detailed drawings," and so on. The federal government, moreover, served as its point of reference, for the NRC planned to locate its bureau in Washington, where it would enjoy "the facilities and encouragement which the Government would naturally be disposed to extend to [such] an institution."[36] The committee envisioned a bureau that would serve a federation of railroads in ways that paralleled the federal government's relationship to the states:

> The Bureau would in its functions be analogous, in a degree, to our Federal Government, as upon it would devolve the care of those matters in which all the railways of the country have a common property independent of the individual rivalries of competing lines,

[33] NRC, 5/1867, p. 32.

[34] NRC, 10/1866, p. 5.

[35] The committee's report is reprinted in NRC, 5/1867, pp. 25–31; on Fink's role, see pp. 26, 30. On Fink's career as an organizer, see Ellen Fink Milton, *A Biography of Albert Fink* (n.p., 1951), pp. 16–18, 44; Chandler, *Visible Hand*, pp. 116–19, 138–41; D. T. Gilchrist, "Albert Fink and the Pooling System," *Business History Review* 34 (1960): 24–49.

[36] NRC, 5/1867, p. 29.

and in these matters the business of the institution would be, in the language of our Federal Constitution, "to provide for the common defense and promote the general welfare."[37]

The bureau would have no powers of compulsion, of course, but the committee thought the bureau's work, if handled by a permanent staff, would be of sufficient caliber to make its recommendations "virtually *authoritative.*"[38]

Yet, despite their optimism and carefully drawn-up plans, the national association did not survive. In the fragmented American political context, not even so able an organizer as Albert Fink could sustain a national association. For American railroad men soon had to contend not only with competition among themselves and with the postmaster general's initiatives but also—unlike Prussian roads—with intervention by a multiplicity of state governments that quickly resumed their efforts to regulate the railroads through Granger legislation and the like.[39] A variety of more limited, functional associations emerged in the railroad industry during and after the Civil War,[40] but no permanent national association appeared until the 1880s.

Instead, railroad officials continued their efforts to promote harmony through regional organizations. This proved increasingly difficult as through traffic expanded in the early 1870s and competition intensified. When depression came in 1873, competition quickly es-

[37] Ibid., p. 27.

[38] Ibid. (original emphasis).

[39] Miller, *Railroads and the Granger Laws;* Maxwell Ferguson, *State Regulation of Railroads in the South,* Ph.D. diss., Columbia University (New York: n.p., 1916).

[40] On the brotherhoods of locomotive engineers, conductors, and firemen, see Licht, *Working for the Railroad,* pp. 239–43; Reed C. Richardson, *The Locomotive Engineer, 1863–1963: A Century of Railway Labor Relations and Work Rules* (Ann Arbor: Bureau of Industrial Relations, Graduate School of Business Administration, University of Michigan, 1963). On the National Car Masters' Association (later the Master Car-Builders' Association) and the American Railway Master Mechanics' Association, see *History and Early Reports of the Master Car-Builders' Association Including the First Six Annual Reports of the Association for the Years 1867, 1868, 1869, 1870, 1871 and 1872* (New York: Martin B. Brown, 1885); *The First and Second Annual Reports of the American Railway Master Mechanics' Association, in Convention at Cleveland, Ohio., Sept'r 30th and Oct'r 1st, 1868, and Pittsburgh, Pa., Sept'r 15th and 16th, 1869* (Cincinnati: Wilstach, Baldwin and Co., 1873). On the NRC's only legacy, two regional patent associations, see the report of the Committee on Patents and Patent Laws in NRC, 5/1867, pp. 20–22; Eastern Railroad Association, *Annual Reports,* 1868–1893; and Steven W. Usselman, "Patents Purloined: Railroads, Inventors, and the Diffusion of Innovation in 19th-Century America," *Technology and Culture* 32 (1991): 1047–75.

calated into rate wars. Albert Fink now proved instrumental in creating the equivalent of the Prussian *Tarifverbände*, two great regional
pools in the South and the East in 1875 and 1877, respectively. A third
was organized in the Southwest in 1876, and others followed in the
West. These had little practical effect after 1878, however, and were
declared illegal under the Sherman Antitrust Act of 1890. By then,
the trunk-lines had already developed an alternative strategy,
"system-building," which entailed buying or leasing control of
neighboring lines in order to establish private regulation on a regional
basis.[41] The presidents of the trunk-line systems also continued to
meet twice a year to set through-traffic schedules, their efforts proceeding on a regional basis through the General Time Convention,
which encompassed northeastern and midwestern lines, and the
Southern Railway Time Convention.[42]

Yet, in the early 1880s, a national association finally began to take
shape, when conditions in the industry could hardly have been less
propitious. With its members engaged in a "fast train war," the General Time Convention (GTC) was on the brink of dissolution. Thus,
when several scientific societies pressed the GTC to adopt a standard-
time system in 1881, the railroad men initially took little notice.[43]
Yet, within three years, the GTC had adopted systems of standard time
and uniform signaling; it was in the process of formulating general
telegraph and train operating rules; and it had joined forces with the
Southern Railway Time Convention (SRTC) to form a single national
organization with a broad mandate to consider all matters of interest
to the operation of railroads.

How did American railroad interests finally manage to organize,
even though the industry was now much larger and more diverse and
even though competition had reached unprecedented levels? No
doubt operating requirements brought pressure to bear, and certainly

[41] Gilchrist, "Albert Fink"; Chandler, *Visible Hand*, pp. 137–43.

[42] For details on these associations, see "Proceedings of the General Time Conven-
tion and its Successor the American Railway Association . . . ," American Railway
Association *Proceedings*, April 14, 1886 to October 11, 1893, appendix (hereafter, ARA
Proceedings).

[43] On the initial efforts of the joint secretary of the two time conventions regarding
standard time, see ARA *Proceedings*, pp. 682–84, 687, 689. On the importance of public
pressure, see Ian R. Bartky, "The Adoption of Standard Time," *Technology and Culture*
30 (1989): 25–56. On earlier developments, see Carlene Stephens, " 'The Most Reliable
Time': William Bond, the New England Railroads, and Time Awareness in 19th-
Century America," *Technology and Culture* 30 (1989): 1–24.

the joint secretary of the time conventions, William F. Allen, worked strenuously to achieve unity. But the GTC itself had suspended operation, and the railroad men had more pressing problems to divert their attention. What lent the necessary urgency to their efforts was not the condition of the industry but the political straits in which the railroads found themselves.

By the early 1880s, political agitation focused not only on the more familiar problem of interstate rates but also on other aspects of railroad operations.[44] Both of the issues that the GTC took up when it reassembled in late 1882 and 1883—standard time and uniform signaling—were then the subject of pending legislation. In fact, Connecticut had already established New York City time as the standard for the state,[45] and the prospect of a "mosaic" of state-level legislation threatened to play havoc with the railroads' schedules.[46] "[W]e should settle this question among ourselves," Secretary Allen warned the GTC in early 1883, "and not entrust it to the infinite wisdom of the several State legislatures." Legislation also threatened from "above," for now both the Railway Mail Service and the U.S. Naval Observatory were pressing for a national standard time, and a bill introduced in Congress in 1883 would have established a single standard time for the entire country. It had not passed, but only for lack of time, the GTC learned, not because it faced opposition. By the end of the year, both the GTC and the SRTC had taken preemptive action and adopted Allen's standard-time system.[47]

Time and again, reports of pending legislation, either in the state legislatures or in Congress, galvanized the railroad men. "[I]t certainly seems to us much better," a GTC committee reported in 1884, "that the railroads should, for themselves, adopt a [signal] code that would be uniform, rather than be subjected to the confusion and

[44] Most of the literature focuses on the issue of interstate rates. See Gabriel Kolko, *Railroads and Regulation, 1877–1916* (New York: W. W. Norton, 1970), pp. 7–44; Ari and Olive Hoogenboom, *A History of the ICC: From Panacea to Palliative* (New York: W. W. Norton & Company, 1976), pp. 1–13; and Skowronek, *Building a New American State*, pp. 138–50.

[45] Leonard Waldo, *First Annual Report of the Astronomer in Charge of the Horological and Thermometric Bureaus of the Winchester Observatory of Yale College* (1880–1881), pp. 23–24. I am indebted to Carlene E. Stephens for this reference. See also Bartky, "Adoption of Standard Time," p. 39.

[46] As noted earlier, I have borrowed "mosaic" from Scheiber, "Federalism and the American Economic Order," p. 97.

[47] ARA *Proceedings*, pp. 691, 693–94, 699, 703; Bartky, "Adoption of Standard Time," pp. 39–40, 44.

chance for disaster (to say nothing of the expense) that would result, should it become necessary to change the signals every time that a train crosses a State line."[48] A member of the southern convention agreed:

> It is, perhaps, generally understood, that there is a disposition on the part of legislative bodies, railroad commissioners, etc., to legislate upon this subject, and there is doubtless a wide diversity of opinion among these bodies as to proper codes, etc. It would seem peculiarly proper that such bodies as the Time Conventions embracing the managing officers of the various railroads should be better able than any other body to determine this question from a practical standpoint, and it was thought by the Cincinnati Convention [GTC meeting, April 1884] that a decided expression on our part would be accepted with favor by these legislative bodies.

Before the year was out, the GTC and the SRTC had adopted a common signal system as well.[49]

But political pressure continued to mount, and in the fall of 1884 the chair of the GTC committee on signals, Joel McCrea, warned that the movement for legislated standards had spread. In Congress, he reported, "questions involved in the operations of railroads that are common to all roads are receiving very general consideration." Indeed, the committee had discovered that a bill had been introduced in Congress to regulate car couplings and that the state governments had taken up the issue, too. Public agitation would doubtless continue, McCrea argued:

> That the public, solely interested in their own safety, will continue to demand more uniformity in matters of operation common to all roads is beyond doubt, and if such is not provided for by some authorized body of this character, it will be found to come through State and National enactments, which, however desirable, may not be directed by the more practical experience that it would receive from a body such as yours.[50]

Finally, in 1885 the GTC recognized the obvious: it formally broadened its functions and invited the SRTC's cooperation.[51] The following

---

[48] ARA *Proceedings*, p. 704.
[50] Ibid., p. 717.
[49] Ibid., p. 748.
[51] Ibid., pp. 736–37.

spring, the two associations consolidated, forming a single organization called the American Railway Association.

Political pressure had finally forced the railroads to overcome the obstacles to collective action, at least with respect to technology and operations. After nearly four decades, a national association could finally offer American railroads a credible "promise of a harmony of action."[52] To be sure, neither the incentives generated by the unitary Prussian structure nor those created by congressional policy-making in the United States proved strong enough to offset the centrifugal pressures of competition in this capital-intensive industry. The rate problem remained outside the purview of both associations and, instead, became the object of national policy in both countries in the 1880s. Nonetheless, in the intervening years, the Prussian structure effectively accelerated efforts to standardize the Prussian railroad system, while the American structure retarded a similar movement in the United States.

In the end, the conventional images of the American and Prussian states as the prototypical strong and weak states turn out to contain more than a kernel of truth—but only after the railroads' capital intensity had, in effect, transformed both political structures. Earlier, the two states, viewed through the lens of early railroad policy, did not conform to conventional images. The Prussian state's much-vaunted "strength" proved largely illusory when it confronted the new, capital-intensive technology, while the American state governments began the railroad era with a strong tradition of state promotion *and* regulation behind them, a tradition now largely obscured by the difficulties that beset them in the 1850s. When federalism is taken seriously and functional equivalents—the Prussian central state and the American state governments—are compared, the "American state" appears the stronger of the two during the early years.

Eventually, however, the railroads' capital intensity and geographic reach precipitated a transformation of both states, altering the formal structure of the Prussian state while shifting the seat of regulatory power within the American structure. In Prussia, the problem of raising the extraordinary sums of capital that railroad construction demanded pushed the issue of political liberalization to the point of revolution. Only after the Prussian political structure had undergone

----

52 Ibid., p. 6.

a degree of liberalization was the state able to exercise the authority that it had possessed in theory from the outset. In light of the interventionist tendencies that the American state legislatures exhibited in the 1830s and 1840s, this outcome does not seem at all paradoxical. Over the long term, however, the Prussian state, partially liberalized but unencumbered by federalism and separation of powers, proved better equipped to regulate the first "big business."

In the United States, in contrast, the peculiarities of railroad rates quickly challenged the legislatures' traditional authority; and then, when the legislatures confronted interstate railroads in the 1850s, their power eroded. Unlike the Prussian state, the American state governments lacked jurisdiction beyond their boundaries and they had no means of coordinating policy across state lines. Consequently, they did not have the capacity to sustain their policies, for the railroads used the political structure itself to fend off the state legislatures, eventually helping to force policy-making to the national level. Only after several decades of political struggle, and a civil war that facilitated a permanent expansion of federal power, was the American state's authority to regulate industrial capitalism partially reconstituted at the national level.[53] The conflict that the railroads unleashed, and the underlying "structural problem," as Naomi Lamoreaux terms it, persists to this day.[54] Nonetheless, the fact that policy-making authority had shifted to the center gave American railroad men the institutional wherewithal "to force unity from diversity,"[55] enabling them finally to forge a technological consensus—and a national system of railroads—as the Prussians had decades earlier.

[53] Skowronek, *Building the New American State*; Bensel, *Yankee Leviathan*.
[54] Lamoreaux, *Great Merger Movement*, pp. 162–73.
[55] Hughes, "Evolution of Large Technological Systems," p. 52.

Bibliography

Archival Collections

National Archives, Washington, D.C.
> Record Group 28, Post Office Department, Letters Received
> Record Group 77, Entry 250, Reports on Internal Improvements, 1823–39

Smithsonian Institution, National Museum of American History, Washington, D.C.
> Dibner Collection
> Division of Engineering and Industry, Baltimore and Ohio Collection

Staatsarchiv Dresden, Federal Republic of Germany
> RBD Dresden
> [Finanz Ministerium]

Staatsarchiv Hamburg, Federal Republic of Germany
> Senat. [Materials on the Berlin-Hamburg Railroad]

Staatsarchiv Magdeburg, Federal Republic of Germany
> Rep. C20. Ober-Präsidium der Provinz Sachsen

Staatsbibliothek Preußischer Kulturbesitz, Berlin
> Musikabteilung, Mendelssohn-Archiv, Bankhaus Mendelssohn & Co., MA Nachl. 5

Zentrales Staatsarchiv, Historische Abteilung II, Merseburg, Federal Republic of Germany
> Rep. 93E, Ministerium für öffentliche Arbeiten, Eisenbahnangelegenheiten
> Rep. 77, Ministerium des Innern
> Rep. 2.2.1, Geh. Zivilkabinett
> Rep. 2.4.1, Ministerium der auswärtigen Angelegenheiten
> Rep. 90a, Staatsministerium

Primary Sources

An Act to Incorporate the New-York, Providence, and Boston Rail Road Company, Passed at the June Session, 1832. Providence: B. Cranston & Co., 1836.

An Act to Incorporate the Wilmington and Raleigh R. R. Co. Passed at the Session of 1833 of the Legislature of North Carolina: With an Act to Amend the Same Passed at the Session of 1835. Raleigh: T. Loring, n.d.

Address of the Directors of the Camden and Amboy Rail Road and Delaware and Raritan Canal Companies, to the People of New Jersey. Trenton: Press of the Emporium, 1846.

Address of the Joint Board of Directors of the Delaware and Raritan Canal and Camden and Amboy Railroad Companies, to the People of New Jersey, June—1848. Trenton: Sherman and Harron, 1848.

Address of the President of the Va. Central Railroad Co., to the Stockholders, on the Subject of Withdrawal of the Mails by the Postmaster General. Richmond: MacFarlane & Ferguson, 1864.

Allgemeine Zeitung. Augsburg. Various issues, 1835–39.

American Railroad Journal, various issues.

Annual Report of the Board of Directors of the South Carolina Canal & Rail Road Company to the Stockholders, with Accompanying Documents, Submitted at their Meeting, May 7, 1832. Charleston: William S. Blain, 1832.

Annual Report of the Board of Directors of the South-Carolina Canal & Rail-Road Company to the Stockholders, with Accompanying Documents submitted at their Meeting May 6, 1833. Charleston: A. E. Miller, 1833.

Baader, Joseph Ritter von. *Über die neuesten Verbesserungen und die zweckmäßige Einrichtung der Eisenbahnen.* Munich: A. E. Fleischmann, [1826].

———. *Die Unmöglichkeit, Dampfwagen auf gewöhnlichen Strassen mit Vortheil als allgemeines Transportmittel einzuführen, und die Ungereimheit aller Projekte, die Eisenbahnen dadurch entbehrlich zu machen.* Nürnberg: Riegel und Weißner, 1835.

Bericht des Comité an die Actionairs der Berlin-Stettiner Eisenbahn. Stettin, February, 1837.

Bericht des Comité zur Begründung eines Actien-Vereins für die Eisenbahn-Verbindung zwischen Berlin und Hamburg. Berlin, 1842.

Bericht des Comite für die Eisenbahn von Köln nach der belgischen Gränze, erstattet am 25. August 1835 und gedruckt auf Beschluß der Rheinischen Eisenbahn-Gesellschaft, zur Vertheilung an die Mitglieder desselben. Cologne, [1835].

Bericht der Direktion der Köln-Mindener Eisenbahn-Gesellschaft über den Bau und Betrieb der unter ihrer Verwaltung stehenden Eisenbahnen im Jahre 1856.

[Berlin-Stettin Railroad, Annual Report of the Directors], May 15, 1841.

Beschorner, Julius Herrmann. *Das deutsche Eisenbahnrecht mit besonderer Berücksichtigung des Actien- und Expropriationsrechtes.* Erlangen: Verlag von Ferdinand Enke, 1858.

Bessel, August, and Kühlwetter, Eduard. *Das Preussische Eisenbahnrecht.* Part 1, Cologne: Franz Carl Eisen, 1855; Part 2, Cologne: F. C. Eisen, 1857.

Bishop, William S., comp. *The General Rail Road Law of the State of New York. With Notes and References.* Rochester: D. Hoyt, 1853.

Black, Alexander. *Report, Exhibiting the Present State of the Work and Probable Progress of Operations on the Charleston and Hamburg Rail Road, Submitted to the Direction, October 18, 1831.* Charleston, 1831.

Bliss, George. *Historical Memoir of the Western Railroad.* Springfield, Mass.: Samuel Bowles & Co., Printers, 1863.

_____. *Reply to a Late Letter of the Post-Master General, and Report of the First Assistant Post-Master General.* Springfield: Wood and Rupp, 1842.

By-Laws of the Board of Directors, [Adopted April and May, 1847.] Together with the Charter of the Pennsylvania Railroad Company, Its Supplement, and Other Laws Relating to Railroads Projected from Cumberland to Pittsburg and from Pittsburg East. Philadelphia: United States Book and Job Printing Office, 1847.

[Carey, Henry C.] *Review of an Address of the Joint Board of Directors of the Delaware and Raritan Canal and Camden and Amboy Railroad Companies, to the People of New Jersey. By a Citizen of Burlington.* Philadelphia: C. Sherman, 1848.

The Charter and Other Acts of the Legislature, in Relation to the South-Carolina Rail Road Company . . . Charleston: Steam-Power Press of Walker and James, 1851.

Charter of the Richmond and Ohio Railroad Company. N.p., [1847].

Chevalier, Michel. *Society, Manners and Politics in the United States, Being a Series of Letters on North America.* Boston, 1839; reprint ed., New York: Burt Franklin, 1969.

Crelle, A. L. *Einiges allgemein Verständliche über Eisenbahnen, insbesondere als Privat-Unternehmungen.* Berlin: G. Reimer, 1835.

Dieterici, C.F.W. *Der Volkswohlstand im Preußischen Staate.* Berlin: Ernst Siegfried Mittler, 1846.

Dritter Generalbericht der Direction der Berlin-Hamburger Eisenbahn-Gesellschaft. Berlin: E. S. Mittler, 1846.

Dritter Jahresbericht des Directorium der Berlin-Stettiner Eisenbahn-Gesellschaft über den Fortgang des Unternehmens im Jahre vom May 1842 bis 1843 zum Vortrag in der General-Versammlung der Aktionaire am 26. May 1843.

Eastern Railroad Association. *First [etc.] Annual Report of the Executive Committee of the Eastern Railroad Association to the Members, for the Year Ending . . . .* 1868–1893.

Examiner, pseud. *The Reading Railroad Company: Their Policy and Prospects. Being a Series of Articles published in the Pennsylvanian, in January, February, and March, 1844.* Philadelphia, 1844.

Exhibit of the Lafayette and Indianapolis Railroad Company. New York: Oliver & Brother, 1851.

First and Second Annual Reports of the American Railway Master Mechanics' Association, in Convention at Cleveland, O., Sept'r 30th and Oct'r 1st, 1868, and Pittsburgh, Pa., Sept'r 15th and 16th, 1869, The. Cincinnati: Wilstach, Baldwin and Co., 1873.

First Report of Edward Miller, Engineer in Chief of the Sunbury and Erie Railroad, to the Managers. January 12, 1839. Philadelphia: John C. Clark, 1839.

First Semi-Annual Report, to the President and Directors of the South-Carolina Canal and Rail-Road Company, by Their Committee of Inquiry. Charleston: A. E. Miller, 1828.

[Gaines, Edmund P.] *To the Young Men of the States of the American Union, Civil and Military*. N.p., n.d.

Gerstner, Franz Anton Ritter von. *Berichte aus den Vereinigten Staaten von Nordamerica, über Eisenbahnen, Dampfschiffahrten, Banken und andere öffentliche Unternehmungen*. Leipzig: C. P. Melzer, 1839.

————. *Die innern Communicationen der Vereinigten Staaten von Nordamerica*. 2 vols. Vienna: L. Förster, 1842–43.

————. *Railroads in the Kingdom of Belgium Compared with Those in the United States* Cincinnati, 1839.

————. "Ueber die Vortheile einer Eisenbahn von St. Petersburg nach Zarskoe-Selo und Powlowsk." *Eisenbahn-Journal*, no. 23 (1836): 36–43 and no. 24 (1836): 54–59.

Geschäfts-Bericht des Directoriums der Magdeburg-Cöthen-Halle-Leipziger Eisenbahn-Gesellschaft für das Jahr . . . . 1843–1848 (title varies slightly).

"Gesetz über die Eisenbahn-Unternehmungen, vom 3. November 1838." In *Gesetz-Sammlung für die Königlichen Preußischen Staaten*, no. 35. Reprinted in, among other places, Wolfgang Klee, *Preußische Eisenbahngeschichte* (Stuttgart: Verlag W. Kohlhammer, 1982), Appendix.

Ghega, Carl. *Die Baltimore-Ohio-Eisenbahn über das Alleghany-Gebirg. Mit besonderer Berücksichtigung der Steigungs- und Krümmungs-Verhältnisse. Mit einer Beschreibung und Berechnung über die Leistungsfähigkeit einiger nordamerikanischen Locomotiven*. Vienna: Kaulfuß Wwe., Prandel & Co., 1844.

Gordon, Alexander. *The Fitness of Turnpike Roads and Highways for the Most Expeditious, Safe, Convenient and Economical Internal Communication*. London: Roake and Varty, 1835.

Gregg, W. P., and Pond, Benjamin, comps. *The Railroad Laws and Charters of the United States*. 2 vols. Boston, Charles C. Little and James Brown, 1851.

Handbuch über den königlich preußischen Hof und Staat für das Jahr 1839. Berlin: Deckersche Geh. Ober-Hofbuchdruckerei, [1839].

Handbuch über den königlich preußischen Hof und Staat für das Jahr 1845. Berlin: Deckersche Geh. Ober-Hofbuchdruckerei, [1845].

Hansemann, David. *Die Eisenbahnen und deren Aktionäre in ihrem Verhältniß zum Staat*. Leipzig and Halle: Renger'sche Verlagsbuchhandlung, 1837.

————. *Kritik des Preussischen Eisenbahn-Gesetzes vom 3. November 1838*. Aachen and Leipzig: A. J. Mayer, 1841.

————. *Über die Ausführung des Preußischen Eisenbahn-Systems*. Berlin: Alexander Duncker, 1843.

History and Early Reports of the Master Car-Builders' Association Including the First Six Annual Reports of the Association for the Years 1867, 1868, 1869, 1870, 1871 and 1872. New York: Martin B. Brown, 1885.

Horry, Elias. *An Address Respecting the Charleston & Hamburgh Rail-Road; and on the Rail-Road System as Regards a Large Portion of the Southern and Western States of the North-American Union.* Charleston: A. E. Miller, 1833.

Howard, William C. *Report on the Charleston and Hamburg Rail-Road.* Charleston, 1829. Reprinted in House Exec. Doc. 7, 21st Cong., 1st Sess., 1829-30.

Jahresbericht des Direktoriums der Berlin-Stettiner Eisenbahn-Gesellschaft für die am 30sten Mai 1851 zusammentretende ordentliche General-Versammlung.

Journal für die Baukunst. Berlin. Various issues, 1829–51.

Journal of the Proceedings of the General Railroad Association, at their Meeting Holden in New York, November 23d, 1854. Newark: Daily Advertiser Print, 1855.

Journal of the Proceedings of the General Railroad Association, at their Second Convention, Holden at Springfield, November 10th, 1852: New Haven: T. J. Stafford, 1852.

Journal of the Proceedings of the General Railroad Convention, Held at Springfield, August 24th and 25th, 1852. New Haven: T. J. Stafford, 1852.

Kirkland, Charles P. *An Inquiry into the Merits of the Suit Brought by the Attorney-General of the State of New York, (now pending and soon to be tried,) against the New York Central Railroad Company, to Recover Five Millions of Dollars of Tolls, Alleged to Be Unpaid, and to Establish the Liability of the Company to Pay Tolls Annually for an Indefinite Period Thereafter.* New York: Wm. C. Bryant, 1860.

Knight, Jonathan, and Benjamin H. Latrobe. *Report Upon the Locomotive Engines, and the Police and Management of Several of the Principal Rail Roads in the Northern and Middle States . . .* Baltimore: Lucas & Deaver, 1838.

_____ *Report Upon the Plan of Construction of Several of the Principal Rail Roads in the Northern and Middle States . . .* Baltimore: Lucas & Deaver, 1838.

Kreeft, Christopher. *First Russian Railroad From St. Petersburg to Zarscoe-Selo and Powlowsk . . .* Trans. from the German. London: Charles Skipper and East, 1837.

Lardner, Dionysius. *Railway Economy: A Treatise on the New Art of Transport, Its Management, Prospects, and Relations, Commercial, Financial, and Social.* London: Taylor, Walton, and Maberly, 1850.

Laws and Ordinances Relating to the Baltimore and Ohio Rail Road Company. Baltimore: Jas. Lucas and E. K. Deaver, 1834.

List, Friedrich. *Über ein sächsiches Eisenbahn-System als Grundlage eines allgemeinen deutschen Eisenbahn-Systems.* Leipzig: A. G. Liebeskind, 1833.

Memorial of the Atchison, Topeka and Santa Fe Railroad Company, to the Senate and House of Representatives of the State of Kansas. Topeka: George W. Martin, 1879.

Michaelis, Julius. *Deutschlands Eisenbahnen: Ein Handbuch für Ge-*

schäftsleute, Privatpersonen, Capitalisten und Speculanten. Leipzig: C. F. Amelang's Verlag, 1854.

Nineteenth Annual Report of the President and Directors to the Stockholders of the Philadelphia, Wilmington and Baltimore Rail Road Company, for the Year Ending November 30, 1857. Made January 12th, 1857. Philadelphia: James H. Bryson, 1857.

Objections to Yielding to Northerners the Control of the Baltimore and Ohio Rail Road, on Which Depends the Development of the Farms, Mines, Manufactures and Trade of the State of Maryland, by a Marylander. Baltimore, 1860.

Owen, Robert Dale. *A Brief Practical Treatise on the Construction and Management of Plank Roads.* New Albany: Kent and Norman, 1850.

[Philadelphia and Reading Railroad]. *Report from the Friends of This Improvement.* Philadelphia? 1833.

Poor, Henry V. *History of the Railroads and Canals of the United States of America.* New York, 1860.

Proceedings, at a Meeting of the Stockholders of the Central Rail Road and Banking Company of Georgia, on the 9th and 11th Days of March, 1843. Savannah: Thomas Purse, 1843.

Proceedings of an Adjourned Meeting of the Presidents of the Five Atlantic Trunk Lines, Held at Willard's Hotel, Washington City. Monday, January 21, 1861. New York, 1861.

Proceedings of a Convention Held in the City of Baltimore, May 19th, 1854, on the Recommendation to Reduce the Pay for Mail Service to Rail Road Companies. Together with the Report of the Committee Appointed on That Occasion. Baltimore: John Murphy and Co., 1854.

Proceedings of a Convention of the Executive Officers of the Rail Road Companies between August and Charleston and the Virginia Springs, Held in Petersburg, April 27th, 1858. Richmond: Chas. H. Wynne, 1858.

Proceedings of a Convention of the Rail Roads of Ohio and Indiana: Held at Columbus, Ohio, on the 21st and 22d of September, 1854. Columbus: Ohio State Journal Company, 1854.

Proceedings of a Meeting of Citizens of Charleston City and Neck, and Report of Committee in Relation to Charlotte Railroad. Charleston: Walker and Burke, 1847.

Proceedings of a Meeting of Representatives of the Several Railroad Companies between New York, Boston, Philadelphia and Baltimore, Chicago, Cincinnati, and the Ohio and Mississippi Rivers, Held at Cleveland, November 28th, 1854. Cleveland: Sanford and Hayward, 1854.

Proceedings of Meetings of General Managers and Passenger Agents of Railroads Forming Lines between New York and Chicago, Held at the St. Nicholas Hotel, New York, on the 18th and 19th November, 1863. New York, 1863.

Proceedings of the Convention of Rail Road and Canal Companies of the State of Virginia, Held in the City of Richmond, December 8, 1857 . . . Richmond: Whig Book and Job Shop, 1857.

Proceedings of the Convention of the Northern Lines of Railway, held at Boston, in December, 1850, and January, 1851. Boston: J. B. Yerrinton &Son, 1851.

Proceedings of the General Railroad Association of the Eastern, Middle, and Western States; Also of the General Ticket Agents' Association, Convened at the Monongahela House, Pittsburg, March 13, 1855. Philadelphia: T. K. and P. G. Collins, 1855.

Proceedings of the Meeting of the Four Atlantic Trunk Lines, Held at the St. Nicholas Hotel, New York, May 22d and 23d, 1866, Together with the Proceedings of the Conventions held at Buffalo, New York, May 2d, 1866, and at Indianapolis, Indiana, May 10, 1866. Baltimore: The Printing Office, 1866.

Proceedings of the National Railway Convention, at the Musical Fund Hall, Philadelphia, Pa. July 4th & 5th, 1866. Philadelphia: E. C. Markley and Son, 1966.

Proceedings of the National Railway Convention, at the St. Nicholas Hotel, New York, October 24 and 25, 1866. New York: Hosford and Ketcham, 1866.

Proceedings of the National Railway Convention, at the St. Nicholas Hotel, New York, May 8th and 9th, 1867. New York: Chas. F. Ketcham, 1867.

Proceedings of the Railroad Convention Held at the St. Nicholas Hotel, New York. August 15, 1854. New York: New York and Erie Railroad Company's Printing Office, 1854.

Proceedings of the Rail-Road Convention, Held at the St. Nicholas Hotel, in New York, September 25, 1858. New York, 1858.

Proceedings of the Rail-Road Convention, Held at the St. Nicholas Hotel, in New York. July 18, 1860. Albany: Weed, Parsons and Co., 1860.

Proceedings of the Rail-Road Convention, Held at the United States Hotel, Saratoga. Saturday, July 28th, 1860. Albany: Weed, Parsons and Co., 1860.

Proceedings of the Various Conventions Held for the Purpose of Establishing Union Offices in New York & Boston, During April, May, June, July, and August, 1863. Philadelphia: Crissy & Markley, 1863.

Protocoll der ersten Generalversammlung der Actionairs der Berlin-Hamburger Eisenbahn-Gesellschaft nebst Bericht des Ausschusses an dieselben. Berlin: E. S. Mittler, 1845.

Protocoll der zweiten Generalversammlung der Actionairs der Berlin-Hamburger Eisenbahn-Gesellschaft nebst Bericht des Ausschusses an dieselben. Berlin: E. S. Mittler, 1846.

Records of the New England Association of Railway Superintendents. Washington, D.C.: Gibson Brothers, 1910.

Reden, Friedrich Wilhelm Freiherr, von. *Eisenbahn-Jahrbuch für Bahn-Beamte und Staats-Behörden* 2 (1847).

_____. *Die Eisenbahnen Deutschlands,* 1. Abt., 1. Abschnitt: *Allgemeines über die deutschen Eisenbahnen.* Berlin: Ernst Siegfried Mittler, 1843.

Reden, Friedrich Wilhelm Freiherr, von. *Die Eisenbahnen Deutschlands*, I. Abt., 2. Abschnitt: *Statistisch-geschichtliche Darstellung ihrer Entstehung, ihres Verhältnisses zu der Staatsgewalt, so wie ihrer Verwaltungs- und Betriebs-Einrichtungen*. Berlin: Ernst Siegfried Mittler, 1844.

Reply of the Executive Committee of the Delaware and Raritan Canal and Camden and Amboy Railroad and Transportation companies, to a Letter Addressed to the Hon. G. W. Hopkins, Chairman of the Committee of Post Offices and Post Roads of the House of Representatives of the U.S. by the Hon. Cave Johnson, Post Master General. Trenton: Arnold and Brittain, 1847.

Report of a Committee Appointed January 4th, 1855, by the Directors of the New York Central Railroad Company, at the Request of the Stockholders, Authorizing Certain Examinations to Be Made of the 'Acts and Doings of the Directors and Treasurer,' Subsequent to the Consolidation. Boston: J. H. Eastburn's Press, 1855.

Report of a Committee of Directors of the Boston and Worcester Rail-road Corporation. On the Proposition of the Directors of the Western Railroad, to reduce the rates of fare and freight on the two Rail-roads Boston: Samuel N. Dickinson, 1840.

Report of a Committee of the Joint Board of Directors of the Delaware and Raritan Canal and Camden & Amboy R. R. & Transportation Co's, on the Subject of the Transportation of the Mails between New York and Philadelphia, October, 1846. Trenton: Arnold and Brittain, 1847.

Report of a Committee of the Stockholders of the Baltimore and Susquehannah Rail Road Company: Appointed May 9, 1839. N.p., n.d.

Report of a Committee on the Boston and Lowell Rail Road. Boston, 1831.

Report of a Special Committee Appointed by the Chamber of Commerce to Inquire into the Cost, Revenue and Advantages of a Rail Road Communication between the City of Charleston and the Towns of Hamburg & Augusta. Charleston: A. E. Miller, 1828.

Report of Proceedings of the Ohio Railroad Convention, Held in Columbus, December 7th and 8th, 1852. Columbus: Scott and Bascom, 1852.

Report of the Committee Appointed to Examine and Report the Causes of Railroad Accidents, the Means of Preventing Their Recurrence, &c. Transmitted to the Legislature January 14, 1853. Albany: C. Van Benthuysen, 1853.

Report of the Committee on Cars, to the Direction of the South-Carolina Canal & Rail-Road Company Submitted to the Stockholders on Wednesday, 20th November 1833. Charleston, 1833.

Report of the Directors of the Boston & Worcester Rail Road, to the Stockholders, at Their Ninth Annual Meeting, June 1, 1840. Boston: Samuel N. Dickinson, 1840.

Report of the Directors Representing the City in the Baltimore & Ohio Rail Road Company, to the Mayor and City Council of Baltimore. Baltimore: James Lucas & Son, 1855.

Report of the Engineers, on the Reconnoissance and Surveys, Made in Reference to the Baltimore and Ohio Rail Road. Baltimore, 1828.

Report of the Proceedings of a Convention of Delegates from Railroad Companies, Held in Columbus, May 4, 1852. Columbus, 1852.

Report of the Proceedings of the Ohio Rail Road Convention, Held in Columbus, on the 18th Day of January, 1854. Columbus: Scott and Bascom, 1854.

Report of the State Directors of the Delaware and Raritan Canal and Camden and Amboy Railroad Companies to the Legislature of New Jersey. Trenton: True American Office, 1852.

Report of William Milnor Roberts, Chief Engineer of the Cumberland Valley Rail Road Company, Made to the Board, on the 23d October, 1835. Annapolis: Jeremiah Hughes, 1836.

Semi-Annual Report of the Direction of the South-Carolina Canal and Rail-Road Company, to July, 1838. Charleston: Burges & James, 1838.

Semi-Annual Report of the Direction of the South-Carolina Canal and Rail-Road Company, to the Stockholders, October 31, 1834. Charleston: J. S. Burgess, 1834.

Semi-Annual Report of the Direction of the South-Carolina Canal & Rail-Road Company to the Stockholders, November 4th, 1833, With Accompanying Documents. Charleston: A. E. Miller, 1833.

Semi-Annual Report of the South-Carolina Canal and Rail Road Company, Accepted Jan. 18th, 1839. Charleston: A. E. Miller, 1839.

Siebenter General-Bericht der Direction der Berlin-Hamburger Eisenbahn-Gesellschaft für das Jahr 1849. Berlin: G. Bernstein, 1850.

[Smith, William Prescott]. *A History and Description of the Baltimore and Ohio Rail Road.* Baltimore: John Murphy & Co., 1853.

Tell-Poussin, G. *Öffentliche Bauwerke in den Vereinigten-Staaten von Amerika. Part II: Eisenbahnen.* Trans. by H. F. Lehritter. Regensburg: Friedrich Pustet, 1837.

Tenth Annual Report of the President and Directors to the Stockholders of the Baltimore and Ohio Rail Road Company. Baltimore: Lucas & Deaver, 1836.

Tredgold, Thomas. *A Practical Treatise on Rail-Roads and Carriages . . .* London: J. B. Nichols and Son, 1825.

Twelfth Annual Report of the President and Directors of the Stockholders of the Baltimore and Susquehanna Rail Road Company. October, 1839. Baltimore: Joseph Robinson, 1840.

Twenty-Second Annual Report of the President and Directors of the Baltimore & Susquehanna Rail-Road Company. Baltimore: James Lucas, 1849.

Verein deutscher Eisenbahn-Verwaltungen. *Deutsche Eisenbahn-Statistik für das Betriebs-Jahr . . . . 1851–1877.*

Wiebe, Eduard. *Einige Mängel der bestehenden Eisenbahnen nebst Andeutungen zu deren Abhülfe.* Potsdam, 1838.

Wood, Nicholas. *A Practical Treatise on Rail-Roads.* London: Knight and Lacey, 1825.

Zimpel, Charles F. *Das Eisenbahnwesen von Nordamerika, England und anderen Ländern.* Vienna, 1840.

Zur Feier des Fünfundzwanzigsten Jahrestages der Eröffnung des Betriebes auf der Oberschlesischen Eisenbahn, den 22. Mai 1867. Breslau: Wilh. Gottl. Korn, 1867.

Zweiter Jahresbericht des Direktorii der Berlin-Stettiner Eisenbahn-gesellschaft über den Fortgang des Unternehmens im Jahre vom Mai 1841 bis 1842, vorgetragen in der General-Versammlung der Aktionaire am 26. Mai 1842.

Secondary Sources

Adler, Dorothy R. *British Investment in American Railways, 1834–1898.* Edited by Muriel E. Hidy. Charlottesville: University Press of Virginia for the Eleutherian Mills-Hagley Foundation, 1970.

Allen, Ann Taylor. "'Let Us Live with Our Children': Kindergarten Movements in Germany and the United States, 1840–1914." *History of Education Quarterly* 28 (1988): 23–48.

Alt, James E., and Shepsle, Kenneth A., eds. *Perspectives on Positive Political Economy.* Cambridge: Cambridge University Press: 1990.

Alvarez, Eugene. *Travel on Southern Antebellum Railroads, 1828–1860.* University, Ala.: University of Alabama Press, 1974.

Angermann, Erich. *Challenges of Ambiguity: Doing Comparative History.* German Historical Institute Annual Lecture Series, no. 4. New York: Berg, 1991.

Angermann, Erich, and Frings, Marie-Luise, eds. *Oceans Apart? Comparing Germany and the United States; Studies in Commemoration of the 150th Anniversary of the Birth of Carl Schurz.* Stuttgart: Klett-Cotta, 1981.

Ashworth, John. *'Agrarians' and 'Aristocrats': Party Political Ideology in the United States, 1837–1846.* Cambridge: Cambridge University Press, 1987.

Bartky, Ian R. "The Adoption of Standard Time." *Technology and Culture* 30 (1989): 25–56.

Bendix, John; Ollman, Bertell; Sparrow, Bartholomew H.; and Mitchell, Timothy P. "Controversy: Going Beyond the State?" *American Political Science Review* 86 (December 1992): 1007–21.

Bensel, Richard Franklin. *Yankee Leviathan: The Origins of Central State Authority in America, 1859–1877.* Cambridge: Cambridge University Press, 1990.

Benson, Barbara, ed. *Benjamin Henry Latrobe & Moncure Robinson: The Engineer as Agent of Technological Transfer.* Greenville, Del.: Eleutherian Mills Historical Library, 1975.

Berger, Suzanne, ed. *Organizing Interests in Western Europe: Pluralism, Corporatism, and the Transformation of Politics.* Cambridge: Cambridge University Press, 1981.

Berk, Gerald. "Constituting Corporations and Markets: Railroads in Gilded Age Politics." *Studies in American Political Development* 4 (1990): 130–68.

Bestor, Arthur. "The American Civil War as a Constitutional Crisis." In *American Law and the Constitutional Order: Historical Perspectives,* edited by Lawrence M. Friedman and Harry N. Scheiber, pp. 219–36. Cambridge: Harvard University Press, 1978.

Beyer, Peter. *Leipzig und die Anfänge des deutschen Eisenbahnbaus: Die Strecke nach Magdeburg als zweitälteste deutsche Fernverbindung und das Ringen der Kaufleute um ihr Entstehen, 1829–1840.* Weimar: Verlag Hermann Böhlaus Nachfolger, 1978.

Bijker, Wiebe E.; Hughes, Thomas P.; and Pinch, Trevor, eds. *The Social Construction of Technological Systems.* Cambridge: M.I.T. Press, 1987.

Black, Paul V. "Experiment in Bureaucratic Centralization: Employee Blacklisting on the Burlington Railroad, 1877–1892." *Business History Review* 51 (Winter 1977): 444–59.

Blackbourn, David, and Eley, Geoff. *Mythen deutscher Geschichtsschreibung: Die gescheiterte bürgerliche Revolution von 1848.* Trans. by Ulla Haselstein. Frankfurt/M: Verlag Ullstein, 1980.

_____. *The Peculiarities of German History: Bourgeois Society and Politics in Nineteenth-Century Germany.* Oxford: Oxford University Press, 1984.

Bleiber, Helmut. "Staat und bürgerliche Umwälzung in Deutschland: Zum Charakter besonders des preußischen Staates in der ersten Hälfte des 19. Jahrhunderts." In *Preußen in der deutschen Geschichte nach 1789,* edited by Gustav Seeber and Karl-Heinz Noack, pp. 82–115. Berlin: Akademie-Verlag, 1983.

Bloch, Marc. *The Historian's Craft.* Trans. by Peter Putnam. New York: Vintage Books, 1953.

_____. "Toward a Comparative History of European Societies." In *Enterprise and Secular Change: Readings in Economic History,* edited by Frederick C. Lane and Jelle C. Riermersma, pp. 494–521. Homewood, Ill.: Richard D. Irwin, Inc., 1953.

Bogen, Jules I. *The Anthracite Railroads: A Study in American Railroad Enterprise.* New York: Ronald Press, 1927.

Bonin, Udo von. *Geschichte des Ingenieurkorps und der Pioniere in Preußen.* 2 vols. Berlin, 1877–78; reprint ed., Wiesbaden: LTR-Verlag, 1981.

Borchardt, Knut. *Perspectives on Modern German Economic History and Policy.* Trans. by Peter Lambert. Cambridge: Cambridge University Press, 1991.

_____. "Zur Frage des Kapitalmangels in der ersten Hälfte des 19. Jahrhunderts in Deutschland." *Jahrbuch für Nationalökonomie und Statistik* 173 (1961): 401–21.

Bösselmann, Kurt. *Die Entwicklung des deutschen Aktienwesens im 19. Jahrhundert: Ein Beitrag zur Frage der Finanzierung gemein-*

wirtschaftlicher Unternehmungen und zu den Reformen des Ak-tienrechts. Berlin: Walter de Gruyter, 1939.

Bourgin, Frank. *The Great Challenge: The Myth of Laissez-Faire in the Early Republic.* New York: George Braziller, 1989.

Bowman, Shearer Davis. "Antebellum Planters and *Vormärz* Junkers in Comparative Perspective." *American Historical Review* 85 (1980): 779–808.

————. "Honor and Martialism in the U.S. South and Prussian East Elbia during the Mid-Nineteenth Century." In *What Made the South Different?,* edited by Kees Gispen, pp. 19–48. Jackson: University Press of Mississippi, 1990.

————. "Planters and Junkers: A Comparative Study of Two Nineteenth-Century Elites and Their Regional Societies." Ph.D. diss., University of California, Berkeley, 1986.

Bridges, Amy. "Becoming American: The Working Classes in the United States before the Civil War." In *Working Class Formation: Nineteenth-Century Patterns in Western Europe and the United States,* edited by Ira Katznelson and Aristide R. Zolberg, pp. 157–96. Princeton: Princeton University Press, 1986.

Brittan, Samuel. *A Restatement of Economic Liberalism.* Atlantic Highlands, N.J.: Humanities Press International, 1988.

Brophy, James M. "Capitulation or Negotiated Settlement? Entrepreneurs and the Prussian State, 1848–1866." Ph.D. diss., Indiana University, Bloomington, 1991.

Brose, Eric Dorn. *The Politics of Technological Change in Prussia: Out of the Shadow of Antiquity, 1809–1848.* Princeton: Princeton University Press, 1993.

Broude, Henry W. "The Role of the State in American Industrial Development, 1820–1890." In *United States Economic History: Selected Readings,* edited by Harry N. Scheiber, pp. 114–35. New York: Alfred A. Knopf, 1964.

Burgess, George H., and Kennedy, Miles C. *Centennial History of the Pennsylvania Railroad Company, 1846–1946.* Philadelphia: The Pennsylvania Railroad Company, 1949.

Burke, John G. "Bursting Boilers and the Federal Power." *Technology and Culture* 7 (Winter 1966): 1–23.

Calhoun, Daniel Hovey. *The American Civil Engineer: Origins and Conflict.* Cambridge, Mass.: Technology Press, 1960.

Callender, Guy S. "The Early Transportation and Banking Enterprises of the States in Relation to the Growth of Corporations." *Quarterly Journal of Economics* 17 (November 1902): 111–62.

Cameron, Rondo. "A New View of European Industrialization." *Economic History Review,* 2d ser., 38 (February 1985): 1–23.

Campbell, E. G. "Railroads in National Defense, 1829–1848." *Mississippi Valley Historical Review* 27 (December 1940): 361–78.

Carlson, W. Bernard. "The Pennsylvania Society for the Promotion of Internal Improvements: A Case Study in the Political Uses of Technological Knowledge, 1824–1826." *Canal History and Technology Proceedings* 8 (1988): 175–206.

Carr, William. *A History of Germany, 1815–1945.* 2d ed. New York: St. Martin's Press, 1979.

Chandler, Alfred D., Jr. *The Essential Alfred Chandler: Essays Toward a Historical Theory of Big Business.* Edited and with an introduction by Thomas K. McCraw. Boston: Harvard Business School, 1988.

_____ *Henry Varnum Poor: Business Editor, Analyst, and Reformer.* Cambridge: Harvard University Press, 1956.

_____. "The Railroads: Pioneers in Modern Corporate Management." *Business History Review* 39 (1965): 16–40.

_____. *Scale and Scope: The Dynamics of Industrial Capitalism.* Cambridge: Harvard University Press, Belknap Press, 1990.

_____. *The Visible Hand: The Managerial Revolution in American Business.* Cambridge: Harvard University Press, Belknap Press, 1977.

_____, comp. and ed. *The Railroads: The Nation's First Big Business, Sources and Readings.* New York: Harcourt, Brace & World, Inc., 1965.

Chandler, Alfred D., Jr., and Herman Daems, eds. *Managerial Hierarchies: Comparative Perspectives on the Rise of the Modern Industrial Enterprise.* Cambridge: Harvard University Press, 1980.

Clapham, J. H. *The Economic Development of France and Germany, 1815–1914.* 4th ed. Cambridge: Cambridge University Press, 1963.

Coase, Ronald H. *The Firm, The Market, and the Law.* Chicago: University of Chicago Press, 1988.

_____. "The New Institutional Economics." *Journal of Institutional and Theoretical Economics* 140 (1984): 229–31.

Cochran, Thomas. *Railroad Leaders, 1845–1890: The Business Mind in Action.* New York: Russell & Russell, 1965.

Cowan, Ruth Schwartz. *More Work for Mother: The Ironies of Household Technology from the Open Hearth to the Microwave.* New York: Basic Books, 1983.

Cullum, George E. *Biographical Register of the Officers and Graduates of the U.S. Military Academy.* 2 vols. Boston: Houghton, Mifflin and Company, Riverside Press, 1891.

Cutcliffe, Stephen H., and Post, Robert C., eds. *In Context: History and the History of Technology.* Bethlehem: Lehigh University Press; London: Associated University Presses, 1989.

David, Paul A. "Heroes, Herds and Hysteresis in Technological History: Thomas Edison and 'The Battle of the Systems' Reconsidered." *Industrial and Corporate Change* 1 (1992): 129–80.

Deane, Phyllis. *The Evolution of Economic Ideas.* Cambridge: Cambridge University Press, 1978.

Degler, Carl N. "In Pursuit of an American History." *American Historical Review* 92 (February 1987): 1–12.

Derrick, Samuel Melanchthon. *Centennial History of South Carolina Railroad*. Columbia, S.C.: The State Company, 1930.

Douglas, George H. *All Aboard! The Railroad in American Life*. New York: Paragon House, 1992.

Doukas, Kimon A. *The French Railroads and the State*. New York: Columbia University Press, 1945.

Dubofsky, Melvin. "Technological Change and American Worker Movements, 1870–1970." In *Technology, The Economy, and Society: The American Experience*, edited by Joel Colton and Stuart Bruchey, pp. 162–85. New York: Columbia University Press, 1987.

Dunlavy, Colleen A. "Political Structure, State Policy, and Industrial Change: Early Railroad Policy in the United States and Prussia." In *Structuring Politics: Historical Institutionalism in Comparative Analysis*, edited by Sven Steinmo, Kathleen Thelen, and Frank Longstreth, pp. 114–54. Cambridge: Cambridge University Press, 1992.

———. "Politics and Industrialization: Early Railroads in the United States and Prussia." Ph.D. diss., Massachusetts Institute of Technology, 1988.

———. "Mirror Images: Political Structure and Early Railroad Policy in the United States and Prussia." *Studies in American Political Development* 5 (Spring 1991): 1–35.

———. "Organizing Railroad Interests: The Creation of National Railroad Associations in the United States and Prussia." *Business and Economic History*, 2d ser., 19 (1990): 133–42.

———. "Der 'Vater der deutschen Eisenbahnen' in den Vereinigten Staaten von Amerika: Friedrich List und Früheisenbahnbauweisen." *Wissenschaftliche Zeitschrift* (Dresden), Sonderheft 54: *Friedrich List— Leben und Werk* (1990): 51–60.

Dupuy, R. Ernest. *Men of West Point: The First 150 Years of the United States Military Academy*. New York: William Sloane Associates, 1951.

———. *Where They Have Trod: The West Point Tradition in American Life*. New York: Frederick A. Stokes Company, 1940.

Eichholtz, Dietrich. *Junker und Bourgeoisie vor 1848 in der Preussischen Eisenbahngeschichte*. Deutsche Akademie der Wissenschaften zu Berlin, Schriften des Instituts für Geschichte. Berlin: Akademie-Verlag, 1962.

Elazar, Daniel J. *Exploring Federalism*. Tuscaloosa: University of Alabama Press, 1987.

———. "Federalism." *International Encyclopedia of the Social Sciences*, vol. 5 (1968), pp. 355–57.

Ellis, David Maldwyn. "Rivalry between the New York Central and the Erie Canal." *New York History* 29 (1948): 268–300.

Enkling, Josef. *Die Stellung des Staates zu den Privateisenbahnen in der Anfangszeit des preußischen Eisenbahnwesens (1830–1848)*. Kettwig: F. Flothmann, 1935.

Evans, Peter B.; Rueschemeyer, Dietrich; and Skocpol, Theda, eds. *Bringing the State Back In*. Cambridge: Cambridge University Press, 1985.

Evans, Richard J. "The New Nationalism and the Old History: Perspectives on the West German *Historikerstreit.*" *Journal of Modern History* 59 (December 1987): 761–97.

Ferguson, Maxwell. *State Regulation of Railroads in the South.* Ph.D. diss., Columbia University; New York, n.p., 1916.

Festschrift über die Thätigkeit des Vereins deutscher Eisenbahn-Verwaltungen in den ersten 50 Jahren seines Bestehens, 1846–1896. Berlin: Nauck'schen Buchdruckerei, 1896.

Field, Alexander James. "Land Abundance, Interest/Profit Rates, and Nineteenth-Century American and British Technology." *Journal of Economic History* 43 (June 1983): 405–31.

Fiorina, Morris P. "Legislator Uncertainty, Legislative Control, and the Delegation of Legislative Power." *Journal of Law, Economics, and Organization* 2 (1986): 33–51.

Fischer, David Hackett. *Historians' Fallacies: Toward a Logic of Historical Thought.* New York: Harper & Row, 1970.

Fischer, Wolfram. "Government Activity and Industrialization in Germany (1815–70)." In *The Economics of Take-Off into Sustained Growth,* edited by W. W. Rostow, pp. 83–94. London: Macmillan & Co.; New York: St. Martin's Press, 1963.

Fish, Carl Russell. "The Northern Railroads, April, 1861." *American Historical Review* 22 (July 1917): 778–93.

Fisher, Charles E. "The West Point Foundry." Railroad and Locomotive Historical Society *Bulletin* 52 (1940): 36–40.

Fishlow, Albert. *American Railroads and the Transformation of the Ante-Bellum Economy.* Cambridge: Harvard University Press, 1965.

Fogel, Robert W. "Notes on the Social Saving Controversy." *Journal of Economic History* 39 (March 1979): 1–54.

_____. *Railroads and American Economic Growth: Essays in Econometric History.* Baltimore: Johns Hopkins University Press, 1964.

_____. *The Union Pacific Railroad: A Case in Premature Enterprise.* Baltimore: Johns Hopkins University Press, 1960.

Foner, Eric, ed. *The New American History.* Philadelphia: Temple University Press, 1990.

Frederickson, George M. "Giving a Comparative Dimension to American History: Problems and Opportunities." *Journal of Interdisciplinary History* 16 (Summer 1985): 107–10.

Fremdling, Rainer. *Eisenbahnen und deutsches Wirtschaftswachstum 1840–1879: Ein Beitrag zur Entwicklungstheorie und zur Theorie der Infrastruktur* 2d ed., enl., Untersuchungen zur Wirtschafts-, Sozial- und Technikgeschichte, vol. 2. Dortmund: Gesellschaft für Westfälische Wirtschaftsgeschichte e.V., 1985.

_____. "Railroads and German Economic Growth: A Leading Sector Analysis with a Comparison to the United States and Great Britain." *Journal of Economic History* 37 (September 1977): 586–87.

Fremdling, Rainer, and Knieps, Günter. "Competition, Regulation and Nationalization: The Prussian Railroad System in the 19th Century." Institute of Economic Research, Faculty of Economics, University of Groningen, Research Memorandum no. 397, November 1990.

Fremdling, Rainer, and Tilly, Richard H., eds. *Industrialisierung und Raum: Studien zur regionalen Differenzierung im Deutschland des 19. Jahrhunderts.* Historisch-Sozialwissenschaftliche Forschungen, vol. 7. Stuttgart: Klett-Cotta, 1979.

Freyer, Tony. *Forums of Order: The Federal Courts and Business in American History.* Greenwich, Conn.: JAI Press, 1979.

Friedman, Lawrence M. *A History of American Law.* New York: Simon & Schuster, Touchstone Books, 1973.

Friedman, Milton, with the assistance of Rose Friedman. *Capitalism and Freedom.* Chicago: University of Chicago Press, 1962.

Friedrich, Carl J. *Trends of Federalism in Theory and Practice.* New York: Frederick A. Praeger, 1968.

Galambos, Louis. *Competition and Cooperation: The Emergence of a National Trade Association.* Baltimore: Johns Hopkins University Press, 1966.

Gallman, Robert E. "The United States Capital Stock in the Nineteenth Century." In *Long-Term Factors in American Economic Growth,* edited by Stanley L. Engerman and Robert E. Gallman, pp. 165–213. Chicago: University of Chicago Press, 1986.

Gamst, Frederick C. "Franz Anton Ritter von Gerstner, Student of America's Pioneering Railroads." *Railroad History,* no. 163 (1990): 13–27.

Gerschenkron, Alexander. *Economic Backwardness in Historical Perspective: A Book of Essays.* Cambridge: Harvard University Press, Belknap Press, 1966.

Gilchrist, D. T. "Albert Fink and the Pooling System." *Business History Review* 34 (1960): 24–49.

Gilligan, Thomas W.; Marshall, William J.; and Weingast, Barry R. "Regulation and the Theory of Legislative Choice: The Interstate Commerce Act of 1887." *Journal of Law & Economics* 32 (1989): 35–61.

Gleim. "Zum dritten November 1888." *Archiv für Eisenbahnwesen* 11 (1888): 797–839.

Goodrich, Carter B. *Government Promotion of American Canals and Railroads, 1800–1890.* New York: Columbia University Press, 1960.

———. "Internal Improvements Reconsidered." *Journal of Economic History* 30 (June 1970): 289–311.

———. "The Revulsion Against Internal Improvements." *Journal of Economic History* 10 (November 1950): 145–69.

———. "State In, State Out—A Pattern of Development Policy." *Journal of Economic Issues* 2 (1968): 365–83.

———. "The Virginia System of Mixed Enterprise: A Study of State Planning of Internal Improvements." *Political Science Quarterly* 64 (1949): 355–87.

Gordon, Robert W. "Critical Legal Histories." In *Critical Legal Studies,* edited by Allan C. Hutchinson, pp. 79–103. Totowa, N.J.: Rowman & Littlefield, 1989.

Grew, Raymond. "The Comparative Weakness of American History." *Journal of Interdisciplinary History* 16 (Summer 1985): 87–101.

Gunn, L. Ray. *The Decline of Authority: Public Economic Policy and Political Development in New York State, 1800–1860.* Ithaca: Cornell University Press, 1988.

Hahn, Erich. "Ministerial Responsibility and Impeachment in Prussia, 1848–63." *Central European History* 10 (1977): 3–27.

Hahn, Steven. "Class and State in Postemancipation Societies: Southern Planters in Comparative Perspective." *American Historical Review* 95 (1990): 75–98.

Hall, John A. *Liberalism: Politics, Ideology and the Market.* Chapel Hill: University of North Carolina Press, 1987.

Hall, Peter A. *Governing the Economy: The Politics of State Intervention in Britain and France.* New York: Oxford University Press, 1986.

———. "Patterns of Economic Policy: An Organizational Approach." In *The State in Capitalist Europe,* edited by S. Born, D. Held, and J. Krieger, pp. 21–53. London: Allen and Unwin, 1983.

Halsey, Harlen I. "The Choice between High-Pressure and Low-Pressure Steam Power in America in the Early Nineteenth Century." *Journal of Economic History* 41 (December 1981): 723–44.

Handlin, Oscar, and Handlin, Mary Flug. *Commonwealth: A Study of the Role of Government in the American Economy: Massachusetts, 1774–1861.* Rev. ed. Cambridge: Harvard University Press, Belknap Press, 1969.

Haney, Lewis. *A Congressional History of Railways in the United States,* vol. 2. New York: Augustus M. Kelley, 1968.

Hardach, Karl W. "Some Remarks on German Economic Historiography and its Understanding of the Industrial Revolution in Germany." *Journal of European Economic History* 1 (Spring 1972): 37–99.

Hardtwig, Wolfgang. *Vormärz: Der monarchische Staat und das Bürgertum.* Munich: Deutscher Taschenbuch Verlag, 1985.

Hare, Jay V. *History of the Reading.* Serial in *The Pilot* and *Philadelphia & Reading Railway Men,* May 1909–February 1914; reprinted in book form, Philadelphia: John Henry Strock, 1966.

Harnisch, Hartmut. "Zum Stand der Diskussion um die Probleme des 'preußischen Weges' kapitalistischer Agrarentwicklung in der deutschen Geschichte." In *Preußen in der deutschen Geschichte nach 1789,* edited by Gustav Seeber and Karl-Heinz Noack, pp. 116-44. Berlin: Akademie-Verlag, 1983.

Hartz, Louis. *Economic Policy and Democratic Thought: Pennsylvania, 1776–1860.* Cambridge: Harvard University Press, 1948; reprint ed., Chicago: Quadrangle Books, Quadrangle Paperbacks, 1968.

Hattam, Victoria. "Economic Visions and Political Strategies: American Labor and the State, 1865–1896." *Studies in American Political Development* 4 (1990): 82–129.

Hattam, Victoria. *Labor Visions and State Power: The Origins of Business Unionism in the United States.* Princeton: Princeton University Press, 1992.

Haywood, Richard M. "The 'Ruler Legend': Tsar Nicholas I and the Route of the St. Petersburg-Moscow Railway, 1842–43." *Slavic Review* 37 (1978): 640–50.

Heath, Milton Sydney. *Constructive Liberalism: The Role of the State in Economic Development in Georgia to 1860.* Cambridge: Harvard University Press, 1954.

Heffter, Heinrich. "Der nachmärzliche Liberalismus: die Reaktion der fünfziger Jahre." In *Moderne deutsche Sozialgeschichte,* edited by Hans-Ulrich Wehler, pp. 177–96. 5th ed. Cologne: Kiepenheuer & Witsch, 1976.

———. *Die deutsche Selbstverwaltung im 19. Jahrhundert: Geschichte der Ideen und Institutionen.* Stuttgart, 1950.

Henderson, W. O. *Frederick List: Economist and Visionary, 1789–1846.* Totowa, N.J.: Frank Cass, 1983.

———. *The Rise of German Industrial Power, 1834–1914.* Berkeley and Los Angeles: University of California Press, 1975.

———. *The State and the Industrial Revolution in Prussia, 1740–1870.* Liverpool: Liverpool University Press, 1958.

Henning, Friedrich-Wilhelm. *Die Industrialisierung in Deutschland 1800 bis 1914.* Wirtschafts- und Sozialgeschichte, vol. 2. 6th ed. Paderborn: Ferdinand Schöningh, 1984.

Hill, Forest G. *Roads, Rails, and Waterways: The Army Engineers and Early Transportation.* Norman: University of Oklahoma Press, 1957.

Hindle, Brooke. "'The Exhilaration of Early American Technology': A New Look." In *The History of American Technology: Exhilaration or Discontent?,* edited by David A. Hounshell, pp. 3-28. Greenville, Del.: Hagley Papers, 1984.

———, ed. *America's Wooden Age: Aspects of Its Early Technology.* Tarrytown, N.Y.: Sleepy Hollow Press, 1975.

———, ed. *Material Culture of the Wooden Age.* Tarrytown, N.Y.: Sleepy Hollow Press, 1981.

Hippel, Wolfgang v.; Stephan, Joachim; Gleber, Peter; and Enzwieler, Hans-Jürgen. *Eisenbahn-Fieber: Badens Aufbruch ins Eisenbahnzeitalter.* Landesmuseum für Technik und Arbeit in Mannheim. Ubstadt-Weiher: Verlag Regionalkultur, 1990.

History of the Railway Mail Service; A Chapter in the History of Postal Affairs in the United States. Washington: Government Printing Office, 1885.

History of Transportation in the United States before 1860. Prepared under the direction of Balthasar H. Meyer by Caroline E. MacGill and a staff of collaborators. Washington, D.C.: Carnegie Institution, 1917.

Hoffmann, Walther G. "The Take-Off in Germany." In *The Economics of Take-Off into Sustained Growth,* edited by W. W. Rostow, pp. 95–118. London: Macmillan & Co.; New York: St. Martin's Press, 1963.

_____. *Das Wachstum der deutschen Wirtschaft seit der Mitte des 19. Jahrhunderts*. Berlin: Springer-Verlag, 1965.

Holmes, Oliver W., and Rohrbach, Peter T. *Stagecoach East: Stagecoach Days in the East from the Colonial Period to the Civil War*. Washington, D.C.: Smithsonian Institution Press, 1983.

Hoogenboom, Ari and Olive. *A History of the ICC: From Panacea to Palliative*. New York: W. W. Norton & Company, 1976.

Horwitz, Morton J. *The Transformation of American Law, 1780–1860*. Cambridge and London: Harvard University Press, 1977.

Hoskin, Keith W., and Macve, Richard H. "The Genesis of Accountability: The West Point Connections." *Accounting, Organizations and Society* 13 (1988): 37–73.

Hounshell, David A. "Commentary: On the Discipline of the History of American Technology." *Journal of American History* 67 (March 1981): 854–65.

_____. *From the American System to Mass Production, 1800–1932: The Development of Manufacturing Technology in the United States*. Baltimore: Johns Hopkins University Press, 1984.

_____. "Rethinking the History of 'American Technology.'" In *In Context: History and the History of Technology*, edited by Stephen H. Cutcliffe and Robert C. Post, 216–29. Bethlehem: Lehigh University Press; London: Associated University Presses, 1989.

_____, ed. *The History of American Technology: Exhilaration or Discontent?* Greenville, Del.: Hagley Papers, 1984.

Huang, Hsien-Ju. *State Taxation of Railways in the United States*. New York: Columbia University Press, 1928.

Hughes, Thomas P. *American Genesis: A Century of Invention and Technological Enthusiasm*. New York: Penguin, 1989.

_____. "The Evolution of Large Technical Systems." In *The Social Construction of Technological Systems*, edited by Wiebe E. Bijker, Thomas P. Hughes, and Trevor Pinch, pp. 51–82. Cambridge: M.I.T. Press, 1987.

_____. *Networks of Power: Electrification in Western Society, 1880–1930*. Baltimore: Johns Hopkins University Press, 1983.

_____. "The Order of the Technological World." *History of Technology* 5 (1980): 1–16.

_____. "A Technological Frontier: The Railway." In *The Railroad and the Space Program: An Exploration in Historical Analogy*, edited by Bruce Mazlish, pp. 53–73. Cambridge: M.I.T. Press, 1965.

Hungerford, Edward. *The Story of the Baltimore & Ohio Railroad, 1827–1927*. New York and London: G. P. Putnam's Sons, 1928.

Hunt, Robert S. *Law and Locomotives: The Impact of the Railroad on Wisconsin Law in the Nineteenth Century*. Madison: State Historical Society of Wisconsin, 1958.

Hurst, J. Willard. *Law and the Conditions of Freedom in the Nineteenth-Century United States*. Madison: University of Wisconsin, 1956.

Immergut, Ellen. "The Rules of the Game: The Logic of Health Policy-

Making in France, Switzerland, and Sweden." In *Structuring Politics: Historical Institutionalism in Comparative Analysis*, edited by Sven Steinmo, Kathleen Thelen, and Frank Longstreth, pp. 57–89. New York: Cambridge University Press, 1992.

Jaeger, Hans. *Geschichte der Wirtschaftsordnung in Deutschland*. Frankfurt/Main: Suhrkamp Verlag, 1988.

Jenks, Leland. "Railroads as an Economic Force in American Development." *Journal of Economic History* 4 (May 1944): 1–20.

Johnston, James Houston, comp. *Western and Atlantic Railroad of the State of Georgia*. Atlanta, 1931.

Kasson, John. *Civilizing the Machine: Technology and Republican Values in America, 1776–1900*. New York: Penguin Books, 1976.

Kirkland, Edward C. *Industry Comes of Age: Business, Labor, and Public Policy, 1860–1897*. Economic History of the United States, vol. 6. New York: Holt, Rinehart and Winston, 1961.

———. *Men, Cities, and Transportation: A Study in New England History, 1820–1900*. 2 vols. Cambridge, Mass.: Harvard University Press, 1948; reprint ed., New York: Russell & Russell, 1968.

Klee, Wolfgang. *Preußische Eisenbahngeschichte*. Stuttgart: Verlag W. Kohlhammer, 1982.

Klein, Hans-Günter. "Das 'Bankarchiv' der Mendelssohns." Staatsbibliothek Preussischer Kulturbesitz, *Mitteilungen* 16 (1984): 94–105.

Kobschätzky, Hans. *Streckenatlas der deutschen Eisenbahnen, 1835–1892*. Düsseldorf: Alba Buchverlag, 1971.

Kocka, Jürgen. "Eisenbahnverwaltung in der industriellen Revolution: Deutsch-Amerikanische Vergleiche." In *Historia Socialis et Oeconomica: Festschrift für Wolfgang Zorn zum 65. Geburtstag*, edited by Hermann Kellenbenz and Hans Pohl, pp. 259–77. Stuttgart: Franz Steiner Verlag Wiesbaden GmbH, 1987.

———. "Entrepreneurs and Managers in German Industrialization." In *Cambridge Economic History of Europe*, vol. 7: *The Industrial Economies: Capital, Labour, and Enterprise*, part 1, *Britain, France, Germany, and Scandinavia*, edited by Peter Mathias and M. M. Postan, pp. 492–589. Cambridge: Cambridge University Press, 1977.

———. "Germany: Cooperation and Competition." In "*Scale and Scope*: A Review Colloquium." *Business History Review* 64 (1990): 711–16.

———. "The Rise of the Modern Industrial Enterprise in Germany." In *Managerial Hierarchies: Comparative Perspectives on the Rise of the Modern Industrial Enterprise*, edited by Alfred D. Chandler, Jr., and Herman Daems, pp. 77–116. Cambridge: Harvard University Press, 1980.

———. *White Collar Workers in America, 1890–1940: A Social-Political History in International Perspective*. Trans. by Maura Kealey. SAGE Studies in 20th Century History, vol. 10. London and Beverly Hills: SAGE Publications, 1980.

Kolchin, Peter. *Unfree Labor: American Slavery and Russian Serfdom*. Cambridge: Harvard University Press, Belknap Press, 1987.

Kolko, Gabriel. *Railroads and Regulation, 1877–1916.* Princeton, N.J.: Princeton University Press, 1965; New York: W. W. Norton, 1970.

Köllmann, Wolfgang, ed. *Quellen zur Bevölkerungs-, Sozial- und Wirtschaftsstatistik Deutschlands 1815–1875.* Vol. 1: *Quellen zur Bevölkerungsstatistik Deutschlands 1815-1875.* Prepared by Antje Kraus. Boppard am Rhein: Harald Boldt Verlag, 1980.

Koselleck, Reinhart. "Altständische Rechte, außerständische Gesellschaft und Beamtenherrschaft im Vormärz." In *Preussen in der deutschen Geschichte,* edited by Dirk Blasius, pp. 219–36. Königstein/Ts.: Verlagsgruppe Athenäum-Hain-Scriptor-Hanstein, 1980.

———. "Staat und Gesellschaft in Preußen 1815–1848." In *Moderne deutsche Sozialgeschichte,* edited by Hans-Ulrich Wehler, pp. 55–84. 5th ed. Cologne: Verlag Kiepenheuer & Witsch, 1976.

Kulik, Gary. "Dams, Fish, and Farmers: Defense of Public Rights in Eighteenth-Century Rhode Island." In *The Countryside in the Age of Capitalist Transformation: Essays in the Social History of Rural America,* edited by Steven Hahn and Jonathan Prude, pp. 25–50. Chapel Hill: University of North Carolina Press, 1985.

Kutler, Stanley I. *Privilege and Creative Destruction: The Charles River Bridge Case.* J. B. Lippincott, 1971; New York: W. W. Norton, 1978.

Lamoreaux, Naomi. *The Great Merger Movement in American Business, 1895–1904.* Cambridge: Cambridge University Press, 1985.

Lardner, Dionysius. *Railway Economy: A Treatise on the New Art of Transport, Its Management, Prospects, and Relations, Commercial, Financial, and Social.* London: Taylor, Walton, and Maberly, 1850.

Larkin, F. Daniel. *John B. Jervis: An American Engineering Pioneer.* Ames: Iowa State University Press, 1990.

Lazonick, William. "Technological Change and the Control of Work: The Development of Capital-Labour Relations in US Mass Production Industries." In *Managerial Strategies and Industrial Relations: An Historical and Comparative Study,* edited by Craig R. Littler and Howard F. Gospel, pp. 111-36. London: Heineman, 1983.

Lee, W. R. "Economic Development and the State in Nineteenth-Century Germany." *Economic History Review,* 2d ser., 41 (1988): 346–67.

———, ed. *German Industry and German Industrialization: Essays in German Economic and Business History in the Nineteenth and Twentieth Centuries.* London: Routledge, 1991.

Leuchtenburg, William E. "The Pertinence of Political History: Reflections on the Significance of the State in America." *Journal of American History* 73 (December 1986): 585–600.

Levy, Leonard W. *The Laws of the Commonwealth and Chief Justice Shaw: The Evolution of American Law, 1830–1860.* New York: Harper & Row, Harper Torchbooks, 1957.

Leyen, von der. "Die Entstehung der Magdeburg-Leipziger Eisenbahn." *Archiv für Eisenbahnwesen* 5 (1880): 215–83.

Licht, Walter. *Working for the Railroad: The Organization of Work in the Nineteenth Century.* Princeton: Princeton University Press, 1983.

Linters, A., ed. *Spoorwegen in België/Chemins de Fer en Belgique/Railways in Belgium.* Gent: GOFF pvba, 1985.

Lively, Robert A. "The American System: A Review Article." *Business History Review* 29 (March 1955): 81–96.

Livesay, Harold C. "Entrepreneurial Dominance in Businesses Large and Small, Past and Present." *Business History Review* 63 (1989): 1–21.

Lukes, Steven. *Power: A Radical View.* London and Basingstoke: The Macmillan Press, Ltd., 1974.

Lundgreen, Peter. "Measures for Objectivity in the Public Interest: The Role of Scientific Expertise in the Politics of Technical Regulation: Germany and the U.S., 1865–1916." In *Standardization, Testing, and Regulation: Studies in the History of the Science-based Regulatory State (Germany and the U.S.A., 19th and 20th Centuries).* Forschungsschwerpunkt Wissenschaftsforschung. Bielefeld: B. Kleine, 1986.

———. *Techniker in Preussen während der frühen Industrialisierung: Ausbildung und Berufsfeld einer entstehenden sozialen Gruppe.* Berlin: Colloquium Verlag, 1975.

McCraw, Thomas K. *Prophets of Regulation: Charles Francis Adams, Louis D. Brandeis, James M. Landis, Alfred E. Kahn.* Cambridge: Harvard University Press, Belknap Press, 1984.

McDougall, Walter A. *. . . the Heavens and the Earth: A Political History of the Space Age.* New York: Basic Books, 1985.

Maddison, Angus. *Dynamic Forces in Capitalist Development: A Long-Run Comparative View.* Oxford: Oxford University Press, 1991.

Maier, Charles. *The Unmasterable Past: History, Holocaust, and German National Identity.* Cambridge: Harvard University Press, 1988.

March, James G., and Olsen, Johan P. *Rediscovering Institutions: The Organizational Basis of Politics.* New York: Free Press, 1989.

Marks, Gary. *Unions in Politics: Britain, Germany, and the United States in the Nineteenth and Early Twentieth Centuries.* Princeton: Princeton University Press, 1989.

Mazlish, Bruce, ed. *The Railroad and the Space Program: An Exploration in Historical Analogy.* Cambridge: M.I.T. Press, 1965.

Meinke, Bernhard. "Die ältesten Stimmen über die militärische Bedeutung der Eisenbahnen, 1833–1842." *Archiv für Eisenbahnwesen* 41 (1918): 921–34 and 42 (1919): 46–74.

Merk, Frederick. "Eastern Antecedents of the Grangers." *Agricultural History* 23 (January 1949): 1–8.

Meyer, Balthasar Henry. *Railway Legislation in the United States.* New York: MacMillan Company, 1903.

Miller, George H. *Railroads and the Granger Laws.* Madison: University of Wisconsin Press, 1971.

Milton, Ellen Fink. *A Biography of Albert Fink.* N.p., 1951.

Mitchell, Timothy. "The Limits of the State: Beyond Statist Approaches and

Their Critics." *American Political Science Review* 85 (March 1991): 77–96.

Mokyr, Joel. "Technological Inertia in Economic History." *Journal of Economic History* 52 (June 1992): 325–38.

Molloy, Peter M. "Technical Education and the Young Republic: West Point as America's École Polytechnique, 1802–1833." Ph.D. diss., Brown University, 1975.

Moore, Linda Ann. "The Failure of Federal Social Programs in the Early 19th Century." Paper presented to the Society for the History of the Early American Republic, Madison, Wis., July 26–28, 1991.

Morrison, James L., Jr. *"The Best School in the World": West Point, the Pre-Civil War Years, 1833–1866.* Kent, Ohio: Kent State University Press, 1986.

Nipperdey, Thomas. *Deutsche Geschichte, 1800–1866: Bürgerwelt und starker Staat.* Munich: Verlag C. H. Beck, 1983.

Noble, David F. *America By Design: Science, Technology, and the Rise of Corporate Capitalism.* Oxford: Oxford University Press, 1977.

_____. *Forces of Production: A Social History of Industrial Automation.* New York: Alfred A. Knopf, 1984.

North, Douglass C. *Institutions, Institutional Change and Economic Performance.* Cambridge: Cambridge University Press, 1990.

_____. *Structure and Change in Economic History.* New York: W. W. Norton, 1981.

North, Douglass C., and Weingast, Barry R. "Constitutions and Commitment: The Evolution of Institutions Governing Public Choice in Seventeenth-Century England." *Journal of Economic History* 49 (December 1989): 803–32.

Obermann, Karl. "Zur Beschaffung des Eisenbahn-Kapitals in Deutschland in den Jahren 1835–1855." *Revue Internationale d'Histoire de la Banque* 5 (1972): 315–52.

O'Brien, P. K. "Do We Have a Typology for the Study of European Industrialization in the XIXth Century?" *Journal of European Economic History* 15 (Fall 1986): 291–333.

O'Brien, Patrick. *The New Economic History of Railways.* London: Croom Helm, 1977.

_____, ed. *Railways and the Economic Development of Western Europe, 1830–1914.* New York: St. Martin's Press, 1983.

O'Connell, Charles F., Jr. "The Corps of Engineers and the Rise of Modern Management, 1827–1856." In *Military Enterprise and Technological Change: Perspectives on the American Experience*, edited by Merritt Roe Smith, pp. 87–116. Cambridge: M.I.T. Press, 1985.

Offe, Claus, and Wiesenthal, Helmut. "Two Logics of Collective Action: Theoretical Notes on Social Class and Organization Form." *Political Power and Social Theory* 1 (1980): 67–115.

Olson, Mancur. *The Logic of Collective Action: Public Goods and the Theory of Groups.* Cambridge: Harvard University Press, 1965; reprint ed., 1971.

Parks, Robert J. *Democracy's Railroads: Public Enterprise in Jacksonian Michigan*. Port Washington, N.Y., and London: Kennikat Press, Inc., 1972.

Parris, Henry. *Government and the Railways in Nineteenth-Century Britain*. London: Routledge & Kegan Paul; Toronto: University of Toronto Press, 1965.

Paul, Helmut. "Die preußische Eisenbahnpolitik von 1835–1838: Ein Beitrag zur Geschichte der Restauration und Reaktion in Preußen." *Archiv für Eisenbahnwesen* 50 (1938): 250–303.

Peal, David. "The Politics of Populism: Germany and the American South in the 1890s." *Comparative Studies in Society and History* 31 (April 1989): 340–62.

Phillips, Ulrich Bonnell. "An American State-Owned Railroad: The Western and Atlantic." *Yale Review* 15 (November 1906): 259–82.

———. *A History of Transportation in the Eastern Cotton Belt to 1860*. New York: Columbia University Press, 1908; reprint ed., Octagon Books, Inc., 1968.

Pierce, Harry H. *Railroads of New York: A Study of Government Aid, 1826–1875*. Cambridge: Harvard University Press, 1953.

Pierenkemper, Toni. "Die Zusammensetzung des Führungspersonals und die Lösung unternehmerischer Probleme in frühen Eisenbahn-Gesellschaften." *Tradition* 21 (1976): 37–49.

Piore, Michael J., and Sabel, Charles F. *The Second Industrial Divide: Possibilities for Prosperity*. New York: Basic Books, 1984.

Pisani, Donald J. "Promotion and Regulation: Constitutionalism and the American Economy." *Journal of American History* 74 (December 1987): 740–68.

Platt, D.C.M. *Foreign Finance in Continental Europe and the United States, 1815–1870: Quantities, Origins, Functions and Distribution*. London: George Allen & Unwin, 1984.

Porter, Glenn. *The Rise of Big Business, 1860–1920*. 2d ed. Arlington Heights, Ill.: Harlan Davidson, 1992.

Porter, Kirk H. *A History of Suffrage*. Chicago: University of Chicago, 1918.

Poschinger, H. *Erinnerungen aus dem Leben von Hans Viktor von Unruh*. Stuttgart: Deutsche Verlags-Anstalt, 1895.

Pratt, Edwin A. *The Rise of Rail-Power in War and Conquest, 1833–1914*. London: P. S. King & Son, 1915.

"Die Preussische Eisenbahnpolitik des Jahres 1848." *Archiv für Eisenbahnwesen* (1880): 141–49.

Primm, James N. *Economic Policy in the Development of a Western State: Missouri, 1820–1860*. Cambridge: Harvard University Press, 1954.

"Proceedings of the General Time Convention and its Successor the American Railway Association. . . ." American Railway Association *Proceedings*, April 14, 1886 to October 11, 1893, Appendix.

Puhle, Hans-Jürgen. "Comparative Approaches from Germany: The 'New Nation' in Advanced Industrial Capitalism, 1860–1940—Integration,

Stabilization and Reform." *Reviews in American History* 14 (December 1986): 614–28.

Radkau, Joachim. *Technik in Deutschland: Vom 18. Jahrhundert bis zur Gegenwart.* Frankfurt/Main: Suhrkamp, 1989.

Ramsdell, Charles W. "The Confederate Government and the Railroads." *American Historical Review* 22 (July 1917): 794–810.

Rapmund, F. *Die finanzielle Betheiligung des Preußischen Staats bei den Preußischen Privateisenbahnen.* Berlin: Verlag der Königlichen Geheimen Ober-Hofbuchdruckerei (R. v. Decker), 1869.

Reed, M. C. *Investment in Railways in Britain, 1820–1844.* London: Oxford University Press, 1974.

Richardson, Reed C. *The Locomotive Engineer, 1863–1963: A Century of Railway Labor Relations and Work Rules.* Ann Arbor: Bureau of Industrial Relations, Graduate School of Business Administration, University of Michigan, 1963.

Ritter, Ulrich Peter. *Die Rolle des Staates in den Frühstadien der Industrialisierung: Die preußische Industrieförderung in der ersten Hälfte des 19. Jahrhunderts.* Berlin: Duncker and Humblot, 1961.

Röll, Louis. *Die Entstehungsgeschichte der Thüringischen Eisenbahn.* 1910.

Rosenberg, Nathan. *Technology and American Economic Growth.* New York: M. E. Sharpe, Inc., 1972.

Rubin, Julius. "Canal or Railroad? Imitation and Innovation in the Response to the Erie Canal in Philadelphia, Baltimore, and Boston." *Transactions of the American Philosophical Society*, n.s. 51, part 7 (1961): 5–106.

Rückblick auf die Thätigkeit des Vereins deutscher Eisenbahn-Verwaltungen in technischer Beziehung, 1850–1900. Berlin: Felgentreff and Co., 1900.

Russo, David J. "The Major Political Issues of the Jacksonian Period and the Development of Party Loyalty in Congress, 1830–1840." *Transactions of the American Philosophical Society*, n.s. 62, pt. 5 (1972): 1–49.

Sabel, Charles, and Zeitlin, Jonathan. "Historical Alternatives to Mass Production: Politics, Markets and Technology in Nineteenth-Century Industrialization." *Past and Present*, no. 108 (August 1985): 133–76.

Salsbury, Stephen. *The State, the Investor, and the Railroad: The Boston & Albany, 1825–1867.* Cambridge: Harvard University Press, 1967.

Sautter. "General Postmeister von Nagler und seine Stellung zu den Eisenbahnen." *Archiv für Post und Telegraphie* 7 (1916): 223–38.

Schäfer, Hans-Peter. *Die Entstehung des mainfränkischen Eisenbahn-Netzes.* Part 1: *Planung und Bau der Hauptstrecken bis 1879.* Würzburger geographische Arbeiten, no. 48. Würzburg: Institut für Geographie der Universität Würzburg, 1979.

Scheiber, Harry N. "Federalism and the American Economic Order, 1789–1910." *Law & Society Review* 10 (Fall 1975): 57–118.

———. "Government and the Economy: Studies of the 'Commonwealth'

Policy in Nineteenth-Century America." *Journal of Interdisciplinary History* 3 (Summer 1972): 135–51.

———. *Ohio Canal Era: A Case Study of Government and the Economy, 1820–1861.* Athens, Ohio: Ohio University Press, 1969.

———. "Public Economic Policy and the American Legal System: Historical Perspectives." *Wisconsin Law Review* (1980): 1159–89.

———. "The Rate-Making Power of the State in the Canal Era: A Case Study." *Political Science Quarterly* 77 (1962): 397–413.

———. "Regulation, Property Rights, and Definition of 'The Market': Law and the American Economy." *Journal of Economic History* 41 (March 1981): 103–9.

———. "The Transportation Revolution and American Law: Constitutionalism and Public Policy." In *Transportation and the Early Nation*, pp. 1–29. Papers presented at an Indiana American Revolution Bicentennial Symposium. Indianapolis: Indiana Historical Society, 1982.

Scheiber, Harry N., and Salsbury, Stephen. "Reflections on George Rogers Taylor's *The Transportation Revolution, 1815–1860*: A Twenty-five Year Retrospect." *Business History Review* 51 (Spring 1977): 79–89.

Schivelbusch, Wolfgang. *The Railway Journey: The Industrialization of Time and Space in the 19th Century.* Translation of *Geschichte der Eisenbahnreise.* New York: Urizen Books, 1979; Berkeley: University of California, 1986.

Schlenke, Manfred, ed. *Preußen-Ploetz: Eine historische Bilanz in Daten und Deutungen.* Würzburg: Verlag Ploetz, 1983.

Scholl, Lars Ulrich. *Ingenieure in der Frühindustrialisierung: Staatliche und private Techniker im Königreich Hannover und an der Ruhr (1815–1873).* Göttingen: Vandenhoeck and Ruprecht, 1978.

Schotter, H. W. *The Growth and Development of the Pennsylvania Railroad Company: A Review of the Charter and Annual Reports of the Pennsylvania Railroad Company 1846 to 1926, Inclusive.* Philadelphia: n.p., 1927.

Schreiber, K. *Die Preussischen Eisenbahnen und ihr Verhältniss zum Staat, 1834–1874.* Berlin: Ernst & Korn, 1874.

Schütz, Rüdiger. *Preußen und die Rheinlande: Studien zur preußischen Integrationspolitik im Vormärz.* Wiesbaden: Franz Steiner Verlag, 1979.

Scranton, Philip. "Diversity in Diversity: Flexible Production and American Industrialization, 1880–1930." *Business History Review* 65 (1991): 27–90.

———. *Proprietary Capitalism: The Textile Manufacture at Philadelphia, 1800–1885.* Cambridge: Cambridge University Press, 1983.

Searight, Thomas B. *The Old Pike: A History of the National Road.* Uniontown, Pa.: By the Author, 1894.

Sewell, William H. "Marc Bloch and the Logic of Comparative History." *History and Theory* 6 (1967): 208–18.

Shallat, Todd. "Building Waterways, 1802–1861: Science and the United

States Army in Early Public Works." *Technology and Culture* 31 (January 1990): 18–50.

Shaw, Robert B. *A History of Railroad Accidents, Safety Precautions and Operating Practices.* 2d ed. Robert B. Shaw, 1978.

Showalter, Dennis E. *Railroads and Rifles: Soldiers, Technology, and the Unification of Germany.* Hamden, Conn.: Shoe String Press, 1975; Archon Book, 1986.

Sieferle, Rolf Peter. *Fortschrittsfeinde? Opposition gegen Technik und Industrie von der Romantik bis zur Gegenwart.* Munich: C. H. Beck, 1984.

Skocpol, Theda. "Bringing the State Back In: Strategies of Analysis in Current Research." In *Bringing the State Back In,* edited by Peter B. Evans, Dietrich Rueschemeyer, and Theda Skocpol, pp. 3–37. Cambridge: Cambridge University Press, 1985.

———. "Political Response to Capitalist Crisis: Neo-Marxist Theories of the State and the Case of the New Deal." *Politics and Society* 10 (1980): 155–201.

Skocpol, Theda, and Somers, Margaret. "The Uses of Comparative History in Macrosocial Inquiry." *Comparative Studies in Society and History* 22 (April 1980): 174–97.

Skowronek, Stephen. *Building a New American State: The Expansion of National Administrative Capacities, 1877–1920.* Cambridge: Cambridge University Press, 1982.

Slotten, Hugh R. "Patronage, Politics, and Practice in Nineteenth-Century American Science: Alexander Dallas Bache and the U.S. Coast Survey." Ph.D. diss., University of Wisconsin-Madison, 1991.

Smith, Adam. *An Inquiry into the Nature and Causes of the Wealth of Nations.* Edited by Edwin Cannan. Chicago: University of Chicago Press, 1976.

Smith, Cecil O., Jr. "The Longest Run: Public Engineers and Planning in France." *American Historical Review* 95 (June 1990): 657–92.

Smith, David G. "Liberalism." *International Encyclopedia of the Social Sciences,* vol. 9 (1968), p. 278.

Smith, Merritt Roe. "Becoming Engineers in Early Industrial America." Program in Science, Technology, and Society Working Paper no. 13, Massachusetts Institute of Technology.

———. *Harper's Ferry and the New Technology: The Challenge of Change.* Ithaca: Cornell University Press, 1977.

Smith, Merritt Roe, ed. *Military Enterprise and Technological Change: Perspectives on the American Experience.* Cambridge: M.I.T. Press, 1985.

Smith, Rogers M. "Political Jurisprudence, The New Institutionalism, and the Future of Public-Law." *American Political Science Review* 82 (1988): 89–108.

Sperber, Jonathan. "State and Civil Society in Prussia: Thoughts on a New Edition of Reinhart Koselleck's *Preußen zwischen Reform und Revolution.*" *Journal of Modern History* 57 (June 1985): 280–84.

Stapleton, Darwin H. "Neither Tocqueville nor Trollope: Michel Chevalier and the Industrialization of America and Europe." In *The World of the Industrial Revolution: Comparative and International Aspects of Industrialization*, Essays from the Lowell Conference on Industrial History, 1984. Edited by Robert Weible, pp. 21–34. North Andover, Mass.: Museum of American Textile History, 1986.

———. "The Origin of American Railroad Technology, 1825–1840." *Railroad History*, no. 139 (1978): 65–77.

———. *The Transfer of Early Industrial Technologies to America*. Philadelphia: American Philosophical Society, 1987.

Stapleton, Darwin, and Hounshell, David A. "The Discipline of the History of Technology: An Exchange." *Journal of American History* 68 (March 1982): 897–902.

Staudenmaier, John M. "Recent Trends in the History of Technology." *American Historical Review* 95 (1990): 715–25.

———. *Technology's Storytellers: Reweaving the Human Fabric*. Cambridge: Society for the History of Technology and M.I.T. Press, 1985.

Steinisch, Irmgard. *Arbeitszeitverkürzung und sozialer Wandel. Der Kampf um die Achtstundenschicht in der deutschen und amerikanischen Eisen- und Stahlindustrie 1880–1929*. Berlin and New York: Walter de Gruyter, 1986.

Steinmo, Sven; Thelen, Kathleen; and Longstreth, Frank, eds. *Structuring Politics: Historical Institutionalism in Comparative Analysis*. New York: Cambridge University Press, 1992.

Steitz, Walter. *Die Entstehung der Köln-Mindener Eisenbahngesellschaft: Ein Beitrag zur Frühgeschichte der deutschen Eisenbahnen und des preussischen Aktienwesens*. Schriften zur Rheinisch-Westfälischen Wirtschaftsgeschichte, vol. 27. Cologne: Rheinisch-Westfälischen Wirtschaftsarchiv zu Köln, 1974.

Stephan, H. *Geschichte der Preußischen Post von ihrem Ursprunge bis auf die Gegenwart*. Berlin: Verlag der Königlichen Geheimen Ober-Hofbuchdruckerei (R. Decker), 1859.

Stephens, Carlene. "'The Most Reliable Time': William Bond, the New England Railroads, and Time Awareness in 19th-Century America." *Technology and Culture* 30 (1989): 1–24.

Stevens, Frank Walker. *The Beginnings of the New York Central Railroad: A History*. New York: G. P. Putnam's Sons, 1926.

Stover, John F. *American Railroads*. Chicago: University of Chicago Press, 1961; Midway Reprint, 1976.

———. *History of the Baltimore and Ohio Railroad*. West Lafayette, Ind.: Purdue University Press, 1987.

Stromquist, Shelton. *A Generation of Boomers: The Pattern of Railroad Labor Conflict in Nineteenth-Century America*. Urbana: University of Illinois Press, 1987.

Summers, Mark W. *Railroads, Reconstruction, and the Gospel of Prosper-*

ity: Aid under the Radical Republicans, 1865–1877. Princeton: Princeton University Press, 1984.

Tarlton, C. D. "Symmetry and Asymmetry as Elements of Federalism: A Theoretical Speculation." *Journal of Politics* 27 (1965): 861–74.

Taylor, George Rogers. "Railroad Investment before the Civil War: Comment." In National Bureau of Economic Research, *Trends in the American Economy in the Nineteenth Century: Studies in Income and Wealth*, pp. 524–44. Princeton: Princeton University Press, 1960.

———. *The Transportation Revolution, 1815–1860.* New York: Holt, Rinehart and Winston, 1951; New York: Harper & Row, Harper Torchbooks, 1968.

Taylor, George Rogers, and Neu, Irene D. *The American Railroad Network, 1861–1890.* Cambridge: Harvard University Press, 1956.

Taylor, Tom. "The Transition to Adulthood in Comparative Perspective: Professional Males in Germany and the United States at the Turn of the Century." *Journal of Social History* 21 (1987–88): 635–58.

Temin, Peter. "Labor Scarcity and the Problem of American Industrial Efficiency in the 1850's." *Journal of Economic History* 26 (September 1966): 277–98.

Tilly, Richard H. "Capital Formation in Germany in the Nineteenth Century." In *Cambridge Economic History of Europe*, vol. 7: *The Industrial Economies: Capital, Labour, and Enterprise*, part 1, *Britain, France, Germany, and Scandinavia*, edited by Peter Mathias and M. M. Postan, pp. 382–441. Cambridge: Cambridge University Press, 1977.

———. "Germany, 1815–1870." In *Banking in the Early Stages of Industrialization: A Study in Comparative Economic History*, edited by Rondo Cameron, pp. 151–82. New York: Oxford University Press, 1967.

———. "The Political Economy of Public Finance and the Industrialization of Prussia, 1815–1866." *Journal of Economic History* 26 (December 1966): 484–97. Reprinted as "Die politische Ökonomie der Finanzpolitik und die Industrialisierung Preußens, 1815–1866." In *Preussen in der deutschen Geschichte*, edited by Dirk Blasius, pp. 203–17. Königstein/Ts.: Verlag Anton Hain Meisenheim, 1980.

———. "The 'Take-Off' in Germany." In *Oceans Apart? Comparing Germany and the United States; Studies in Commemoration of the 150th Anniversary of the Birth of Carl Schurz*, edited by Erich Angermann and Marie-Luise Frings, pp. 47–59. Stuttgart: Klett-Cotta, 1981.

———. *Vom Zollverein zum Industriestaat: Die wirtschaftlich-soziale Entwicklung Deutschlands 1834 bis 1914.* Munich: Deutscher Taschenbuch Verlag, 1990.

———. "Zur Entwicklung des Kapitalmarktes und Industrialisierung im 19. Jahrhundert unter besonderer Berücksichtigung Deutschlands." *Vierteljahrschrift für Sozial- und Wirtschaftsgeschichte* 60 (1973): 145–65.

Tipton, Frank B., Jr. *Regional Variations in the Economic Development of*

Germany During the Nineteenth Century. Middletown, Conn.: Wesleyan University Press, 1976.

Tolliday, Steven, and Zeitlin, Jonathan, eds. *The Power to Manage? Employers and Industrial Relations in Comparative-Historical Perspective.* London: Routledge, 1991.

Towles, John K. "Early Railroad Monopoly and Discrimination in Rhode Island, 1835–55." *Yale Review* 18 (November 1909): 299–319.

Trebilcock, Clive. *The Industrialization of the Continental Powers, 1780–1914.* New York: Longman Inc., 1981.

Treue, Wilhelm. "Das Bankhaus Mendelssohn als Beispiel einer Privatbank im 19. und 20. Jahrhundert." *Mendelssohn Studien* 1 (1972): 29–80.

Turner, Frederick Jackson. "The Significance of the Section in American History." In *Frontier and Section: Selected Essays of Frederick Jackson Turner,* pp. 115–35. Englewood Cliffs, N.J.: Prentice-Hall, Inc., Spectrum Books, 1961.

Usselman, Steven W. "Patents Purloined: Railroads, Inventors, and the Diffusion of Innovation in 19th-Century America." *Technology and Culture* 32 (1991): 1047–75.

Van Metre, Thurman W. *Early Opposition to the Steam Railroad.* N.p., n.d.

Der Verein für Eisenbahnkunde zu Berlin, 1842 bis 1892, Festschrift zur Feier des fünfzigjährign Bestehens des Vereins am 11. Oktober 1892. N.p., n.d.

"Die Verhandlungen der Vereinigten ständischen Ausschüsse über die Eisenbahnfrage in Preussen im Jahre 1842." *Archiv für Eisenbahnwesen* (1881): 1–21.

Vorsteher, Dieter. *Borsig: Eisengießerei und Maschinenbauanstalt zu Berlin.* Berlin: Siedler Verlag, 1983.

Wagenblass, Horst. *Der Eisenbahnbau und das Wachstum der deutschen Eisen- und Maschinenbauindustrie 1835 bis 1860: Ein Beitrag zur Geschichte der Industrialisierung Deutschlands.* Stuttgart: Gustav Fischer Verlag, 1973.

Waldo, Leonard. *First Annual Report of the Astronomer in Charge of the Horological and Thermometric Bureaus of the Winchester Observatory of Yale College.* 1880–1881.

Ward, James A. *J. Edgar Thomson: Master of the Pennsylvania.* Westport, Conn.: Greenwood Press, 1980.

———. *Railroads and the Character of America, 1820–1887.* Knoxville: University of Tennessee Press, 1986.

Weaver, Charles Clinton. *Internal Improvements in North Carolina Previous to 1860.* Johns Hopkins University Studies in Historical and Political Science, ser. 21, March–April 1903. Reprint ed., Spartanburg, S.C.: The Reprint Company, 1971.

Weigley, Russell F. *History of the United States Army.* Enlarged ed. Bloomington: Indiana University Press, Midland Books, 1984.

Weisbrod, Bernd. "Der englische 'Sonderweg' in der neueren Geschichte." *Geschichte und Gesellschaft* 16 (1990): 233–52.

Welskopp, Thomas. "Arbeit und Macht im Hüttenwerk. Arbeits- und industrielle Beziehungen in der deutschen und amerikanischen Eisen- und Stahlindustrie von den 1860er bis zu den 1930er Jahren." Ph.D. diss., Freie Universität Berlin, 1991.

White, John W., Jr. *A History of the American Locomotive, Its Development: 1830–1880.* New York: Dover Publications, Inc., 1968.

Wiedenfeld, Kurt. "Deutsche Eisenbahn-Gestalter aus Staatsverwaltung und Wirtschaftsleben im 19. Jahrhundert (1815–1914)." *Archiv für Eisenbahnwesen* 63 (1940): 733–824.

Williamson, Oliver. *The Economic Institutions of Capitalism: Firms, Markets, Relational Contracting.* New York: The Free Press, 1985.

Winner, Langdon. *The Whale and the Reactor: A Search for Limits in an Age of High Technology.* Chicago: University of Chicago Press, 1986.

Wisely, William H. *The American Civil Engineer, 1852–1974: The History, Traditions and Development of the American Society of Civil Engineers.* New York: American Society of Civil Engineers, 1974.

Wood, Richard George. *Stephen Harriman Long, 1784–1864: Army Engineer, Explorer, Inventor.* Glendale, Calif.: Arthur H. Clark Co., 1966.

Yago, Glenn. *The Decline of Transit: Urban Transportation in German and U.S. Cities, 1900–1970.* Cambridge: Cambridge University Press, 1984.

Index